Connecting Networks Companion Guide

Cisco Networking Academy

Cisco Press

800 East 96th Street

Indianapolis, Indiana 46240 USA

Connecting Networks Companion Guide

Published by:
Cisco Press
800 East 96th Street
Indianapolis, IN 46240 USA

Printed in the United States of America

First Printing May 2014

Library of Congress Control Number: 2014933762

ISBN-13: 978-1-58713-332-9

ISBN-10: 1-58713-332-6

Warning and Disclaimer

This book is designed to provide information about the Connecting Networks course. Every effort has been made to make this book as complete and as accurate as possible, but no warranty or fitness is implied.

The information is provided on an "as is" basis. The authors, Cisco Press, and Cisco Systems, Inc. shall have neither liability nor responsibility to any person or entity with respect to any loss or damages arising from the information contained in this book or from the use of the discs or programs that may accompany it.

The opinions expressed in this book belong to the author and are not necessarily those of Cisco Systems, Inc.

This book is part of the Cisco Networking Academy® series from Cisco Press. The products in this series support and complement the Cisco Networking Academy curriculum. If you are using this book outside the Networking Academy, then you are not preparing with a Cisco trained and authorized Networking Academy provider.

For more information on the Cisco Networking Academy or to locate a Networking Academy, Please visit www.cisco.com/edu.

CISCO.

Publisher	Paul Boger
Associate Publisher	Dave Dusthimer
Business Operation Manager, Cisco Press	Jan Cornelssen
Executive Editor	Mary Beth Ray
Managing Editor	Sandra Schroeder
Development Editor	Ellie C. Bru
Project Editor	Mandie Frank
Copy Editor	Keith Cline
Technical Editor	Kathleen Page
Editorial Assistant	Vanessa Evans
Designer	Mark Shirar
Composition	Trina Wurst
Indexer	Ken Johnson
Proofreader	Dan Knott

Trademark Acknowledgements

All terms mentioned in this book that are known to be trademarks or service marks have been appropriately capitalized. Cisco Press or Cisco Systems, Inc., cannot attest to the accuracy of this information. Use of a term in this book should not be regarded as affecting the validity of any trademark or service mark.

Special Sales

For information about buying this title in bulk quantities, or for special sales opportunities (which may include electronic versions; custom cover designs; and content particular to your business, training goals, marketing focus, or branding interests), please contact our corporate sales department at corpsales@pearsoned.com or (800) 382-3419.

For government sales inquiries, please contact governmentsales@pearsoned.com.

For questions about sales outside the U.S., please contact international@pearsoned.com.

Feedback Information

At Cisco Press, our goal is to create in-depth technical books of the highest quality and value. Each book is crafted with care and precision, undergoing rigorous development that involves the unique expertise of members from the professional technical community.

Readers' feedback is a natural continuation of this process. If you have any comments regarding how we could improve the quality of this book, or otherwise alter it to better suit your needs, you can contact us through email at feedback@ciscopress.com. Please make sure to include the book title and ISBN in your message.

We greatly appreciate your assistance.

CISCO

Americas Headquarters
Cisco Systems, Inc.
170 West Tasman Drive
San Jose, CA 95134-1706
USA
www.cisco.com
Tel: 408 526-4000
800 553-NETS (6387)
Fax: 408 527-0883

Asia Pacific Headquarters
Cisco Systems, Inc.
168 Robinson Road
#28-01 Capital Tower
Singapore 068912
www.cisco.com
Tel: +65 6317 7777
Fax: +65 6317 7799

Europe Headquarters
Cisco Systems International BV
Haarlerbergpark
Haarlerbergweg 13-19
1101 CH Amsterdam
The Netherlands
www-europe.cisco.com
Tel: +31 0 800 020 0791
Fax: +31 0 20 357 1100

Cisco has more than 200 offices worldwide. Addresses, phone numbers, and fax numbers are listed on the Cisco Website at **www.cisco.com/go/offices.**

About the Contributing Authors

Rick Graziani teaches computer science and computer networking courses at Cabrillo College in Aptos, California. Prior to teaching, Rick worked in the information technology field for Santa Cruz Operation, Tandem Computers, and Lockheed Missiles and Space Corporation. He holds an M.A. in Computer Science and Systems Theory from California State University Monterey Bay. Rick is also a member of the Curriculum Development team for the Cisco Networking Academy since 1999.

Rick has authored multiple books for Cisco Press and multiple online courses for the Cisco Networking Academy. Rick is the author of the Cisco Press book *IPv6 Fundamentals* and has presented on IPv6 at several Cisco Academy conferences. He is the coauthor of the Cisco Press book *Routing Protocols Companion Guide*.

When Rick is not working, he is most likely surfing at one of his favorite Santa Cruz surf breaks.

Bob Vachon is a professor in the Computer Systems Technology program at Cambrian College in Sudbury, Ontario, Canada, where he teaches networking infrastructure courses. He has over 30 years of work and teaching experience in the computer networking and information technology field.

Since 2001, Bob has collaborated as team lead, lead author, and subject matter expert on various CCNA, CCNA-S, and CCNP projects for Cisco and the Cisco Networking Academy. He also authored the *CCNA Accessing the WAN Companion Guide* and the *CCNA Security (640-554) Portable Command Guide*. He is the coauthor of the Cisco Press book *Routing Protocols Companion Guide*.

In his downtime, Bob enjoys playing the guitar, shooting darts or pool, and either working in his gardens or white-water canoe tripping.

Contents At a Glance

Contents

Syntax Conventions

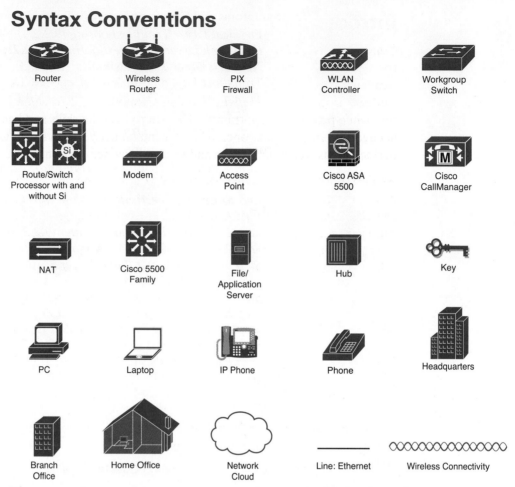

The conventions used to present command syntax in this book are the same conventions used in the IOS Command Reference. The Command Reference describes these conventions as follows:

- **Boldface** indicates commands and keywords that are entered literally as shown. In actual configuration examples and output (not general command syntax), boldface indicates commands that are manually input by the user (such as a **show** command).

- *Italic* indicates arguments for which you supply actual values.

- Vertical bars (|) separate alternative, mutually exclusive elements.

- Square brackets ([ ]) indicate an optional element.

- Braces ({ }) indicate a required choice.

- Braces within brackets ([{ }]) indicate a required choice within an optional element.

Introduction

Connecting Networks Companion Guide is the official supplemental textbook for the Cisco Network Academy Connecting Networks course. Cisco Networking Academy is a comprehensive program that delivers information technology skills to students around the world. The curriculum emphasizes real-world practical application while providing opportunities for you to gain the skills and hands-on experience needed to design, install, operate, and maintain networks in small- to medium-sized businesses, as well as enterprise and service provider environments.

As a textbook, this book provides a ready reference to explain the same networking concepts, technologies, protocols, and devices as the online curriculum. This book emphasizes key topics, terms, and activities and provides some alternate explanations and examples as compared with the course. You can use the online curriculum as directed by your instructor and then use this Companion Guide's study tools to help solidify your understanding of all the topics.

Who Should Read This Book

This book is intended for students enrolled in the Cisco Networking Academy Connecting Networks course. The book, as well as the course, is designed as an introduction to data network technology for those pursuing careers as network professionals as well as those who need only an introduction to network technology for professional growth. Topics are presented concisely, starting with the most fundamental concepts and progressing to a comprehensive understanding of network communication. The content of this text provides the foundation for additional Cisco Academy courses, and preparation for the CCENT and CCNA Routing and Switching certifications.

Book Features

The educational features of this book focus on supporting topic coverage, readability, and practice of the course material to facilitate your full understanding of the course material.

Topic Coverage

The following features give you a thorough overview of the topics covered in each chapter so that you can make constructive use of your study time:

- **Objectives:** Listed at the beginning of each chapter, the objectives reference the core concepts covered in the chapter. The objectives match the objectives stated in the corresponding chapters of the online curriculum; however, the question format in the Companion Guide encourages you to think about finding the answers as you read the chapter.

- **"How-to" feature:** When this book covers a set of steps that you need to perform for certain tasks, the text lists the steps as a how-to list. When you are studying, the icon helps you easily refer to this feature as you skim through the book.

- **Notes:** These are short sidebars that point out interesting facts, timesaving methods, and important safety issues.

- **Chapter summaries:** At the end of each chapter is a summary of the chapter's key concepts. It provides a synopsis of the chapter and serves as a study aid.

- **Practice:** At the end of each chapter, there is a full list of all the labs, class activities, and Packet Tracer activities to refer back to for study time.

Readability

The following features have been updated to assist your understanding of the networking vocabulary:

- **Key terms:** Each chapter begins with a list of key terms, along with a page-number reference from inside the chapter. The terms are listed in the order in which they are explained in the chapter. This handy reference allows you to find a term, flip to the page where the term appears, and see the term used in context. The glossary defines all the key terms.

- **Glossary:** This book contains an all-new glossary with 195 terms.

Practice

Practice makes perfect. This new Companion Guide offers you ample opportunities to put what you learn into practice. You will find the following features valuable and effective in reinforcing the instruction that you receive:

- **Check Your Understanding questions and answer key**: Updated review questions are presented at the end of each chapter as a self-assessment tool. These questions match the style of questions that you see in the online course. Appendix A, "Answers to the 'Check Your Understanding' Questions," provides an answer key to all the questions and includes an explanation of each answer.

Packet Tracer
☐ Activity

Video

- **Labs and activities**: Throughout each chapter, you will be directed back to the online course to take advantage of the activities created to reinforce concepts. In addition, at the end of each chapter, there is a "Practice" section that collects a list of all the labs and activities to provide practice with the topics introduced in this chapter. The labs and class activities are available in the companion *Connecting Networks Lab Manual* (ISBN 978-1-58713-331-2). The Packet Tracer activity PKA files are found in the online course.

- **Page references to online course**: After headings, you will see, for example, (1.1.2.3). This number refers to the page number in the online course so that you can easily jump to that spot online to view a video, practice an activity, perform a lab, or review a topic.

Lab Manual

The supplementary book *Connecting Networks Lab Manual*, by Cisco Press (ISBN 978-1-58713-331-2), contains all the labs and class activities from the course.

Practice and Study Guide

Additional Study Guide exercises, activities, and scenarios are available in *CCNA Routing and Switching Practice and Study Guide* (978-158713-344-2) book by Allan Johnson. The Practice and Study Guide coordinates with the recommended curriculum sequence. The CCNA edition follows the course outlines for Scaling Networks and Connecting Networks.

About Packet Tracer Software and Activities

```
Packet Tracer
☐ Activity
```

Interspersed throughout the chapters, you'll find many activities to work with the Cisco Packet Tracer tool. Packet Tracer allows you to create networks, visualize how packets flow in the network, and use basic testing tools to determine whether the network would work. When you see this icon, you can use Packet Tracer with the listed file to perform a task suggested in this book. The activity files are available in the course. Packet Tracer software is available only through the Cisco Networking Academy website. Ask your instructor for access to Packet Tracer.

How This Book Is Organized

This book corresponds closely to the Cisco Academy Connecting Networks course and is divided into nine chapters, one appendix, and a glossary of key terms:

- **Chapter 1, "Hierarchical Network Design"**: Structured engineering principles of network design are examined. The three layers of hierarchical design and the Cisco Enterprise Architecture model are discussed. Three business architectures are examined: Borderless Network Architecture, Collaboration Network Architecture, and Data Center/Virtualizing Network Architecture.

- **Chapter 2, "Connecting to the WAN"**: Basic WAN operations and services are examined. Private and public WAN technologies are discussed. Includes how to select the appropriate WAN protocol and service for a specific network requirement.

- **Chapter 3, "Point-to-Point Connections"**: Examines point-to-point serial communications using HDLC and PPP. Describes the features and benefits of PPP over HDLC. The PPP layered architecture is discussed as well as the functions of LCP and NCP. PPP authentication is included.

- **Chapter 4, "Frame Relay"**: Examines the benefits and operations of Frame Relay. Bandwidth control mechanisms and basic Frame Relay PVC configuration are discussed.

- **Chapter 5, "Network Address Translation for IPv4"**: Describes the characteristics, benefits and drawbacks of NAT. Configuration of static NAT, dynamic NAT, and PAT are discussed. Port forwarding and NAT64 are introduced.

- **Chapter 6, "Broadband Solutions"**: Introduces various broadband solutions including DSL and cable. Broadband wireless options are described. PPPoE operation and configuration are discussed.

- **Chapter 7, "Securing Site-to-Site Connectivity":** Describes the benefits of VPN technology. Site-to-site and remote-access VPNs are introduced. The purpose, benefits, and configuration of GRE tunnels are examined. IPsec characteristics and protocol framework are examined. How AnyConnect and clientless SSL remote-access VPM implementations support business requirements are discussed. The chapter also compares IPsec and SSL remote-access VPNs.

- **Chapter 8, "Monitoring the Network":** Focuses on monitoring the network including syslog, SNMP, and NetFlow operations. The operations, configuration, and monitoring capabilities of each technology are examined.

- **Chapter 9, "Troubleshooting the Network":** Examines how to develop network documentation that is used to troubleshoot network issues. Describes the general troubleshooting process, along with the systematic layer approach to troubleshooting. Troubleshooting tools are examined and how they are used to gather and analyze symptoms of network problems. Includes determining symptoms and causes of network problems using the layered model.

- **Appendix A, "Answers to the 'Check Your Understanding' Questions":** This appendix lists the answers to the "Check Your Understanding" review questions that are included at the end of each chapter.

- **Glossary:** The glossary provides you with definitions for all the key terms identified in each chapter.

CHAPTER 1

Hierarchical Network Design

Objectives

Upon completion of this chapter

- What are the structured engineering principles of network design?

- How do you apply the three hierarchical network layers in network design?

- What are the four basic modules in an enterprise campus network architecture that interconnect via the core?

- How do the modules of the Cisco Enterprise Architecture model differ?

- What are some trends that are challenging enterprise network architectures?

- How do the Borderless Network, Collaboration Network, and Data Center/Virtualization Network architectures address the network challenges?

Key Terms

This chapter uses the following key terms. You can find the definitions in the glossary.

Introduction (1.0.1.1)

Networks must meet the current needs of organizations and be able to support emerging technologies as new technologies are adopted. Network design principles and models can help a network engineer design and build a network that is flexible, resilient, and manageable.

This chapter introduces network design concepts, principles, models, and architectures. It covers the benefits that are obtained by using a systematic design approach. Emerging technology trends that will affect network evolution are also discussed.

Class Activity 1.0.1.2: Design Hierarchy

A network administrator is tasked with designing an expanded network for the company.

After speaking with network administrators in other branches of the company, it was decided to use the Cisco three-layer hierarchical network design model to influence the expansion. This model was chosen for its simple influence upon network planning.

The three layers of the expanded network design include

- Access
- Distribution
- Core

Hierarchical Network Design Overview (1.1)

The Cisco hierarchical (three-layer) internetworking model is an industry wide adopted model for designing a reliable, scalable, and cost-efficient internetwork. In this section, you will learn about the access, distribution, and core layers and their role in the hierarchical network model.

Enterprise Network Campus Design (1.1.1)

An understanding of network scale and knowledge of good structured engineering principles is recommended when discussing network campus design.

Network Requirements (1.1.1.1)

When discussing network design, it is useful to categorize networks based on the number of devices serviced:

- *Small network*: Provides services for up to 200 devices.

- *Medium-size network*: Provides services for 200 to 1,000 devices.

- *Large network*: Provides services for 1,000+ devices.

Network designs vary depending on the size and requirements of the organizations. For example, the networking infrastructure needs of a small organization with fewer devices will be less complex than the infrastructure of a large organization with a significant number of devices and connections.

There are many variables to consider when designing a network. For instance, consider the example in Figure 1-1. The sample high-level topology diagram is for a large enterprise network that consists of a main campus site connecting small, medium, and large sites.

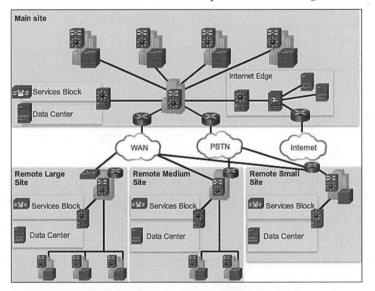

Figure 1-1   Large Enterprise Network Design

Network design is an expanding area and requires a great deal of knowledge and experience. The intent of this section is to introduce commonly accepted network design concepts.

Note

The Cisco Certified Design Associate (CCDA®) is an industry-recognized certification for network design engineers, technicians, and support engineers who demonstrate the skills required to design basic campus, data center, security, voice, and wireless networks.

Structured Engineering Principles (1.1.1.2)

Regardless of network size or requirements, a critical factor for the successful implementation of any network design is to follow good structured engineering principles. These principles include

- **Hierarchy:** A hierarchical network model is a useful high-level tool for designing a reliable network infrastructure. It breaks the complex problem of network design into smaller and more manageable areas.

- **Modularity:** By separating the various functions that exist on a network into modules, the network is easier to design. Cisco has identified several modules, including the enterprise campus, services block, data center, and Internet edge.

- **Resiliency:** The network must remain available for use under both normal and abnormal conditions. Normal conditions include normal or expected traffic flows and traffic patterns, as well as scheduled events such as maintenance windows. Abnormal conditions include hardware or software failures, extreme traffic loads, unusual traffic patterns, denial-of-service (DoS) events, whether intentional or unintentional, and other unplanned events.

- **Flexibility:** The ability to modify portions of the network, add new services, or increase capacity without going through a major forklift upgrade (i.e., replacing major hardware devices).

To meet these fundamental design goals, a network must be built on a hierarchical network architecture that allows for both flexibility and growth.

Hierarchical Network Design (1.1.2)

This topic discusses the three functional layers of the hierarchical network model: the access, distribution, and core layers.

Network Hierarchy (1.1.2.1)

Early networks were deployed in a flat topology as shown in Figure 1-2.

Hubs and switches were added as more devices needed to be connected. A flat network design provided little opportunity to control broadcasts or to filter undesirable traffic. As more devices and applications were added to a flat network, response times degraded, making the network unusable.

A better network design approach was needed. For this reason, organizations now use a hierarchical network design as shown in Figure 1-3.

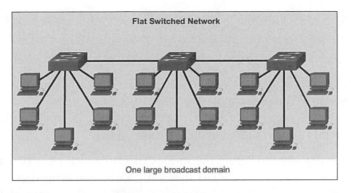

Figure 1-2   Flat Switched Network

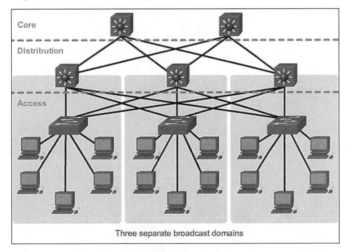

Figure 1-3   Hierarchical Network

A hierarchical network design involves dividing the network into discrete layers. Each layer, or tier, in the hierarchy provides specific functions that define its role within the overall network. This helps the network designer and architect to optimize and select the right network hardware, software, and features to perform specific roles for that network layer. Hierarchical models apply to both LAN and WAN design.

The benefit of dividing a flat network into smaller, more manageable blocks is that local traffic remains local. Only traffic that is destined for other networks is moved to a higher layer. For example, in Figure 1-3 the flat network has now been divided into three separate broadcast domains.

A typical enterprise hierarchical LAN campus network design includes the following three layers:

- **Access layer:** Provides workgroup/user access to the network
- **Distribution layer:** Provides policy-based connectivity and controls the boundary between the access and core layers
- **Core layer:** Provides fast transport between distribution switches within the enterprise campus

Another sample three-layer hierarchical network design is displayed in Figure 1-4. Notice that each building is using the same hierarchical network model that includes the access, distribution, and core layers.

Figure 1-4   Multi Building Enterprise Network Design

Note

There are no absolute rules for the way a campus network is physically built. While it is true that many campus networks are constructed using three physical tiers of switches, this is not a strict requirement. In a smaller campus, the network might have two tiers of switches in which the core and distribution elements are combined in one physical switch. This is referred to as a collapsed core design.

The Access Layer (1.1.2.2)

In a LAN environment, the *access layer* highlighted grants end devices access to the network. In the WAN environment, it may provide teleworkers or remote sites access to the corporate network across WAN connections.

As shown in Figure 1-5, the access layer for a small business network generally incorporates Layer 2 switches and access points providing connectivity between workstations and servers.

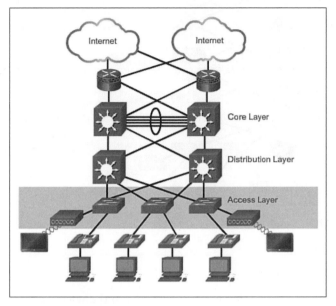

Figure 1-5   Access Layer

The access layer serves a number of functions, including

- Layer 2 switching

- High availability

- Port security

- QoS classification and marking and trust boundaries

- Address Resolution Protocol (ARP) inspection

- Virtual access control lists (VACLs)

- Spanning tree

- Power over Ethernet (PoE) and auxiliary VLANs for VoIP

The Distribution Layer (1.1.2.3)

The *distribution layer* aggregates the data received from the access layer switches before it is transmitted to the core layer for routing to its final destination. In Figure 1-6, the distribution layer is the boundary between the Layer 2 domains and the Layer 3 routed network.

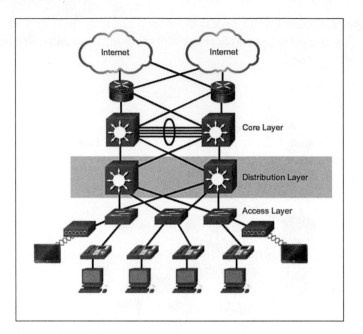

Figure 1-6   Distribution Layer

The distribution layer device is the focal point in the wiring closets. Either a router or a multilayer switch is used to segment workgroups and isolate network problems in a campus environment.

A distribution layer switch may provide upstream services for many access layer switches.

The distribution layer can provide

- Aggregation of LAN or WAN links.

- Policy-based security in the form of access control lists (ACLs) and filtering.

- Routing services between LANs and VLANs and between routing domains (e.g., EIGRP to OSPF).

- Redundancy and load balancing.

- A boundary for route aggregation and summarization configured on interfaces toward the core layer.

- Broadcast domain control, because routers or multilayer switches do not forward broadcasts. The device acts as the demarcation point between broadcast domains.

The Core Layer (1.1.2.4)

The *core layer* is also referred to as the network backbone. The core layer consists of high-speed network devices such as the Cisco Catalyst 6500 or 6800. These are designed to switch packets as fast as possible and interconnect multiple campus components, such as distribution modules, service modules, the data center, and the WAN edge.

As shown in Figure 1-7, the core layer is critical for interconnectivity between distribution layer devices (for example, interconnecting the distribution block to the WAN and Internet edge).

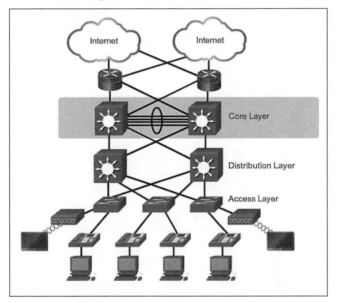

Figure 1-7   Core Layer

The core should be highly available and redundant. The core aggregates the traffic from all the distribution layer devices, so it must be capable of forwarding large amounts of data quickly.

Considerations at the core layer include

- Providing high-speed switching (i.e., fast transport)

- Providing reliability and fault tolerance

- Scaling by using faster, and not more, equipment

- Avoiding CPU-intensive packet manipulation caused by security, inspection, quality of service (QoS) classification, or other processes

Two-Tier Collapsed Core Design (1.1.2.5)

The *three-tier hierarchical design* maximizes performance, network availability, and the ability to scale the network design.

However, many small enterprise networks do not grow significantly larger over time. Therefore, a *two-tier hierarchical design* where the core and distribution layers are collapsed into one layer is often more practical. A *"collapsed core"* is when the distribution layer and core layer functions are implemented by a single device. The primary motivation for the collapsed core design is reducing network cost, while maintaining most of the benefits of the three-tier hierarchical model.

The example in Figure 1-8 has collapsed the distribution layer and core layer functionality into multilayer switch devices.

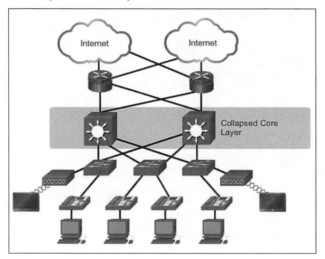

Figure 1-8   Two-Tier Hierarchical Design

The hierarchical network model provides a modular framework that allows flexibility in network design and facilitates ease of implementation and troubleshooting.

Interactive Graphic

Activity 1.1.2.6: Identify Hierarchical Network Characteristics

Go to the course online to perform this practice activity.

Cisco Enterprise Architecture (1.2)

The Cisco Enterprise Architecture is a modular approach to network design. This section identifies enterprise architecture modules that are commonly found in medium-to-large organizations.

Modular Design (1.2.1.1)

While the hierarchical network design works well within the campus infrastructure, networks have expanded beyond these borders. As shown in Figure 1-9, networks have become more sophisticated and complex. The central campus site now requires connections to branch sites and support for teleworking employees working from home offices or other remote locations. Large organizations may also require dedicated connections to offsite data centers.

Figure 1-9   Expanding Beyond the Campus Infrastructure

As the complexity of the network increased to meet these demands, it became necessary to adjust the network design to one that uses a more modular approach.

A *modular network design* separates the network into various functional network modules, each targeting a specific place or purpose in the network. The modules represent areas that have different physical or logical connectivity. They designate where different functions occur in the network. Using a modular approach has several benefits, including

- Failures that occur within a module can be isolated from the remainder of the network, providing for simpler problem detection and higher overall system availability.

- Network changes, upgrades, or the introduction of new services can be made in a controlled and staged fashion, allowing greater flexibility in the maintenance and operation of the campus network.

- When a specific module no longer has sufficient capacity or is missing a new function or service, it can be updated or replaced by another module that has the same structural role in the overall hierarchical design.

- Security can be implemented on a modular basis allowing for more granular security control.

The use of modules in network design enables flexibility and facilitates implementation and troubleshooting.

Modules in the Enterprise Architecture (1.2.1.2)

A modular approach to network design further divides the three-layer hierarchical design by pulling out specific blocks or modular areas. These basic modules are connected together via the core of the network.

Basic network modules include

- **Access-distribution:** Also called the distribution block, this is the most familiar element and fundamental component of a campus design (see Figure 1-10).

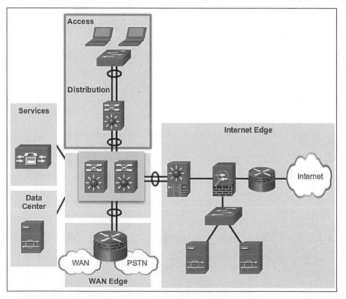

Figure 1-10   Access-Distribution Module

- **Services:** This is a generic block used to identify services such as centralized Lightweight Access Point Protocol (LWAPP) wireless controllers, unified communications services, policy gateways, and more (see Figure 1-11).

Figure 1-11   Services Module

- **Data center:** Originally called the server farm. This block is responsible for managing and maintaining many data systems that are vital to modern business operations. Employees, partners, and customers rely on data and resources in the data center to effectively create, collaborate, and interact (see Figure 1-12).

Figure 1-12   Data Center Module

■ **Enterprise edge:** Consists of the Internet edge and the WAN edge. These blocks offer connectivity to voice, video, and data services outside the enterprise (see Figure 1-13).

Figure 1-13 Enterprise Edge Module

Activity 1.2.1.3: Identify Modules in a Network Design

Go to the course online to perform this practice activity.

Cisco Enterprise Architecture Model (1.2.2)

The Cisco Enterprise Architecture is a modular approach to network design. This topic discusses the enterprise campus module, enterprise edge module, and the service provider edge module.

Cisco Enterprise Architecture Model (1.2.2.1)

To accommodate the need for modularity in network design, Cisco developed the *Cisco Enterprise Architecture model*. This model provides all the benefits of the hierarchical network design on the campus infrastructure, and facilitates the design of larger, more scalable networks.

The Cisco Enterprise Architecture model separates the enterprise network into functional areas that are referred to as modules. The modularity that is built in to the architecture allows flexibility in network design and facilitates implementation and troubleshooting.

As shown in Figure 1-14, the following are the primary Cisco Enterprise Architecture modules:

- Enterprise campus

- Enterprise edge

- Service provider edge

Figure 1-14   Cisco Enterprise Architecture Modules

Connected to the service provider edge are the remote modules, including

- Enterprise branch

- Enterprise teleworker

- Enterprise data center

Cisco Enterprise Campus (1.2.2.2)

A campus network is a building or group of buildings connected into one enterprise network that consists of many LANs. A campus is generally limited to a fixed geographic area, but it can span several neighboring buildings (for example, an industrial complex or business park environment). Regional offices, SOHOs, and mobile workers may need to connect to the central campus for data and information.

The *enterprise campus module* describes the recommended methods to create a scalable network while addressing the needs of campus-style business operations.

The architecture is modular and can easily expand to include additional campus buildings or floors as the enterprise grows.

As shown in Figure 1-15, the enterprise campus module consists of the following submodules:

- Building access
- Building distribution
- Campus core
- Data center

Figure 1-15   Enterprise Campus Module

Together these submodules

- Provide high availability through a resilient hierarchical network design
- Integrate IP communications, mobility, and advanced security
- Utilize multicast traffic and QoS to optimize network traffic
- Provide increased security and flexibility using access management, VLANs, and IPsec VPNs

The enterprise campus module architecture provides the enterprise with high availability through a resilient multilayer design, redundant hardware and software features, and automatic procedures for reconfiguring network paths when failures occur. Integrated security protects against and mitigates the impact of worms, viruses, and other attacks on the network, even at the switch port level.

A high-capacity, centralized data center module can provide internal server resources to users. The data center module typically also supports network management services for the enterprise, including monitoring, logging, troubleshooting, and other common management features from end to end. The data center submodule typically contains internal email and corporate servers that provide application, file, print, email, and Domain Name System (DNS) services to internal users.

Cisco Enterprise Edge (1.2.2.3)

The *enterprise edge module* provides connectivity for voice, video, and data services outside the enterprise. This module often functions as a liaison between the enterprise campus module and the other modules.

As shown in Figure 1-16, the enterprise edge module consists of submodules providing

- E-commerce services
- Internet connectivity
- Remote access and VPN access
- WAN site-to-site VPN access

Figure 1-16   Enterprise Edge Submodules

Specifically, these submodules consist of:

- **E-commerce networks and servers:** The e-commerce submodule enables enterprises to support e-commerce applications through the Internet. It uses the high-availability designs of the data center module. Devices located in the e-commerce submodule include web, application, and database servers; firewall and firewall routers; and network intrusion prevention systems (IPS).

- **Internet connectivity and demilitarized zone (DMZ) :** The Internet submodule of the enterprise edge provides internal users with secure connectivity to Internet services such as public servers, email, and DNS. Connectivity to one or several Internet service providers (ISPs) is also provided. Components of this submodule include firewall and firewall routers, Internet edge routers, FTP and HTTP servers, SMTP relay servers, and DNS servers.

- **Remote access and VPN:** The VPN/remote access submodule of the enterprise edge provides remote-access termination services, including authentication for remote users and sites. Components of this submodule include firewalls, dial-in access concentrators, Cisco Adaptive Security Appliances (ASA), and network intrusion prevention system (IPS) appliances.

- **WAN:** The WAN submodule uses various WAN technologies for routing traffic between remote sites and the central site. Enterprise WAN links include technologies such as Multiprotocol Label Switching (MPLS), Metro Ethernet, leased lines, Synchronous Optical Network (SONET) and Synchronous Digital Hierarchy (SDH), PPP, Frame Relay, ATM, cable, digital subscriber line (DSL), and wireless.

Service Provider Edge (1.2.2.4)

Enterprises use service providers (SPs) to link to other sites. As shown in Figure 1-17, the *SP edge module* can include

- Internet service providers (ISPs)
- WAN services such as Frame Relay, ATM, and MAN
- Public switched telephone network (PSTN) services

Figure 1-17   Service Provider Edge Module

The SP edge provides connectivity between the enterprise campus module to the remote enterprise data center, enterprise branch, and enterprise teleworker modules.

The SP edge module

- Spans across large geographic areas in a cost effective manner
- Converges voice, video, and data services over a single IP communications network
- Supports QoS and service level agreements
- Supports security using VPNs (IPsec / MPLS) over Layer 2 and Layer 3 WANs

When acquiring Internet services from an ISP, redundancy or failover should be considered. Redundant Internet connections vary depending if the enterprise is connecting to a single ISP or multiple ISPs.

As shown in Figure 1-18, redundant connections to a single ISP can include

- **Single-homed:** A single connection to an ISP
- **Dual-homed:** Two or more connections to a single ISP

Figure 1-18 Connecting to a Single ISP

Alternatively, it is possible to set up redundancy using multiple ISPs, as shown in Figure 1-19. Options for connecting to multiple ISPs include

- **Multihomed:** Connections to two or more ISPs
- **Dual-multihomed:** Multiple connections to two or more ISPs

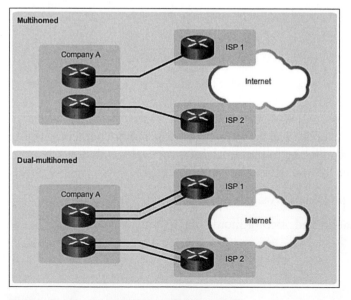

Figure 1-19 Connecting to Multiple ISPs

Remote Functional Area (1.2.2.5)

The remote functional area is responsible for remote connectivity options and includes the following modules, as shown in Figure 1-20.

Figure 1-20   Remote Connectivity Areas

Enterprise Branch

The *enterprise branch module* includes remote branches that allow employees to work at noncampus locations. These locations are typically responsible for providing security, telephony, and mobility options to employees, as well as general connectivity into the campus network and the different components located inside the enterprise campus. The enterprise branch module allows enterprises to extend head-office applications and services, such as security, Cisco Unified Communications, and advanced application performance, to the remote branches. The edge device connecting the remote site to the central site varies depending on the needs and size of the site. Large remote sites may use high-end Cisco Catalyst switches, while smaller sites may use an ISR G2 router. These remote sites rely on the SP edge to provide services and applications from the main site. In Figure 1-20, the enterprise branch module connects to the enterprise campus site primarily using a WAN link. However, it also has an Internet link as a backup. The Internet link uses site-to-site IPsec VPN technology to encrypt corporate data.

Enterprise Teleworker

The *enterprise teleworker module* is responsible for providing connectivity for workers who operate out of different geographically dispersed locations, including home offices, hotels, or customer/client sites. The teleworker module recommends that mobile users connect to the Internet using the services of a local ISP, such as cable modem or DSL. VPN services can then be used to secure communications between the mobile worker and central campus. Integrated security- and identity-based networking services enable the enterprise to extend campus security policies to the teleworker. Staff can securely log in to the network over the VPN and gain access to authorized applications and services from a single cost-effective platform.

Enterprise Data Center

The *enterprise data center module* is a data center with all of the same functional options as a campus data center, but exists at a remote location. This provides an added layer of security as the offsite data center can provide disaster recovery and business continuance services for the enterprise. High-end switches such as the Cisco Nexus series switch use fast WAN services such as Metro Ethernet (MetroE) to connect the enterprise campus to the remote enterprise data center. Redundant data centers provide backup using synchronous and asynchronous data and application replication. Additionally, the network and devices offer server and application load balancing to maximize performance. This solution allows the enterprise to scale without major changes to the infrastructure.

Interactive Graphic

Activity 1.2.2.6: Identify Modules of the Cisco Enterprise Architecture

Go to the course online to perform this practice activity.

Evolving Network Architectures (1.3)

New technologies are constantly challenging network administrators. This section discusses new networking architecture trends.

IT Challenges (1.3.1.1)

As businesses have grown more dependent on networks for success, network architectures have evolved over the years. Traditionally, users, data, and applications were housed on premise. Users could only access network resources with company-owned computers. The network had distinct borders and access requirements. Maintaining security, productivity, and services was simpler. Today, the network border has shifted, creating new challenges for IT departments. Networks are transforming from a data-only transportation system of connected LAN devices to a system that enables the connections of people, devices, and information in a media-rich, converged network environment.

As new technologies and end-user devices come to market, businesses and consumers must continue to adjust to this ever-changing environment. There are several new networking trends that continue to effect organizations and consumers. Some of the top trends include

- Bring your own device (BYOD)
- Online collaboration
- Video communication
- Cloud computing

These trends, while allowing for more advanced services than ever before, also introduce new security risks that IT must address.

Emerging Enterprise Architectures (1.3.1.2)

The speed of change in market and business environments is requiring IT to be more strategic than ever before. Evolving business models are creating complex technology challenges that IT must address.

To address these emerging network trends, new business network architectures are necessary. These architectures must account for the network design principles established in the Cisco Enterprise Architecture, as well as the overlaying policies and technologies that allow organizations to support emerging trends in a safe and manageable way.

To meet this need, Cisco has introduced the following three network architectures:

- Cisco Borderless Network Architecture
- Collaboration Architecture
- Data Center/Virtualization Architecture

Note

Network architectures continually evolve. The intent of this section is to provide an introduction and overview of emerging architecture trends.

Emerging Network Architectures (1.3.2)

Cisco has been at the forefront of network design for decades. They consistently adopt existing networks and develop new network architectures. This topic introduces the Cisco Borderless Network Architecture, the Collaboration Architecture, and the Data Center and Virtualization Architecture.

Cisco Borderless Networks (1.3.2.1)

The *Cisco Borderless Network Architecture* is a network solution that allows organizations and individuals to connect securely, reliably, and seamlessly to the corporate network in a BYOD environment. It is based on wired, wireless, routing, switching, security, and application optimization devices working in harmony to help IT balance demanding business challenges and changing business models.

It is not a static solution, but an evolving solution to help IT evolve its infrastructure to deliver secure, reliable, and seamless user experiences in a world with many new and shifting borders.

It enables an IT department to architect and deploy its systems and policies efficiently to all end user devices that require connection to the network. In doing this, it provides secure, reliable, and seamless access to resources from multiple locations, from multiple devices, and to applications that can be located anywhere.

Specifically, the Cisco Borderless Network Architecture delivers two primary sets of services:

- **Borderless end-point/user services:** As highlighted in Figure 1-21, borderless end-point/user services connect the various devices to provide access to network services. Devices that can connect to the borderless network can range from PCs to tablets and smartphones. It removes the location and device borders, providing unified access to wired and wireless devices. End-point/user services define the user experience and enable the attributes of secure, reliable, and seamless performance on a broad range of devices and environments, as shown in Figure 1-21. For example, most smartphones and tablets can download and use the Cisco AnyConnect software. It enables the device to establish a secure, persistent, policy-based connection for a seamless user experience.

- **Borderless network services:** As highlighted in Figure 1-22, borderless network services unify the approach to securely deliver applications to users in a highly distributed environment. It securely connects internal users and remote users and provides access to network resources. The crucial element to scaling secure access is a policy-based architecture that allows IT to implement centralized access controls.

Figure 1-21   Borderless Network Architecture

Figure 1-22   Services Supported in Borderless Networks

The borderless network architecture supports a highly secure, high-performing network that is accessible to a wide range of devices. It needs to be flexible enough to scale in its support for future growth in terms of business expansion, including BYOD, mobility and cloud computing and must be able to support the growing requirements for online voice and video.

Collaboration Architecture (1.3.2.2)

Working in a collaborative environment helps increase productivity. Collaboration and other types of groupware are used to bring people together for one reason or another: such as to socialize, to work together, to cooperate and contribute to the production of something, and to innovate.

The *Cisco Collaboration Architecture* comprises a portfolio of products, applications, software development kits (SDKs), and APIs. The individual components work together to provide a comprehensive solution.

As shown in Figure 1-23, Cisco's collaboration architecture is composed of three layers:

- **Application and Devices:** This layer contains unified communications and conference applications such as Cisco WebEx Meetings, WebEx Social, Cisco Jabber, and TelePresence. The applications within this layer help users stay connected and productive. These applications include voice, video, web conferencing, messaging, mobile applications, and enterprise social software.

- **Collaboration Services:** This layer supports collaboration applications including the following services: presence, location, session management, contact management, client frameworks, tagging, and policy and security management.

- **Network and Computer Infrastructure:** This layer is responsible for allowing collaboration anytime, from anywhere, on any device. It includes virtual machines, the network, and storage.

Figure 1-23   Cisco Collaboration Architecture

Data Center and Virtualization (1.3.2.3)

The *Cisco Data Center/Virtualization Architecture* is built upon Cisco Data Center 3.0. It comprises a comprehensive set of virtualization technologies and services that bring the network, computing, storage, and virtualization platforms together.

The Data Center Architecture consists of three components, as shown in Figure 1-24:

- **Cisco Unified Management Solutions:** Management solutions simplify and automate the process of deploying IT infrastructure and services with speed and enterprise reliability. Solutions operate transparently across physical and virtual resources in cloud environments.

- **Unified Fabric Solutions:** Flexible network solutions deliver network services to servers, storage, and applications, providing transparent convergence, scalability, and sophisticated intelligence. Solutions include Cisco Nexus switches, Catalyst switches, Cisco Fabric Manager, and Cisco NX-OS software.

- **Unified Computing Solutions:** Cisco's next-generation data center system unites computing, network, storage access, and virtualization into a cohesive system designed to reduce total cost of ownership (TCO) and increase business agility. The Cisco Unified Computing System (Cisco UCS) is built with blade servers, rack-mount servers, fabric interconnects, and virtual interface cards (VICs).

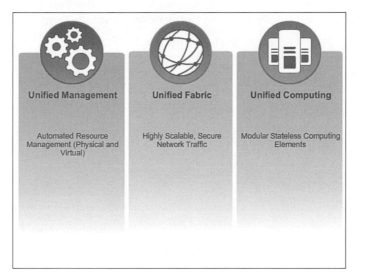

Figure 1-24   Components of the Data Center Architecture

Video 1.3.2.3: Cisco Unified Fabric

Go to the course to see a short video on the Cisco Unified Fabric.

Expanding the Network (1.3.2.4)

These three architectures are built on an infrastructure of scalable and resilient hardware and software. Components of the architecture come together to build network systems that span an organization from network access to the cloud, and provide organizations with the services they need.

Building off the basic network infrastructure, organizations can use these network architectures to grow their network over time, adding features and functionality in an integrated solution.

One of the first steps in growing the network is expanding from the campus infrastructure to a network that connects remote sites through the Internet and through the WAN.

Interactive Graphic

Video 1.3.2.4: Evolution of a Corporate WAN

Go to the course to see a short video on the evolution of a network to a WAN infrastructure.

Interactive Graphic

Activity 1.3.2.5: Identify Evolving Network Architecture Terminology

Go to the course online to perform this practice activity.

Summary (1.4)

Class Activity 1.4.1.1: Borderless Innovations - Everywhere

You are the network administrator for your small- to medium-size business. Borderless network services interest you as you plan your network's future.

While planning for network policies and services, you realize that your wired and wireless networks need manageability and deployment design.

Therefore, this leads you to consider the following Cisco borderless services as possible options for your business:

- **Security:** TrustSec
- **Mobility:** Motion
- **Application performance:** App Velocity
- **Multimedia performance:** Medianet
- **Energy management:** EnergyWise

Packet Tracer
☐ Activity

Packet Tracer Activity 1.4.1.2: Skills Integration Challenge

This Packet Tracer Activity provides an opportunity to review skills from previous coursework.

Your business has just expanded into a different town and needs to expand its presence across the Internet. You are tasked with completing the upgrades to the enterprise network, which includes dual-stacked IPv4 and IPv6 as well as a variety of addressing and routing technologies.

Packet Tracer
☐ Activity

Packet Tracer Activity 1.4.1.3: Skills Integration Challenge - EIGRP

You are a network technician new to a company that has lost its last technician in the middle of a system upgrade. You are tasked with completing upgrades to the network infrastructure that has two locations. Half of the enterprise network uses IPv4 addressing, and the other half uses IPv6 addressing. The requirements also include a variety of routing and switching technologies.

The structured engineering principles of good network design include hierarchy, modularity, resiliency, and flexibility.

A typical enterprise hierarchical LAN campus network design includes the access layer, distribution layer, and the core layer. In smaller enterprise networks, a "collapsed core" hierarchy, where the distribution layer and core layer functions are implemented in a single device, can be more practical. The benefits of a hierarchical network include scalability, redundancy, performance, and maintainability.

A modular design that separates the functions of a network enables flexibility and facilitates implementation and management. The basic module blocks that are connected by the core include the access distribution block, the services block, the data center, and the enterprise edge. The Cisco Enterprise Architecture modules are used to facilitate the design of large, scalable networks. The primary modules include the enterprise campus, enterprise edge, service provider edge, enterprise data center, enterprise branch, and enterprise teleworker.

Practice

The following activities provide practice with the topics introduced in this chapter. The Labs and Class Activities are available in the companion Connecting Networks Lab Manual (978-1-58713-331-2). The Packet Tracer Activity PKA files are found in the online course.

Class Activities

Class Activity 1.0.1.2: Design Hierarchy

Class Activity 1.4.1.1: Borderless Innovations - Everywhere

Packet Tracer
☐ Activity

Packet Tracer Activities

Packet Tracer Activity 1.4.1.2: Skills Integration Challenge - OSPF

Packet Tracer Activity 1.4.1.3: Skills Integration Challenge - EIGRP

Check Your Understanding Questions

Complete all the review questions listed here to test your understanding of the topics and concepts in this chapter. The appendix, "Answers to the 'Check Your Understanding' Questions," lists the answers.

1. What are the four structured design principles?

   A. Availability, flexibility, modularity, and security

   B. Availability, hierarchy, modularity, quality of service (QoS)

   C. Flexibility, hierarchy, modularity, resiliency

   D. Flexibility, modularity, resiliency, and security

   E. Hierarchy, quality of service (QoS), resiliency, and security

   F. Hierarchy, modularity, resiliency, and security

   G. Modularity, quality of service (QoS), resiliency, and security

2. Which layer of the hierarchical network design model is often called the backbone?

   A. Access

   B. Core

   C. Distribution

   D. Network

   E. WAN

   F. Workgroup

3. Which network architecture combines individual components to provide a comprehensive solution allowing people to cooperate and contribute to the production of something?

   A. Cisco Collaboration Architecture

   B. Cisco Enterprise Campus Architecture

   C. Cisco Enterprise Branch Architecture

   D. Cisco Enterprise Data Center Architecture

   E. Cisco Borderless Network Architecture

   F. Cisco Enterprise Teleworker module

4. At which layer of the hierarchical network model do users connect to the network?

   A. Access

   B. Application

   C. Core

   D. Distribution

   E. Network

5. Which two statements regarding the Cisco AnyConnect software are true? (Choose two.)

   A. It is part of the borderless end-point/user services.

   B. It is part of the borderless network services.

   C. It is used to connect any device to the network.

   D. It is used to connect from anywhere.

   E. It is used to connect without an Internet connection.

   F. It is used to establish a secure, persistent, policy-based connection.

6. Which three devices are found in the access layer of the hierarchical network model? (Choose three.)

   A. Firewall appliance

   B. Layer 2 switch

   C. Layer 3 switch

   D. Modular multilayer switch

   E. VoIP phones

   F. Wireless access point

7. Which two statements correctly describe a collapsed core network design? (Choose two.)

   A. Also called a two-tier hierarchical network design

   B. Also called a three-tier hierarchical network design

   C. Consists of the access layer and distribution layer in one device

   D. Consists of the access layer and core layer in one device

   E. Consists of the distribution and core layer in one device

8. Which goal can be accomplished by implementing the Cisco enterprise teleworker module?

   A. It allows the enterprise to add large branch sites that span geographic areas.

   B. It allows the enterprise to deliver secure voice and data services to workers no matter where or when they work.

   C. To reduce remote security threats, it forces users who are located at main sites to log on to resources.

   D. It satisfies telephony requirements for users who are located at medium to large enterprise sites.

9. What should be considered first when starting the network design?

   A. Connectivity to the data center

   B. Connectivity to the branch site

   C. Protocols required

   D. Size of the network

   E. Type of security implemented

   F. Type of applications

10. Which network architecture functions through a combination of technologies that include wired, wireless, security, and more?

    A. Cisco Borderless Network

    B. Cisco Enterprise Branch

    C. Cisco Enterprise Campus

    D. Cisco Enterprise Edge

    E. Cisco Enterprise Teleworker

11. What does the application and device layer of the Cisco Collaboration Architecture do?

    A. It contains applications such as Cisco WebEx Meetings, Cisco Jabber, and TelePresence to help users stay connected and productive.

    B. It is responsible for allowing collaboration anytime, from anywhere, on any device.

    C. It supports collaboration applications with presence, location, session management, contact management, client frameworks, tagging, and policy and security management.

CHAPTER 2

Connecting to the WAN

Objectives

Upon completion of this chapter

- What is the purpose of a WAN?

- How does a circuit-switched network differ from a packet-switched network?

- How do service provider networks connect to enterprise networks?

- How do the link connection options available from private WAN infrastructures and public WAN infrastructures differ?

- What questions should you answer when choosing a WAN link connection?

Key Terms

This chapter uses the following key terms. You can find the definitions in the glossary.

service provider   page 38

digital subscriber line (DSL)   page 40

Point-to-Point Protocol (PPP)   page 45

Frame Relay   page 45

Asynchronous Transfer Mode (ATM) page 45

High-Level Data Link Control (HDLC) page 45

customer premises equipment (CPE) page 46

data communications equipment (DCE)   page 46

data terminal equipment (DTE)   page 46

demarcation point   page 46

local loop   page 47

central office (CO)   page 47

toll network   page 47

dialup modem   page 47

access server   page 48

broadband modem   page 48

channel service unit / data service unit (CSU/ DSU)   page 48

circuit-switched network   page 48

Integrated Services Digital Network (ISDN)   page 49

packet-switched network (PSN)   page 50

virtual circuit (VC)   page 50

private WAN infrastructure   page 51

public WAN infrastructure   page 51

Synchronous Optical Networking (SONET)   page 52

Synchronous Digital Hierarchy (SDH) page 52

light-emitting diodes (LEDs)   page 52

dense wavelength-division multiplexing (DWDM)   page 53

leased lines   page 54

Basic Rate Interface (BRI)   page 57

Introduction (2.0.1.1)

Businesses must connect local-area networks (LANs) together to provide communications between them, even when these LANs are far apart. Wide-area networks (WANs) are used to connect remote LANs together. A WAN may cover a city, country, or global region. A WAN is owned by a service provider, and a business pays a fee to use the provider's WAN network services.

Different technologies are used for WANs than for LANs. This chapter introduces WAN standards, technologies, and purposes. It covers selecting the appropriate WAN technologies, services, and devices to meet the changing business requirements of an evolving enterprise.

Class Activity 2.0.1.2: Branching Out

Your medium-size company is opening a new branch office to serve a wider, client-based network. This branch will focus on regular day-to-day network operations, but will also provide TelePresence, web conferencing, IP telephony, video on demand, and wireless services.

Although you know that an ISP can provide WAN routers and switches to accommodate the branch office connectivity for the network, you prefer to use your own customer premises equipment (CPE). To ensure interoperability, Cisco devices have been used in all other branch-office WANs.

As the branch-office network administrator, it is your responsibility to research possible network devices for purchase and use over the WAN.

WAN Technologies Overview (2.1)

As an organization expands, WAN connections are necessary. This section discusses the purpose of WANs, introduces WAN terminology, WAN devices, and circuit-switch / packet-switch networks.

Why a WAN? (2.1.1.1)

A WAN operates beyond the geographic scope of a LAN. As shown in Figure 2-1, WANs are used to interconnect the enterprise LAN to remote LANs in branch sites and telecommuter sites.

Figure 2-1   WANs Interconnect Users and LANs

A WAN is owned by a *service provider*. An organization must pay a fee to use the provider's network services to connect remote sites. WAN service providers include carriers, such as a telephone network, cable company, or satellite service. Service providers provide links to interconnect remote sites for the purpose of transporting data, voice, and video.

In contrast, LANs are typically owned by the organization and used to connect local computers, peripherals, and other devices within a single building or other small geographic area.

Are WANs Necessary? (2.1.1.2)

Without WANs, LANs would be a series of isolated networks. LANs provide both speed and cost-efficiency for transmitting data over relatively small geographic areas. However, as organizations expand, businesses require communication among geographically separated sites. The following are some examples:

- Regional or branch offices of an organization need to be able to communicate and share data with the central site.

- Organizations need to share information with other customer organizations. For example, software manufacturers routinely communicate product and promotional information to distributors that sell their products to end users.

- Employees who travel on company business frequently need to access information that resides on their corporate networks.

Home computer users also need to send and receive data across increasingly larger distances. Here are some examples:

- Consumers now commonly communicate over the Internet with banks, stores, and a variety of providers of goods and services.

- Students do research for classes by accessing library indexes and publications located in other parts of their country and in other parts of the world.

It is not feasible to connect computers across a country, or around the world, with physical cables. Therefore, different technologies have evolved to support this communication requirement. Increasingly, the Internet is being used as an inexpensive alternative to enterprise WANs. New technologies are available to businesses to provide security and privacy for their Internet communications and transactions. WANs used by themselves, or in concert with the Internet, allow organizations and individuals to meet their wide-area communication needs.

Evolving Networks (2.1.1.3)

Every business is unique, and how an organization grows depends on many factors. These factors include the type of products or service the business sells, the management philosophy of the owners, and the economic climate of the country in which the business operates.

In slow economic times, many businesses focus on increasing their profitability by improving the efficiency of their existing operations, increasing employee productivity, and lowering operating costs. Establishing and managing networks can represent significant installation and operating expenses. To justify such a large expense, companies expect their networks to perform optimally and to be able to deliver an ever increasing array of services and applications to support productivity and profitability.

The example used in this chapter is of a fictitious company called SPAN Engineering. The following topics provide an example of how the network requirements of SPAN Engineering change as the company grows from a small local business into a global enterprise.

Small Office (2.1.1.4)

SPAN Engineering is an environmental consulting firm that has developed a special process for converting household waste into electricity. SPAN Engineering is developing a small pilot project for a municipal government in its local area. The company, which has been in business for 4 years, has grown to include 15 employees: 6 engineers, 4 computer-aided drawing (CAD) designers, a receptionist, 2 senior partners, and 2 office assistants.

SPAN Engineering's management is working to win full-scale contracts after the pilot project successfully demonstrates the feasibility of their process. Until then, the company must manage its costs carefully.

For their small office, SPAN Engineering uses a single LAN to share information between computers, and to share peripherals, such as a printer, a large-scale plotter (to print engineering drawings), and fax equipment. They have recently upgraded their LAN to provide inexpensive Voice over IP (VoIP) service to save on the costs of separate phone lines for their employees.

The SPAN Engineering network consists of a small office as shown in Figure 2-2.

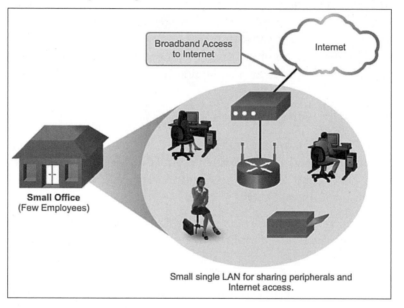

Figure 2-2   Connecting a Small Office

Connection to the Internet is through a common broadband service called *digital subscriber line (DSL)*, which is supplied by their local telephone service provider. With so few employees, bandwidth is not a significant problem.

The company cannot afford in-house IT support staff, and uses support services purchased from the DSL provider. The company also uses a hosting service rather than purchasing and operating its own FTP and email servers.

Campus Network (2.1.1.5)

Five years later, SPAN Engineering has grown rapidly. The company was contracted to design and implement a full-size waste-conversion facility soon after the successful implementation of their first pilot plant. Since then, SPAN has won other projects in neighboring municipalities, and in other parts of the country.

To handle the additional workload, the business has hired more staff and leased more office space. It is now a small- to medium-size business with several hundred employees. Many projects are being developed at the same time, and each requires a project manager and support staff. The company has organized itself into functional departments, with each department having its own organizational team. To meet its growing needs, the company has moved into several floors of a larger office building, as shown in Figure 2-3.

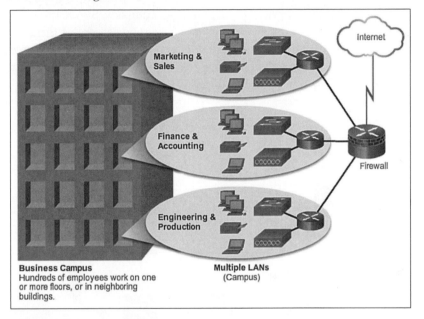

Figure 2-3   Connecting a Campus Network

As the business has expanded, the network has also grown. Instead of a single small LAN, the network now consists of several subnetworks, each devoted to a different department. For example, all the engineering staff is on one LAN, while the marketing staff is on another LAN.

These multiple LANs are joined to create a company-wide campus network which spans several floors of the building.

The business now has in-house IT staff to support and maintain the network. The network includes dedicated servers for email, data transfer, and file storage, and web-based productivity tools and applications. There is also a company intranet to provide in-house documents and information to employees. An extranet provides project information to designated customers.

Branch Networks (2.1.1.6)

Another 6 years later, SPAN Engineering has been so successful with its patented process that demand for its services has skyrocketed. New projects are underway in multiple cities. To manage those projects, the company has opened small branch offices closer to the project sites.

This situation presents new challenges to the IT team. To manage the delivery of information and services throughout the company, SPAN Engineering now has a data center, which houses the various databases and servers of the company. To ensure that all parts of the business are able to access the same services and applications regardless of where the offices are located, the company must now implement a WAN, as shown in Figure 2-4.

Figure 2-4   Connecting Branch Networks

Connecting to its branch sites may occur over dedicated private lines or by using the Internet. For its branch office that is in a nearby city, the company decides to use private dedicated lines through their local service provider. However, for its regional office and remote office located in another country, the Internet is an attractive WAN connection option. Although connecting offices through the Internet is economical, it introduces security and privacy issues that the IT team must address.

Distributed Network (2.1.1.7)

SPAN Engineering has now been in business for 20 years and has grown to thousands of employees distributed in offices worldwide. The cost of the network and its related services is a significant expense. The company is looking to provide its employees with the best network services at the lowest cost. Optimized network services would allow each employee to work at a high rate of efficiency.

To increase profitability, SPAN Engineering must reduce its operating expenses. It has relocated some of its office facilities to less-expensive areas. The company is also encouraging teleworking and virtual teams. Web-based applications, including web conferencing, e-learning, and online collaboration tools, are being used to increase productivity and reduce costs. Site-to-site and remote access virtual private networks (VPNs) enable the company to use the Internet to connect easily and securely with employees and facilities around the world. To meet these requirements, the network must provide the necessary converged services and secure Internet WAN connectivity to remote offices and individuals, as shown in Figure 2-5.

Figure 2-5   Connecting a Global Enterprise Network

As seen in this example, network requirements of a company can change dramatically as the company grows over time. Distributing employees saves costs in many ways, but it puts increased demands on the network. Not only must a network meet the day-to-day operational needs of the business, but it must also be able to adapt and grow as the company changes. Network designers and administrators meet these challenges by carefully choosing network technologies, protocols, and service providers, and by optimizing their networks using many of the network design techniques and architectures described in this course.

Interactive Graphic

Activity 2.1.1.8: Identify WAN Topologies

Go to the course online to perform this practice activity.

WAN Operations (2.1.2)

This topic introduces common WAN terminology and devices and differentiates between circuit-switch and packet-switch networks.

WANs in the OSI Model (2.1.2.1)

As shown in Figure 2-6, WAN operations focus primarily on the physical layer (OSI Layer 1) and the data link layer (OSI Layer 2).

Figure 2-6   WANs Operate in Layer 1 and Layer 2

WAN access standards typically describe both physical layer delivery methods and data link layer requirements, including physical addressing, flow control, and encapsulation.

WAN access standards are defined and managed by a number of recognized authorities, including the

- Telecommunication Industry Association and the Electronic Industries Alliance (TIA/EIA)

- International Organization for Standardization (ISO)

- Institute of Electrical and Electronics Engineers (IEEE)

Layer 1 protocols describe how to provide electrical, mechanical, operational, and functional connections to the services of a communications service provider.

Layer 2 protocols define how data is encapsulated for transmission toward a remote location, and the mechanisms for transferring the resulting frames. A variety of different technologies are used, such as the *Point-to-Point Protocol (PPP)*, *Frame Relay*, and *Asynchronous Transfer Mode (ATM)*. Some of these protocols use the same basic framing or a subset of the *High-Level Data Link Control (HDLC)* mechanism.

Most WAN links are point to point. For this reason, the address field in the Layer 2 frame is usually not used.

Common WAN Terminology (2.1.2.2)

One primary difference between a WAN and a LAN is that an organization must subscribe to an outside WAN service provider and use the WAN carrier network services to interconnect its sites and users. A WAN uses data links provided by carrier services to access the Internet and connect different locations of an organization to each other, to locations of other organizations, to external services, and to remote users.

The physical layer of a WAN describes the physical connections between the company network and the service provider network. As illustrated in Figure 2-7, common terminology is used to describe WAN components and reference points.

Figure 2-7   Common WAN Terminology

Specifically, these terms include

- *Customer premises equipment (CPE)*: The devices and inside wiring located on the enterprise edge connecting to a carrier link. The subscriber either owns the CPE or leases the CPE from the service provider. A subscriber, in this context, is a company that arranges for WAN services from a service provider.

- *Data communications equipment (DCE)*: Also called data circuit-terminating equipment, the DCE consists of devices that put data on the local loop. The DCE primarily provides an interface to connect subscribers to a communication link on the WAN cloud.

- *Data terminal equipment (DTE)*: The customer devices that pass the data from a customer network or host computer for transmission over the WAN. The DTE connects to the local loop through the DCE.

- *Demarcation point*: A point established in a building or complex to separate customer equipment from service provider equipment. Physically, the demarcation point is the cabling junction box, located on the customer premises, that connects the CPE wiring to the local loop. It is usually placed for easy access by a technician. The demarcation point is the place where the responsibility for the connection changes from the user to the service provider. When problems arise, it is necessary to determine whether the user or the service provider is responsible for troubleshooting or repair.

- *Local loop*: The actual copper or fiber cable that connects the CPE to the CO of the service provider. The local loop is also sometimes called the "last mile."

- *Central office (CO)*: The CO is the local service provider facility or building that connects the CPE to the provider network.

- *Toll network*: This consists of the long-haul, all-digital, fiber-optic communications lines, switches, routers, and other equipment inside the WAN provider network.

WAN Devices (2.1.2.3)

As illustrated in Figure 2-8, there are various methods, and therefore devices, that are used to access the WAN connection. Service providers also have specific WAN devices within their network and devices that are required to interconnect to other WAN providers.

Figure 2-8   WAN Devices

The example in the figure identifies the following WAN devices:

- *Dialup modem*: Considered to be a legacy WAN technology, a voiceband modem converts (i.e., modulates) the digital signals produced by a computer into voice frequencies that can be transmitted over the analog lines of the public telephone network. On the other side of the connection, another modem converts the sounds back into a digital signal (i.e., demodulates) for input to a computer or network connection.

- *Access server*: Devices used to concentrate the dial-in and dial-out user communications of dialup modems. Considered to be a legacy technology, an access server may have a mixture of analog and digital interfaces and support hundreds of simultaneous users.

- *Broadband modem*: A type of digital modem used with high-speed DSL or cable Internet service. Both operate in a similar manner to the voiceband modem, but use higher broadband frequencies and transmission speeds.

- *Channel service unit / data service unit (CSU/DSU)*: Digital leased lines require a CSU and a DSU. A CSU/DSU can be a separate device like a modem or it can be an interface on a router. The CSU provides termination for the digital signal and ensures connection integrity through error correction and line monitoring. The DSU converts the line frames into frames that the LAN can interpret and vice versa.

- **WAN switch**: A multiport internetworking device used in service provider networks. These devices typically switch traffic, such as Frame Relay or ATM and operate at Layer 2.

- **Router**: This is a CPE device that provides internetworking and WAN access interface ports used to connect to the service provider network. These interfaces may be serial connections, Ethernet, or other WAN interfaces. With some types of WAN interfaces, an external device, such as a DSU/CSU or modem (analog, cable, or DSL), is required to connect the router to the local service provider.

- **Core router/multilayer switch**: These are the routers and multilayer switches that reside within the service provider WAN backbone. To fulfill this role, the devices must be able to support routing protocols being used in the core and multiple high speed interfaces used in the WAN core backbone. They must also be able to forward IP packets at full speed on all of those interfaces. Key core routers interconnect to other provider core routers.

Note

The preceding list is not exhaustive, and other devices may be required depending on the WAN access technology chosen.

The type of devices used depends on the WAN technology implemented. These WAN technologies are implemented over either circuit-switched or packet-switched networks.

Circuit-Switched Networks (2.1.2.4)

A *circuit-switched network* is one that establishes a dedicated circuit (or channel) between nodes and terminals before the users may communicate. As illustrated in

Figure 2-9, circuit switching dynamically establishes a dedicated virtual connection for voice or data between a sender and a receiver. Before communication can start, it is necessary to establish the connection through the network of the service provider. It is important to note that the circuit must remain established and never change or communication will be terminated.

Figure 2-9   Circuit-Switched Connection

As an example, when a subscriber makes a telephone call, the dialed number is used to set switches in the exchanges along the route of the call so that there is a continuous circuit from the caller to the called party. Because of the switching operation used to establish the circuit, the telephone system is called a circuit-switched network. If the telephones are replaced with modems, then the switched circuit is able to carry computer data.

If the circuit carries computer data, the usage of this fixed capacity may not be efficient. For example, if the circuit is used to access the Internet, there is a burst of activity on the circuit while a web page is transferred. This could be followed by no activity while the user reads the page, and then another burst of activity while the next page is transferred. This variation in usage between none and maximum is typical of computer network traffic. Because the subscriber has sole use of the fixed capacity allocation, switched circuits are generally an expensive way of moving data.

The two most common types of circuit-switched WAN technologies are the public switched telephone network (PSTN) and the *Integrated Services Digital Network (ISDN)*.

Video 2.1.2.4: Circuit-Switched Network

Video

Go to the course and play the animation to see how a circuit-switch network connects host A to host B.

Packet-Switched Networks (2.1.2.5)

In contrast to circuit switching, packet switching splits traffic data into packets that are routed over a shared network. Packet-switching networks do not require a circuit to be established, and they allow many pairs of nodes to communicate over the same channel.

The routers in a *packet-switched network (PSN)* determine the links that packets must be sent over based on the addressing information in each packet. The following are two approaches to this link determination:

- **Connectionless systems:** Full addressing information must be carried in each packet. Each router must evaluate the address to determine where to send the packet. An example of a connectionless system is the Internet.

- **Connection-oriented systems:** The network predetermines the route for a packet, and each packet only has to carry an identifier. The router determines the onward route by looking up the identifier in tables held in memory. The set of entries in the tables identifies a particular route or circuit through the system. When the circuit is established temporarily while a packet is traveling through it, and then breaks down again, it is called a *virtual circuit (VC)*. An example of a connection-oriented system is Frame Relay. In the case of Frame Relay, the identifiers used are called data-link connection identifiers (DLCIs).

Because the internal links between the switches are shared between many users, the cost of packet switching is lower than that of circuit-switching. However, delays (latency) and variability of delay (jitter) are greater in packet-switched networks than in circuit-switched networks. This is because the links are shared and because packets must be entirely received at one switch before moving to the next. Despite the latency and jitter inherent in shared networks, modern technology allows satisfactory transport of voice and video communications on these networks.

Video

Video 2.1.2.5: Packet-Switched Network

Go to the course and play the animation to see how a packet-switch network connects host A to host B. In the animation, SRV1 is sending data to SRV2. As the packet traverses the provider network, it arrives at the second provider switch. The packet is added to the queue and forwarded after the other packets in the queue have been forwarded. Eventually, the packet reaches SRV2.

Interactive Graphic

Activity 2.1.2.6: Identify WAN Terminology

Go to the course online to perform this practice activity.

Selecting a WAN Technology (2.2)

Corporate networks can be interconnected using private WAN infrastructures and public WAN infrastructures. This section discusses both types of infrastructures.

WAN Link Connection Options (2.2.1.1)

There are several WAN access connection options that ISPs can use to connect the local loop to the enterprise edge. These WAN access options differ in technology, speed, and cost. Each has distinct advantages and disadvantages. Familiarity with these technologies is an important part of network design.

As summarized in Figure 2-10, an enterprise can get WAN access over a

- *Private WAN infrastructure*: Service providers may offer dedicated point-to-point leased lines, circuit-switched links, such as PSTN or ISDN, and packet-switched links, such as Ethernet WAN, ATM, or Frame Relay.

- *Public WAN infrastructure*: Service provider may offer broadband Internet access using digital subscriber line (DSL), cable, and satellite access. Broadband connection options are typically used to connect small offices and telecommuting employees to a corporate site over the Internet. Data traveling between corporate sites over the public WAN infrastructure should be protected using VPNs.

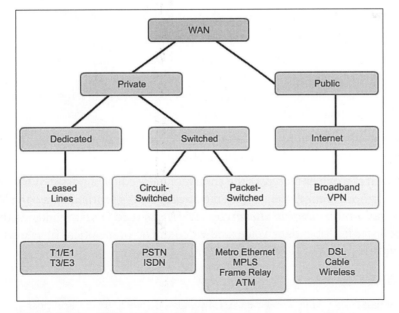

Figure 2-10   WAN Access Options

The topology in Figure 2-11 illustrates some of these WAN access technologies.

Figure 2-11   WAN Access Technologies

Service Provider Network Infrastructure (2.2.1.2)

When a WAN service provider receives data from a client at a site, it must forward the data to the remote site for final delivery to the recipient. In some cases, the remote site may be connected to the same service provider as the originating site. In other cases, the remote site may be connected to a different ISP, and the originating ISP must pass the data to the connecting ISP.

Long-range communications are usually those connections between ISPs or between branch offices in very large companies.

Service provider networks are complex. They consist mostly of high-bandwidth fiber-optic media, using either the *Synchronous Optical Networking (SONET)* or *Synchronous Digital Hierarchy (SDH)* standard. These standards define how to transfer multiple data, voice, and video traffic over optical fiber using lasers or *light-emitting diodes (LEDs)* over great distances.

Note

SONET is an American-based ANSI standard, while SDH is a European-based ETSI and ITU standard. Both are essentially the same and, therefore, often listed as SONET/SDH.

A newer fiber-optic media development for long-range communications is called *dense wavelength-division multiplexing (DWDM)*. DWDM multiplies the amount of bandwidth that a single strand of fiber can support. As illustrated in Figure 2-12, DWDM assigns incoming signals specific color wavelengths. These signals are transmitted over the fiber-optic cable to the end device, which then separates the traffic accordingly.

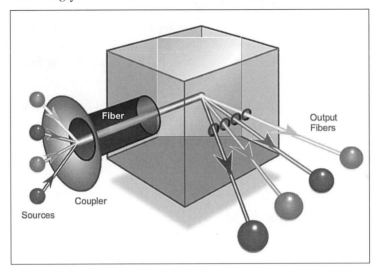

Figure 2-12   DWDM Concept

DWDM circuits are used in all modern submarine communications cable systems and other long-haul circuits.

Specifically, DWDM

- Enables bidirectional communications over one strand of fiber

- Assigns incoming optical signals to specific wavelengths of light (i.e., frequencies)

- Each channel is capable of carrying a 10-Gbps multiplexed signal

- Can multiplex more than 80 different channels of data (i.e., wavelengths) onto a single fiber

- Can amplify these wavelengths to boost the signal strength

- Supports SONET and SDH standards

Activity 2.2.1.3: Classify WAN Access Options

Interactive Graphic

Go to the course online to perform this practice activity.

Private WAN Infrastructures (2.2.2)

In this topic, private WAN infrastructures are discussed including leased lines, dialup access, ISDN, Frame Relay, ATM, MPLS, and Ethernet WANs, and VSAT.

Leased Lines (2.2.2.1)

When permanent dedicated connections are required, a point-to-point link is used to provide a pre-established WAN communications path from the customer premises to the provider network. Point-to-point lines are usually leased from a service provider and are called *leased lines*.

Leased lines have existed since the early 1950s, and for this reason are referred to by different names, such as leased circuits, serial link, serial line, point-to-point link, and T1/E1 or T3/E3 lines. The term leased line refers to the fact that the organization pays a monthly lease fee to a service provider to use the line. Leased lines are available in different capacities and are generally priced based on the bandwidth required and the distance between the two connected points.

In North America, service providers use the T-carrier system to define the digital transmission capability of a serial copper media link, while Europe uses the E-carrier system, as shown in Figure 2-13.

Figure 2-13   Sample Leased Line Topology

For instance, a T1 link supports 1.544 Mbps, an E1 supports 2.048 Mbps, a T3 supports 43.7 Mbps, and an E3 connection supports 34.368 Mbps. Optical Carrier (OC) transmission rates are used to define the digital transmitting capacity of a fiber-optic network.

The advantages of leased lines include

- **Simplicity:** Point-to-point communication links require minimal expertise to install and maintain.

- **Quality:** Point-to-point communication links usually offer high service quality, if they have adequate bandwidth. The dedicated capacity removes latency or jitter between the endpoints.

- **Availability:** Constant availability is essential for some applications, such as e-commerce. Point-to-point communication links provide permanent, dedicated capacity, which is required for VoIP or Video over IP.

The disadvantages of leased lines include

- **Cost:** Point-to-point links are generally the most expensive type of WAN access. The cost of leased line solutions can become significant when they are used to connect many sites over increasing distances. In addition, each endpoint requires an interface on the router, which increases equipment costs.

- **Limited flexibility:** WAN traffic is often variable, and leased lines have a fixed capacity, so that the bandwidth of the line seldom matches the need exactly. Any change to the leased line generally requires a site visit by ISP personnel to adjust capacity.

The Layer 2 protocol is usually HDLC or PPP.

Dialup (2.2.2.2)

Dialup WAN access may be required when no other WAN technology is available. For example, a remote location could use a modem and analog dialed telephone lines to provide low-capacity and dedicated switched connections. Dialup access is suitable when intermittent, low-volume data transfers are needed.

Traditional telephony uses a copper cable for the local loop to connect the telephone handset in the subscriber premises to the CO. The signal on the local loop during a call is a continuously varying electronic signal that is a translation of the subscriber voice into an analog signal.

Traditional local loops can transport binary computer data through the voice telephone network using a modem. The modem modulates the binary data into an analog signal at the source and demodulates the analog signal to binary data at the destination. The physical characteristics of the local loop and its connection to the PSTN limit the rate of the signal to less than 56 Kbps.

For small businesses, these relatively low-speed dialup connections are adequate for the exchange of sales figures, prices, routine reports, and email. Using automatic dial-up at night or on weekends for large file transfers and data backup can take advantage of lower off-peak tariffs (toll charges). Tariffs are based on the distance between the endpoints, time of day, and the duration of the call.

The advantages of modem and analog lines are simplicity, availability, and low implementation cost. The disadvantages are the low data rates and a relatively long connection time. The dedicated circuit has little delay or jitter for point-to-point traffic, but voice or video traffic does not operate adequately at these low bit rates.

Figure 2-14 displays a sample topology of two remote sites interconnecting with dialup modems.

WAN built with an on demand connection using a modem and the voice telephone network.

Figure 2-14   Sample Dialup Topology

Note

Although very few enterprises support dialup access, it is still a viable solution for remote areas with limited WAN access options.

ISDN (2.2.2.3)

Integrated Services Digital Network (ISDN) is a circuit-switching technology that enables the local loop of a PSTN to carry digital signals, resulting in higher-capacity switched connections.

ISDN changes the internal connections of the PSTN from carrying analog signals to time-division multiplexed (TDM) digital signals. TDM allows two or more signals, or bit streams, to be transferred as subchannels in one communication channel. The signals appear to transfer simultaneously; but physically, the signals are taking turns on the channel.

Figure 2-15 displays a sample ISDN topology. The ISDN connection may require a terminal adapter (TA), which is a device used to connect ISDN Basic Rate Interface (BRI) connections to a router.

Figure 2-15   Sample ISDN Topology

ISDN turns the local loop into a TDM digital connection. This change enables the local loop to carry digital signals that result in higher-capacity switched connections. The connection uses 64-Kbps bearer channels (B) for carrying voice or data and a signaling delta channel (D) for call setup and other purposes.

There are two types of ISDN interfaces:

- *Basic Rate Interface (BRI)*: ISDN BRI is intended for the home and small enterprise and provides two 64-Kbps B channels and one 16-Kbps D channel. The BRI D channel is designed for control and often underused, because it has only two B channels to control (Figure 2-16).

Figure 2-16   ISDN BRI

- *Primary Rate Interface (PRI)*: ISDN is also available for larger installations. In North America, PRI delivers 23 B channels with 64 Kbps and 1 D channel with 64 Kbps for a total bit rate of up to 1.544 Mbps. This includes some additional overhead for synchronization. In Europe, Australia, and other parts of the world, ISDN PRI provides 30 B channels and 1 D channel, for a total bit rate of up to 2.048 Mbps, including synchronization overhead (see Figure 2-17).

Figure 2-17 ISDN PRI

BRI has a call setup time that is less than a second, and the 64-Kbps B channel provides greater capacity than an analog modem link. If greater capacity is required, a second B channel can be activated to provide a total of 128 Kbps. Although inadequate for video, this permits several simultaneous voice conversations in addition to data traffic.

Another common application of ISDN is to provide additional capacity as needed on a leased line connection. The leased line is sized to carry average traffic loads while ISDN is added during peak demand periods. ISDN is also used as a backup if the leased line fails. ISDN tariffs are based on a per-B-channel basis and are similar to those of analog voice connections.

With PRI ISDN, multiple B channels can be connected between two endpoints. This allows for videoconferencing and high-bandwidth data connections with no latency or jitter. However, multiple connections can be very expensive over long distances.

Note

Although ISDN is still an important technology for telephone service provider networks, it is declining in popularity as an Internet connection option with the introduction of high-speed DSL and other broadband services.

Frame Relay (2.2.2.4)

Frame Relay is a simple Layer 2 nonbroadcast multiaccess (NBMA) WAN technology used to interconnect enterprise LANs. A single router interface can be used to connect to multiple sites using PVCs. PVCs are used to carry both voice and data traffic between a source and destination, and support data rates up to 4 Mbps, with some providers offering even higher rates.

An edge router only requires a single interface, even when multiple virtual circuits (VCs) are used. The short-leased line to the Frame Relay network edge allows cost-effective connections between widely scattered LANs.

Frame Relay creates PVCs, which are uniquely identified by a data-link connection identifier (DLCI). The PVCs and DLCIs ensure bidirectional communication from one DTE device to another.

For instance, in the example in Figure 2-18 R1 will use DLCI 102 to reach R2, while R2 will use DLCI 201 to reach R1.

Figure 2-18   Sample Frame Relay Topology

ATM (2.2.2.5)

Asynchronous Transfer Mode (ATM) technology is capable of transferring voice, video, and data through private and public networks. It is built on a cell-based architecture rather than on a frame-based architecture. ATM cells are always a fixed length of 53 bytes. The ATM cell contains a 5-byte ATM header followed by 48 bytes of ATM payload. Small fixed-length cells are well-suited for carrying voice and video traffic because this traffic is intolerant of delay. Video and voice traffic do not have to wait for larger data packets to be transmitted.

The 53-byte ATM cell is less efficient than the bigger frames and packets of Frame Relay. Furthermore, the ATM cell has at least 5 bytes of overhead for each 48-byte payload. When the cell is carrying segmented network layer packets, the overhead is higher because the ATM switch must be able to reassemble the packets at the destination. A typical ATM line needs almost 20 percent greater bandwidth than Frame Relay to carry the same volume of network layer data.

ATM was designed to be extremely scalable and to support link speeds of T1/E1 to OC-12 (622 Mbps) and faster.

ATM offers both PVCs and SVCs, although PVCs are more common with WANs. As with other shared technologies, ATM allows multiple VCs on a single leased-line connection to the network edge.

In the example in Figure 2-19, the ATM switch transmits four different traffic flows consisting of video, VoIP, web, and email.

Figure 2-19   Sample ATM Topology

Ethernet WAN (2.2.2.6)

Ethernet was originally developed to be a LAN access technology. At that time however, it really was not suitable as a WAN access technology because the maximum cable length supported was only up to a kilometer. However, newer Ethernet standards using fiber-optic cables have made Ethernet a reasonable WAN access option. For instance, the IEEE 1000BASE-LX standard supports fiber-optic cable lengths of 5 km, while the IEEE 1000BASE-ZX standard supports up to 70 km cable lengths.

Service providers now offer Ethernet WAN service using fiber-optic cabling. The Ethernet WAN service can go by many names, including *Metropolitan Ethernet (MetroE)*, *Ethernet over MPLS (EoMPLS)*, and *Virtual Private LAN Service (VPLS)*.

Figure 2-20 displays a sample Ethernet WAN topology.

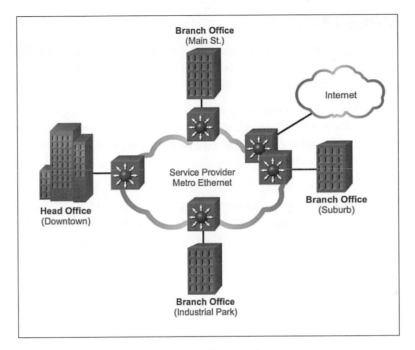

Figure 2-20 Sample Ethernet WAN Topology

Benefits of Ethernet WAN include

- **Reduced expenses and administration:** Ethernet WAN provides a switched, high-bandwidth Layer 2 network capable of managing data, voice, and video all on the same infrastructure. This characteristic increases bandwidth and eliminates expensive conversions to other WAN technologies. The technology enables businesses to inexpensively connect numerous sites, in a metropolitan area, to each other and to the Internet.

- **Easy integration with existing networks:** Ethernet WAN connects easily to existing Ethernet LANs, reducing installation costs and time.

- **Enhanced business productivity:** Ethernet WAN enables businesses to take advantage of productivity-enhancing IP applications that are difficult to implement on TDM or Frame Relay networks, such as hosted IP communications, VoIP, and streaming and broadcast video.

Note

Ethernet WANs have gained in popularity and are now commonly being used to replace the traditional Frame Relay and ATM WAN links.

MPLS (2.2.2.7)

Multiprotocol Label Switching (MPLS) is a multiprotocol high-performance WAN technology that directs data from one router to the next based on short path labels rather than IP network addresses.

MPLS has several defining characteristics. It is multiprotocol, meaning it has the ability to carry any payload including IPv4, IPv6, Ethernet, ATM, DSL, and Frame Relay traffic. It uses labels that tell a router what to do with a packet. The labels identify paths between distant routers rather than endpoints, and while MPLS actually routes IPv4 and IPv6 packets, everything else is switched.

MPLS is a service provider technology. Leased lines deliver bits between sites, and Frame Relay and Ethernet WAN deliver frames between sites. However, MPLS can deliver any type of packet between sites. MPLS can encapsulate packets of various network protocols. It supports a wide range of WAN technologies, including T-carrier / E-carrier links, Carrier Ethernet, ATM, Frame Relay, and DSL.

The sample topology in Figure 2-21 illustrates how MPLS is used.

Figure 2-21   Sample MPLS Topology

Notice that the different sites can connect to the MPLS cloud using different access technologies. In the figure, CE refers to the customer edge, PE is the provider edge router, which adds and removes labels, while P is an internal provider router, which switches MPLS labeled packets.

Note

MPLS is primarily a service provider WAN technology.

VSAT (2.2.2.8)

All private WAN technologies discussed so far used either copper or fiber-optic media. What if an organization needs connectivity in a remote location where there are no service providers that offer WAN service?

Very small aperture terminal (VSAT) is a solution that creates a private WAN using satellite communications. A VSAT is a small satellite dish similar to those used for home Internet and TV. VSATs create a private WAN while providing connectivity to remote locations.

Specifically, a router connects to a satellite dish that is pointed to a service provider's satellite in a geosynchronous orbit in space. The signals must travel approximately 35,786 km (22,236 miles) to the satellite and back.

The example in Figure 2-22 displays a VSAT dish on the roofs of the buildings communicating with a satellite dish thousands of kilometers away in space.

Figure 2-22   Sample VSAT Topology

Interactive Graphic

Activity 2.2.2.9: Identify Private WAN Infrastructure Terminology

Go to the course online to perform this practice activity.

Public WAN Infrastructure (2.2.3)

In this topic, public WAN infrastructures are discussed, including DSL, cable, wireless, 3G/4G cellular, as well as the need to secure data using site-to-site VPNs and remote-access VPNs.

DSL (2.2.3.1)

DSL technology is an always-on connection technology that uses existing twisted-pair telephone lines to transport high-bandwidth data, and provides IP services to subscribers. A *DSL modem* converts an Ethernet signal from the user device to a DSL signal, which is transmitted to the central office.

Multiple DSL subscriber lines are multiplexed into a single high-capacity link using a *DSL access multiplexer (DSLAM)* at the provider location. DSLAMs incorporate TDM technology to aggregate many subscriber lines into a single medium, generally a T3 (DS3) connection. Current DSL technologies use sophisticated coding and modulation techniques to achieve fast data rates.

There is a wide variety of DSL types, standards, and emerging standards. DSL is now a popular choice for enterprise IT departments to support home workers. Generally, a subscriber cannot choose to connect to an enterprise network directly, but must first connect to an ISP, and then an IP connection is made through the Internet to the enterprise. Security risks are incurred in this process, but can be mediated with security measures.

The topology in Figure 2-23 displays a sample DSL WAN connection.

Figure 2-23   Sample DSL Topology

Cable (2.2.3.2)

Coaxial cable is widely used in urban areas to distribute television signals. Network access is available from many cable television providers. This allows for greater bandwidth than the conventional telephone local loop.

Cable modems provide an always-on connection and a simple installation. A subscriber connects a computer or LAN router to the cable modem, which translates the digital signals into the broadband frequencies used for transmitting on a cable television network. The local cable TV office, which is called the cable *headend*, contains the computer system and databases needed to provide Internet access. The most important component located at the headend is the *cable modem termination system (CMTS)*, which sends and receives digital cable modem signals on a cable network and is necessary for providing Internet services to cable subscribers.

Cable modem subscribers must use the ISP associated with the service provider. All the local subscribers share the same cable bandwidth. As more users join the service, available bandwidth may be below the expected rate.

The topology in Figure 2-24 displays a sample cable WAN connection.

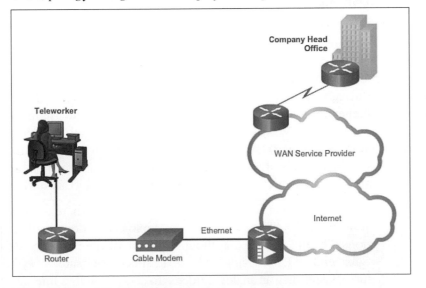

Figure 2-24   Sample Cable Topology

Wireless (2.2.3.3)

Wireless technology uses the unlicensed radio spectrum to send and receive data. The unlicensed spectrum is accessible to anyone who has a wireless router and wireless technology in the device they are using.

Until recently, one limitation of wireless access has been the need to be within the local transmission range (typically less than 100 feet) of a wireless router or a wireless modem that has a wired connection to the Internet. The following new developments in broadband wireless technology are changing this situation:

- *Municipal Wi-Fi*: Many cities have begun setting up municipal wireless networks. Some of these networks provide high-speed Internet access for free or for substantially less than the price of other broadband services. Others are for city use only, allowing police and fire departments and other city employees to do certain aspects of their jobs remotely. To connect to a municipal Wi-Fi, a subscriber typically needs a wireless modem, which provides a stronger radio and directional antenna than conventional wireless adapters. Most service providers provide the necessary equipment for free or for a fee, much like they do with DSL or cable modems.

- *WiMAX*: Worldwide Interoperability for Microwave Access (WiMAX) is a new technology that is just beginning to come into use. It is described in the IEEE standard 802.16. WiMAX provides high-speed broadband service with wireless access and provides broad coverage like a cell phone network rather than through small Wi-Fi hotspots. WiMAX operates in a similar way to Wi-Fi, but at higher speeds, over greater distances, and for a greater number of users. It uses a network of WiMAX towers that are similar to cell phone towers. To access a WiMAX network, subscribers must subscribe to an ISP with a WiMAX tower within 30 miles of their location. They also need some type of WiMAX receiver and a special encryption code to get access to the base station.

- *Satellite Internet*: Typically used by rural users where cable and DSL are not available. A VSAT provides two-way (upload and download) data communications. The upload speed is about one-tenth of the 500 Kbps download speed. Cable and DSL have higher download speeds, but satellite systems are about 10 times faster than an analog modem. To access satellite Internet services, subscribers need a satellite dish, two modems (uplink and downlink), and coaxial cables between the dish and the modem.

Figure 2-25 displays an example of a WiMAX network.

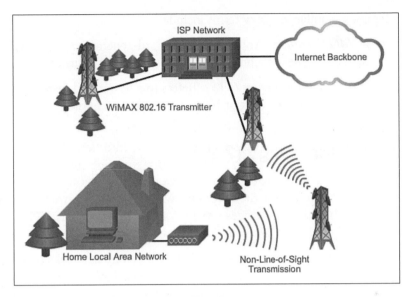

Figure 2-25 Sample Wireless Topology

3G/4G Cellular (2.2.3.4)

Increasingly, cellular service is another wireless WAN technology being used to connect users and remote locations where no other WAN access technology is available. Many users with smartphones and tablets can use cellular data to email, surf the Web, download apps, and watch videos.

Phones, tablet computers, laptops, and even some routers can communicate through to the Internet using cellular technology. As shown in Figure 2-26, these devices use radio waves to communicate through a nearby mobile phone tower.

Figure 2-26 Sample Cellular Topology

The device has a small radio antenna, and the provider has a much larger antenna sitting at the top of a tower somewhere within miles of the phone.

Common cellular industry terms include

- *3G/4G Wireless*: Abbreviation for third-generation and fourth-generation cellular access. These technologies support wireless Internet access.

- *Long Term Evolution (LTE)*: Refers to a newer and faster technology and is considered to be part of fourth generation (4G) technology.

VPN Technology (2.2.3.5)

Security risks are incurred when a teleworker or a remote office worker uses broadband services to access the corporate WAN over the Internet. To address security concerns, broadband services provide capabilities for using VPN connections to a VPN server, which is typically located at the corporate site.

A VPN is an encrypted connection between private networks over a public network, such as the Internet. Instead of using a dedicated Layer 2 connection, such as a leased line, a VPN uses virtual connections called VPN tunnels, which are routed through the Internet from the private network of the company to the remote site or employee host.

Benefits of VPN include the following:

- **Cost savings:** VPNs enable organizations to use the global Internet to connect remote offices and remote users to the main corporate site, thus eliminating expensive dedicated WAN links and modem banks.

- **Security:** VPNs provide the highest level of security by using advanced encryption and authentication protocols that protect data from unauthorized access.

- **Scalability:** Because VPNs use the Internet infrastructure within ISPs and devices, it is easy to add new users. Corporations are able to add large amounts of capacity without adding significant infrastructure.

- **Compatibility with broadband technology**: VPN technology is supported by broadband service providers such as DSL and cable, so mobile workers and telecommuters can take advantage of their home high-speed Internet service to access their corporate networks. Business-grade high-speed broadband connections can also provide a cost-effective solution for connecting remote offices.

There are two types of VPN access:

- *Site-to-site VPNs*: Site-to-site VPNs connect entire networks to each other; for example, they can connect a branch office network to a company headquarters network, as shown in Figure 2-27. Each site is equipped with a VPN gateway, such as a router, firewall, VPN concentrator, or security appliance. In the figure, a remote branch office uses a site-to-site-VPN to connect with the corporate head office.

Figure 2-27   Sample Site-to-Site VPN Topology

■ *Remote-access VPNs*: Remote-access VPNs enable individual hosts, such as tele-commuters, mobile users, and extranet consumers, to access a company network securely over the Internet. Each host (Teleworker 1 and Teleworker 2) typically has VPN client software loaded or uses a web-based client, as shown in Figure 2-28.

Figure 2-28   Sample Remote-Access VPN Topology

Interactive Graphic

Activity 2.2.3.6: Identify Public WAN Infrastructure Terminology

Go to the course online to perform this practice activity.

Selecting WAN Services (2.2.4)

Many factors influence the choice of service provider. This topic discusses how the purpose of the WAN, the geographic scope of the WAN, and the traffic requirements all factor in when choosing service providers.

Choosing a WAN Link Connection (2.2.4.1, 2.2.4.2)

There are many important factors to consider when choosing an appropriate WAN connection. For a network administrator to decide which WAN technology best meets the requirements of their specific business, they must answer the following questions:

What Is the Purpose of the WAN?

Considerations include

- Will the enterprise connect local branches in the same city area, connect remote branches, or connect to a single branch?

- Will the WAN be used to connect internal employees, or external business partners and customers, or all three?

- Will the enterprise connect to customers, connect to business partners, connect to employees, or some combination of these?

- Will the WAN provide authorized users limited or full access to the company intranet?

What Is the Geographic Scope?

Considerations include

- Is the WAN local, regional, or global?

- Is the WAN one to one (single branch), one to many branches, or many to many (distributed)?

What Are the Traffic Requirements?

Considerations include

- What type of traffic must be supported (data only, VoIP, video, large files, streaming files)? This determines the quality and performance requirements.

- What volume of traffic type (voice, video, or data) must be supported for each destination? This determines the bandwidth capacity required for the WAN connection to the ISP.

- What quality of service is required? This may limit the choices. If the traffic is highly sensitive to latency and jitter, eliminate any WAN connection options that cannot provide the required quality.

- What are the security requirements (data integrity, confidentiality, and security)? These are important factors if the traffic is of a highly confidential nature, or if it provides essential services, such as emergency response.

In addition to gathering information about the scope of the WAN, the administrator must also determine

- **Should the WAN use a private or public infrastructure?** A private infrastructure offers the best security and confidentiality, whereas the public Internet infrastructure offers the most flexibility and lowest ongoing expense. The choice depends on the purpose of the WAN, the types of traffic it carries, and available operating budget. For example, if the purpose is to provide a nearby branch with high-speed, secure services, a private dedicated or switched connection may be best. If the purpose is to connect many remote offices, a public WAN using the Internet may be the best choice. For distributed operations, a combination of options may be the solution.

- **For a private WAN, should it be dedicated or switched?** Real-time high-volume transactions have special requirements that could favor a dedicated line, such as traffic flowing between the data center and the corporate head office. If the enterprise is connecting to a local single branch, a dedicated leased line could be used. However, that option would become very expensive for a WAN connecting multiple offices. In that case, a switched connection might be better.

- **For a public WAN, what type of VPN access is required?** If the purpose of the WAN is to connect a remote office, a site-to-site VPN may be the best choice. To connect teleworkers or customers, remote-access VPNs are a better option. If the WAN is serving a mixture of remote offices, teleworkers, and authorized customers, such as a global company with distributed operations, a combination of VPN options may be required.

- **Which connection options are available locally?** In some areas, not all WAN connection options are available. In this case, the selection process is simplified, although the resulting WAN may provide less-than-optimal performance. For example, in a rural or remote area, the only option may be VSAT or cellular access.

- **What is the cost of the available connection options?** Depending on the option chosen, the WAN can be a significant ongoing expense. The cost of a particular option must be weighed against how well it meets the other requirements. For example, a dedicated leased line is the most expensive option, but the expense may be justified if it is critical to ensure secure transmission of high volumes of real-time data. For less-demanding applications, a less-expensive switched or Internet connection option may be more suitable.

Using the guidelines described here, as well as those described by the Cisco Enterprise Architecture, a network administrator should be able to choose an appropriate WAN connection to meet the requirements of different business scenarios.

Lab 2.2.4.3: Researching WAN Technologies

In this lab, you will complete the following objectives:

- Part 1: Investigate Dedicated WAN Technologies and Providers
- Part 2: Investigate a Dedicated Leased Line Service Provider in Your Area

Summary (2.3)

Class Activity 2.3.1.1: WAN Device Modules

Your medium-size company is upgrading its network. To make the most of the equipment currently in use, you decide to purchase WAN modules instead of new equipment.

All branch offices use either Cisco 1900 or 2911 series ISRs. You will be updating these routers in several locations. Each branch has its own ISP requirements to consider.

To update the devices, focus on the following WAN modules access types:

- Ethernet
- Broadband
- T1/E1 and ISDN PRI
- BRI
- Serial
- T1 and E1 trunk voice and WAN
- Wireless LANs and WANs

A business can use private lines or the public network infrastructure for WAN connections. A public infrastructure connection can be a cost-effective alternative to a private connection between LANs, as long as security is also planned.

WAN access standards operate at Layers 1 and 2 of the OSI model, and are defined and managed by the TIA/EIA, ISO, and IEEE. A WAN may be circuit switched or packet switched.

There is common terminology used to identify the physical components of WAN connections and who, the service provider or the customer, is responsible for which components.

Service provider networks are complex and the service provider's backbone networks consist primarily of high-bandwidth fiber-optic media. The device used for interconnection to a customer is specific to the WAN technology that is implemented.

Permanent, dedicated, point-to-point connections are provided by using leased lines. Dialup access, although slow, is still viable for remote areas with limited WAN options. Other private connection options include ISDN, Frame Relay, ATM, Ethernet WAN, MPLS, and VSAT.

Public infrastructure connections include DSL, cable, wireless, and 3G/4G cellular. Security over public infrastructure connections can be provided by using remote-access or site-to-site virtual private networks (VPNs).

Practice

The following activities provide practice with the topics introduced in this chapter. The Labs and Class Activities are available in the companion *Connecting Networks Lab Manual* (978-1-58713-331-2).

Class Activities

Class Activity 2.0.1.2: Branching Out

Class Activity 2.3.1.1: WAN Device Modules

Labs

Lab 2.2.4.3: Researching WAN Technologies

Check Your Understanding Questions

Complete all the review questions listed here to test your understanding of the topics and concepts in this chapter. The appendix, "Answers to the 'Check Your Understanding' Questions," lists the answers.

1. A broadband service such as DSL available through a local Internet service provider is suitable for what type of organization?

   A. A small company with 10 employees that uses a single LAN to share information

   B. A medium-size company with 500 employees that uses multiple LANs to share information

   C. A large company with 2,000 employees, in multiple locations and in a multi-LAN environment.

2. Which device is a data terminal equipment?

   A. Cable modem

   B. CSU/DSU

   C. Dialup modem

   D. DSL modem

   E. Router

3. Which two devices are used when digital leased lines interconnect a client with a provider? (Choose two.)

   A. Access server

   B. Channel service unit (CSU)

   C. Data service unit (DSU)

   D. Dialup modem

   E. Layer 2 switch

   F. Router

4. Which statements are true regarding connection-orientated packet-switched networks? (Choose three.)

   A. A virtual circuit is created for the duration of the packet delivery.

   B. Each packet has to carry only an identifier.

   C. Ethernet is an example.

   D. Full addressing information must be carried in each data packet.

   E. The Internet is an example.

   F. The network predetermines the route for each packet.

5. Which technology supports long distance SONET and SDH connections using fiber-optic media?

   A. ATM

   B. DSL

   C. DWDM

   D. Frame Relay

   E. ISDN

   F. MPLS

   G. Municipal Wi-Fi

   H. VPN

   I. VSAT

   J. WiMAX

6. What WAN technology is designed to deliver data, voice, and video simultaneously built on a cell-based architecture?

A. ATM

B. DSL

C. DWDM

D. Frame Relay

E. ISDN

F. MPLS

G. Municipal Wi-Fi

H. VPN

I. VSAT

J. WiMAX

7. ISDN PRI is composed of how many B channels in North America?

A. 2

B. 16

C. 23

D. 30

E. 64

8. The ability to connect securely to a private network over a public network is provided by which WAN technology?

A. ATM

B. DSL

C. DWDM

D. Frame Relay

E. ISDN

F. MPLS

G. VPN

H. VSAT

I. WiMAX

9. What term describes the cabling that connects the customer site to the nearest exchange of the WAN service provider?

    A. CO

    B. DCE

    C. DTE

    D. Local loop

10. Which two statements about a circuit-switched network are true? (Choose two.)

    A. A dedicated secure circuit is established between each pair of communicating nodes.

    B. A connection through the service provider network is established quickly before communications start.

    C. Multiple pairs of nodes can communicate over the same network channel.

    D. The communication costs are lower.

CHAPTER 3

Point-to-Point Connections

Objectives

Upon completion of this chapter

- What are the fundamentals of point-to-point serial communications across a WAN?

- How do you configure HDLC encapsulation on a point-to-point serial link?

- What are the benefits of using PPP over HDLC in a WAN?

- What is the PPP layered architecture and the functions of LCP and NCP?

- How is a PPP session established?

- How do you configure PPP encapsulation on a point-to-point serial link?

- How do you configure PPP authentication protocols?

- How are the **show** and **debug** commands used to troubleshoot PPP?

Key Terms

This chapter uses the following key terms. You can find the definitions in the glossary.

Introduction (3.0.1.1)

One of the most common types of WAN connections, especially in long-distance communications, is a *point-to-point connection*, also called a serial or leased line connection. Because these connections are typically provided by a carrier, such as a telephone company, boundaries between what is managed by the carrier and what is managed by the customer must be clearly established.

This chapter covers the terms, technology, and protocols used in serial connections. The High-Level Data Link Control (HDLC) and Point-to-Point Protocol (PPP) are introduced. PPP is a protocol that is able to handle authentication, compression, error detection, monitor link quality, and logically bundles multiple serial connections together to share the load.

Class Activity 3.0.1.2: PPP Persuasion

Your network engineering supervisor recently attended a networking conference where Layer 2 protocols were discussed. He knows that you have Cisco equipment on the premises, but he would also like to offer security and advanced TCP/IP options and controls on that same equipment by using the Point-to-Point Protocol (PPP).

After researching the PPP protocol, you find it offers some advantages over the HDLC protocol, currently used on your network.

Create a matrix listing the advantages and disadvantages of using the HDLC vs. PPP protocols. When comparing the two protocols, include

- Ease of configuration
- Adaptability to non-proprietary network equipment
- Security options
- Bandwidth usage and compression
- Bandwidth consolidation

Share your chart with another student or class. Justify whether or not you would suggest sharing the matrix with the network engineering supervisor to justify a change being made from HDLC to PPP for Layer 2 network connectivity.

Serial Point-to-Point Overview (3.1)

This section gives an overview of point-to-point serial communications. A basic understanding of point-to-point serial communications is essential to understanding protocols that are used over these types of serial links. HDLC encapsulation and configuration is discussed later in this section.

Serial Communications (3.1.1)

The earliest form of computer communications involved serial links between mainframe computers. Serial communications is still a widely used method of connecting two networks usually over long distances.

Serial and Parallel Ports (3.1.1.1)

One of the most common types of WAN connections is the point-to-point connection. As shown in Figure 3-1, point-to-point connections are used to connect LANs to service provider WANs, and to connect LAN segments within an enterprise network.

Figure 3-1   Serial Point-to-Point Communications

A LAN-to-WAN point-to-point connection is also referred to as a serial connection or leased line connection. This is because the lines are leased from a carrier (usually a telephone company) and are dedicated for use by the company leasing the lines. Companies pay for a continuous connection between two remote sites, and the line is continuously active and available. Leased lines are a frequently used type of WAN access, and they are generally priced based on the bandwidth required and the distance between the two connected points.

Understanding how point-to-point serial communication across a leased line works is important to an overall understanding of how WANs function.

Communications across a serial connection is a method of data transmission in which the bits are transmitted sequentially over a single channel. This is equivalent to a pipe only wide enough to fit one ball at a time. Multiple balls can go into the pipe, but only one at a time, and they only have one exit point, the other end of the pipe. A serial port is bidirectional, and often referred to as a bidirectional port or a communications port.

This is in contrast to parallel communications in which bits can be transmitted simultaneously over multiple wires. As shown in Figure 3-2, a parallel connection theoretically transfers data eight times faster than a serial connection. Based on this theory, a parallel connection sends a byte (eight bits) in the time that a serial connection sends a single bit. However, parallel communications do have issues with crosstalk across wires, especially as the wire length increases. *Clock skew* is also an issue with parallel communications. Clock skew occurs when data across the various wires does not arrive at the same time, creating synchronization issues. Finally, most parallel communications support only one-direction, outbound-only communication from the hard drive.

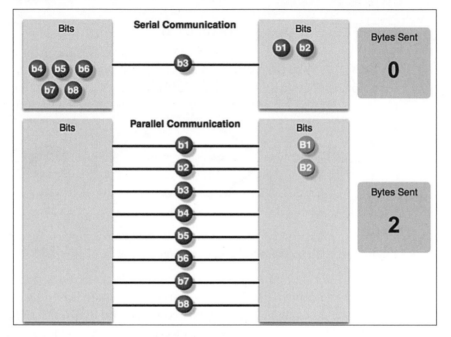

Figure 3-2   Serial and Parallel Communications

At one time, most PCs included both serial and parallel ports. Parallel ports were used to connect printers, computers, and other devices that required relatively high bandwidth. Parallel ports were also used between interior components. For external communications, a serial bus was primarily used for signal conversion. Because of their bidirectional ability, serial communications are considerably less expensive to implement. Serial communications use fewer wires, cheaper cables, and fewer connector pins.

On most PCs, parallel ports and RS-232 serial ports have been replaced by the higher speed serial Universal Serial Bus (USB) interfaces. However, for long-distance communication, many WANs use still serial transmission.

Serial Communication (3.1.1.2)

Figure 3-3 shows a simple representation of a serial communication across a WAN. Data is encapsulated by the communications protocol used by the sending router. The encapsulated frame is sent on a physical medium to the WAN. There are various ways to traverse the WAN, but the receiving router uses the same communications protocol to de-encapsulate the frame when it arrives.

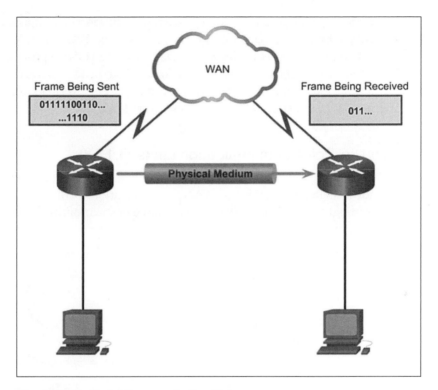

Figure 3-3   Serial Communication Process

There are many different serial communication standards, each one using a different signaling method. There are three important serial communication standards affecting LAN-to-WAN connections:

- **RS-232:** Most serial ports on personal computers conform to the RS-232C or newer RS-422 and RS-423 standards. Both 9-pin and 25-pin connectors are used. A serial port is a general-purpose interface that can be used for almost any type of device, including modems, mice, and printers. These types of peripheral devices for computers have been replaced by new and faster standards such as USB but many network devices use RJ-45 connectors that conform to the original RS-232 standard.

- **V.35:** Typically used for modem-to-multiplexer communication, this ITU standard for high-speed, synchronous data exchange combines the bandwidth of several telephone circuits. In the U.S., V.35 is the interface standard used by most routers and DSUs that connect to T1 carriers. V.35 cables are high-speed serial assemblies designed to support higher data rates and connectivity between DTEs and DCEs over digital lines. There is more on DTEs and DCEs later in this section.

- **HSSI:** A High-Speed Serial Interface (HSSI) supports transmission rates up to 52 Mbps. Engineers use HSSI to connect routers on LANs with WANs over high-speed lines, such as T3 lines. Engineers also use HSSI to provide high-speed connectivity between LANs, using Token Ring or Ethernet. HSSI is a DTE/DCE interface developed by Cisco Systems and T3 Plus Networking to address the need for high-speed communication over WAN links.

Point-to-Point Communication Links (3.1.1.3)

When permanent dedicated connections are required, a point-to-point link is used to provide a single, pre-established WAN communications path from the customer premises, through the provider network, to a remote destination, as shown in Figure 3-4.

Figure 3-4   Point-to-Point Communication Links

A point-to-point link can connect two geographically distant sites, such as a corporate office in New York and a regional office in London. For a point-to-point line, the carrier dedicates specific resources for a line that is leased by the customer (leased line).

Note

Point-to-point connections are not limited to connections that cross land. There are hundreds of thousands of miles of undersea fiber-optic cables that connect countries and continents worldwide. An Internet search of "undersea Internet cable map" produces several cable maps of these undersea connections.

Point-to-point links are usually more expensive than shared services. The cost of leased line solutions can become significant when used to connect many sites over increasing distances. However, there are times when the benefits outweigh the cost of the leased line. The dedicated capacity removes latency or jitter between the endpoints. Constant availability is essential for some applications such as VoIP or video over IP.

Time-Division Multiplexing (3.1.1.4)

With a leased line, despite the fact that customers are paying for dedicated services, and dedicated bandwidth is provided to the customer, the carrier still uses multiplexing technologies within the network. Multiplexing refers to a scheme that allows multiple logical signals to share a single physical channel. Two common types of multiplexing are *time-division multiplexing (TDM)* and *statistical time-division multiplexing (STDM)*.

TDM

Bell Laboratories originally invented TDM to maximize the amount of voice traffic carried over a medium. Before multiplexing, each telephone call required its own physical link. This was an expensive and unscalable solution. TDM divides the bandwidth of a single link into separate time slots. TDM transmits two or more channels (*data stream*) over the same link by allocating a different time slot for the transmission of each channel. In effect, the channels take turns using the link.

TDM is a physical layer concept. It has no regard for the nature of the information that is multiplexed on to the output channel. TDM is independent of the Layer 2 protocol that has been used by the input channels.

TDM can be explained by an analogy to highway traffic. To transport traffic from four roads to another city, all traffic can be sent on one lane if the roads are equally serviced and the traffic is synchronized. If each of the four roads puts a car on to the main highway every four seconds, the highway gets a car at the rate of one each second. As long as the speed of all the cars is synchronized, there is no collision. At the destination, the reverse happens and the cars are taken off the highway and fed to the local roads by the same synchronous mechanism.

This is the principle used in synchronous TDM when sending data over a link. TDM increases the capacity of the *transmission link* by dividing transmission time into smaller, equal intervals so that the link carries the bits from multiple input sources.

In Figure 3-5, a multiplexer (MUX) at the transmitter accepts three separate signals. The MUX breaks each signal into segments. The MUX puts each segment into a single channel by inserting each segment into a time slot.

Figure 3-5   Time-Division Multiplexing

A MUX at the receiving end reassembles the TDM stream into the three separate data streams based only on the timing of the arrival of each bit. A technique called bit interleaving keeps track of the number and sequence of the bits from each specific transmission so that they can be quickly and efficiently reassembled into their original form upon receipt. Byte interleaving performs the same functions, but because there are eight bits in each byte, the process needs a bigger or longer time slot.

The operations of TDM are summarized as follows:

■ TDM shares available transmission time on a medium by assigning a time slot to users.

■ The MUX accepts input from attached devices in an alternating sequence (round-robin) and transmits the data in a recurrent pattern.

■ T1/E1 and ISDN telephone lines are common examples of synchronous TDM.

Statistical Time-Division Multiplexing (3.1.1.5)

In another analogy, compare TDM to a train with 32 railroad cars. Each car is owned by a different freight company, and every day the train leaves with the 32 cars attached. If one of the companies has cargo to send, the car is loaded. If the company has nothing to send, the car remains empty, but stays on the train. Shipping empty containers is not very efficient. TDM shares this inefficiency when traffic is intermittent, because the time slot is still allocated even when the channel has no data to transmit.

STDM

STDM was developed to overcome this inefficiency. As shown in Figure 3-6, STDM uses a variable time slot length allowing channels to compete for any free slot space. It employs a buffer memory that temporarily stores the data during periods of peak traffic. STDM does not waste high-speed line time with inactive channels using this scheme. STDM requires each transmission to carry identification information or a channel identifier.

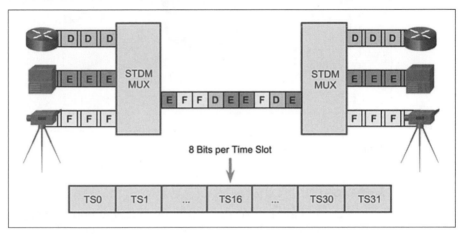

Figure 3-6   Statistical Time-Division Multiplexing

TDM Examples – Sonet and SDM (3.1.1.6)

On a larger scale, the telecommunications industry uses the Synchronous Optical Networking (SONET) or Synchronous Digital Hierarchy (SDH) standard for optical transport of TDM data. SONET, used in North America, and SDH, used elsewhere, are two closely related standards that specify interface parameters, rates, framing formats, multiplexing methods, and management for synchronous TDM over fiber.

Figure 3-7 displays SONET, which is an example of STDM. SONET/SDH takes n bit streams, multiplexes them, and optically modulates the signals. It then sends the signals out using a light emitting device over fiber with a bit rate equal to (incoming bit rate) ´ n. Thus, traffic arriving at the SONET multiplexer from four places at 2.5 Gbps goes out as a single stream at 4 ´ 2.5 Gbps, or 10 Gbps. This principle is illustrated in the figure, which shows an increase in the bit rate by a factor of four in time slot T.

Figure 3-7   TDM Example: SONET

Demarcation Point (3.1.1.7)

Prior to deregulation in North America and other countries, telephone companies owned the local loop, including the wiring and equipment on the premises of the customers. The local loop refers to the line from the premises of a telephone subscriber to the telephone company central office. Deregulation forced telephone companies to unbundle their local loop infrastructure to allow other suppliers to provide equipment and services. This led to a need to delineate which part of the network the telephone company owned and which part the customer owned. This point of delineation is the *demarcation point*, or demarc. The demarcation point marks the point where your network interfaces with a network that is owned by another organization. In telephone terminology, this is the interface between customer premises equipment (CPE) and network service provider equipment. The demarcation point is the point in the network where the responsibility of the service provider ends, as shown in Figure 3-8.

The differences in demarcation points can best be shown using ISDN. In the United States, a service provider provides the local loop into the customer premises, and the customer provides the active equipment such as the channel service unit / data service unit (CSU/DSU) on which the local loop is terminated. This termination often occurs in a telecommunications closet, and the customer is responsible for maintaining, replacing, or repairing the equipment. In other countries, the network terminating unit (NTU) is provided and managed by the service provider. This allows the service provider to actively manage and troubleshoot the local loop with the demarcation point occurring after the NTU. The customer connects a CPE device, such as a router or Frame Relay access device, to the NTU using a V.35 or RS-232 serial interface.

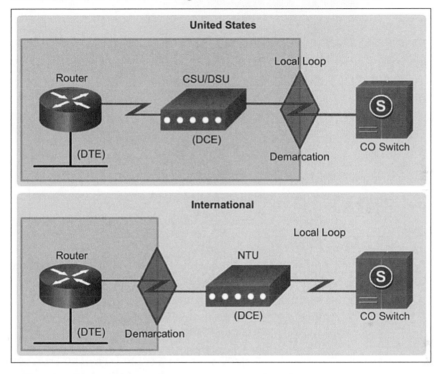

Figure 3-8   Demarcation Point

A router serial port is required for each leased line connection. If the underlying network is based on the T-carrier or E-carrier technologies, the leased line connects to the network of the carrier through a CSU/DSU. The purpose of the CSU/DSU is to provide a clocking signal to the customer equipment interface from the DSU and terminate the channelized transport media of the carrier on the CSU. The CSU also provides diagnostic functions such as a loopback test.

As shown in Figure 3-9, most T1 or E1 TDM interfaces on current routers include CSU/DSU capabilities. A separate CSU/DSU is not required because this functionality is embedded in the interface. IOS commands are used to configure the CSU/DSU operations.

Figure 3-9   T1/E1 with Embedded CSU/DSU

DTE-DCE (3.1.1.8)

From the point of view of connecting to the WAN, a serial connection has a data terminal equipment (DTE) device at one end of the connection and a data circuit-terminating equipment or data communications equipment (DCE) device at the other end. The connection between the two DCE devices is the WAN service provider transmission network, as shown in Figure 3-10. In this example

- The CPE, which is generally a router, is the DTE. The DTE could also be a terminal, computer, printer, or fax machine if they connect directly to the service provider network.

- The DCE, commonly a modem or CSU/DSU, is the device used to convert the user data from the DTE into a form acceptable to the WAN service provider transmission link. This signal is received at the remote DCE, which decodes the signal back into a sequence of bits. The remote DCE then signals this sequence to the remote DTE.

The Electronics Industry Association (EIA) and the International Telecommunication Union Telecommunications Standardization Sector (ITU-T) have been most active in the development of standards that allow DTEs to communicate with DCEs.

Figure 3-10   Serial DCE and DTE WAN Connections

Serial Cables (3.1.1.9)

Originally, the concept of DCEs and DTEs was based on two types of equipment: terminal equipment that generated or received data, and the communication equipment that only relayed data. In the development of the RS-232 standard, there were reasons why 25-pin RS-232 connectors on these two types of equipment must be wired differently. These reasons are no longer significant, but there are two different types of cables remaining: one for connecting a DTE to a DCE, and another for connecting two DTEs directly to each other.

The DTE/DCE interface for a particular standard defines the following specifications:

- **Mechanical/physical:** Number of pins and connector type

- **Electrical:** Defines voltage levels for 0 and 1

- **Functional:** Specifies the functions that are performed by assigning meanings to each of the signaling lines in the interface

- **Procedural:** Specifies the sequence of events for transmitting data

The original RS-232 standard only defined the connection of DTEs with DCEs, which were modems. However, to connect two DTEs, such as two computers or two routers in a lab, a special cable called a null modem eliminates the need for a DCE. In other words, the two devices can be connected without a modem. A *null modem* is a communication method to directly connect two DTEs using an RS-232 serial cable. With a null modem connection, the transmit (Tx) and receive (Rx) lines are cross-linked, as shown in Figure 3-11.

Note the crosslinks: Pin 2 to Pin 3 and Pin 3 to Pin 2

Connector 1	Connector 2	Function
2	3	Rx ← Tx
3	2	Tx → Rx
5	5	Signal ground

Figure 3-11   Null Modem to Connect Two DTEs

The cable for the DTE to DCE connection is a shielded serial transition cable. The router end of the shielded serial transition cable may be a DB-60 connector, which connects to the DB-60 port on a serial WAN interface card, as shown in Figure 3-12. The other end of the serial transition cable is available with the connector appropriate for the standard that is to be used. The WAN provider or the CSU/DSU usually dictates this cable type. Cisco devices support the EIA/TIA-232, EIA/TIA-449, V.35, X.21, and EIA/TIA-530 serial standards, as shown in Figure 3-13.

Figure 3-12   DB-60 Router Connection

To support higher port densities in a smaller form factor, Cisco has introduced a Smart Serial cable, as shown in Figure 3-14. The router interface end of the Smart Serial cable is a 26-pin connector that is significantly more compact than the DB-60 connector.

Figure 3-13   WAN Serial Connection Options

Figure 3-14   Smart Serial Connector

When using a null modem, synchronous connections require a clock signal. An external device can generate the signal, or one of the DTEs can generate the clock signal. When a DTE and DCE are connected, the serial port on a router is the DTE end of the connection, by default, and the clock signal is typically provided by a CSU/DSU, or similar DCE device. However, when using a null modem cable in a router-to-router connection, one of the serial interfaces must be configured as the DCE end to provide the clock signal for the connection, as shown in Figure 3-15.

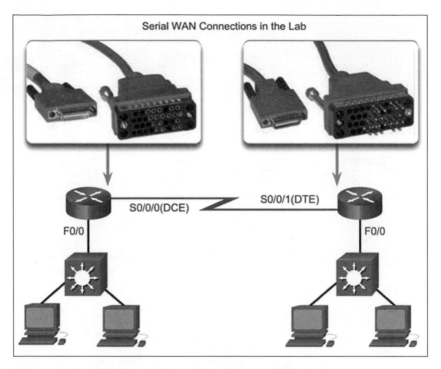

Figure 3-15 Smart Serial Connections in the Lab

Serial Bandwidth (3.1.1.10)

Bandwidth refers to the rate at which data is transferred over the communication link. The underlying carrier technology depends on the bandwidth available. There is a difference in bandwidth points between the North American (T-carrier) specification and the European (E-carrier) system. Optical networks also use a different bandwidth hierarchy, which again differs between North America and Europe. In the United States, Optical Carrier (OC) defines the bandwidth points.

In North America, the bandwidth is usually expressed as a *DS (digital signal level)* number (DS0, DS1, etc.), which refers to the rate and format of the signal. The most fundamental line speed is 64 Kbps, or DS-0, which is the bandwidth required for an uncompressed, digitized phone call. Serial connection bandwidths can be incrementally increased to accommodate the need for faster transmission. For example, 24 DS0s can be bundled to get a DS1 line (also called a T1 line) with a speed of 1.544 Mbps. Also, 28 DS1s can be bundled to get a DS3 line (also called a T3 line) with a speed of 44.736 Mbps. Leased lines are available in different capacities and are generally priced based on the bandwidth required and the distance between the two connected points.

OC transmission rates are a set of standardized specifications for the transmission of digital signals carried on SONET fiber-optic networks. The designation uses OC, followed by an integer value representing the base transmission rate of 51.84 Mbps. For example, OC-1 has a transmission capacity of 51.84 Mbps, whereas an OC-3 transmission medium would be three times 51.84 Mbps, or 155.52 Mbps.

Table 3-1 lists the most common line types and the associated bit rate capacity of each.

Table 3-1   Carrier Transmission Rates

Line Type	Bit Rate Capacity
56	56 Kbps
64	64 Kbps
T1	1.544 Mbps
E1	2.048 Mbps
J1	2.048 Mbps
E3	34.064 Mbps
T3	44.736 Mbps
OC-1	51.84 Mbps
OC-3	155.54 Mbps
OC-9	466.56 Mbps
OC-12	622.08 Mbps
OC-18	933.12 Mbps
OC-24	1.244 Gbps
OC-36	1.866 Gbps
OC-48	2.488 Gbps
OC-96	4.976 Gbps
OC-192	9.954 Gbps
OC-768	39.813 Gbps

Note

E1 (2.048 Mbps) and *E3* (34.368 Mbps) are European standards like T1 and T3, but with different bandwidths and frame structures.

Interactive Graphic

Activity 3.1.1.11: Identify the Serial Communications Terminology

Go to the course online to perform this practice activity.

HDLC Encapsulation (3.1.2)

HDLC is a synchronous data link layer protocol developed by the International Organization for Standardization (ISO). Although HDLC can be used for point-to-multipoint connections, the most common usage of HDLC is for point-to-point serial communications.

WAN Encapsulation Protocols (3.1.2.1)

On each WAN connection, data is encapsulated into frames before crossing the WAN link. To ensure that the correct protocol is used, the appropriate Layer 2 encapsulation type must be configured. The choice of protocol depends on the WAN technology and the communicating equipment. Figure 3-16 displays the more common WAN protocols and where they are used. The following are short descriptions of each type of WAN protocol:

- **HDLC:** The default encapsulation type on point-to-point connections, dedicated links, and circuit-switched connections when the link uses two Cisco devices. HDLC is now the basis for synchronous PPP used by many servers to connect to a WAN, most commonly the Internet.

- **PPP:** Provides router-to-router and host-to-network connections over synchronous and asynchronous circuits. PPP works with several network layer protocols, such as IPv4 and IPv6. PPP uses the HDLC encapsulation protocol, but also has built-in security mechanisms such as PAP and CHAP.

- **Serial Line Internet Protocol (SLIP):** A standard protocol for point-to-point serial connections using TCP/IP. SLIP has been largely displaced by PPP.

- **X.25/Link Access Procedure, Balanced (LAPB):** An ITU-T standard that defines how connections between a DTE and DCE are maintained for remote terminal access and computer communications in public data networks. X.25 specifies LAPB, a data link layer protocol. X.25 is a predecessor to Frame Relay.

- **Frame Relay:** An industry standard, switched, data link layer protocol that handles multiple virtual circuits. Frame Relay is a next-generation protocol after X.25. Frame Relay eliminates some of the time-consuming processes (such as error correction and flow control) employed in X.25.

- **ATM:** The international standard for cell relay in which devices send multiple service types, such as voice, video, or data, in fixed-length (53-byte) cells. Fixed-length cells allow processing to occur in hardware; thereby, reducing transit delays. ATM takes advantage of high-speed transmission media such as E3, SONET, and T3.

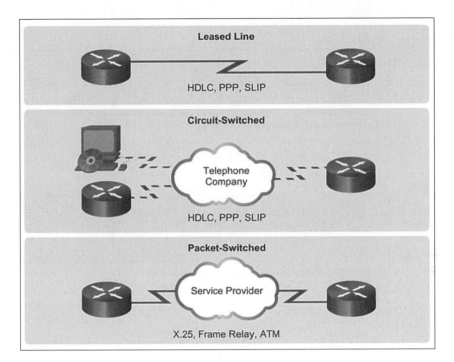

Figure 3-16 WAN Encapsulation Protocols

HDLC Encapsulation (3.1.2.2)

HDLC is a *bit-oriented* synchronous data link layer protocol developed by the International Organization for Standardization (ISO). The current standard for HDLC is ISO 13239. HDLC was developed from the *Synchronous Data Link Control (SDLC)* standard proposed in the 1970s. HDLC provides both connection-oriented and connectionless service.

HDLC uses synchronous serial transmission to provide error-free communication between two points. HDLC defines a Layer 2 framing structure that allows for flow control and error control through the use of acknowledgments. Each frame has the same format, whether it is a data frame or a control frame.

When frames are transmitted over synchronous or asynchronous links, those links have no mechanism to mark the beginning or end of frames. For this reason, HDLC uses a frame delimiter, or flag, to mark the beginning and the end of each frame.

Cisco has developed an extension to the HLDC protocol to solve the inability to provide multiprotocol support. Although Cisco HLDC (also referred to as cHDLC) is proprietary, Cisco has allowed many other network equipment vendors to implement it. Cisco HDLC frames contain a field for identifying the network protocol being encapsulated. Figure 3-17 compares standard HLDC to Cisco HLDC.

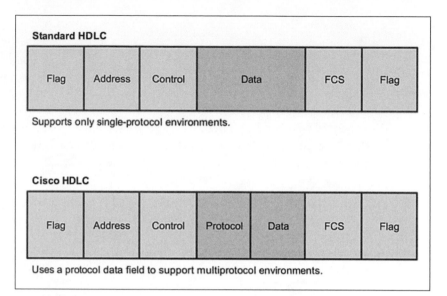

Figure 3-17   Standard and Cisco HLDC Frame Format

HDLC Frame Types (3.1.2.3)

HDLC defines three types of frames, each with a different control field format.

Flag

The Flag field initiates and terminates error checking. The frame always starts and ends with an 8-bit Flag field. The bit pattern is 01111110. Because there is a likelihood that this pattern occurs in the actual data, the sending HDLC system always inserts a 0 bit after every five consecutive 1s in the data field, so in practice the flag sequence can only occur at the frame ends. The receiving system strips out the inserted bits. When frames are transmitted consecutively, the end flag of the first frame is used as the start flag of the next frame.

Address

The Address field contains the HDLC address of the secondary station. This address can contain a specific address, a group address, or a broadcast address. A primary address is either a communication source or a destination, which eliminates the need to include the address of the primary.

Control

The Control field, shown in Figure 3-18, uses three different formats, depending on the type of HDLC frame used:

- **Information (I) frame:** I-frames carry upper layer information and some control information. This frame sends and receives sequence numbers, and the poll final (P/F) bit performs flow and error control. The send sequence number refers to the number of the frame to be sent next. The receive sequence number provides the number of the frame to be received next. Both sender and receiver maintain send and receive sequence numbers. A *primary station* uses the P/F bit to tell the secondary whether it requires an immediate response. A secondary station uses the P/F bit to tell the primary whether the current frame is the last in its current response.

- **Supervisory (S) frame:** S-frames provide control information. An S-frame can request and suspend transmission, report on status, and acknowledge receipt of I-frames. S-frames do not have an information field.

- **Unnumbered (U) frame:** U-frames support control purposes and are not sequenced. Depending on the function of the U-frame, its Control field is 1 or 2 bytes. Some U-frames have an Information field.

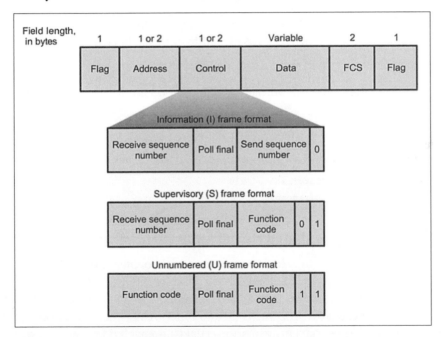

Figure 3-18   HDLC Frame Types

Protocol

Only used in Cisco HDLC. This field specifies the protocol type encapsulated within the frame (e.g., 0x0800 for IP).

Data

The Data field contains a path information unit (PIU) or exchange identification (XID) information.

Frame Check Sequence (FCS)

The FCS precedes the ending flag delimiter and is usually a cyclic redundancy check (CRC) calculation remainder. The CRC calculation is redone in the receiver. If the result differs from the value in the original frame, an error is assumed.

Configuring HDLC Encapsulation (3.1.2.4)

Cisco HDLC is the default encapsulation method used by Cisco devices on synchronous serial lines.

Use Cisco HDLC as a point-to-point protocol on leased lines between two Cisco devices. If connecting non-Cisco devices, use synchronous PPP.

If the default encapsulation method has been changed, use the **encapsulation hdlc** command in privileged EXEC mode to reenable HDLC.

There are two steps to re-enable HDLC encapsulation:

Step 1.   Enter the interface configuration mode of the serial interface.

Step 2.   Enter the **encapsulation hdlc** command to specify the encapsulation protocol on the interface.

The following shows an example of HDLC reenabled on a serial interface:

```
R2(config)# interface s0/0/0
R2(config-if)# encapsulation hdlc
```

Troubleshooting a Serial Interface (3.1.2.5)

The output of the **show interfaces serial** command displays information specific to serial interfaces. When HDLC is configured, **encapsulation HDLC** should be reflected in the output, as highlighted in Example 3-1. **Serial 0/0/0 is up, line protocol is up** indicates that the line is up and functioning; **encapsulation HDLC** indicates that the default serial encapsulation (HDLC) is enabled.

Example 3-1   Displaying Serial Interface Information

```
R1# show interface serial 0/0/0
Serial0/0/0 is up, line protocol is up
  Hardware is GT96K Serial
  Internet address is 172.16.0.1/30
  MTU 1500 bytes, BW 1544 Kbit/sec, DLY 20000 usec,
```

```
     reliability 255/255, txload 1/255, rxload 1/255
Encapsulation HDLC, loopback not set
Keepalive set (10 sec)
CRC checking enabled
<Output omitted for brevity>
```

The **show interfaces serial** command returns one of six possible states:

- Serial x is up, line protocol is up.

- Serial x is down, line protocol is down.

- Serial x is up, line protocol is down.

- Serial x is up, line protocol is up (looped).

- Serial x is up, line protocol is down (disabled).

- Serial x is administratively down, line protocol is down.

Of the six possible states, there are five problem states. Table 3-2 lists the five problem states, the issues associated with that state, and how to troubleshoot the issue.

Table 3-2   Troubleshooting a Serial Interface

Status Line Condition	Possible Problem	Solution
Serial x is up, line protocol is up.	This is proper status line condition.	No action is required.
Serial x is down, line protocol is down.	The router is not sensing a carrier detect (CD) signal (that is, the CD is not active). The line is down or is not connected on the far end. Cabling is faulty or incorrect. Hardware failure has occurred (CSU/DSU).	1. Check the CD LEDs on the CSU/DSU to see whether the CD is active, or insert a breakout box on the line to check for the CD signal. 2. Verify that the proper cable and interface are being used by looking at the hardware installation documentation. 3. Insert a breakout box and check all control leads. 4. Contact the leased line or other carrier service to see whether there is a problem. 5. Swap faulty parts. 6. If you suspect faulty router hardware, change the serial line to another port. If the connection comes up, the previously connected interface has a problem.

Status Line Condition	Possible Problem	Solution
Serial x is up, line protocol is down (DCE mode).	The **clock rate** interface configuration command is missing. The DTE device does not support or is not set up for SCTE mode (terminal timing). The remote CSU or DSU has failed.	1. Add the **clockrate** interface configuration command on the serial interface. Syntax: **clock rate** *bps* Syntax Description: ■ *bps*: Desired clock rate in bits per second: 1200, 2400, 4800, 9600, 19200, 38400, 56000, 64000, 72000, 125000, 148000, 250000, 500000, 800000, 1000000, 1300000, 2000000, 4000000, or 8000000. 2. If the problem appears to be on the remote end, repeat Step 1 on the remote modem, CSU or DSU. 3. Verify that the correct cable is being used. 4. If the line protocol is still down, there is a possible hardware failure or cabling problem. Insert a breakout box and observe leads. 5. Replace faulty parts as necessary.
Serial *x* is up, line protocol is up (looped).	A loop exists in the circuit. The sequence number in the keepalive packet changes to a random number when a loop is initially detected. If the same random number is returned over the link, a loop exists.	1. Use the **show running-config** privileged exec command to look for any **loopback** interface configuration command entries. 2. If you find a **loopback** interface configuration command entry, use the **no loopback** interface configuration command to remove the loop. 3. If you do not find the **loopback** interface configuration command, examine the CSU/DSU to determine whether they are configured in manual loopback mode. If they are, disable manual loopback. 4. Reset the CSU/DSU, and inspect the line status. If the line protocol comes up, no other action is needed. 5. If the CSU/DSU is not configured in manual loopback mode, contact the leased line or other carrier service for line troubleshooting assistance.

Status Line Condition	Possible Problem	Solution
Serial *x* is up, line protocol is down (disabled) .	A high error rate has occurred due to a remote device problem. A CSU or DSU hardware problem has occurred. Router hardware (interface) is bad.	1. Troubleshoot the line with a serial analyzer and breakout box. Look for toggling CTS and DSR signals. 2. Loop CSU/DSU (DTE loop). If the problem continues, it is likely that there is a hardware problem. If the problem does not continue, it is likely that there is a telephone company problem. 3. Swap out bad hardware, as required (CSU, DSU, switch, local or remote router).
Serial *x* is administratively down, line protocol is down.	The router configuration includes the shutdown interface configuration command. A duplicate IP address exists.	1. Check the router configuration for the **shutdown** command. 2. Use the **no shutdown** interface configuration command to remove the **shutdown** command. 3. Verify that there are no identical IP addresses using the **show running-config** privileged exec command or the **show interfaces** exec command. 4. If there are duplicate addresses, resolve the conflict by changing one of the IP addresses.

The **show controllers** command is another important diagnostic tool when troubleshooting serial lines, as shown in Example 3-2. The output indicates the state of the interface channels and whether a cable is attached to the interface. In example 3-2, interface serial 0/0/0 has a V.35 DCE cable attached. The command syntax varies depending on the platform. *Cisco 7000* series routers use a cBus controller card for connecting serial links. With these routers, use the **show controllers cbus** command.

If the electrical interface output displays as UNKNOWN instead of V.35, EIA/TIA-449, or some other electrical interface type, the likely problem is an improperly connected cable. A problem with the internal wiring of the card is also possible. If the electrical interface is unknown, the corresponding display for the **show interfaces serial** command shows that the interface and line protocol are down.

Example 3-2   Displaying Controller Hardware Information on a Serial Interface

```
R1# show controllers serial 0/0/0
Interface Serial0/0/0
Hardware is GT96K
DCE V.35, clock rate 64000
idb at 0x66855120, driver data structure at 0x6685C93C
wic_info 0x6685CF68
```

```
Physical Port 0, SCC Num 0
MPSC Registers:
<Output omitted for brevity>
```

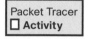

Activity 3.1.2.6: Troubleshooting a Serial Interface

Go to the course online to use the Syntax Checker to perform troubleshooting on a serial interface.

Packet Tracer Activity 3.1.2.7: Troubleshooting Serial Interfaces

Background/Scenario

You have been asked to troubleshoot WAN connections for a local telephone company (Telco). The Telco router is supposed to communicate with four remote sites, but none of them are working. Use your knowledge of the OSI model and a few general rules to identify and repair the errors in the network.

PPP Operation (3.2)

This section discusses the PPP operations, including the benefits of PPP, LCP, and NCP protocols, and establishing a PPP session.

Benefits of PPP (3.2.1)

PPP has several advantages over its predecessor HDLC. In this section, PPP is introduced along with examining the benefits of PPP.

Introducing PPP (3.2.1.1)

Recall that HDLC is the default serial encapsulation method when connecting two Cisco routers. With an added protocol type field, the Cisco version of HDLC is proprietary. Thus, Cisco HDLC can only work with other Cisco devices. However, when there is a need to connect to a non-Cisco router, PPP encapsulation should be used, as shown in the Figure 3-19.

HDLC is the default encapsulation method on a serial link.

Use PPP encapsulation to connect a Cisco router to a non-Cisco router.

Figure 3-19   What is PPP?

PPP encapsulation has been carefully designed to retain compatibility with most commonly used supporting hardware. PPP encapsulates data frames for transmission over Layer 2 physical links. PPP establishes a direct connection using serial cables, phone lines, *trunk lines*, cellular telephones, specialized radio links, or fiber-optic links.

PPP contains three main components:

- HDLC-like framing for transporting multiprotocol packets over point-to-point links.

- Extensible *Link Control Protocol (LCP)* for establishing, configuring, and testing the data-link connection.

- Family of *Network Control Protocols (NCPs)* for establishing and configuring different network layer protocols. PPP allows the simultaneous use of multiple network layer protocols. Some of the more common NCPs are Internet Protocol (IPv4) Control Protocol, IPv6 Control Protocol, AppleTalk Control Protocol, *Novell IPX* Control Protocol, Cisco Systems Control Protocol, *SNA Control Protocol*, and Compression Control Protocol.

Advantages of PPP (3.2.1.2)

PPP originally emerged as an encapsulation protocol for transporting IPv4 traffic over point-to-point links. PPP provides a standard method for transporting multiprotocol packets over point-to-point links.

There are many advantages to using PPP including the fact that it is not proprietary. PPP includes many features not available in HDLC:

- The link quality management feature, as shown in Figure 3-20, monitors the quality of the link. If too many errors are detected, PPP takes the link down.

- PPP supports PAP and CHAP authentication. This feature is explained and practiced in a later section.

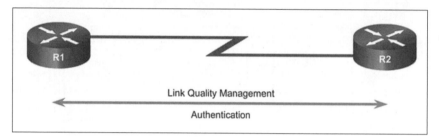

Figure 3-20   Advantages of PPP

LCP and NCP (3.2.2)

LCP and NCP are two key components to PPP. An understanding of these two protocols will help you understand and troubleshoot PPP operations.

PPP Layered Architecture (3.2.2.1)

A layered architecture is a logical model, design, or blueprint that aids in communication between interconnecting layers. Figure 3-21 maps the layered architecture of PPP against the Open System Interconnection (OSI) model. PPP and OSI share the same physical layer, but PPP distributes the functions of LCP and NCP differently.

At the physical layer, you can configure PPP on a range of interfaces, including

- Asynchronous serial, such as leased line services

- Synchronous serial, such as those that use basic telephone service for modem dialup connections

- HSSI

- ISDN

Figure 3-21   PPP Layered Architecture

PPP operates across any DTE/DCE interface (RS-232-C, RS-422, RS-423, or V.35). The only absolute requirement imposed by PPP is a full-duplex circuit, either dedicated or switched, that can operate in either an asynchronous or synchronous bit-serial mode, transparent to PPP link layer frames. PPP does not impose any restrictions regarding transmission rate other than those imposed by the particular DTE/DCE interface in use.

Most of the work done by PPP is at the data link and network layers by the LCP and NCPs. The LCP sets up the PPP connection and its parameters, the NCPs handle higher layer protocol configurations, and the LCP terminates the PPP connection.

PPP – Link Control Protocol (LCP) (3.2.2.2)

The LCP functions within the data link layer and has a role in establishing, configuring, and testing the data-link connection. The LCP establishes the point-to-point link. The LCP also negotiates and sets up control options on the WAN data link, which are handled by the NCPs.

The LCP provides automatic configuration of the interfaces at each end, including

- Handling varying limits on packet size
- Detecting common misconfiguration errors
- Terminating the link
- Determining when a link is functioning properly or when it is failing

After the link is established, PPP also uses the LCP to agree automatically on encapsulation formats such as authentication, compression, and error detection. Figure 3-21 shows the relationship of LCP to the physical layer and NCP.

PPP – Network Control Protocol (NCP) (3.2.2.3)

PPP permits multiple network layer protocols to operate on the same communications link. For every network layer protocol used, PPP uses a separate NCP, as shown in Figure 3-21. For example, IPv4 uses the IP Control Protocol (IPCP) and IPv6 uses IPv6 Control Protocol (IPv6CP).

NCPs include functional fields containing standardized codes to indicate the network layer protocol that PPP encapsulates. Table 3-3 lists the PPP protocol field numbers. Each NCP manages the specific needs required by its respective network layer protocols. The various NCP components encapsulate and negotiate options for multiple network layer protocols.

Table 3-3 Protocol Fields

Value (in hex)	Protocol Name
8021	Internet Protocol (IPv4) Control Protocol
8057	Internet Protocol Version 6 (IPv6) Control Protocol
8023	OSI Network Layer Control Protocol
8029	Appletalk Control Protocol
802b	Novell IPX Control Protocol
c021	Link Control Protocol
c023	Password Authentication Protocol
c223	Challenge Handshake Authentication Protocol

PPP Frame Structure (3.2.2.4)

A PPP frame consists of six fields. The following descriptions summarize the PPP frame fields illustrated in Figure 3-22:

- **Flag:** A single byte that indicates the beginning or end of a frame. The Flag field consists of the binary sequence 01111110. In successive PPP frames, only a single Flag character is used.

- **Address:** A single byte that contains the binary sequence 11111111, the standard broadcast address. PPP does not assign individual station addresses.

- **Control:** A single byte that contains the binary sequence 00000011, which calls for transmission of user data in an unsequenced frame. This provides a connectionless link service that does require the establishment of data links or links stations. On a point-to-point link, the destination node does not need to be addressed. Therefore, for PPP, the Address field is set to 0xFF, the broadcast address. If both PPP peers agree to perform Address and Control field compression during the LCP negotiation, the Address field is not included.

- **Protocol:** Two bytes that identify the protocol encapsulated in the information field of the frame. The 2-byte Protocol field identifies the protocol of the PPP payload. If both PPP peers agree to perform Protocol field compression during LCP negotiation, the Protocol field is 1 byte for the protocol identification in the range 0x00-00 to 0x00-FF. The most up-to-date values of the Protocol field are specified in the most recent Assigned Numbers Request For Comments (RFC).

- **Data:** Zero or more bytes that contain the datagram for the protocol specified in the Protocol field. The end of the Information field is found by locating the closing flag sequence and allowing 2 bytes for the FCS field. The default maximum length of the Information field is 1500 bytes. By prior agreement, consenting PPP implementations can use other values for the maximum Information field length.

- **Frame Check Sequence (FCS):** Normally 16 bits (2 bytes). By prior agreement, consenting PPP implementations can use a 32-bit (4-byte) FCS for improved error detection. If the receiver's calculation of the FCS does not match the FCS in the PPP frame, the PPP frame is silently discarded.

Figure 3-22   PPP Frame Fields

LCPs can negotiate modifications to the standard PPP frame structure. Modified frames, however, are always distinguishable from standard frames.

Activity 3.2.2.5: Troubleshooting a Serial Interface

Go to the course online to perform this practice activity.

PPP Sessions (3.2.3)

Understanding PPP session establishment, LCP and NCP are important parts of implementing and troubleshooting PPP. These topics are discussed next.

Establishing a PPP Session (3.2.3.1)

There are three phases of establishing a PPP session, as shown in Figure 3-23:

- **Phase 1: Link establishment and configuration negotiation:** Before PPP exchanges any network layer datagrams, such as IP, the LCP must first open the connection and negotiate configuration options. This phase is complete when the receiving router sends a configuration-acknowledgment frame back to the router initiating the connection.

- **Phase 2: Link quality determination (optional):** The LCP tests the link to determine whether the link quality is sufficient to bring up network layer protocols. The LCP can delay transmission of network layer protocol information until this phase is complete.

- **Phase 3: Network layer protocol configuration negotiation:** After the LCP has finished the link quality determination phase, the appropriate NCP can separately configure the network layer protocols, and bring them up and take them down at any time. If the LCP closes the link, it informs the network layer protocols so that they can take appropriate action.

Figure 3-23   Establishing a PPP Session

The link remains configured for communications until explicit LCP or NCP frames close the link, or until some external event occurs such as an inactivity timer expiring, or an administrator intervening.

The LCP can terminate the link at any time. This is usually done when one of the routers requests termination, but can happen because of a physical event, such as the loss of a carrier or the expiration of an idle-period timer.

LCP Operation (3.2.3.2)

LCP operation includes provisions for link establishment, link maintenance, and link termination. LCP operation uses three classes of LCP frames to accomplish the work of each of the LCP phases:

- Link-establishment frames establish and configure a link (Configure-Request, Configure-Ack, Configure-Nak, and Configure-Reject).

- Link-maintenance frames manage and debug a link (Code-Reject, Protocol-Reject, Echo-Request, Echo-Reply, and Discard-Request).

- Link-termination frames terminate a link (Terminate-Request and Terminate-Ack).

Link Establishment

Link establishment is the first phase of LCP operation, as seen in Figure 3-24. This phase must complete successfully, before any network layer packets can be exchanged. During link establishment, the LCP opens the connection and negotiates the configuration parameters. The link establishment process starts with the initiating device sending a Configure-Request frame to the responder. The Configure-Request frame includes a variable number of configuration options needed to set up on the link.

Figure 3-24 PPP Link Establishment

The initiator includes the options for how it wants the link created, including protocol or authentication parameters. The responder processes the request:

- If the options are not acceptable or not recognized, the responder sends a Configure-Nak or Configure-Reject message. If this occurs and the negotiation fails, the initiator must restart the process with new options.

- If the options are acceptable, the responder responds with a Configure-Ack message and the process moves on to the authentication stage. The operation of the link is handed over to the NCP.

When NCP has completed all necessary configurations, including validating authentication if configured, the line is available for data transfer. During the exchange of data, LCP transitions into link maintenance.

Link Maintenance

During link maintenance, LCP can use messages to provide feedback and test the link, as shown in Figure 3-25.

- **Echo-Request, Echo-Reply, and Discard-Request:** These frames can be used for testing the link.

- **Code-Reject and Protocol-Reject:** These frame types provide feedback when one device receives an invalid frame due to either an unrecognized LCP code (LCP frame type) or a bad protocol identifier. For example, if an uninterpretable packet is received from the peer, a Code-Reject packet is sent in response. The sending device will resend the packet.

Figure 3-25 PPP Link Maintenance

Link Termination

After the transfer of data at the network layer completes, the LCP terminates the link, as shown in Figure 3-26. NCP only terminates the network layer and NCP link. The link remains open until the LCP terminates it. If the LCP terminates the link before NCP, the NCP session is also terminated.

Figure 3-26   PPP Link Termination

PPP can terminate the link at any time. This might happen because of the loss of the carrier, authentication failure, link quality failure, the expiration of an idle-period timer, or the administrative closing of the link. The LCP closes the link by exchanging Terminate packets. The device initiating the shutdown sends a Terminate-Request message. The other device replies with a Terminate-Ack. A termination request indicates that the device sending it needs to close the link. When the link is closing, PPP informs the network layer protocols so that they may take appropriate action.

LCP Packet (3.2.3.3)

Figure 3-27 shows the fields in an LCP packet:

- **Code:** The Code field is 1 byte in length and identifies the type of LCP packet.

- **Identifier:** The Identifier field is 1 byte in length and is used to match packet requests and replies.

- **Length:** The Length field is 2 bytes in length and indicates the total length (including all fields) of the LCP packet.

- **Data:** The Data field is 0 or more bytes as indicated by the length field. The format of this field is determined by the code.

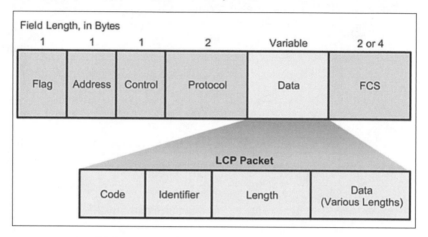

Figure 3-27   LCP Packet Codes

Each LCP packet is a single LCP message consisting of an LCP Code field identifying the type of LCP packet, an identifier field so that requests and replies can be matched, and a Length field indicating the size of the LCP packet and LCP packet type-specific data.

Each LCP packet has a specific function in the exchange of configuration information depending on its packet type. The Code field of the LCP packet identifies the packet type according to Table 3-4.

Table 3-4   LCP Packet Fields

LCP Code	LCP Packet Type	Description
1	Configure-Request	Sent to open or reset a PPP connection. Configure-Request contains a list of LCP options with changes to default option values.
2	Configure-Ack	Sent when all of the values of all of the LCP options in the last Configure-Request received are recognized and acceptable. When both PPP peers send and receive Configure-Acks, the LCP negotiation is complete.
3	Configure-Nak	Sent when all the LCP options are recognized, but the values of some options are not acceptable. Configure-Nak includes the mismatching options and their acceptable values.

LCP Code	LCP Packet Type	Description
4	Configure-Reject	Set when LCP options are not recognized or not acceptable for negotiation. Configure-Reject includes the unrecognized or non-negotiable options.
5	Terminate-Request	Optionally sent to close the PPP connection.
6	Terminate-Ack	Sent in response to a Terminate-Request.
7	Code-Reject	Sent when the LCP code is unknown. The Code-Request message includes the rejected LCP packet.
8	Protocol-Reject	Sent when the PPP frame contains an unknown Protocol ID. The Protocol-Reject message includes the rejected LCP packet. Protocol-Reject is typically sent by a PPP peer in response to PPP NCP for a LAN protocol not enabled on the PPP peer.
9	Echo-Request	Optionally sent to test PPP connection.
10	Echo-Reply	Sent in response to an Echo-Request. The PPP Echo-Request and Echo-Reply are not related to the ICMP Echo Request and Echo Reply messages.
11	Discard-Request	Optionally sent to exercise the link in the outbound direction.

PPP Configuration Options (3.2.3.4)

PPP can be configured to support various optional functions, as shown in Figure 3-28. These optional functions include

- Authentication using either PAP or CHAP

- Compression using either Stacker or Predictor

- Multilink that combines two or more channels to increase the WAN bandwidth

To negotiate the use of these PPP options, the LCP link-establishment frames contain option information in the data field of the LCP frame, as shown in Figure 3-29. If a configuration option is not included in an LCP frame, the default value for that configuration option is assumed.

Figure 3-28 PPP Configuration Options

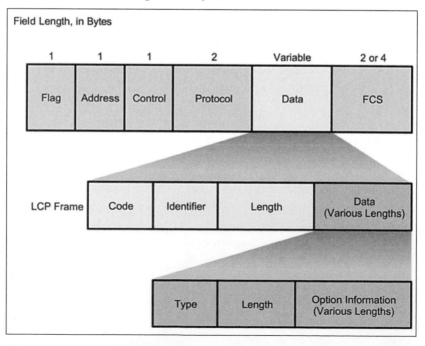

Figure 3-29 LCP Option Fields

This phase is complete when a configuration acknowledgment frame has been sent and received.

NCP Explained (3.2.3.5)

After the link has been initiated, the LCP passes control to the appropriate NCP.

NCP Process

Although initially designed for IP packets, PPP can carry data from multiple network layer protocols by using a modular approach in its implementation. PPP's modular model allows LCP to set up the link and then transfer the details of a network protocol to a specific NCP. Each network protocol has a corresponding NCP and each NCP has a corresponding RFC.

There are NCPs for IPv4, IPv6, IPX, AppleTalk, and many others. NCPs use the same packet format as the LCPs.

After the LCP has configured and authenticated the basic link, the appropriate NCP is invoked to complete the specific configuration of the network layer protocol being used. When the NCP has successfully configured the network layer protocol, the network protocol is in the open state on the established LCP link. At this point, PPP can carry the corresponding network layer protocol packets.

IPCP Example

As an example of how the NCP layer works, the NCP configuration of IPv4, which is the most common Layer 3 protocol, is shown in Figure 3-30. After LCP has established the link, the routers exchange IPCP messages, negotiating options specific to the IPv4 protocol. IPCP is responsible for configuring, enabling, and disabling the IPv4 modules on both ends of the link. IPv6CP is an NCP with the same responsibilities for IPv6.

IPCP negotiates two options:

- **Compression:** Allows devices to negotiate an algorithm to compress TCP and IP headers and save bandwidth. The Van Jacobson TCP/IP header compression reduces the size of the TCP/IP headers to as few as 3 bytes. This can be a significant improvement on slow serial lines, particularly for interactive traffic.

- **IPv4-Address:** Allows the initiating device to specify an IPv4 address to use for routing IP over the PPP link, or to request an IPv4 address for the responder. Prior to the advent of broadband technologies such as DSL and cable modem services, dialup network links commonly used the IPv4 address option.

Figure 3-30   PPP NCP Operation

After the NCP process is complete, the link goes into the open state, and LCP takes over again in a link maintenance phase. Link traffic consists of any possible combination of LCP, NCP, and network layer protocol packets. When data transfer is complete, NCP terminates the protocol link; LCP terminates the PPP connection.

Interactive Graphic

Activity 3.2.3.6: Identify the Steps in the LCP Link Negotiation Process

Go to the course online to perform this practice activity.

Configure PPP (3.3)

This section describes the configuration of PPP. Basic PPP configuration is discussed along with optional PPP features and PPP authentication.

Configure PPP (3.3.1)

Basic PPP configuration commands are discussed next along with PPP compression, PPP quality link monitoring, and PPP Multilink.

PPP Configuration Options (3.3.1.1)

In the previous section, configurable LCP options were introduced to meet specific WAN connection requirements. PPP may include the following LCP options:

- **Authentication:** Peer routers exchange authentication messages. Two authentication choices are *Password Authentication Protocol (PAP)* and *Challenge Handshake Authentication Protocol (CHAP)*.

- **Compression:** Increases the effective throughput on PPP connections by reducing the amount of data in the frame that must travel across the link. The protocol decompresses the frame at its destination. Two compression protocols available in Cisco routers are Stacker and Predictor.

- **Error detection:** Identifies fault conditions. The Quality and Magic Number options help ensure a reliable, loop-free data link. The Magic Number field helps in detecting links that are in a looped-back condition. Until the Magic-Number Configuration Option has been successfully negotiated, the Magic-Number must be transmitted as zero. Magic numbers are generated randomly at each end of the connection.

- **PPP Callback:** PPP callback is used to enhance security. With this LCP option, a Cisco router can act as a callback client or a callback server. The client makes the initial call, requests that the server call it back, and terminates its initial call. The callback router answers the initial call and makes the return call to the client based on its configuration statements. The command is **ppp callback [accept | request]**.

- **Multilink:** This alternative provides load balancing over the router interfaces that PPP uses. Multilink PPP, also referred to as MP, MPPP, MLP, or Multilink, provides a method for spreading traffic across multiple physical WAN links while providing packet *fragmentation* and *reassembly*, proper sequencing, multivendor interoperability, and load balancing on inbound and outbound traffic.

When options are configured, a corresponding field value is inserted into the LCP option field, shown in Table 3-5.

Table 3-5 Configurable Options Field Codes

Option Name	Option Type	Option Length	Description
Authentication Protocol	3	5 or 6	This field indicates the authentication protocol, either PAP or CHAP.
Protocol Compression	7	2	A flag indicating that the PPP protocol ID be compressed to a single octet when the 2-byte protocol field is in the range of 0x00-00 to 0x00-FF.

Option Name	Option Type	Option Length	Description
Address and Control Field Compression	8	2	A flag indicating that the PPP Address field (always set to 0xFF) and the PPP Control field (always set to 0x03) be removed from the PPP header.
Magic Number (Error Detection)	5	6	This is a random number chosen to distinguish a peer and detect looped back lines.
Callback	13 or 0x0D	3	A 1-octet indicator of how callback is to be determined.

PPP Basic Configuration Command (3.3.1.2)

Basic PPP configuration is very straightforward. After PPP is configured on an interface the network administrator can then apply one or more PPP options.

Enabling PPP on an Interface

To set PPP as the encapsulation method used by a serial interface, use the **encapsulation ppp** interface configuration command.

The following example enables PPP encapsulation on interface serial 0/0/0:

```
R3# configure terminal
R3(config)# interface serial 0/0/0
R3(config-if)# encapsulation ppp
```

The **encapsulation ppp** interface command has no arguments. Remember that if PPP is not configured on a Cisco router, the default encapsulation for serial interfaces is HDLC.

Figure 3-31 and the listing that follows, shows that routers R1 and R2 have been configured with both an IPv4 and an IPv6 address on the serial interfaces. PPP is a Layer 2 encapsulation that supports various Layer 3 protocols including IPv4 and IPv6.

Figure 3-31   PPP Basic Configuration

Partial running-config for R1

```
hostname R1
!
interface Serial 0/0/0
 ip address 10.0.1.1 255.255.255.252
 ipv6 address 2001:db8:cafe:1::1/64
 encapsulation ppp
```

Parital running-config for R2

```
hostname R2
!
interface Serial 0/0/0
 ip address 10.0.1.2 255.255.255.252
 ipv6 address 2001:db8:cafe:1::2/64
 encapsulation ppp
```

PPP Compression Commands (3.3.1.3)

Point-to-point software compression on serial interfaces can be configured after PPP encapsulation is enabled. Because this option invokes a software compression process, it can affect system performance. If the traffic already consists of compressed files, such as .zip, .tar, or .mpeg, do not use this option. The command syntax for the **compress** command is

```
Router(config-if)# compress [ predictor | stac ]
```

- **predictor** (optional): Specifies that a predictor compression algorithm will be used

- **stac** (optional): Specifies that a Stacker (LZS) compression algorithm will be used

To configure compression over PPP, enter the following commands:

```
R2(config)# interface serial 0/0/0
R2(config-if)# encapsulation ppp
R2(config-if)# compress [ predictor | stac ]
```

The following example shows predictor compression used between R1 and R2:

Partial running-config for R1

```
hostname R1
!
interface Serial 0/0/0
 ip address 10.0.1.1 255.255.255.252
 ipv6 address 2001:db8:cafe:1::1/64
```

```
encapsulation ppp

compress predictor
```

Partial running-config for R2

```
hostname R2
!
interface Serial 0/0/0
  ip address 10.0.1.2 255.255.255.252
  ipv6 address 2001:db8:cafe:1::2/64
  encapsulation ppp
  compress predictor
```

PPP Link Quality Monitoring Command (3.3.1.4)

Recall that LCP provides an optional link quality determination phase. In this phase, LCP tests the link to determine whether the link quality is sufficient to use Layer 3 protocols. The **ppp quality** *percentage* command ensures that the link meets the quality requirement set; otherwise, the link closes down. The command syntax for the **ppp quality** command is

```
Router(config-if)# ppp quality percentage
```

- *percentage*: Specifies the link quality threshold. Range is 1 to 100.

The percentages are calculated for both incoming and outgoing directions. The outgoing quality is calculated by comparing the total number of packets and bytes sent to the total number of packets and bytes received by the destination node. The incoming quality is calculated by comparing the total number of packets and bytes received to the total number of packets and bytes sent by the destination node.

If the link quality percentage is not maintained, the link is deemed to be of poor quality and is taken down. Link Quality Monitoring (LQM) implements a time lag so that the link does not bounce up and down.

The following configuration example monitors the data dropped on the link and avoids frame looping:

```
R2(config)# interface serial 0/0/0
R2(config-if)# encapsulation ppp
R2(config-if)# ppp quality 80
```

Use the **no ppp quality** command to disable LQM. The following example shows link quality being used between R1 and R2:

Partial running-config for R1

```
hostname R1
!
interface Serial 0/0/0
 ip address 10.0.1.1 255.255.255.252
 ipv6 address 2001:db8:cafe:1::1/64
 encapsulation ppp
 ppp quality 80
```

Partial running-config for R2

```
hostname R2
!
interface Serial 0/0/0
 ip address 10.0.1.2 255.255.255.252
 ipv6 address 2001:db8:cafe:1::2/64
 encapsulation ppp
 ppp quality 80
```

Interactive Graphic

Activity 3.3.1.4: PPP Link Quality Monitoring Command

Go to the course online to use the checker to LQM on R1's serial 0/0/1 interface.

PPP Multilink Commands (3.3.1.5)

Multilink PPP (also referred to as MP, MPPP, MLP, or Multilink) provides a method for spreading traffic across multiple physical WAN links, as shown in Figure 3-32. Multilink PPP also provides packet fragmentation and reassembly, proper sequencing, multivendor interoperability, and load balancing on inbound and outbound traffic.

Figure 3-32   PPP Multilink

MPPP allows packets to be fragmented and sends these fragments simultaneously over multiple point-to-point links to the same remote address. The multiple physical links come up in response to a user-defined load threshold. MPPP can measure the load on just inbound traffic, or on just outbound traffic, but not on the combined load of both inbound and outbound traffic.

Configuring MPPP requires two steps.

Step 1.   Create a multilink bundle.

The **interface multilink** `number` command creates the multilink interface.

In interface configuration mode, an IP address is assigned to the multilink interface. In this example, both IPv4 and IPv6 addresses are configured on routers R3 and R4.

The interface is enabled for multilink PPP.

The interface is assigned a multilink group number.

Step 2.   Assign interfaces to the multilink bundle. Each interface that is part of the multilink group:

Is enabled for PPP encapsulation.

Is enabled for multilink PPP.

Is bound to the multilink bundle using the multilink group number configured in Step 1.

The following example shows multilink PPP configured between R3 and R4:

Partial running-config for R3

```
hostname R3
!
interface Multilink 1
 ip address 10.0.1.1 255.255.255.252
 ipv6 address 2001:db8:cafe:1::1/64
 ppp multilink
 ppp multilink group 1
!
interface Serial 0/1/0
 no ip address
 encapsulation ppp
 ppp multilink
 ppp multilink group 1
!
interface Serial 0/1/1
 no ip address
 encapsulation ppp
 ppp multilink
 ppp multilink group 1
```

Partial running-config for R4

```
hostname R4
!
interface Multilink 1
 ip address 10.0.1.2 255.255.255.252
 ipv6 address 2001:db8:cafe:1::2/64
 ppp multilink
 ppp multilink group 1
!
interface Serial 0/0/0
 no ip address
 encapsulation ppp
 ppp multilink
 ppp multilink group 1
!
interface Serial 0/0/1
 no ip address
 encapsulation ppp
 ppp multilink
 ppp multilink group 1
```

To disable PPP multilink, use the **no ppp multilink** command.

Verifying PPP Configuration (3.3.1.6)

Use the **show interfaces serial** command to verify proper configuration of HDLC or PPP encapsulation. Example 3-3 shows a PPP configuration.

Example 3-3   Using **show interfaces serial** to Verify a PPP Encapsulation

```
R2#show interfaces serial 0/0/0
Serial0/0/0 is up, line protocol is up
  Hardware is GT96K Serial
  Internet address is 10.0.1.2/30
  MTU 1500 bytes, BW 1544 Kbit/sec, DLY 20000 usec,
     reliability 255/255, txload 1/255, rxload 1/255
  Encapsulation PPP, LCP Open
  Open: IPCP, IPV6CP, CCP, CDPCP,, loopback not set
  Keepalive set (10 sec)
  CRC checking enabled
<Output omitted for brevity>
```

When you configure HDLC, the output of the **show interfaces serial** command should display **encapsulation HDLC**. When PPP is configured, the LCP and NCP states also display. Notice that NCPs IPCP and IPv6CP are open for IPv4 and IPv6 because R1 and R2 were configured with both IPv4 and IPv6 addresses.

Table 3-6 summarizes commands used when verifying PPP.

Table 3-6   Verifying PPP Commands

Command	Description
show interfaces	Displays statistics for all interfaces configured on the router.
show interfaces serial	Displays information about a serial interface.
show ppp multilink	Displays information about a PPP multilink interface.

The **show ppp multilink** command verifies that PPP multilink is enabled on R3, as shown in Example 3-4. The output indicates the interface Multilink 1, the hostnames of both the local and remote endpoints, and the serial interfaces assigned to the multilink bundle.

Example 3-4   Verifying PPP Multilink

```
R3# show ppp multilink
Multilink1
  Bundle name: R4
  Remote Endpoint Discriminator: [1] R4
  Local Endpoint Discriminator: [1] R3
  Bundle up for 00:01:20, total bandwidth 3088, load 1/255
  Receive buffer limit 24000 bytes, frag timeout 1000 ms
    0/0 fragments/bytes in reassembly list
    0 lost fragments, 0 reordered
    0/0 discarded fragments/bytes, 0 lost received
    0x2 received sequence, 0x2 sent sequence
  Member links: 2 active, 0 inactive (max 255, min not set)
    Se0/1/1, since 00:01:20
    Se0/1/0, since 00:01:06
No inactive multilink interfaces
R3#
```

PPP Authentication (3.3.2)

PPP authentication protocols and configuration of PPP authentication is discussed in this section.

PPP Authentication Protocols (3.3.2.1)

PPP defines an extensible LCP that allows negotiation of an authentication protocol for authenticating its peer before allowing network layer protocols to transmit over the link. RFC 1334 defines two protocols for authentication, PAP and CHAP, as shown in Figure 3-33.

Figure 3-33   PPP Authentication Protocols

PAP is a very basic two-way process. There is no encryption. The username and password are sent in plaintext. If it is accepted, the connection is allowed. CHAP is more secure than PAP. It involves a three-way exchange of a shared secret.

The authentication phase of a PPP session is optional. If used, the peer is authenticated after LCP establishes the link and chooses the authentication protocol. If it is used, authentication takes place before the network layer protocol configuration phase begins.

The authentication options require that the calling side of the link enter authentication information. This helps to ensure that the user has the permission of the network administrator to make the call. Peer routers exchange authentication messages.

Password Authentication Protocol (PAP) (3.3.2.2)

One of the many features of PPP is that it performs Layer 2 authentication in addition to other layers of authentication, encryption, access control, and general security procedures.

Initiating PAP

PAP provides a simple method for a remote node to establish its identity using a two-way handshake. PAP is not interactive. When the **ppp authentication pap** command is used, the username and password are sent as one LCP data package, rather than the server sending a login prompt and waiting for a response, as shown in Figure 3-34. After PPP completes the link establishment phase, the remote node repeatedly sends a username-password pair across the link until the receiving node acknowledges it or terminates the connection.

Figure 3-34   Initiating PAP

Completing PAP

At the receiving node, the username-password is checked by an authentication server that either allows or denies the connection. An accept or reject message is returned to the requester, as shown in Figure 3-35.

PAP is not a strong authentication protocol. Using PAP, passwords are sent across the link in plaintext, and there is no protection from playback or repeated trial-and-error attacks. The remote node is in control of the frequency and timing of the login attempts.

Nonetheless, there are times when using PAP can be justified. For example, despite its shortcomings, PAP may be used in the following environments:

- A large installed base of client applications that do not support CHAP
- Incompatibilities between different vendor implementations of CHAP
- Situations where a plaintext password must be available to simulate a login at the remote host

Figure 3-35   Completing PAP

Challenge Handshake Authentication Protocol (CHAP) (3.3.2.3)

After authentication is established with PAP, it does not reauthenticate. This leaves the network vulnerable to attack. Unlike PAP, which only authenticates once, CHAP conducts periodic challenges to make sure that the remote node still has a valid password value. The password value is variable and changes unpredictably while the link exists.

After the PPP link establishment phase is complete, the local router sends a challenge message to the remote node, as shown in Figure 3-36.

Figure 3-36   Initiating CHAP

The remote node responds with a value calculated using a one-way hash function, which is typically *message digest 5 (MD5)* based on the password and challenge message, as shown in Figure 3-37.

Figure 3-37   Responding CHAP

The local router checks the response against its own calculation of the expected hash value. If the values match, the initiating node acknowledges the authentication, as shown in Figure 3-38. If the value does not match, the initiating node immediately terminates the connection.

Figure 3-38   Completing CHAP

CHAP provides protection against playback attack by using a variable challenge value that is unique and unpredictable. Because the challenge is unique and random, the resulting hash value is also unique and random. The use of repeated challenges limits the time of exposure to any single attack. The local router or a third-party authentication server is in control of the frequency and timing of the challenges.

PPP Encapsulation and Authentication Process (3.3.2.4)

The flowchart in Figure 3-39 can be used to help understand the PPP authentication process when configuring PPP. The flowchart provides a visual example of the logic decisions made by PPP.

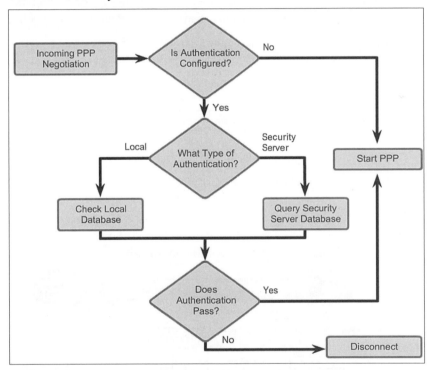

Figure 3-39   PPP Encapsulation and Authentication Process

For example, if an incoming PPP request requires no authentication, then PPP progresses to the next level. If an incoming PPP request requires authentication, then it can be authenticated using either the local database or a security server. As illustrated in the flowchart, successful authentication progresses to the next level, while an authentication failure disconnects and drops the incoming PPP request.

Follow the steps to view R1 establishing an authenticated PPP CHAP connection with R2.

Step 1.   As shown in Figure 3-40, R1 initially negotiates the link connection using LCP with router R2 and the two systems agree to use CHAP authentication during the PPP LCP negotiation.

Figure 3-40   Establishing a Link

Step 2.   As shown in Figure 3-41, R2 generates an ID and a random number, and sends that and its username as a CHAP challenge packet to R1.

Figure 3-41   Sending a CHAP Challenge to R1

Step 3.   As shown in Figure 3-42, R1 uses the username of the challenger (R2) and cross references it with its local database to find its associated password. R1 then generates a unique MD5 hash number using the R2's username, ID, random number and the shared secret password. In this example, the shared secret password is boardwalk.

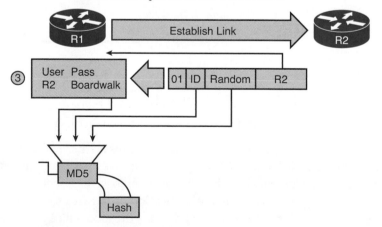

Figure 3-42   R1 Validates R2

Step 4.   As shown in Figure 3-43, Router R1 then sends the challenge ID, the hashed value, and its username (R1) to R2.

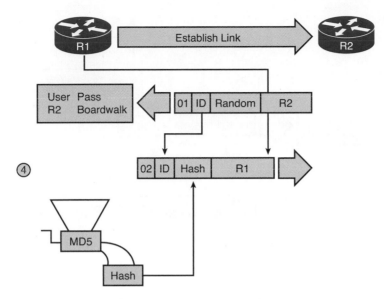

Figure 3-43   R1 Sends the Challenge to R2

Step 5.   As shown in Figure 3-44, R2 generates its own hash value using the ID, the
shared secret password, and the random number it originally sent to R1.

Figure 3-44   R2 Validates R1

Step 6.   As shown in Figure 3-45, R2 compares its hash value with the hash value
sent by R1. If the values are the same, R2 sends a link established response
to R1.

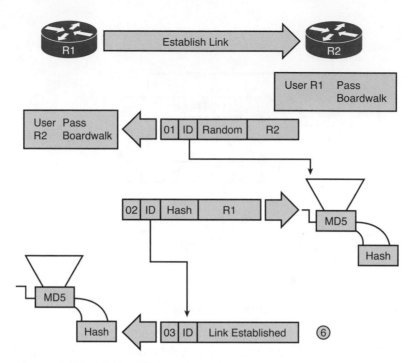

Figure 3-45   R2 Establishes the Link

If the authentication failed, a CHAP failure packet is built from the following components:

- 04 = CHAP failure message type

- id = copied from the response packet

- "Authentication failure" or some similar text message, which is meant to be a user-readable explanation

The shared secret password must be identical on R1 and R2.

Configuring PPP Authentication (3.3.2.5)

To specify the order in which the CHAP or PAP protocols are requested on the interface, use the **ppp authentication** interface configuration command:

```
Router(config-if)# ppp authentication {chap | chap pap | pap chap | pap} [if needed]
    [list-name | default] [callin]
```

- Use the **no** form of the command to disable this authentication.

Table 3-7 explains the syntax for the **ppp authentication** interface configuration command.

Table 3-7 PPP Command Syntax

chap	Enables CHAP on serial interface.
pap	Enables PAP on serial interface.
chap pap	Enables both CHAP and PAP on serial interface, and performs CHAP authentication before PAP.
pap chap	Enables both CHAP and PAP on serial interface, and performs PAP authentication before CHAP.
if-needed (Optional)	Used with TACACS and XTACACS. Do not perform CHAP or PAP authentication if the user has already provided authentication. This option is available only on asynchronous interfaces.
list-name (Optional)	Used with AAA/TACACS+. Specifies the name of a list of TACACS+ methods of authentication to use. If no list name is specified, the system uses the default. Lists are created with the **aaa authentication ppp** command.
default (Optional)	Used with AAA/TACACS+. Created with the **aaa authentication ppp** command.
Callin	Specifies authentication on incoming (received) calls only.

After you have enabled CHAP or PAP authentication, or both, the local router requires the remote device to prove its identity before allowing data traffic to flow. This is done as follows:

- PAP authentication requires the remote device to send a name and password to be checked against a matching entry in the local username database or in the remote *TACACS/TACACS+* database.

- CHAP authentication sends a challenge to the remote device. The remote device must encrypt the challenge value with a shared secret and return the encrypted value and its name to the local router in a response message. The local router uses the name of the remote device to look up the appropriate secret in the local username or remote TACACS/TACACS+ database. It uses the looked-up secret to encrypt the original challenge and verify that the encrypted values match.

Note

Authentication, authorization, and accounting (AAA)/TACACS is a dedicated server used to authenticate users. TACACS clients send a query to a TACACS authentication server. The server can authenticate the user, authorize what the user can do, and track what the user has done.

Either PAP or CHAP or both can be enabled. If both methods are enabled, the first method specified is requested during link negotiation. If the peer suggests using the second method or simply refuses the first method, the second method should be tried. Some remote devices support CHAP only and some PAP only. The order in which you specify the methods is based on your concerns about the ability of the remote device to correctly negotiate the appropriate method as well as your concern about data line security. PAP usernames and passwords are sent as plaintext strings and can be intercepted and reused. CHAP has eliminated most of the known security holes.

Configuring PPP with Authentication (3.3.2.6)

The procedure outlined in the table describes how to configure PPP encapsulation and PAP/CHAP authentication protocols. Correct configuration is essential, because PAP and CHAP use these parameters to authenticate.

Configuring PAP Authentication

Figure 3-46 shows the topology used in an example of a two-way PAP authentication configuration, with the configuration in the following listing. Both routers authenticate and are authenticated, so the PAP authentication commands mirror each other. The PAP username and password that each router sends must match those specified with the **username** *name* **password** *password* command of the other router.

Figure 3-46   Topology for PPP

Partial running-config for R1

```
hostname R1
username R2 password sameone
!
interface Serial0/0/0
 ip address 10.0.1.1 255.255.255.252
 ipv6 address 2001:DB8:CAFE:1::1/64
 encapsulation ppp
 ppp authentication pap
 ppp pap sent-username R2 password sameone
```

Partial running-config for R2

```
hostname R2
username R1 password 0 sameone
!
interface Serial 0/0/0
```

```
ip address 10.0.1.2 255.255.255.252
ipv6 address 2001:db8:cafe:1::2/64
encapsulation ppp
ppp authentication pap
ppp pap sent-username R2 password sameone
```

PAP provides a simple method for a remote node to establish its identity using a two-way handshake. This is done only on initial link establishment. The hostname on one router must match the username the other router has configured for PPP. The passwords must also match. Specify the username and password parameters, use the following command: **ppp pap sent-username** *name* **password** *password*.

Interactive Graphic

Activity 3.3.2.6: PPP PAP Authentication

Go to the course online to use the Syntax Checker to configure PAP authentication on router R1's serial 0/0/1 interface.

Configuring CHAP Authentication

CHAP periodically verifies the identity of the remote node using a three-way handshake. The hostname on one router must match the username the other router has configured. The passwords must also match. This occurs on initial link establishment and can be repeated any time after the link has been established. The following is an example of a CHAP configuration.

Partial running-config for R1

```
hostname R1
username R2 password sameone
!
interface Serial0/0/0
 ip address 10.0.1.1 255.255.255.252
 ipv6 address 2001:DB8:CAFE:1::1/64
 encapsulation ppp
 ppp authentication chap
```

Partial running-config for R2

```
hostname R2
username R1 password 0 sameone
!
interface Serial 0/0/0
 ip address 10.0.1.2 255.255.255.252
 ipv6 address 2001:db8:cafe:1::2/64
 encapsulation ppp
 ppp authentication chap
```

Interactive Graphic

Activity 3.3.2.6: PPP CHAP Authentication

Go to the course online to use the Syntax Checker to configure CHAP authentication on router R1's serial 0/0/1 interface.

Packet Tracer ☐ Activity

Packet Tracer Activity 3.3.2.7: Configuring PAP and CHAP Authentication

Background/Scenario

In this activity, you will practice configuring PPP encapsulation on serial links. You will also configure PPP PAP authentication and PPP CHAP authentication.

Lab 3.3.2.8: Configuring Basic PPP with Authentication

In this lab, you will complete the following objectives:

- Part 1: Configure Basic Device Settings
- Part 2: Configure PPP Encapsulation
- Part 3: Configure PPP CHAP Authentication

Troubleshoot WAN Connectivity (3.4)

Troubleshooting is an important component to understanding and implementing any technology. This section discusses troubleshooting WAN connectivity, specifically point-to-point serial communications using PPP.

Troubleshoot PPP (3.4.1)

Similar to other protocols implemented on a router, troubleshooting PPP involves a combination of **debug** and **show** commands. This section discusses how to use these commands to troubleshoot PPP negotiation and authentication.

Troubleshooting PPP Serial Encapsulation (3.4.1.1)

Recall that the **debug** command is used for troubleshooting and is accessed from privileged EXEC mode of the command-line interface. A **debug** output displays information about various router operations, related traffic generated or received by the router, and any error messages. It can consume a significant amount of resources, and the router is forced to process-switch the packets being debugged. The **debug** command must not be used as a monitoring tool; rather, it is meant to be used for a short period of time for troubleshooting.

Use the **debug ppp** command to display information about the operation of PPP.

```
Router# debug ppp {packet | negotiation | error | authentication | compression |
    cbcp}
```

Table 3-8 shows the command syntax. Use the no form of this command to disable debugging output.

Table 3-8 `debug ppp` Command Parameters

Parameter	Usage
packet	Displays PPP packets being sent and received. (This command displays low-level packet dumps.)
negotiation	Displays PPP packets transmitted during PPP startup, where PPP options are negotiated.
error	Displays protocol errors and error statistics associated with PPP connection negotiation and operation.
authentication	Displays authentication protocol messages, including Challenge Authentication Protocol (CHAP) packet exchanges and Password Authentication Protocol (PAP) exchanges.
compression	Displays information specific to the exchange of PPP connections using MPPC. This command is useful for obtaining incorrect packet sequence number information where MPPC compression is enabled.
cbcp	Displays protocol errors and statistics associated with PPP connection negotiations using MSCB.

Use the **debug ppp** command when trying to search the following:

- NCPs that are supported on either end of a PPP connection
- Any loops that might exist in a PPP internetwork
- Nodes that are (or are not) properly negotiating PPP connections
- Errors that have occurred over the PPP connection
- Causes for CHAP session failures
- Causes for PAP session failures
- Information specific to the exchange of PPP connections using the Callback Control Protocol (CBCP), used by Microsoft clients
- Incorrect packet sequence number information where MPPC compression is enabled

Debug PPP (3.4.1.2)

In addition to the **debug ppp** command, there are other commands that are available for troubleshooting a PPP connection.

A good command to use when troubleshooting serial interface encapsulation is the **debug ppp packet** command, as shown in Example 3-5. The example depicts packet exchanges under normal PPP operation, including LCP state, LQM procedures, and the LCP magic number.

Example 3-5   Output of **debug ppp packet** Command

```
R1# debug ppp packet
PPP packet display debugging is on
R1#
*Apr  1 16:15:17.471: Se0/0/0 LQM: O state Open magic 0x1EFC37C3 len 48
*Apr  1 16:15:17.471: Se0/0/0 LQM:    LastOutLQRs 70 LastOutPackets/Octets 194/9735
*Apr  1 16:15:17.471: Se0/0/0 LQM:    PeerInLQRs 70 PeerInPackets/Discards/Errors/
  Octets 0/0/0/0
*Apr  1 16:15:17.471: Se0/0/0 LQM:    PeerOutLQRs 71 PeerOutPackets/Octets 197/9839
*Apr  1 16:15:17.487: Se0/0/0 PPP: I pkt type 0xC025, datagramsize 52 link[ppp]
*Apr  1 16:15:17.487: Se0/0/0 LQM: I state Open magic 0xFE83D624 len 48
*Apr  1 16:15:17.487: Se0/0/0 LQM:    LastOutLQRs 71 LastOutPackets/Octets 197/9839
*Apr  1 16:15:17.487: Se0/0/0 LQM:    PeerInLQRs 71 PeerInPackets/Discards/Errors/
  Octets 0/0/0/0
*Apr  1 16:15:17.487: Se0/0/0 LQM:    PeerOutLQRs 71 PeerOutPackets/Octets 196/9809
*Apr  1 16:15:17.535: Se0/0/0 LCP: O ECHOREQ [Open] id 36 len 12 magic 0x1EFC37C3
*Apr  1 16:15:17.539: Se0/0/0 LCP-FS: I ECHOREP [Open] id 36 len 12 magic 0xFE83D624
*Apr  1 16:15:17.539: Se0/0/0 LCP-FS: Received id 36, sent id 36, line up
R1# undebug all
```

Example 3-6 displays the **debug ppp negotiation** command in a normal negotiation, where both sides agree on NCP parameters. In this case, protocol types IPv4 and IPv6 are proposed and acknowledged. The **debug ppp negotiation** command enables the network administrator to view the PPP negotiation transactions, identify the problem or stage when the error occurs, and develop a resolution. The output includes the LCP negotiation, authentication, and NCP negotiation.

Example 3-6   Output of **debug ppp negotiation** Command

```
R1# debug ppp negotiation
PPP protocol negotiation debugging is on
R1#
*Apr  1 18:42:29.831: %LINK-3-UPDOWN: Interface Serial0/0/0, changed state to up
*Apr  1 18:42:29.831: Se0/0/0 PPP: Sending cstate UP notification
*Apr  1 18:42:29.831: Se0/0/0 PPP: Processing CstateUp message
```

```
*Apr   1 18:42:29.835: PPP: Alloc Context [66A27824]
*Apr   1 18:42:29.835: ppp2 PPP: Phase is ESTABLISHING
*Apr   1 18:42:29.835: Se0/0/0 PPP: Using default call direction
*Apr   1 18:42:29.835: Se0/0/0 PPP: Treating connection as a dedicated line
*Apr   1 18:42:29.835: Se0/0/0 PPP: Session handle[4000002] Session id[2]
*Apr   1 18:42:29.835: Se0/0/0 LCP: Event[OPEN] State[Initial to Starting]
*Apr   1 18:42:29.835: Se0/0/0 LCP: O CONFREQ [Starting] id 1 len 23
*Apr   1 18:42:29.835: Se0/0/0 LCP:    AuthProto CHAP (0x0305C22305)
*Apr   1 18:42:29.835: Se0/0/0 LCP:    QualityType 0xC025 period 1000
  (0x0408C025000003E8)
*Apr   1 18:42:29.835: Se0/0/0 LCP:    MagicNumber 0x1F887DD3 (0x05061F887DD3)
<Output omitted>
*Apr   1 18:42:29.855: Se0/0/0 PPP: Phase is AUTHENTICATING, by both
*Apr   1 18:42:29.855: Se0/0/0 CHAP: O CHALLENGE id 1 len 23 from "R1"
<Output omitted>
*Apr   1 18:42:29.871: Se0/0/0 IPCP: Authorizing CP
*Apr   1 18:42:29.871: Se0/0/0 IPCP: CP stalled on event[Authorize CP]
*Apr   1 18:42:29.871: Se0/0/0 IPCP: CP unstall
<Output omitted>
*Apr   1 18:42:29.875: Se0/0/0 CHAP: O SUCCESS id 1 len 4
*Apr   1 18:42:29.879: Se0/0/0 CHAP: I SUCCESS id 1 len 4
*Apr   1 18:42:29.879: Se0/0/0 PPP: Phase is UP
*Apr   1 18:42:29.879: Se0/0/0 IPCP: Protocol configured, start CP. state[Initial]
*Apr   1 18:42:29.879: Se0/0/0 IPCP: Event[OPEN] State[Initial to Starting]
*Apr   1 18:42:29.879: Se0/0/0 IPCP: O CONFREQ [Starting] id 1 len 10
*Apr   1 18:42:29.879: Se0/0/0 IPCP:    Address 10.0.1.1 (0x03060A000101)
*Apr   1 18:42:29.879: Se0/0/0 IPCP: Event[UP] State[Starting to REQsent]
*Apr   1 18:42:29.879: Se0/0/0 IPV6CP: Protocol configured, start CP. state[Initial]
*Apr   1 18:42:29.883: Se0/0/0 IPV6CP: Event[OPEN] State[Initial to Starting]
*Apr   1 18:42:29.883: Se0/0/0 IPV6CP: Authorizing CP
*Apr   1 18:42:29.883: Se0/0/0 IPV6CP: CP stalled on event[Authorize CP]
<Output omitted>
*Apr   1 18:42:29.919: Se0/0/0 IPCP: State is Open
*Apr   1 18:42:29.919: Se0/0/0 IPV6CP: State is Open
*Apr   1 18:42:29.919: Se0/0/0 CDPCP: State is Open
*Apr   1 18:42:29.923: Se0/0/0 CCP: State is Open
*Apr   1 18:42:29.927: Se0/0/0 Added to neighbor route AVL tree: topoid 0, address
  10.0.1.2
*Apr   1 18:42:29.927: Se0/0/0 IPCP: Install route to 10.0.1.2
*Apr   1 18:42:39.871: Se0/0/0 LQM: O state Open magic 0x1F887DD3 len 48
*Apr   1 18:42:39.871: Se0/0/0 LQM:    LastOutLQRs 0 LastOutPackets/Octets 0/0
*Apr   1 18:42:39.871: Se0/0/0 LQM:    PeerInLQRs 0 PeerInPackets/Discards/Errors/
  Octets 0/0/0/0
*Apr   1 18:42:39.871: Se0/0/0 LQM:    PeerOutLQRs 1 PeerOutPackets/Octets 3907/155488
*Apr   1 18:42:39.879: Se0/0/0 LQM: I state Open magic 0xFF101A5B len 48
*Apr   1 18:42:39.879: Se0/0/0 LQM:    LastOutLQRs 0 LastOutPackets/Octets 0/0
```

```
*Apr  1 18:42:39.879: Se0/0/0 LQM:     PeerInLQRs 0 PeerInPackets/Discards/Errors/
  Octets 0/0/0/0
*Apr  1 18:42:39.879: Se0/0/0 LQM:     PeerOutLQRs 1 PeerOutPackets/Octets 3909/155225
<Output omitted>
```

The **debug ppp error** command is used to display protocol errors and error statistics associated with PPP connection negotiation and operation, as shown in Example 3-7. These messages might appear when the Quality Protocol option is enabled on an interface that is already running PPP.

Example 3-7   Output of **debug ppp error** Command

```
R1# debug ppp error

PPP Serial3(i): rlqr receive failure. successes = 15
PPP: myrcvdiffp = 159 peerxmitdiffp = 41091
PPP: myrcvdiffo = 2183 peerxmitdiffo = 1714439
PPP: threshold = 25
PPP Serial4(i): rlqr transmit failure. successes = 15
PPP: myxmitdiffp = 41091 peerrcvdiffp = 159
PPP: myxmitdiffo = 1714439 peerrcvdiffo = 2183
PPP: l->OutLQRs = 1 LastOutLQRs = 1
PPP: threshold = 25
PPP Serial3(i): lqr_protrej() Stop sending LQRs.
PPP Serial3(i): The link appears to be looped back.
```

Troubleshooting a PPP Configuration with Authentication (3.4.1.3)

Authentication is a feature that needs to be implemented correctly or the security of your serial connection may be compromised. Always verify your configuration with the **show interfaces serial** command, in the same way as you did without authentication.

Note

Never assume your authentication configuration works without testing it. Debugging allows you to confirm your configuration and correct any deficiencies. For debugging PPP authentication, use the **debug ppp authentication** command.

Example 3-8 shows an example output of the **debug ppp authentication** command.

Example 3-8   Troubleshooting a PPP Configuration with Authentication

```
R2# debug ppp authentication

Serial0/0/0: Unable to authenticate. No name received from peer
Serial0/0/0: Unable to validate CHAP response. USERNAME pioneer not found.
Serial0/0/0: Unable to validate CHAP response. No password defined for USERNAME pio-
  neer
Serial0/0/0: Failed CHAP authentication with remote.
Remote message is Unknown name
Serial0/0/0: remote passed CHAP authentication.
Serial0/0/0: Passed CHAP authentication with remote.
Serial0/0/0: CHAP input code = 4 id = 3 len = 48
```

The following is an interpretation of the output:

Line 1 says that the router is unable to authenticate on interface Serial0/0/0 because the peer did not send a name.

Line 2 says the router was unable to validate the CHAP response because username pioneer was not found.

Line 3 says no password was found for pioneer. Other possible responses at this line might have been no name received to authenticate, unknown name, no secret for given name, short MD5 response received, or MD5 compare failed.

In the last line, the code 4 means that a failure has occurred. Other code values are as follows:

- **1**: Challenge.
- **2**: Response.
- **3**: Success.
- **4**: Failure.
- **id**: 3 is the ID number per LCP packet format.
- **len**: 48 is the packet length without the header.

Packet Tracer Activity 3.4.1.4: Troubleshooting PPP with Authentication

Background/Scenario

The routers at your company were configured by an inexperienced network engineer. Several errors in the configuration have resulted in connectivity issues. Your boss has asked you to troubleshoot and correct the configuration errors and document your work. Using your knowledge of PPP and standard testing methods, find and correct the errors. Make sure that all of the serial links use PPP CHAP authentication, and that all of the networks are reachable. The passwords are cisco and class.

Lab 3.4.1.5: Troubleshooting Basic PPP with Authentication

In this lab, you will complete the following objectives:

Part 1: Build the Network and Load Device Configurations

Part 2: Troubleshoot the Data Link Layer

Part 3: Troubleshoot the Network Layer

Summary (3.5)

Class Activity 3.5.1.1: PPP Validation

Three friends who are enrolled in the Cisco Networking Academy want to check their knowledge of PPP network configuration.

They set up a contest where each person will be tested on configuring PPP with defined PPP scenario requirements and varying options. Each person devises a different configuration scenario.

The next day they get together and test each other's configuration using their PPP scenario requirements.

Packet Tracer
☐ Activity

Packet Tracer Activity 3.5.1.2: Skills Integration Challenge

Background/Scenario

This activity allows you to practice a variety of skills including configuring VLANs, PPP with CHAP, static and default routing, using IPv4 and IPv6. Due to the sheer number of graded elements, feel free to click Check Results and Assessment Items to see if you correctly entered a graded command. Use the passwords cisco and class to access EXEC modes of the CLI for routers and switches.

Serial transmissions sequentially send 1 bit at a time over a single channel. A serial port is bidirectional. Synchronous serial communications require a clocking signal.

Point-to-Point links are usually more expensive than shared services; however, the benefits may outweigh the costs. Constant availability is important for some protocols, such as VoIP.

SONET is an optical network standard that uses STDM for efficient use of bandwidth. In the United States, OC transmission rates are standardized specifications for SONET.

The bandwidth hierarchy used by carriers is different in North America (T-carrier) and Europe (E-carrier). In North America, the fundamental line speed is 64 Kbps, or DS0. Multiple DS0s are bundled together to provide higher line speeds.

The demarcation point is the point in the network where the responsibility of the service provider ends and the responsibility of the customer begins. The CPE, usually a router, is the DTE device. The DCE is usually a modem or CSU/DSU.

A null modem cable is used to connect two DTE devices together without the need for a DCE device by crossing the Tx and Rx lines. When using this cable between routers in a lab, one of the routers must provide the clocking signal.

Cisco HDLC is a bit-oriented synchronous data link layer protocol extension of HDLC and is used by many vendors to provide multiprotocol support. This is the default encapsulation method used on Cisco synchronous serial lines.

Synchronous PPP is used to connect to non-Cisco devices, to monitor link quality, provide authentication, or bundle links for shared use. PPP uses HDLC for encapsulating datagrams. LCP is the PPP protocol used to establish, configure, test, and terminate the data link connection. LCP can optionally authenticate a peer using PAP or CHAP. A family of NCPs are used by the PPP protocol to simultaneously support multiple network layer protocols. Multilink PPP spreads traffic across bundled links by fragmenting packets and simultaneously sending these fragments over multiple links to the same remote address, where they are reassembled.

Practice

The following activities provide practice with the topics introduced in this chapter. The Labs and Class Activities are available in the companion Introduction to Connecting Networks Lab Manual (978-1-58713-331-2). The Packet Tracer Activity PKA files are found in the online course.

Class Activities

Class Activity 3.0.1.2: PPP Persuasion

Class Activity 3.5.1.1: PPP Validation

Labs

Lab 3.3.2.8: Configuring Basic PPP with Authentication

Lab 3.4.1.5: Troubleshooting Basic PPP with Authentication

Packet Tracer
☐ Activity

Packet Tracer Activities

Packet Tracer Activity 3.1.2.7: Troubleshooting Serial Interfaces

Packet Tracer Activity 3.3.2.7: Configuring PAP and CHAP Authentication

Packet Tracer Activity 3.4.1.4: Troubleshooting PPP with Authentication

Packet Tracer Activity 3.5.1.2: Skills Integration Challenge

Check Your Understanding Questions

Complete all the review questions listed here to test your understanding of the topics and concepts in this chapter. The appendix, "Answers to the 'Check Your Understanding' Questions," lists the answers.

1. Match each PPP establishment step with its appropriate sequence number:

   Step 1:

   Step 2:

   Step 3:

   Step 4:

   Step 5:

   A. Test link quality (optional).

   B. Negotiate Layer 3 protocol options.

   C. Send link-establishment frames to negotiate options such as MTU size, compression, and authentication.

   D. Send configuration-acknowledgment frames.

   E. NCP reaches Open state.

2. Which output from the **show interfaces s0/0/0** command indicates that the far end of a point-to-point link has a different encapsulation set than the local router?

   A. Serial 0/0/0 is down, line protocol is down.

   B. Serial 0/0/0 is up, line protocol is down.

   C. Serial 0/0/0 is up, line protocol is up (looped).

   D. Serial 0/0/0 is up, line protocol is down (disabled).

   E. Serial 0/0/0 is administratively down, line protocol is down.

3. What is the default encapsulation for serial interfaces on a Cisco router?

   A. HDLC

   B. PPP

   C. Frame Relay

   D. X.25

4. What is the function of the Protocol field in a PPP frame?

   A. It identifies the application layer protocol that will process the frame.

   B. It identifies the transport layer protocol that will process the frame.

   C. It identifies the data link layer protocol encapsulation in the frame's Data field.

   D. It identifies the network layer protocol encapsulated in the frame's Data field.

5. Match each description with its corresponding term:

Error control:

Authentication protocols:

Allows load balancing:

Compression protocols:

A. Stacker/predictor

B. Magic number

C. Multilink

D. CHAP/PAP

E. Call in

6. Which of the following statements describe the function of statistical time-division multiplexing (STDM)? (Choose three.)

A. Multiple data streams share one common channel.

B. Bit interleaving controls the timing mechanism that places data on the channel.

C. Time slots are used on a first-come, first-served basis.

D. STDM was developed to overcome the inefficiency caused by time slots still being allocated even when the channel has no data to transmit.

E. Sources of data alternate during transmission and are reconstructed at the receiving end.

F. Priority can be dedicated to one data source.

7. Which of the following describes the serial connection between two routers using the High-level Data Link Control (HDLC) protocol?

A. Synchronous or asynchronous bit-oriented transmissions using a universal frame format

B. Synchronous bit-oriented transmissions using a frame format that allows flow control and error detection

C. Asynchronous bit-oriented transmissions using a frame format derived from the Synchronous Data Link Control (SDLC) protocol

D. Asynchronous bit-oriented transmissions using a V.35 DTE/DCE interface

8. If an authentication protocol is configured for PPP operation, when is the client or user workstation authenticated?

    A. Before link establishment

    B. During the link establishment phase

    C. Before the network layer protocol configuration begins

    D. After the network layer protocol configuration has ended

9. Why are Network Control Protocols used in PPP?

    A. To establish and terminate data links

    B. To provide authentication capabilities to PPP

    C. To manage network congestion and to allow quality testing of the link

    D. To allow multiple Layer 3 protocols to operate over the same physical link

10. Which statement describes the PAP authentication protocol?

    A. It sends encrypted passwords by default.

    B. It uses a two-way handshake to establish identity.

    C. It protects against repeated trial-and-error attacks.

    D. It requires the same username to be configured on every router.

11. A technician testing the functionality of a recently installed router is unable to ping the serial interface of a remote router. The technician executes the **show interfaces serial 0/0/0** command on the local router and sees the following line in the router:

    Serial0/0/0 is down, line protocol is down

    What are two possible causes of this command output?

    A. The **clock rate** command is missing.

    B. The carrier detect signal is not sensed.

    C. Keepalives are not being sent.

    D. The interface is disabled due to a high error rate.

    E. The interface is shut down.

    F. The cabling is faulty or incorrect.

12. The network administrator is configuring Router1 to connect to Router2 using three-way handshake authentication. Match each description with the command necessary to configure Router1:

Configure the username and password:

Enter interface configuration mode:

Specify the encapsulation type:

Configure authentication:

A. **username Router2 password cisco**

B. **username Router1 password cisco**

C. **interface serial 0/1/0**

D. **encapsulation ppp**

E. **encapsulation hdlc**

F. **ppp authentication pap**

G. **ppp authentication chap**

13. What is required to successfully establish a connection between two routers using CHAP authentication?

A. The hostnames of both routers must be the same.

B. The usernames of both routers must be the same.

C. The enable secret passwords configured on both routers must be the same.

D. The password configured with the router's username must be the same on both routers.

E. The **ppp chap sent-username** command must be configured the same on both routers.

14. For each characteristic, indicate whether it is associated with PAP or CHAP:

Two-way handshake:

Three-way handshake:

Open to trial-and-error attacks:

Password sent in cleartext:

Periodic verification:

Uses a one-way hash function:

15. For each description, indicate whether it is associated with LCP or NCP:

Negotiates link establishment parameters:

Negotiates Layer 3 protocol parameters:

Maintains/debugs a link:

Can negotiate multiple Layer 3 protocols:

Terminates a link:

16. Describe the functions of LCP and NCP.

17. Describe the five configurable LCP encapsulation options.

18. Refer to the following configurations for Router R1 and Router R3:

```
hostname R1
username R1 password cisco123
!
int serial 0/0
ip address 128.0.1.1 255.255.255.0
encapsulation ppp
ppp authentication pap
----------------------------
hostname R3
username R1 password cisco
!
int serial 0/0
ip address 128.0.1.2 255.255.255.0
encapsulation ppp
ppp authentication CHAP
```

Router R1 is unable to connect with Router R3. On the basis of the information presented, which configuration changes on Router R1 would correct the problem?

CHAPTER 4

Frame Relay

Objectives

Upon completion of this chapter

- What are the benefits of Frame Relay?
- How does Frame Relay operate?
- What are the bandwidth control mechanisms in Frame Relay?
- How do you configure Frame Relay point-to-point subinterfaces?
- How do you use the **show** and **debug** commands to troubleshoot Frame Relay?

Key Terms

This chapter uses the following key terms. You can find the definitions in the glossary.

Introduction (4.0.1.1)

An alternative to dedicated, expensive, leased WAN lines is Frame Relay. Frame Relay is a high-performance WAN protocol that operates at the physical and data link layers of the OSI reference model. Although newer services such as broadband and metro Ethernet have reduced the need for Frame Relay in many locations, Frame Relay is still a viable option in many locales around the world. Frame Relay provides a cost-efficient solution for communications between multiple remote sites by using a single access circuit from each site to the provider.

This chapter introduces the fundamental concepts of Frame Relay. It also covers Frame Relay configuration, verification, and troubleshooting tasks.

Class Activity 4.0.1.2: Emerging WAN Technologies

As the network administrator, in your small- to medium-size business, you have already moved from leased line WAN to Frame Relay connectivity for WAN network communication. You are responsible to keep current with all future network upgrades.

To stay current with emerging and developing technologies, you find that there are some alternate options available for WAN connectivity. Some of these include

- Frame Relay

- Broadband DSL

- Broadband cable modem

- GigaMAN

- VPN

- MPLS

Because you want to offer the best quality, lowest-cost WAN network service to your company, you decide to research at least two emerging and developing technologies. It is your intent to gather information about these two alternate WAN options to intelligently discuss the future goals of your network with your business manager and other network administrators.

Introduction to Frame Relay (4.1)

This section provides in introduction to the standardized WAN technology Frame Relay. With the advent of dedicated broadband services such as DSL and cable modem, along with Ethernet over fiber optics, Frame Relay is becoming lesser-used access technology. However, Frame Relay still remains as a viable option in many areas and quite often the only option in some remote areas.

Benefits of Frame Relay (4.1.1)

Frame Relay provides several benefits over traditional point-to-point leased lines depending on the needs of the organization. We begin with an introduction to Frame Relay, followed by the benefits and flexibility associated with using Frame Relay in a small- to medium-size network.

Introducing Frame Relay (4.1.1.1)

Leased lines provide permanent dedicated capacity and are used extensively for building WANs. They have been the traditional connection of choice, but have a number of disadvantages. One disadvantage is that customers pay for leased lines with a fixed capacity. However, WAN traffic is often variable and leaves some of the capacity unused. In addition, each endpoint needs a separate physical interface on the router, which increases equipment costs. Any change to the leased line generally requires a site visit by the carrier personnel.

Frame Relay is a high-performance WAN protocol that operates at the physical and data link layers of the OSI reference model. Unlike leased lines, Frame Relay requires only a single access circuit to the Frame Relay provider to communicate with other sites connected to the same provider, as shown in Figure 4-1. The capacity between any two sites can vary.

Frame Relay allows communications between all sites using a single access circuit to the provider.

Figure 4-1   Frame Relay Service

Eric Scace, an engineer at Sprint International, invented Frame Relay as a simpler version of the X.25 protocol to use across Integrated Services Digital Network (ISDN) interfaces. Today, it is also used over a variety of other network interfaces. When Sprint first implemented Frame Relay in its public network, they used StrataCom switches. Cisco's acquisition of StrataCom in 1996 marked their entry into the carrier market.

Network providers implement Frame Relay to support voice and data traffic between LANs over a WAN. Each end user gets a private line, or leased line, to a Frame Relay node. The Frame Relay network handles the transmission over a frequently changing path transparent to all end users. As shown in the figure, Frame Relay provides a solution to allow the communications between multiple sites using a single access circuit to the provider.

Historically, Frame Relay was used extensively as a WAN protocol because it was inexpensive compared to dedicated leased lines. In addition, configuring user equipment in a Frame Relay network is very simple. Frame Relay connections are created by configuring customer premise equipment (CPE) routers or other devices to communicate with a service provider Frame Relay switch. The service provider configures the Frame Relay switch, which helps keep end-user configuration tasks to a minimum.

Benefits of Frame Relay WAN Technology (4.1.1.2)

With the advent of broadband services such as DSL and cable modem, Ethernet WAN (point-to-point Ethernet service over fiber-optic cable), VPN, and Multiprotocol Label Switching (MPLS), Frame Relay has become a less-suitable solution for accessing the WAN. However, there are still locations in the world which rely on Frame Relay for connectivity to the WAN.

Frame Relay provides greater bandwidth, reliability, and resiliency than private or leased lines.

Using an example of a large enterprise network helps illustrate the benefits of using a Frame Relay WAN. In Figure 4-2, SPAN Engineering Company has five campuses across North America. Like most organizations, SPAN's bandwidth requirements are varied.

The first thing to consider is the bandwidth requirement of each site. Working from the headquarters, the Chicago-to-New York connection requires a maximum speed of 256 Kbps. Three other sites need a maximum speed of 48 Kbps connecting to the headquarters, while the connection between the New York and Dallas branch offices requires only 12 Kbps.

Before Frame Relay became available, SPAN Engineering Company leased *dedicated lines*.

Figure 4-2   SPAN Engineering Company – Corporate Bandwidth Requirements

---

Note

The bandwidth values used in the leased line and Frame Relay examples throughout this chapter do not necessarily reflect current bandwidths used by many customers today. The bandwidth values used in this chapter are only for comparison purposes.

Dedicated Line Requirements (4.1.1.3)

Using leased lines, each of SPAN's sites is connected through a switch at the local telephone company's central office (CO) through the local loop, and then across the entire network. Figure 4-3 shows the Chicago and New York sites each use a dedicated T1 line (equivalent to 24 DS0 channels) to connect to the switch, while other sites use ISDN connections (56 Kbps), as shown in the figure. Because the Dallas site connects with both New York and Chicago, it has two locally leased lines. The network providers have provided SPAN with one DS0 between the respective COs, except for the larger pipe connecting Chicago to New York, which has four DS0s. DS0s are priced differently from region to region, and usually are offered at a fixed price. These lines are truly dedicated in that the network provider reserves that line for SPAN's own use. There is no sharing, and SPAN is paying for the end-to-end circuit regardless of how much bandwidth it uses.

Figure 4-3   Dedicated Line WAN Requirements

A dedicated line provides little practical opportunity for a one-to-many connection without getting more lines from the network provider. In the example, almost all communication must flow through the corporate headquarters, simply to reduce the cost of additional lines.

Upon further examination of the bandwidth requirements for each site, it becomes apparent that there is a lack of efficiency:

- Of the 24 DS0 channels available in the T1 connection, the Chicago site only uses 7. Some carriers offer fractional T1 connections in increments of 64 Kbps, but this requires a specialized device called a multiplexer at the customer end to channelize the signals. In this case, SPAN has opted for the full T1 service.

- Similarly, the New York site only uses five of its available 24 DS0s.

- Because Dallas must connect to Chicago and New York, there are two lines connecting through the CO to each site.

The leased line design also limits flexibility. Unless circuits are already installed, connecting new sites typically requires new circuit installations and takes considerable time to implement. From a network reliability point of view, imagine the additional costs in money and complexity of adding spare and redundant circuits.

Cost-Effectiveness and Flexibility of Frame Relay (4.1.1.4)

SPAN's Frame Relay network uses permanent virtual circuits (PVCs), as shown in Figure 4-4. A PVC is the logical path along an originating Frame Relay link, through the network, and along a terminating Frame Relay link to its ultimate destination. Compare this to the physical path used by a dedicated connection. In a network with Frame Relay access, a PVC uniquely defines the path between two endpoints. The concept of virtual circuits (VCs) is discussed in more detail later in this section.

Figure 4-4   Frame Relay PVCs

SPAN's Frame Relay solution provides both cost effectiveness and flexibility.

Cost-Effectiveness of Frame Relay

Frame Relay is a more cost-effective option for two reasons. First, with dedicated lines, customers pay for an end-to-end connection, which includes the local loop and the network link. With Frame Relay, customers only pay for the local loop and for the bandwidth they purchase from the network provider. Distance between nodes is not important. While in a dedicated line model, customers use dedicated lines provided in increments of 64 Kbps, and Frame Relay customers can define their virtual circuit needs in far greater granularity, often in increments as small as 4 Kbps.

The second reason for Frame Relay's cost-effectiveness is that it shares bandwidth across a larger base of customers. Typically, a network provider can service 40 or more 56 Kbps customers over one T1 circuit. Using dedicated lines would require more CSU/DSUs (one for each line) and more complicated routing and switching. Network providers save because there is less equipment to purchase and maintain.

> **Note**
>
> Cost can vary significantly depending on location.

The Flexibility of Frame Relay

A virtual circuit provides considerable flexibility in network design. Examining the figure, you can see that SPAN's offices all connect to the Frame Relay cloud over their respective local loops. What happens in the cloud is really of no concern at this time. All that matters is that when any SPAN office wants to communicate with any other SPAN office, all it needs to do is connect to a virtual circuit leading to the other office. In Frame Relay, the end of each connection has a number to identify it called a *data-link connection identifier (DLCI)*. Any station can connect with any other simply by stating the address of that station and DLCI number of the line it must use. In a later section, you will learn that when Frame Relay is configured, all data from all configured DLCIs flows through the same port of the router. Imagine the same flexibility using dedicated lines. Not only is it complicated, but it also requires considerably more equipment.

Interactive Graphic

Activity 4.1.1.5: Identify Frame Relay Terminology and Concepts

Go to the course online to perform this practice activity.

Frame Relay Operation (4.1.2)

Understanding Frame Relay operations is essential to understanding advanced Frame Relay concepts and how to implement Frame Relay. This section discusses basic Frame Relay concepts, terminology and operations.

Virtual Circuits (4.1.2.1)

The connection through a Frame Relay network between two DTEs is a VC. The circuits are virtual because there is no direct electrical connection from end to end. The connection is logical, and data moves from end to end, without a direct electrical circuit. With VCs, Frame Relay shares the bandwidth among multiple users and any single site can communicate with any other single site without using multiple dedicated physical lines.

There are two ways to establish VCs:

- **Switched virtual circuits (SVCs):** Established dynamically by sending signaling messages to the network (CALL SETUP, DATA TRANSFER, IDLE, CALL TERMINATION).

- **Permanent virtual circuits (PVCs):** Preconfigured by the carrier, and after they are set up operate only in DATA TRANSFER and IDLE modes. Note that some publications refer to PVCs as private VCs.

Note

PVCs are more commonly implemented than SVCs.

Figure 4-5 shows a VC between the sending and receiving nodes. The VC follows the path A, B, C, and D. Frame Relay creates a VC by storing input-port to output-port mapping in the memory of each switch and thus links one switch to another until a continuous path from one end of the circuit to the other is identified. A VC can pass through any number of intermediate devices (switches) located within the Frame Relay network.

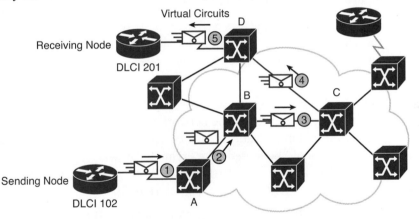

Figure 4-5 Virtual Circuits

DLCI values have local significance, which means that they are unique only to the physical channel on which they reside. Therefore, devices at opposite ends of a connection can use the same DLCI values to refer to different virtual circuits.

VCs provide a bidirectional communication path from one device to another. VCs are identified by DLCIs, as shown in Figure 4-6. DLCI values typically are assigned by the Frame Relay service provider. Frame Relay DLCIs have local significance, which means that the values themselves are not unique in the Frame Relay WAN. A DLCI identifies a VC to the equipment at an endpoint. A DLCI has no significance beyond the single link. Two devices connected by a VC may use a different DLCI value to refer to the same connection.

Figure 4-6   Local Significance of DLCIs

Locally significant DLCIs have become the primary method of addressing because the same address can be used in several different locations while still referring to different connections. Local addressing prevents a customer from running out of DLCIs as the network grows.

Figure 4-7 shows the same network as presented in the previous figure, but this time, as the frame moves across the network, Frame Relay labels each VC with a DLCI. The DLCI is stored in the address field of every frame transmitted to tell the network how the frame should be routed. The Frame Relay service provider assigns DLCI numbers. Usually, DLCIs 0 to 15 and 1008 to 1023 are reserved. Therefore, service providers typically assign DLCIs in the range of 16 to 1007.

In Figure 4-7, the frame uses DLCI 102. It leaves the router (R1) using Port 0 and VC 102. In Figure 4-8, at switch A, the frame exits Port 1 using VC 432. This process of VC-port mapping continues through the WAN until the frame reaches its destination at DLCI 201. The DLCI is stored in the address field of every frame transmitted.

Leg	VC	Port	VC	Port
A	102	0	432	1
B	432	3	119	1
C	119	4	579	3
D	579	4	201	1

Figure 4-7   Identifying DLCIs – DLCI 102

Multiple Virtual Circuits (4.1.2.2)

Frame Relay is statistically multiplexed, meaning that it transmits only one frame at a time, but that many logical connections can coexist on a single physical line. The *Frame Relay Access Device (FRAD)*, or router connected to the Frame Relay network, may have multiple VCs connecting it to various endpoints. Multiple VCs on a single physical line are distinguished because each VC has its own DLCI. Keep in mind that the DLCI has only local significance and may be different at each end of a VC.

Figure 4-8 shows an example of two VCs on a single access line, each with its own DLCI, attaching to a router (R1). Multiple VCs on the same access link are distinguishable by the DLCI.

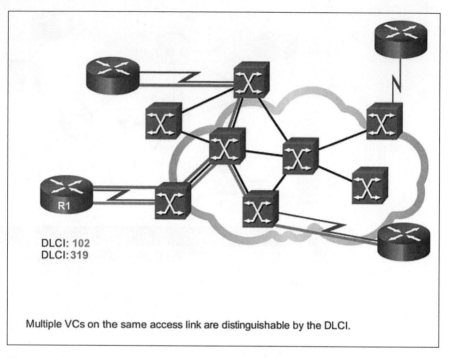

DLCI: 102
DLCI: 319

Multiple VCs on the same access link are distinguishable by the DLCI.

Figure 4-8   Multiple VCs on a Single Access Line

This capability often reduces the equipment and network complexity required to connect multiple devices, making it a very cost-effective replacement for a *mesh* of access lines. With this configuration, each endpoint needs only a single access line and interface. More savings arise as the capacity of the access line is based on the average bandwidth requirement of the VCs, rather than on the maximum bandwidth requirement.

In the example in Figure 4-9, SPAN Engineering has five remote locations, with its headquarters in Chicago. Chicago is connected to the network using five VCs, and each VC is given a DLCI. Notice that SPAN has grown and recently opened an office in San Jose. Using Frame Relay made this expansion relatively easy.

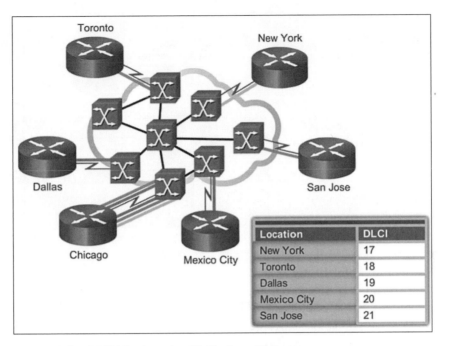

Figure 4-9   SPAN Engineering DLCIs from Chicago

Cost Benefits of Multiple VCs

With Frame Relay, customers pay for the bandwidth they use. In effect, they pay for a Frame Relay port. When the customer increases the number of ports, as described previously, they pay for more bandwidth, but they do not pay for more equipment because the ports are virtual. There is no change to the physical infrastructure. Compare this to purchasing more bandwidth using dedicated lines.

Frame Relay Encapsulation (4.1.2.3)

Frame Relay takes data packets from a network layer protocol, such as IPv4 or IPv6, encapsulates them as the data portion of a Frame Relay frame, and then passes the frame to the physical layer for delivery on the wire. To understand how this works, it is helpful to understand how it relates to the lower levels of the OSI model.

Frame Relay encapsulates data for transport and moves it down to the physical layer for delivery, as shown in Figure 4-10.

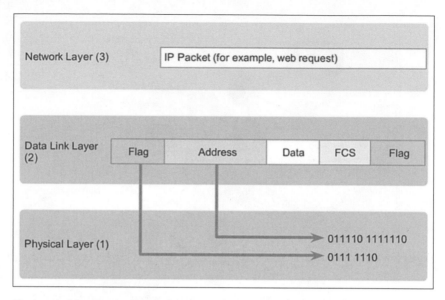

Figure 4-10 Frame Relay Encapsulation and the OSI Model

First, Frame Relay accepts a packet from a network layer protocol, such as IPv4. It then wraps it with an Address field that contains the DLCI and a checksum. Flag fields are added to indicate the beginning and end of the frame. The Flag fields mark the start and end of the frame and are always the same. The flags are represented either as the hexadecimal number 7E or as the binary number 01111110. After the packet is encapsulated, Frame Relay passes the frame to the physical layer for transport.

The CPE router encapsulates each Layer 3 packet inside a Frame Relay header and trailer before sending it across the VC. The header and trailer are defined by the *Link Access Procedure for Frame Relay (LAPF)* Bearer Services specification, ITU Q.922-A. As shown in Figure 4-11, the Frame Relay header (Address field) specifically contains the following:

- **DLCI:** The 10-bit DLCI is one of the most important fields in the Frame Relay header. This value represents the virtual connection between the DTE device and the switch. Each virtual connection that is multiplexed on to the physical channel is represented by a unique DLCI. The DLCI values have local significance only, which means that they are unique only to the physical channel on which they reside. Therefore, devices at opposite ends of a connection can use different DLCI values to refer to the same virtual connection.

- **C/R:** The bit that follows the most significant DLCI byte in the Address field. The C/R bit is not currently defined.

- **Extended Address (EA):** If the value of the EA field is 1, the current byte is determined to be the last DLCI octet. Although current Frame Relay implementations all use a two-octet DLCI, this capability does allow longer DLCIs in the future. The eighth bit of each byte of the Address field indicates the EA.

- *Congestion* control: Consists of 3 Frame Relay congestion-notification bits. These 3 bits are specifically referred to as the *Forward Explicit Congestion Notification (FECN)*, *Backward Explicit Congestion Notification (BECN)*, and Discard Eligible bits.

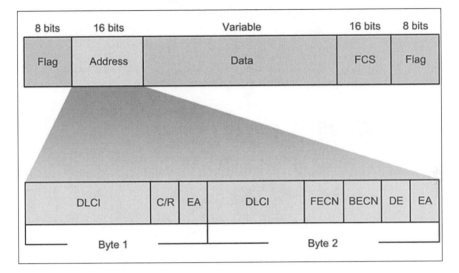

Figure 4-11   Standard Frame Relay Frame

The physical layer is typically EIA/TIA-232, 449 or 530, V.35, or X.21. The Frame Relay frame is a subset of the HDLC frame type; therefore, it is delimited with Flag fields. The 1-byte flag uses the bit pattern 01111110. The FCS determines whether any errors in the Layer 2 Address field occurred during transmission. The FCS is calculated prior to transmission by the sending node, and the result is inserted in the FCS field. At the distant end, a second FCS value is calculated and compared to the FCS in the frame. If the results are the same, the frame is processed. If there is a difference, the frame is discarded. Frame Relay does not notify the source when a frame is discarded. Error control is left to the upper layers of the OSI model.

Frame Relay Topologies (4.1.2.4, 4.1.2.5)

When more than two sites must be connected, the Frame Relay topology, or map, of the connections between the sites must be planned. A network designer must consider the topology from several perspectives to understand the network and the equipment used to build the network. Complete topologies for design, implementation, operation, and maintenance include overview maps, logical connection maps, functional maps, and address maps showing the detailed equipment and channel links.

Cost-effective Frame Relay networks link dozens and even hundreds of sites. Considering that a corporate network might span any number of service providers and include networks from acquired businesses differing in basic design, documenting topologies can be a very complicated process. However, every network or network segment can be viewed as being one of three topology types: star, full mesh, or partial mesh.

Star Topology (Hub and Spoke)

The simplest WAN topology is a *star topology*, as shown in Figure 4-12. In this topology, SPAN Engineering Company has a central site in Chicago that acts as a hub and hosts the primary services. The Chicago router is the hub router with five physical links called hubs.

Figure 4-12   Star Topology

Connections to each of the five remote sites act as spokes. In a star topology, the location of the *hub* is usually chosen by the lowest leased line cost. When implementing a star topology with Frame Relay, each remote site has an access link to the Frame Relay cloud with a single VC.

Figure 4-13 shows the star topology in the context of a Frame Relay cloud. The hub at Chicago has an access link with multiple VCs, one for each remote site. The lines going out from the cloud represent the connections from the Frame Relay service provider and terminate at the customer premises. These are typically lines ranging in speed from 56 Kbps to a T1 (1.544 Mbps) and faster. One or more DLCI numbers are assigned to each line endpoint. Because Frame Relay costs are not distance related, the hub does not need to be in the geographical center of the network.

Figure 4-13   Chicago Hub with One Physical Link Carrying Five VCs

Full-Mesh Topology

Figure 4-14 represents a *full-mesh topology* using dedicated lines. A full-mesh topology suits a situation in which the services to be accessed are geographically dispersed and highly reliable access to them is required. A full-mesh topology connects every site to every other site. Using leased line interconnections, additional serial interfaces and lines add costs. In this example, 10 dedicated lines are required to interconnect each site in a full-mesh topology.

Using Frame Relay mesh, a network designer can build multiple connections simply by configuring additional VCs on each existing link, as shown in Figure 4-15. This software upgrade grows the star topology to a full-mesh topology without the expense of additional hardware or dedicated lines. Because VCs use statistical multiplexing, multiple VCs on an access link generally make better use of Frame Relay than single VCs. Figure 4-15 shows how SPAN has used four VCs on each link to scale its network without adding new hardware. Each DTE has one physical link carrying four VCs. Service providers will charge for the additional bandwidth, but this solution is usually more cost effective than using dedicated lines.

Figure 4-14   Full-Mesh Topology

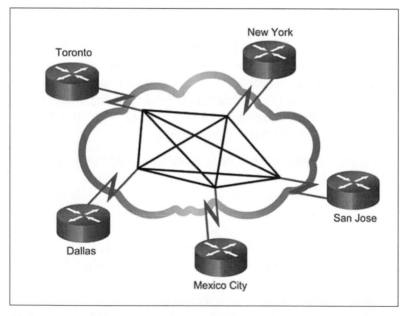

Figure 4-15   Frame Relay Mesh

Partial-Mesh Topology

For large networks, a full-mesh topology is seldom affordable because the number of links required increases exponentially. The issue is not with the cost of the hardware, but because there is a theoretical limit of less than 1,000 VCs per link. In practice, the limit is less than that.

For this reason, larger networks are generally configured in a *partial-mesh topology*. With partial mesh, there are more interconnections than required for a star arrangement, but not as many as for a full mesh. The actual pattern is dependent on the data flow requirements.

Frame Relay Address Mapping (4.1.2.6)

Before a Cisco router is able to transmit data over Frame Relay, it needs to know which local DLCI maps to the Layer 3 address of the remote destination. Cisco routers support all network layer protocols over Frame Relay, such as IPv4, IPv6, IPX, and AppleTalk. This address-to-DLCI mapping can be accomplished either by static or dynamic mapping. Figure 4-16 shows an example topology with DLCI mapping.

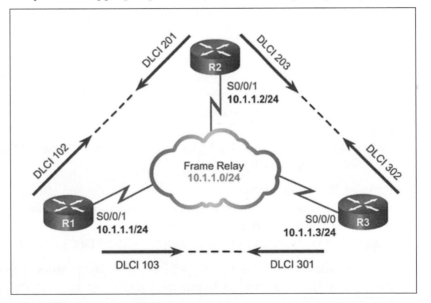

Figure 4-16 Static Frame Relay Mapping

Inverse ARP

A primary tool of Frame Relay is *Inverse Address Resolution Protocol (InARP)*. Whereas ARP translates Layer 3 IPv4 addresses to Layer 2 MAC addresses, Inverse ARP does the opposite. The corresponding Layer 3 IPv4 addresses must be available before VCs can be used.

Note

Frame Relay for IPv6 uses Inverse Neighbor Discovery (IND) to obtain a Layer 3 IPv6 address from a Layer 2 DLCI. A Frame Relay router sends an IND Solicitation message to request a Layer 3 IPv6 address corresponding to a Layer 2 DLCI address of the remote Frame Relay router. At the same time, the IND Solicitation message provides the sender's Layer 2 DLCI address to the remote Frame Relay router.

Dynamic Mapping

Dynamic address mapping relies on Inverse ARP to resolve a next-hop network layer IPv4 address to a local DLCI value. The Frame Relay router sends out Inverse ARP requests on its PVC to discover the protocol address of the remote device connected to the Frame Relay network. The router uses the responses to populate an address-to-DLCI mapping table on the Frame Relay router or access server. The router builds and maintains this mapping table, which contains all resolved Inverse ARP requests, including both dynamic and static mapping entries.

On Cisco routers, Inverse ARP is enabled, by default, for all protocols enabled on the physical interface. Inverse ARP packets are not sent out for protocols that are not enabled on the interface.

Static Frame Relay Mapping

The user can choose to override dynamic Inverse ARP mapping by supplying a manual static map for the next-hop protocol address to a local DLCI. A static map works similarly to dynamic Inverse ARP by associating a specified next-hop protocol address to a local Frame Relay DLCI. You cannot use Inverse ARP and a map statement for the same DLCI and protocol.

An example of using static address mapping is a situation in which the router at the other side of the Frame Relay network does not support dynamic Inverse ARP for a specific network protocol. To provide connectivity, a static mapping is required to complete the remote network layer address to local DLCI resolution.

Another example is on a hub-and-spoke Frame Relay network. Use static address mapping on the spoke routers to provide spoke-to-spoke reachability. Because the spoke routers do not have direct connectivity with each other, dynamic Inverse ARP would not work between them. Dynamic Inverse ARP relies on the presence of a direct point-to-point connection between two ends. In this case, dynamic Inverse ARP only works between hub and spoke, and the spokes require static mapping to provide reachability to each other.

Configuring Static Mapping

Establishing static mapping depends on your network needs. To map between a next hop protocol address and DLCI destination address, use this command: **frame-relay map** *protocol protocol-address dlci* [**broadcast**] [**ietf**] [**cisco**].

Use the keyword **ietf** when connecting to a non-Cisco router.

The configuration of Open Shortest Path First (OSPF) protocol can be greatly simplified by adding the optional **broadcast** keyword when doing this task. The broadcast keyword specifies that broadcast and multicast traffic is allowed over the VC. This configuration permits the use of dynamic routing protocols over the VC.

Example 4-1 provides an example of static mapping on a Cisco router. In this example, static address mapping is performed on interface serial 0/0/1. The Frame Relay encapsulation used on DLCI 102 is CISCO. As seen in the configuration steps, static mapping of the address using the **frame-relay map** command allows users to select the type of Frame Relay encapsulation used on a per-VC basis.

Example 4-1   Static Frame Relay Mapping

```
R1(config)# interface serial 0/0/1
R1(config-if)# ip address 10.1.1.1 255.255.255.0
R1(config-if)# encapsulation frame-relay
R1(config-if)# no frame-relay inverse-arp
R1(config-if)# frame-relay map ip 10.1.1.2 102 broadcast cisco
R1(config-if)# no shutdown
R1(config-if)#
*Mar 31 18:57:38.994: %LINK-3-UPDOWN: Interface Serial0/0/1, changed state to up
R1(config-if)#
```

Example 4-2 shows the output of the **show frame-relay map** command. Notice that the interface is up and the destination IPv4 address is 10.1.1.2. The DLCI identifies the logical connection being used to reach this interface. This value is displayed in decimal value (102), in hexadecimal value (0x66), and its value as it would appear on the wire (0x1860). This is a static entry, not a dynamic entry. The link is using Cisco encapsulation as opposed to IETF encapsulation.

Example 4-2   Address-to-DLCI Mapping Table

```
R1# show frame-relay map
Serial0/0/1 (up): ip 10.1.1.2 dlci 102(0x66,0x1860), static,
              broadcast,
              CISCO, status defined, active
R1#
```

Local Management Interface (LMI) (4.1.2.7)

Another important concept in Frame Relay is the *Local Management Interface (LMI)*. The Frame Relay design provides packet-switched data transfer with minimum end-to-end delays. The original design omits anything that might contribute to delay.

When vendors implemented Frame Relay as a separate technology rather than as one component of ISDN, they decided that there was a need for DTEs to dynamically acquire information about the status of the network. However, the original design did not include this feature. A consortium of Cisco, Digital Equipment Corporation (DEC), Northern Telecom, and StrataCom extended the Frame Relay protocol to provide additional capabilities for complex internetworking environments. These extensions are referred to collectively as the LMI.

Refer to the Frame Relay topology in Figure 4-17. Basically, the LMI is a keepalive mechanism that provides status information about Frame Relay connections between the router (DTE) and the Frame Relay switch (DCE). Every 10 seconds or so, the end device polls the network, either requesting a dumb sequenced response or channel status information. If the network does not respond with the requested information, the user device may consider the connection to be down. When the network responds with a FULL STATUS response, it includes status information about DLCIs that are allocated to that line. The end device can use this information to determine whether the logical connections are able to pass data.

Figure 4-17   LMI Statistics

Example 4-3 shows the output of the **show frame-relay lmi** command. The output shows the LMI type used by the Frame Relay interface and the counters for the LMI status exchange sequence, including errors such as LMI timeouts.

Example 4-3   Displaying LMI Statistics

```
R1# show frame-relay lmi
LMI Statistics for interface Serial0/0/1 (Frame Relay DTE) LMI TYPE = CISCO
  Invalid Unnumbered info 0        Invalid Prot Disc 0
  Invalid dummy Call Ref 0         Invalid Msg Type 0
  Invalid Status Message 0         Invalid Lock Shift 0
  Invalid Information ID 0         Invalid Report IE Len 0
  Invalid Report Request 0        Invalid Keep IE Len 0
  Num Status Enq. Sent 368         Num Status msgs Rcvd 369
  Num Update Status Rcvd 0         Num Status Timeouts 0
  Last Full Status Req 00:00:29    Last Full Status Rcvd 00:00:29
R1#
```

It is easy to confuse the LMI and encapsulation. The LMI is a definition of the messages used between the DTE (R1) and the DCE (the Frame Relay switch owned by the service provider). Encapsulation defines the headers used by a DTE to communicate information to the DTE at the other end of a VC. The switch and its connected router care about using the same LMI. The switch does not care about the encapsulation. The endpoint routers (DTEs) do care about the encapsulation.

LMI Extensions (4.1.2.8)

In addition to the Frame Relay protocol functions for transferring data, the Frame Relay specification includes optional LMI extensions. Some of the extensions include

- **VC status messages:** Provide information about PVC integrity by communicating and synchronizing between devices, periodically reporting the existence of new PVCs and the deletion of already existing PVCs. VC status messages prevent data from being sent into black holes (PVCs that no longer exist).

- **Multicasting:** Allows a sender to transmit a single frame that is delivered to multiple recipients. Multicasting supports the efficient delivery of routing protocol messages and address resolution procedures that are typically sent to many destinations simultaneously.

- **Global addressing:** Provides connection IDs with global rather than local significance, allowing them to be used to identify a specific interface to the Frame Relay network. Global addressing makes the Frame Relay network resemble a LAN in terms of addressing, and ARPs are used as on a LAN.

- **Simple flow control:** Provides for an XON/XOFF flow control mechanism that applies to the entire Frame Relay interface. It is intended for devices that cannot use the congestion notification bits (i.e., FECN and BECN) that would be leveraged by higher layers, but still require some level of flow control.

LMI is used to manage Frame Relay links. Each LMI message is classified by a DLCI appearing in the LMI frame. The 10-bit DLCI field supports 1024 VC IDs: 0 to 1023, as shown in Table 4-1. The LMI extensions reserve some of these VC IDs, thereby reducing the number of permitted VCs. LMI messages are exchanged between the DTE and DCE using these reserved DLCIs.

Table 4-1 Frame Relay Input-Port to Output-Port Mapping

VC Identifiers	VC Types
0	LMI link management (ANSI, ITU)
1–15	Reserved for future use
16–991	Available for VC endpoint assignment
992–1007	Optional layer 2 management information
1008–1018	Reserved for future use (ANSI, ITU)
1019–1022	LMI multicast
1023	LMI link management (Cisco)

There are several LMI types, each of which is incompatible with the others. The LMI type configured on the router must match the type used by the service provider. Three types of LMIs are supported by Cisco routers:

- **CISCO:** Original LMI extension
- **ANSI:** Corresponding to the ANSI standard T1.617 Annex D
- **Q933A:** Corresponding to the ITU standard Q933 Annex A

To display the LMI message information and the associated DLCI numbers, use the **show interfaces** [*type number*] command, as shown in Example 4-4. Cisco uses DLCI 1023 to identify LMI messages used for Frame Relay link management.

Example 4-4 Displaying the LMI Type

```
R1# show interfaces serial 0/0/1
Serial0/0/1 is up, line protocol is up
  Hardware is GT96K Serial
  MTU 1500 bytes, BW 1544 Kbit/sec, DLY 20000 usec,
     reliability 255/255, txload 1/255, rxload 1/255
```

```
    Encapsulation FRAME-RELAY, loopback not set
    Keepalive set (10 sec)
    CRC checking enabled
    LMI enq sent   443, LMI stat recvd 444, LMI upd recvd 0, DTE LMI up
    LMI enq recvd 0, LMI stat sent   0, LMI upd sent   0
    LMI DLCI 1023  LMI type is CISCO   frame relay DTE
    FR SVC disabled, LAPF state down
    Broadcast queue 0/64, broadcasts sent/dropped 1723/0, interface broadcasts 1582
    Last input 00:00:01, output 00:00:01, output hang never
<output omitted>
```

Starting with the Cisco IOS Software Release 11.2, the default LMI autosense feature detects the LMI type supported by the directly connected Frame Relay switch. Based on the LMI status messages it receives from the Frame Relay switch, the router automatically configures its interface with the supported LMI type acknowledged by the Frame Relay switch. If it is necessary to set the LMI type, use the **frame-relay lmi-type [cisco | ansi | q933a]** interface configuration command. Configuring the LMI type disables the autosense feature.

In cases where a Frame Relay switch uses non-default timeout settings, the *keepalive interval* must also be configured on the Frame Relay interface to prevent status exchange messages from timing out. The LMI status exchange messages determine the status of the PVC connection. A large mismatch in the keepalive interval on the router and the switch can cause the switch to declare the router dead. It is important to consult the Frame Relay service provider for information on how to modify the keepalive setting. By default, the keepalive time interval is 10 seconds on Cisco serial interfaces. You can change the keepalive interval with the **keepalive** interface configuration command.

Status messages help verify the integrity of logical and physical links. This information is critical in a routing environment because routing protocols make decisions based on link integrity.

As shown in Figure 4-18, LMI status messages are similar to the Frame Relay frame. In place of the Address field of a Frame Relay frame that is used for data transmission, is an LMI DLCI field. Following the DLCI field are the Control, Protocol Discriminator, and Call Reference fields. These are the same as with standard Frame Relay data frames. The fourth field indicates the LMI message type and includes one of the three LMI message types supported by Cisco.

Standard Frame Relay Frame is the basis for an LMI Frame.

Flag	LMI DLCI	Unnumbered IE	Protocol Discriminator	Call Reference	LMI Message Type	IEs	FCS	Flag
8	16	8	8	8	8	Variable	16	8

Bits — Bits

Figure 4-18   LMI Frame Format

Using LMI and Inverse ARP to Map Addresses (4.1.2.9)

LMI status messages combined with Inverse ARP messages allow a router to associate network layer and data link layer addresses.

In Figure 4-19, when R1 connects to the Frame Relay network, it sends an LMI status inquiry message to the network. The network replies with an LMI status message containing the details of every VC configured on the access link.

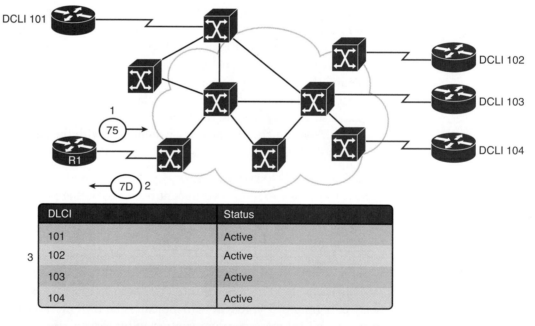

DLCI	Status
101	Active
102	Active
103	Active
104	Active

1 DTE sends Status Enquiry Message (75) to DCE.

2 DCE responds with Status Message (7D) – includes configured DLCIs.

3 DTE learns what VCs it has.

Figure 4-19   Stages of Inverse ARP and LMI Operations

Periodically, the router repeats the status inquiry, but subsequent responses include only status changes. After a set number of these abbreviated responses, the network sends a full status message.

If the router needs to map VCs to network layer addresses, it sends an Inverse ARP message on each VC, as shown in Figure 4-20. Inverse ARP operates similarly to ARP on an Ethernet local network, with the exception that Inverse ARP does not broadcast requests. With ARP, the sending device knows the Layer 3 IP address and sends a broadcast to learn the destination Layer 2 MAC address. With Inverse ARP, the router knows the Layer 2 address, which is the local DLCI, and sends a request for the destination Layer 3 IP address.

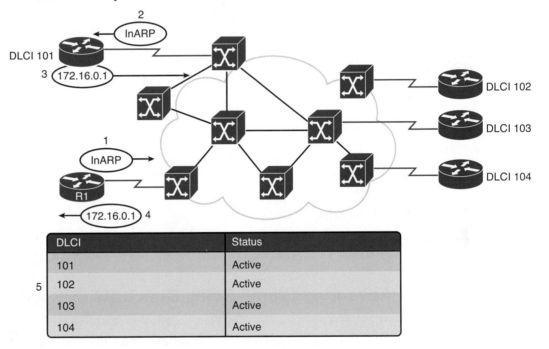

DLCI	Status
101	Active
102	Active
103	Active
104	Active

1,2 DTE sends inverse ARP on a VC, mapping VC to network address.

3,4 Remote DTE replies with Layer 3 address.

5   DTE maps Layer 2–Layer 3.

This process is repeated for each VC and each Layer 3 protocol.

Figure 4-20   Using LMI and Inverse ARP to Map Operations

Inverse ARP Operation

When an interface supporting Inverse ARP becomes active, it initiates the Inverse ARP protocol and formats an Inverse ARP request for the active VC. The Inverse

ARP request includes the source hardware, source Layer 3 protocol address, and the known target hardware address. It then fills the target Layer 3 protocol Address field with all 0s. It encapsulates the packet for the specific network and sends it directly to the destination device using the VC.

Upon receiving an Inverse ARP request, the destination device will use the address of the source device to create its own DLCI-to-Layer 3 map. It will then send an Inverse ARP response that includes its Layer 3 address information. When the source device receives the Inverse ARP response, it completes the DLCI-to-Layer 3 map using the provided information.

When an interface on a Cisco router is configured to use Frame Relay encapsulation, Inverse ARP is enabled by default.

Interactive Graphic

Activity 4.1.2.10: Map the Virtual Circuit to the Port Number

Go to the course online to perform this practice activity.

Interactive Graphic

Activity 4.1.2.11: Match Frame Relay Fields to the Definition

Go to the course online to perform this practice activity.

Interactive Graphic

Activity 4.1.2.12: Identify LMI Terminology and Concepts

Go to the course online to perform this practice activity.

Advanced Frame Relay Concepts (4.1.3)

Frame Relay provides mechanisms to optimize the bandwidth of the access links. This section discusses those mechanisms along with how it implements congestion-notification techniques.

Access Rate and Committed Information Rate (4.1.3.1)

Service providers build Frame Relay networks using very large and very powerful switches, but devices only see the switch interface of the service provider. Customers are usually not exposed to the inner workings of the network, which may be built on very high-speed technologies, such as SONET or SDH.

From a customer's point of view, Frame Relay is a single interface configured with one or more PVCs. Customers buy Frame Relay services from a service provider. Before considering how to pay for Frame Relay services, there are some terms and concepts to learn:

- **Access rate:** Access rate refers to the port speed. From a customer's point of view, the service provider provides a serial connection or access link to the Frame Relay network over a leased line. The access rate is the rate at which your access circuits join the Frame Relay network. These may be 56 Kbps, T1 (1.544 Mbps), or Fractional T1 (a multiple of 56 Kbps or 64 Kbps). Access rates are clocked on the Frame Relay switch. It is not possible to send data at higher than the access rate.

- *Committed information rate (CIR)*: Customers negotiate CIRs with service providers for each PVC. The CIR is the amount of data that the network receives from the access circuit. The service provider guarantees that the customer can send data at the CIR. All frames received at or below the CIR are accepted.

The CIR specifies the maximum average data rate that the network undertakes to deliver under normal conditions. When subscribing to a Frame Relay service, the local access rate is specified (for example, 56 Kbps or T1). Typically, the provider asks the customer to specify a CIR for each DLCI.

If the customer sends information faster than the CIR on a given DLCI, the network marks some frames with a Discard Eligibility (DE) bit. The network does its best to deliver all packets; however, it discards DE packets first if there is congestion.

> **Note**
>
> Many inexpensive Frame Relay services are based on a CIR of zero (0). A CIR of zero means that every frame is a DE frame, and the network throws away any frame when it needs to. The DE bit is within the address field of the Frame Relay frame header.

Frame Relay Example (4.1.3.2)

Aside from any CPE costs, the customer pays for three Frame Relay cost components as follows:

- **Access rate:** The cost of the access line from the DTE to the DCE (customer to service provider). This line is charged based on the port speed that has been negotiated and installed.

- **PVC:** This cost component is based on the PVCs. After a PVC is established, the additional cost to increase CIR is typically small and can be done in small (4 Kbps) increments.

- **CIR:** Customers normally choose a CIR lower than the access rate. This allows them to take advantage of bursts.

In the example in Figure 4-21, the customer is paying for the following:

- An access line with a rate of 64 Kbps connecting their DTE to the DCE of the service provider through serial port S0/0/1.

- Two virtual ports, one at 32 Kbps and the other at 16 Kbps.

- A CIR of 48 Kbps across the entire Frame Relay network. This is usually a flat charge and not connected to the distance.

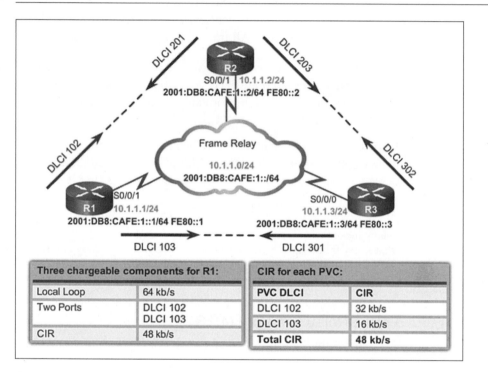

Figure 4-21   Frame Relay Charges - Example

Oversubscription

Service providers sometimes sell more capacity than they have on the assumption that not everyone will demand their entitled capacity all of the time. This oversubscription is analogous to airlines selling more seats than they have in the expectation that some of the booked customers will not show up. Because of oversubscription, there are instances when the sum of CIRs from multiple PVCs to a given location is higher than the port or access channel rate. This can cause congestion and dropped traffic.

Bursting (4.1.3.3)

A great advantage of Frame Relay is that any network capacity that is being unused is made available or shared with all customers, usually at no extra charge. This allows customers to burst over their CIR as a bonus.

Using the previous example, Figure 4-22 shows an access rate on serial port S0/0/1 of router R1 to be 64 Kbps. This is higher than the combined CIRs of the two PVCs. Under normal circumstances, the two PVCs should not transmit more than 32 Kbps and 16 Kbps, respectively. As long as the amount of data the two PVCs send does not exceed the CIR, it should get through the network.

PVC DCLI	CIR (Normal)	Bc (Example)	Be
DCLI 102	32 kb/s	48 kb/s	16 kb/s
DCLI 103	16 kb/s	0 kb/s	48 kb/s
	All frames are forwarded.	Frames are forwarded, but marked DE.	Frames will most likely will be dropped.

Figure 4-22   Frame Relay Bursting

Because the physical circuits of the Frame Relay network are shared between subscribers, there are often times where there is excess bandwidth available. Frame Relay can allow customers to dynamically access this extra bandwidth and burst over their CIR for free.

Bursting allows devices that temporarily need additional bandwidth to borrow it at no extra cost from other devices not using it. For example, if PVC 102 is transferring a large file, it could use any of the 16 Kbps not being used by PVC 103. A device can burst up to the access rate and still expect the data to get through. The duration of a burst transmission should be less than three or four seconds.

Various terms are used to describe burst rates, including the Committed Burst Size (Bc) and *Excess Burst Size (Be)*.

The Bc is a negotiated rate above the CIR that the customer can use to transmit for short burst, and represents the maximum allowed traffic under normal working conditions. It allows traffic to burst to higher speeds, as available network bandwidth permits. However, it cannot exceed the access rate of the link. A device can burst up to the Bc and still expect the data to get through. If long bursts persist, then a higher CIR should be purchased.

For example, DLCI 102 has a CIR of 32 Kbps with an additional Bc of 16 Kbps for a total of up to 48 Kbps. DLCI 103 has a CIR of 16 Kbps. However, DLCI 103 does not have a Bc negotiated; therefore, the Bc is set to 0 Kbps. Frames within the negotiated CIR are not eligible for discard (DE = 0). Frames above the CIR have the DE bit set to 1, marking it as eligible to be discarded, should the network be congested. Frames submitted in the Bc level are marked as *Discard Eligible (DE)* in the frame header but will most likely be forwarded.

The Be describes the bandwidth available above the CIR up to the access rate of the link. Unlike the Bc, it is not negotiated. Frames may be transmitted at this level but are most likely dropped.

Figure 4-23 illustrates the relationship between the various bursting terms.

Figure 4-23   Frame Relay Bursting - Example

Frame Relay Flow Control (4.1.3.4)

Frame Relay reduces network overhead by implementing simple congestion-notification mechanisms, rather than explicit, per-VC flow control. These congestion-notification mechanisms are the Forward Explicit Congestion Notification (FECN) and the Backward Explicit Congestion Notification (BECN).

To help understand the mechanisms, Figure 4-24 shows the structure of the Standard Frame Relay frame for review. FECN and BECN are each controlled by a single bit contained in the frame header. They let the router know that there is congestion and that the router should stop transmission until the condition is reversed. When the DCE sets the BECN bit to 1, it notifies devices in the direction of the source (upstream) that there is congestion on the network. When the DCE sets the FECN bit to 1, it notifies devices in the direction of the destination (downstream) that there is congestion on the network.

Figure 4-24   Standard Frame Relay Frame

The frame header also contains the DE bit, which identifies less-important traffic that can be dropped during periods of congestion. DTE devices can set the value of the DE bit to 1 to indicate that the frame has lower importance than other frames. When the network becomes congested, DCE devices discard the frames with the DE bit set to 1 before discarding those that do not. This reduces the likelihood of critical data being dropped during periods of congestion.

In periods of congestion, the service provider's Frame Relay switch applies the following logic rules to each incoming frame based on whether the CIR is exceeded:

- If the incoming frame does not exceed the Bc, the frame is passed.

- If an incoming frame exceeds the Bc, it is marked as DE.

- If an incoming frame exceeds the Bc and the Be, it is discarded.

Frames arriving at a switch are queued or buffered prior to forwarding. As in any queuing system, it is possible that there will be an excessive buildup of frames at a switch. This causes delays, which lead to unnecessary retransmissions that occur when higher level protocols receive no acknowledgment within a set time. In severe cases, this can cause a serious drop in network throughput. To avoid this problem, Frame Relay incorporates a flow control feature.

Figure 4-25 shows a switch with a filling queue. To reduce the flow of frames to the queue, the switch notifies DTEs of the problem using the Explicit Congestion Notification bits in the frame Address field.

- The FECN bit, indicated by F in Figure 4-25, is set on every frame that the switch receives on the congested link.

- The BECN bit, indicated by B in Figure 4-26, is set on every frame that the switch places onto the congested link.

Figure 4-25   Frame Relay Bandwidth Control: FECN

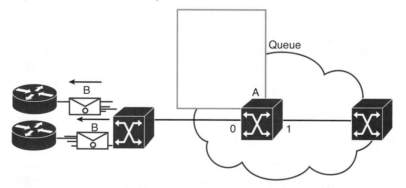

Figure 4-26   Frame Relay Bandwidth Control: BECN

DTEs receiving frames with the ECN bits set are expected to try to reduce the flow of frames until the congestion clears. If the congestion occurs on an internal trunk, DTEs may receive notification even though they are not the cause of the congestion.

Interactive Graphic

Activity 4.1.3.5: Identify Frame Relay Bandwidth and Flow Control Terminology

Go to the course online to perform this practice activity.

Configure Frame Relay (4.2)

This section focuses on the configuration of Frame Relay, both basic Frame Relay and more advanced commands using subinterfaces.

Configure Basic Frame Relay (4.2.1)

Basic Frame Relay configuration involves using static Frame Relay mapping statements between two destinations.

Basic Frame Relay Configuration Commands (4.2.1.1)

Frame Relay is configured on a Cisco router from the Cisco IOS command-line interface (CLI). The required and optional steps for configuring Frame Relay are as follows.

Required tasks

- Enable Frame Relay encapsulation on an interface.

- Configure dynamic or static address mapping.

Optional tasks

- Configure the LMI.

- Configure Frame Relay SVCs.

- Configure Frame Relay traffic shaping.

- Customize Frame Relay for your network.

- Monitor and maintain Frame Relay connections.

Figure 4-27 shows the three router topology that will be used in this section, though initial focus will be on the Frame Relay link between R1 and R2, network 10.1.1.0/24. Notice that all routers have been configured with both IPv4 and IPv6 addresses.

Figure 4-27   Standard Frame Relay Frame

Step 1.   Set the IP Address on the Interface

On a Cisco router, Frame Relay is most commonly supported on synchronous serial interfaces. Use the **ip address** command to set the IPv4 address of the interface. On the link between R1 and R2, R1 S0/0/1 has been assigned 10.1.1.1/24, and R2 S0/0/1 has been assigned IPv4 address 10.1.1.2/24. Using the **ipv6 address** command, routers R1 and R2 have also both been configured with the following IPv6 addresses:

R1 has been configured with the IPv6 global unicast address, 2001:DB8:CAFE:1::1/64 and the static link-local address FE80::1.

R2 has been configured with the IPv6 global unicast address, 2001:DB8:CAFE:1::2/64 and the static link-local address FE80::2.

Note

By default, Cisco IOS uses EUI-64 to automatically generate the IPv6 link-local address on an interface. Configuring static link-local addresses makes it easier to remember and identify the link-local addresses. IPv6 link-local addresses are used by IPv6 routing protocols for routing messages and next-hop addresses in the IPv6 routing table.

Step 2.   Configure Encapsulation

The **encapsulation frame-relay [cisco | ietf]** interface configuration command enables Frame Relay encapsulation and allows Frame Relay processing on the supported interface. There are two encapsulation options to choose from: **cisco** and **ietf**.

The **cisco** encapsulation type is the default Frame Relay encapsulation enabled on supported interfaces. Use this option if connecting to another Cisco router. Many non-Cisco devices also support this encapsulation type. It uses a 4-byte header, with 2 bytes to identify the DLCI and 2 bytes to identify the packet type.

The **ietf** encapsulation type complies with RFC 1490 and RFC 2427. Use this option if connecting to a non-Cisco router.

Step 3. Set the Bandwidth

Use the **bandwidth** command to set the bandwidth of the serial interface. Specify bandwidth in Kbps. This command notifies the routing protocol that bandwidth is statically configured on the link. The EIGRP and OSPF routing protocols use the bandwidth value to calculate and determine the metric of the link.

Step 4. Set the LMI Type (optional)

Manually setting the LMI type is optional, as Cisco routers autosense the LMI type by default. Recall that Cisco supports three LMI types: cisco, ANSI Annex D, and Q933-A Annex A. The default LMI type for Cisco routers is cisco.

Example 4-5 shows the R1 and R2 configurations for enabling Frame Relay.

Example 4-5   Frame Relay Interface Configuration

```
R1:
R1(config)# interface Serial0/0/1
R1(config-if)# bandwidth 64
R1(config-if)# ip address 10.1.1.1 255.255.255.0
R1(config-if)# ipv6 address 2001:db8:cafe:1::1/64
R1(config-if)# ipv6 address fe80::1 link-local
R1(config-if)# encapsulation frame-relay
R2:
R2(config)# interface Serial0/0/1
R2(config-if)# bandwidth 64
R2(config-if)# ip address 10.1.1.2 255.255.255.0
R2(config-if)# ipv6 address 2001:db8:cafe:1::2/64
R2(config-if)# ipv6 address fe80::2 link-local
R2(config-if)# encapsulation frame-relay
```

The **show interfaces serial** command verifies the configuration, including the Layer 2 encapsulation of Frame Relay and the default LMI type of **cisco**, as shown in Example 4-6. Notice that this command shows the IPv4 address, but does not include any of the IPv6 addresses. Use the **show ipv6 interface** or the **show ipv6 interface brief** command to verify IPv6.

Example 4-6   Verifying Frame Relay Configuration

```
R1# show interfaces serial 0/0/1
Serial0/0/1 is up, line protocol is up
  Hardware is GT96K Serial
  Internet address is 10.1.1.1/24
  MTU 1500 bytes, BW 64 Kbit/sec, DLY 20000 usec,
     reliability 255/255, txload 1/255, rxload 1/255
  Encapsulation FRAME-RELAY, loopback not set
  Keepalive set (10 sec)
  CRC checking enabled
  LMI enq sent   481, LMI stat recvd 483, LMI upd recvd 0, DTE LMI up
  LMI enq recvd 0, LMI stat sent   0, LMI upd sent   0
  LMI DLCI 1023  LMI type is CISCO   frame relay DTE
  FR SVC disabled, LAPF state down
  Broadcast queue 0/64, broadcasts sent/dropped 1/0, interface broadcasts 0
  <Output omitted>
```

Note

The **no encapsulation frame-relay** command removes the Frame Relay encapsulation on the interface and returns the interface to the default HDLC encapsulation.

Configuring a Static Frame Relay Map (4.2.1.2)

Cisco routers support all network layer protocols over Frame Relay, such as IPv4, IPv6, IPX, and AppleTalk. The address-to-DLCI mapping can be accomplished either by dynamic or static address mapping.

Dynamic mapping is performed by the Inverse ARP feature. Because Inverse ARP is enabled by default, no additional command is required to configure dynamic mapping on an interface. Figure 4-27 shows the topology used for this topic.

Static mapping is manually configured on a router. Establishing static mapping depends on your network needs. To map between a next hop protocol address and a DLCI destination address, use the command:

frame-relay map *protocol protocol-address dlci* [**broadcast**]

The **frame-relay map** command parameters are

- *protocol*: Defines the supported protocol, bridging, or logical link control: **ip** (IPv4), **ipv6**, **appletalk**, **decnet**, **dlsw**, **ipx**, **llc2**, **rsrb**, **vines** and **xns**.

- *protocol-address*: Defines the network layer address of the destination router interface.

- *dlci*: Defines the local DLCI used to connect to the remote protocol address.

- **broadcast** (optional): Allows broadcasts and multicasts over the virtual circuit. This permits the use of dynamic routing protocols over the VC.

Frame Relay, ATM, and X.25 are *nonbroadcast multiaccess (NBMA)* networks. NBMA networks allow only data transfer from one computer to another, over a VC, or across a switching device. NBMA networks do not support multicast or broadcast traffic, so a single packet cannot reach all destinations. This requires you to replicate the packets manually to all destinations. Using the **broadcast** keyword is a simplified way to forward routing updates. The **broadcast** keyword allows IPv4 broadcasts and multicasts to be propagated to all nodes. It also allows IPv6 multicasts over the PVC. When the keyword is enabled, the router converts the broadcast or multicast traffic into unicast traffic so that other nodes receive the routing updates.

Example 4-7 shows how to use the keywords when configuring static address maps. Notice that the first IPv6 Frame Relay map to a global unicast address does not include the **broadcast** keyword. However, the **broadcast** keyword is used in the mapping to the link-local address. IPv6 routing protocols use link-local addresses for multicast routing updates; therefore, only the link-local address map requires the **broadcast** keyword to forward multicast packets.

Example 4-7   Configuration for R1 and R2

```
R1:
R1(config)# interface Serial0/0/1
R1(config-if)# bandwidth 64
R1(config-if)# ip address 10.1.1.1 255.255.255.0
R1(config-if)# ipv6 address 2001:db8:cafe:1::1/64
R1(config-if)# ipv6 address fe80::1 link-local
R1(config-if)# encapsulation frame-relay
R1(config-if)# frame-relay map ip 10.1.1.2 102 broadcast
R1(config-if)# frame-relay map ipv6 2001:DB8:CAFE:1::2 102
R1(config-if)# frame-relay map ipv6 FE80::2 102 broadcast


R2:
R2(config)# interface Serial0/0/1
R2(config-if)# bandwidth 64
R2(config-if)# ip address 10.1.1.2 255.255.255.0
R2(config-if)# ipv6 address 2001:db8:cafe:1::2/64
R2(config-if)# ipv6 address fe80::2 link-local
R2(config-if)# encapsulation frame-relay
R2(config-if)# frame-relay map ip 10.1.1.1 201 broadcast
R2(config-if)# frame-relay map ipv6 2001:DB8:CAFE:1::2 201
```

The example only shows the configurations to map the VCs between R1 and R2.

> **Note**
>
> Some routing protocols may require additional configuration options. For example, RIP, EIGRP, and OSPF require additional configurations to be supported on NBMA networks.

Verify a Static Frame Relay Map (4.2.1.3)

To verify the Frame Relay mapping, use the **show frame-relay map** command, as shown in Example 4-8. Notice that there are three Frame Relay maps. There is one map for IPv4 and two for IPv6, one for each of the IPv6 addresses.

Example 4-8   Verifying a Static Frame Relay Map for R1 and R2

```
R1:
R1# show frame-relay map
Serial0/0/1 (up): ipv6 2001:DB8:CAFE:1::2 dlci 102(0x66,0x1860), static,
            CISCO, status defined, active
Serial0/0/1 (up): ipv6 FE80::2 dlci 102(0x66,0x1860), static,
            broadcast,
            CISCO, status defined, active
Serial0/0/1 (up): ip 10.1.1.2 dlci 102(0x66,0x1860), static,
            broadcast,
            CISCO, status defined, active
R1#


R2:
R2# show frame-relay map
Serial0/0/1 (up): ipv6 2001:DB8:CAFE:1::1 dlci 201(0xC9,0x3090), static,
            CISCO, status defined, active
Serial0/0/1 (up): ipv6 FE80::1 dlci 201(0xC9,0x3090), static,
            broadcast,
            CISCO, status defined, active
Serial0/0/1 (up): ip 10.1.1.1 dlci 201(0xC9,0x3090), static,
            broadcast,
            CISCO, status defined, active
R2#
```

Interactive Graphic

Activity 4.2.1.3: Configuring Static Frame Relay Mapping

Go to the course online to use the Syntax Checker to configure IPv4 and IPv6 static Frame Relay maps on R1 to forward traffic to R3.

Packet Tracer Activity 4.2.1.4: Configuring Static Frame Relay Maps

Background/Scenario

In this activity, you will configure two static Frame Relay maps on each router to reach two other routers. Although the LMI type is autosensed on the routers, you will statically assign the type by manually configuring the LMI.

Configure Subinterfaces (4.2.2)

One of the benefits of Frame Relay over traditional leased lines is the ability to use a single access link to connect to multiple sites through the use of subinterfaces.

Reachability Issues (4.2.2.1)

By default, most Frame Relay networks provide NBMA connectivity, using a hub-and-spoke topology, between remote sites. In an NBMA Frame Relay topology, when a single multipoint interface must be used to interconnect multiple sites, routing update reachability issues may result. With distance vector routing protocols, reachability issues may result from split horizon and multicast or broadcast replication. With link state routing protocols, issues with the DR/BDR election may result in reachability issues.

Split Horizon

The split horizon rule is a loop prevention mechanism for distance vector routing protocols such as EIGRP and RIP. It is not applicable to link-state routing protocols. The split horizon rule reduces routing loops by preventing a routing update that is received on an interface from being forwarded out the same interface.

For example, in Figure 4-28, which is a hub-and-spoke Frame Relay topology, a remote router R2 (a spoke router) sends an update to the headquarters router R1 (the hub router). R1 is connecting multiple PVCs over a single physical interface. R1 receives the multicast on its physical interface; however, split horizon cannot forward that routing update through the same interface to other remote (spoke) routers.

> **Note**
>
> Split horizon is not an issue if only one PVC (a single remote connection) is configured on a physical interface. This type of connection is point to point.

Figure 4-29 displays a similar example using the reference topology used throughout this chapter. R2, a spoke router, sends a routing update to R1, a hub router. R1 has multiple PVCs on a single physical interface. The split horizon rule prevents R1 from forwarding that routing update through the same physical interface to the other remote spoke router (R3).

Figure 4-28   Split Horizon Problem Example 1

Figure 4-29   Split Horizon Problem Example 2

Multicast and Broadcast Replication

As shown in Figure 4-30, due to split horizon, when a router supports multipoint connections over a single interface, the router must replicate broadcast or multicast packets. In the case of routing updates, the updates must be replicated and sent on each PVC to the remote routers. These replicated packets consume bandwidth and cause significant latency variations in user traffic. The amount of broadcast traffic and the number of VCs terminating at each router should be evaluated during the design phase of a Frame Relay network. Overhead traffic, such as routing updates, can affect the delivery of critical user data, especially when the delivery path contains low-bandwidth (56-Kbps) links.

Figure 4-30   Split Horizon Problem Example 3

Neighbor Discovery: DR and BDR

Link-state routing protocols, such as OSPF, do not use the split horizon rule for loop prevention. However, reachability issues can arise with the DR/BDR. OSPF over NBMA networks work in nonbroadcast network mode, by default, and neighbors are not automatically discovered. Neighbors can be statically configured. However, ensure that the hub router becomes a DR, as shown in Figure 4-31. Recall that an NBMA network behaves like Ethernet, and on Ethernet, a DR is needed to exchange routing information between all routers on a segment. Therefore, only the hub router can act as a DR, because it is the only router that has PVCs with all other routers.

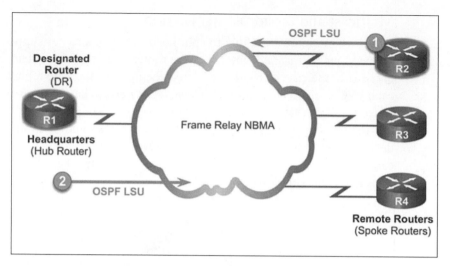

Figure 4-31   Neighbor Discovery: DR/BDR

Solving Reachability Issues (4.2.2.2)

There are several ways to solve the routing reachability issue:

- **Disable split horizon:** One method for solving the reachability issues that are produced by split horizon may be to turn off split horizon. However, disabling split horizon increases the chances of routing loops in your network. Additionally, only IP allows the ability to disable split horizon; IPX and AppleTalk do not.

- **Full-mesh topology:** Another method is to use a full-mesh topology; however, this topology increases costs.

- **Subinterfaces:** In a hub-and-spoke Frame Relay topology, the hub router can be configured with logically assigned interfaces called subinterfaces.

Frame Relay Subinterfaces

Frame Relay can partition a physical interface into multiple virtual interfaces called subinterfaces, as shown in Figure 4-32. A subinterface is simply a logical interface that is directly associated with a physical interface. Therefore, a Frame Relay subinterface can be configured for each of the PVCs coming into a physical serial interface.

Figure 4-32   Single Physical Interface

To enable the forwarding of broadcast routing updates in a Frame Relay network, you can configure the router with logically assigned subinterfaces. Using a subinterface configuration, each VC can be configured as a point-to-point connection. A partially meshed network can be divided into a number of smaller, fully meshed, point-to-point networks. Each point-to-point subnetwork can be assigned a unique network address. This allows each subinterface to act similarly to a leased line. Using a Frame Relay point-to-point subinterface, each pair of the point-to-point routers is on its own subnet. This allows packets received on one subinterface to be sent out another subinterface, even though the packets are being forwarded out the same physical interface.

Frame Relay subinterfaces can be configured in either point-to-point or multipoint mode:

- **Point-to-point mode** (shown in Figure 4-33) : A single point-to-point subinterface establishes one PVC connection to another physical interface or subinterface on a remote router. In this case, each pair of the point-to-point routers is on its own subnet, and each point-to-point subinterface has a single DLCI. In a point-to-point environment, each subinterface is acting like a point-to-point interface. For each point-to-point VC, there is a separate subnet. Therefore, routing update traffic is not subject to the split horizon rule.

- **Multipoint mode** (shown in Figure 4-34) : A single multipoint subinterface establishes multiple PVC connections to multiple physical interfaces or subinterfaces on remote routers. All the participating interfaces are in the same subnet. The subinterface acts like an NBMA Frame Relay interface, so routing update traffic is subject to the split horizon rule. All multipoint VCs belong to the same subnet.

Figure 4-33 Point-to-Point Subinterface

Figure 4-34 Multipoint Subinterface

When configuring subinterfaces, the **encapsulation frame-relay** command is assigned to the physical interface. All other configuration items, such as the network layer address and DLCIs, are assigned to the subinterface.

The multipoint subinterface configurations can be used to conserve addresses. This can be especially helpful if variable-length subnet masking (VLSM) is not being used. However, multipoint configurations may not work properly given the broadcast traffic and split horizon considerations. The point-to-point subinterface option was created to avoid these issues.

To summarize, point-to-point subinterfaces in hub-and-spoke topologies:

- Subinterfaces act as leased lines.

- Each point-to-point subinterface requires its own subnet.

To summarize, multipoint subinterfaces in partial-mesh and full-mesh topologies:

- Subinterfaces act as NBMA so they do not resolve the split horizon issue.

- Can save address space because it uses a single subnet.

Configuring Point-to-Point Subinterfaces (4.2.2.3)

Subinterfaces address the limitations of Frame Relay networks by providing a way to subdivide a partially meshed Frame Relay network into a number of smaller, fully meshed, or point-to-point, subnetworks. Each subnetwork is assigned its own network number and appears to the protocols as if it were reachable through a separate interface.

To create a subinterface, in global configuration mode, use the **interface serial** command followed by the physical port number, a period (.), and the subinterface number. To make troubleshooting easier, use the DLCI as the subinterface number. You must also specify whether the interface is point-to-multipoint or point-to-point using either the **multipoint** or **point-to-point** keyword because there is no default. The interface command syntax for creating subinterfaces with the **interface serial** command is

```
Router(config-if)# interface serial number.subinterface-number [ multipoint | point-
   to-point]
```

The **interface serial** command parameters are

- *number.subinterface-number*: The subinterface number should be in the range of 1 to 4294967293. The interface number that precedes the period (.) must match the physical interface number to which this subinterface belongs.

- **multipoint**: Select this if all routers exist in the same subnet.

- **point-to-point**: Select this in order for each pair of point-to-point routers to have its own subnet. Point-to-point links normally use a subnet mask of 255.255.255.252.

The following command creates a point-to-point subinterface for PVC 103 to R3:

```
R1(config-if)# interface serial 0/0/0.103 point-to-point
```

> **Note**
>
> For simplicity, only IPv4 addresses are used in this section to illustrate subinterfaces. The same concepts and commands also apply when using IPv6 addressing.

If the subinterface is configured as point to point, the local DLCI for the subinterface must also be configured to distinguish it from the physical interface. The DLCI is also required for multipoint subinterfaces for which Inverse ARP is enabled for IPv4. It is not required for multipoint subinterfaces configured with static route maps.

The Frame Relay service provider assigns the DLCI numbers. These numbers range from 16 to 992 and usually have only local significance. The range varies depending on the LMI used.

The **frame-relay interface-dlci** command configures the local DLCI on the subinterface. The interface command syntax for configuring a local DLCI on the subinterface is

```
Router(config-if)# frame-relay interface-dlci dlci-number
```

The **frame-relay interface-dlci** command parameters are

- *dlci-number*: Defines the local DLCI number being linked to the subinterface. This is the only way to link an LMI-derived DLCI to a subinterface because LMI does not know about subinterfaces. Use the **frame-relay interface-dlci** command on subinterfaces only.

The following command defines the local DLCI 103 on R1's subinterface:

```
R1(config-subif)# frame-relay interface-dlci 103
```

Note

Unfortunately, altering an existing Frame Relay subinterface configuration may fail to provide the expected result. In these situations, shut down the physical interface, make the appropriate changes to the subinterfaces and then reenable the physical interface. If the corrected configuration produces unexpected results, then it may be necessary to save the configuration and reload the router.

Example: Configuring Point-to-Point Subinterfaces (4.2.2.4)

Figure 4-35 shows the previous topology but using point-to-point subinterfaces. Each PVC is a separate subnetwork. The router's physical interfaces are divided into subinterfaces, with each subinterface on a separate subnetwork.

In Example 4-9, R1 has two point-to-point subinterfaces. The s0/0/1.102 subinterface connects to R2, and the s0/0/1.103 subinterface connects to R3. Each subinterface is on a different subnet.

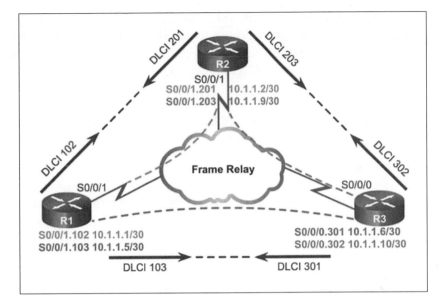

Figure 4-35   Frame Relay Topology with Subinterfaces

Example 4-9   Configuring Point-to-Point Subinterfaces

```
R1(config)# interface serial 0/0/1
R1(config-if)# encapsulation frame-relay
R1(config-if)# no shutdown
R1(config-if)# exit
R1(config)# interface serial 0/0/1.102 point-to-point
R1(config-subif)# ip address 10.1.1.1 255.255.255.252
R1(config-subif)# bandwidth 64
R1(config-subif)# frame-relay interface-dlci 102
R1(config-fr-dlci)# exit
R1(config-subif)# exit
R1(config)# interface serial 0/0/1.103 point-to-point
R1(config-subif)# ip address 10.1.1.5 255.255.255.252
R1(config-subif)# bandwidth 64
R1(config-subif)# frame-relay interface-dlci 103
R1(config-fr-dlci)#
```

To configure subinterfaces on a physical interface, the following steps are required:

Step 1.   Remove any network layer address assigned to the physical interface. If the physical interface has an address, frames are not received by the local subinterfaces.

Step 2.   Configure Frame Relay encapsulation on the physical interface using the **encapsulation frame-relay** command.

Step 3.   For each of the defined PVCs, create a logical subinterface. Specify the port number, followed by a period (.) and the subinterface number. To make troubleshooting easier, it is suggested that the subinterface number matches the DLCI number.

Step 4.   Configure an IP address for the interface and set the bandwidth.

Step 5.   Configure the local DLCI on the subinterface using the **frame-relay interface-dlci** command. Recall that the Frame Relay service provider assigns the DLCI numbers.

Interactive Graphic

Activity 4.2.2.4: Configuring Point-to-Point Subinterfaces on R2

Go to the course online to use the Syntax Checker to configure router R2's physical interface into point-to-point subinterfaces with the appropriate Frame Relay configuration.

Interactive Graphic

Activity 4.2.2.5: Identify Frame Relay Bandwidth and Flow Control Terminology

Go to the course online to perform this practice activity.

Packet Tracer □ Activity

Packet Tracer Activity 4.2.2.6: Configuring Frame Relay Point-to-Point Subinterfaces

Background/Scenario

In this activity, you will configure Frame Relay with two subinterfaces on each router to reach the other two routers. You will also configure EIGRP and verify end-to-end connectivity.

Lab 4.2.2.7: Configuring Frame Relay and Subinterfaces

In this lab, you will complete the following objectives:

- Part 1: Build the Network and Configure Basic Device Settings
- Part 2: Configure a Frame Relay Switch
- Part 3: Configure Basic Frame Relay
- Part 4: Troubleshoot Frame Relay
- Part 5: Configure a Frame Relay Subinterface

Troubleshoot Connectivity (4.3)

Troubleshooting is an important component to understanding and implementing any technology. This section discusses the commands to help troubleshoot and verify Frame Relay.

Troubleshoot Frame Relay (4.3.1)

Troubleshooting Frame Relay requires an understanding of the commands used to verify whether or not Frame Relay is working correctly. Knowing which commands to use and how to analyze the output of these commands is an important skill for any network administrator.

Verifying Frame Relay Operation: Frame Relay Interface (4.3.1.1)

Frame Relay is generally a very reliable service. Nonetheless, there are times when the network performs at less than expected levels and troubleshooting is necessary. For example, users may report slow and intermittent connections across the circuit, or circuits may go down altogether. Regardless of the reason, network outages are very expensive in terms of lost productivity. A recommended best practice is to verify the configuration before problems appear.

In this topic, you will step though a verification procedure to ensure everything is working correctly before a configuration is launched on a live network.

Verify Frame Relay Interfaces

After configuring a Frame Relay PVC and when troubleshooting an issue, verify that Frame Relay is operating correctly on that interface using the **show interfaces** command.

Recall that with Frame Relay, the router is normally considered a DTE device. However, for testing purposes, a Cisco router can be configured as a DCE device to simulate a Frame Relay switch. In such cases, the router becomes a DCE device when it is configured as a Frame Relay switch.

As shown in Example 4-10, the **show interfaces** command displays how the encapsulation is set up, along with useful Layer 1 and Layer 2 status information, including

- LMI DLCI
- LMI type
- Frame Relay DTE/DCE type

Example 4-10   Verifying Frame Relay Operation: Look at the Interfaces

```
R1# show interfaces serial 0/0/1
Serial0/0/1 is up, line protocol is up
  Hardware is GT96K Serial
  MTU 1500 bytes, BW 1544 Kbit/sec, DLY 20000 usec,
      reliability 255/255, txload 1/255, rxload 1/255
  Encapsulation FRAME-RELAY, loopback not set
  Keepalive set (10 sec)
  CRC checking enabled
  LMI enq sent  443, LMI stat recvd 444, LMI upd recvd 0, DTE LMI up
  LMI enq recvd 0, LMI stat sent  0, LMI upd sent  0
  LMI DLCI 1023  LMI type is CISCO  frame relay DTE
  FR SVC disabled, LAPF state down
  Broadcast queue 0/64, broadcasts sent/dropped 1723/0, interface broadcasts 1582
  Last input 00:00:01, output 00:00:01, output hang never
<Output omitted>
```

The first step is always to confirm that the interfaces are properly configured. In the figure, among other things, you can see details about the encapsulation, the DLCI on the Frame Relay-configured serial interface, and the DLCI used for the LMI. Confirm that these values are the expected values; if not, changes may be required.

Verifying Frame Relay Operation: LMI Operations (4.3.1.2)

The next step is to look at some LMI statistics using the **show frame-relay lmi** command. Example 4-11 displays a sample output that shows the number of status messages exchanged between the local router and the local Frame Relay switch. Ensure that the counters between status messages being sent and received are incrementing. This validates that there is active communication between the DTE and the DCE.

Also look for any nonzero `Invalid` items. This helps isolate the problem of Frame Relay communications between the carrier's switch and the client router.

Example 4-11   Verifying Frame Relay Operation: LMI Statistics

```
R1# show frame-relay lmi
LMI Statistics for interface Serial0/0/1 (Frame Relay DTE) LMI TYPE = CISCO
  Invalid Unnumbered info 0           Invalid Prot Disc 0
  Invalid dummy Call Ref 0            Invalid Msg Type 0
  Invalid Status Message 0            Invalid Lock Shift 0
  Invalid Information ID 0            Invalid Report IE Len 0
  Invalid Report Request 0            Invalid Keep IE Len 0
  Num Status Enq. Sent 578            Num Status msgs Rcvd 579
  Num Update Status Rcvd 0            Num Status Timeouts 0
  Last Full Status Req 00:00:28       Last Full Status Rcvd 00:00:28
R1#
```

Verifying Frame Relay Operation: PVC Status (4.3.1.3)

Example 4-12 shows the statistics for the interface.

Example 4-12   Verifying Frame Relay Operation: PVC Status

```
R1# show frame-relay pvc 102
PVC Statistics for interface Serial0/0/1 (Frame Relay DTE)
DLCI = 102, DLCI USAGE = LOCAL, PVC STATUS = ACTIVE, INTERFACE = Serial0/0/1.102
  input pkts 1230          output pkts 1243        in bytes 103826
  out bytes 105929         dropped pkts 0          in pkts dropped 0
  out pkts dropped 0             out bytes dropped 0
  in FECN pkts 0           in BECN pkts 0          out FECN pkts 0
  out BECN pkts 0          in DE pkts 0            out DE pkts 0
  out bcast pkts 1228      out bcast bytes 104952
  5 minute input rate 0 bits/sec, 0 packets/sec
  5 minute output rate 0 bits/sec, 0 packets/sec
  pvc create time 01:38:29, last time pvc status changed 01:26:19
R1#
```

Use the **show frame-relay pvc [interface** *interface***] [***dlci***]** command to view PVC
and traffic statistics. This command is also useful for viewing the number of BECN
and FECN packets received by the router. The PVC status can be active, inactive, or
deleted.

The **show frame-relay pvc** command displays the status of all the PVCs configured
on the router. You can also specify a particular PVC.

After the statistics are gathered, use the **clear counters** command to reset the statistics counters. Wait 5 or 10 minutes after clearing the counters before issuing the
show commands again. Note any additional errors. If you need to contact the carrier,
these statistics help in resolving the issues.

Verifying Frame Relay Operation: Inverse ARP (4.3.1.4)

To clear dynamically created Frame Relay maps that are created using Inverse ARP,
use the **clear frame-relay inarp** command, as shown in Example 4-13.

Example 4-13   Verifying Frame Relay Operation: Clear Frame Relay Maps

```
R1:
R1# clear frame-relay inarp
R1# show frame-relay map
Serial0/0/1.102 (up): point-to-point dlci, dlci 102(0x66,0x1860), broadcast
          status defined, active
Serial0/0/1.103 (up): point-to-point dlci, dlci 103(0x67,0x1870), broadcast
```

```
                 status defined, active
R1#
R2:
R2# clear frame-relay inarp
R2# show frame-relay map
Serial0/0/1.201 (up): point-to-point dlci, dlci 201(0xC9,0x3090), broadcast
          status defined, active
Serial0/0/1.203 (up): point-to-point dlci, dlci 203(0xCB,0x30B0), broadcast
          status defined, active
R2#
```

A final task is to confirm whether the **frame-relay inverse-arp** command resolved a remote IPv4 address to a local DLCI. Use the **show frame-relay map** command to display the current map entries and information about the connections. Example 4-14 shows output from router R3 with a previous Frame Relay configuration on the physical interface, without the use of subinterfaces. Inverse ARP is enabled by default for IPv4. Frame Relay for IPv6 uses Inverse Neighbor Discovery (IND) to obtain a Layer 3 IPv6 address from a Layer 2 DLCI.

Example 4-14   Verifying Frame Relay Operation: Verify Inverse ARP

```
R3# show frame-relay map
Serial0/0/0 (up): ip 10.1.1.9 dlci 302(0x12E,0x48E0), dynamic,
              broadcast,
              CISCO, status defined, active
R3#
```

The output shows the following information:

- 10.1.1.9 is the IPv4 address of the remote router, dynamically learned via the Inverse ARP process.

- 302 is the decimal value of the local DLCI number.

- 0x12E is the hex conversion of the DLCI number, 0x12E = 302 decimal.

- 0x48E0 is the value as it would appear on the wire because of the way the DLCI bits are spread out in the address field of the Frame Relay frame.

- Broadcast/multicast is enabled on the PVC.

- LMI type is cisco.

- PVC status is active.

When an Inverse ARP request is made, the router updates its map table with three possible LMI connection states. These states are

- **ACTIVE:** Indicates a successful end-to-end (DTE to DTE) circuit.

- **INACTIVE:** Indicates a successful connection to the switch (DTE to DCE) without a DTE detected on the other end of the PVC. This can occur due to incorrect configuration on the switch.

- **DELETED:** Indicates that the DTE is configured for a DLCI that the switch does not recognize as valid for that interface.

Troubleshooting Frame Relay Operation (4.3.1.5)

If the verification procedure indicates that your Frame Relay configuration is not working properly, the next step is to troubleshoot the configuration.

Use the **debug frame-relay lmi** command to determine whether the router and the Frame Relay switch are sending and receiving LMI packets properly.

Look at Example 4-15 to examine the output of an LMI exchange.

- `out` is an LMI status message sent by the router.

- `in` is a message received from the Frame Relay switch.

- A full LMI status message is a `type 0`.

- An LMI exchange is a `type 1`.

- `dlci 102, status 0x2` means that the status of DLCI 102 is active.

The possible values of the status field are as follows:

- **0x0:** The switch has this DLCI programmed, but for some reason it is not usable. The reason could possibly be the other end of the PVC is down.

- **0x2:** The Frame Relay switch has the DLCI and everything is operational.

- **0x4:** The Frame Relay switch does not have this DLCI programmed for the router, but it was programmed at some point in the past. This could also be caused by the DLCIs being reversed on the router, or by the PVC being deleted by the service provider in the Frame Relay cloud.

Example 4-15   Troubleshooting Frame Relay Operation

```
R1# debug frame lmi
Frame Relay LMI debugging is on
Displaying all Frame Relay LMI data
R1#
*Apr  1 14:57:43.559: Serial0/0/1(in): Status, myseq 22, pak size 29
*Apr  1 14:57:43.559: RT IE 1, length 1, type 0
*Apr  1 14:57:43.559: KA IE 3, length 2, yourseq 22, myseq 22
```

```
*Apr  1 14:57:43.559: PVC IE 0x7 , length 0x6 , dlci 102, status 0x2 , bw 0
*Apr  1 14:57:43.559: PVC IE 0x7 , length 0x6 , dlci 103, status 0x2 , bw 0
R1#
*Apr  1 14:57:53.555: Serial0/0/1(out): StEnq, myseq 23, yourseen 22, DTE up
*Apr  1 14:57:53.555: datagramstart = 0xED802AF4, datagramsize = 13
*Apr  1 14:57:53.555: FR encap = 0xFCF10309
*Apr  1 14:57:53.555: 00 75 01 01 01 03 02 17 16
*Apr  1 14:57:53.555:
*Apr  1 14:57:53.559: Serial0/0/1(in): Status, myseq 23, pak size 13
*Apr  1 14:57:53.559: RT IE 1, length 1, type 1
*Apr  1 14:57:53.559: KA IE 3, length 2, yourseq 23, myseq 23
R1# undebug all
All possible debugging has been turned off
```

Lab Activity 4.3.1.6: Troubleshooting Basic Frame Relay

In this lab, you will complete the following objectives:

Part 1: Build the Network and Load Device Configurations

Part 2: Troubleshoot Layer 3 Connectivity

Part 3: Troubleshoot Frame Relay

Summary (4.4)

Class Activity 4.4.1.1: Frame Relay Budget Proposal

It has been decided that your company will use Frame Relay technology to provide video connectivity between your main office location and two branch offices. The company will also use the new network for redundancy in case their current ISP network connectivity is interrupted for any reason.

As usual, with any kind of network upgrade, you must develop a cost proposal for your administrator.

After doing some research, you decide to use this Frame Relay website for your cost analysis. Costs listed on the site are representative of real ISP costs; they are referenced only to help you create your cost analysis design.

Packet Tracer Activity 4.4.1.2: Skills Integration Challenge

Packet Tracer
☐ Activity

Background/Scenario

This activity allows you to practice a variety of skills, including configuring Frame Relay, PPP with CHAP, EIGRP, static, and default routing.

Frame Relay is a reliable, packet-switching, connection-oriented technology that is widely used to interconnect remote sites. This is more cost-effective than leased lines because the bandwidth in the service provider's network is shared and an endpoint only needs one physical circuit to the circuit provider to support multiple VCs. Each VC is identified by a DLCI.

Layer 3 data is encapsulated into a Frame Relay frame that has both a Frame Relay header and trailer. It is then passed to the physical layer, which is typically EIA/TIA-232, 449 or 530, V.35, or X.21.

Typical Frame Relay topologies include the star (hub-and-spoke), a full-mesh, and a partial-mesh topology.

Mapping between Layer 2 DLCI addresses and Layer 3 addresses can be achieved dynamically by using Inverse ARP or by manually configuring static maps.

LMI is a protocol for messages sent between the DCE and DTE devices to maintain the status information of the Frame Relay between these devices. The LMI type configured on the router must match that of the service provider.

The Frame Relay circuit cost includes the access rate, the number of PVCs, and the CIR. Some bursting above the CIR is normally allowed without an additional cost. A Bc rate can be negotiated to provide some dependable bursting ability for short-term conditions.

Frame Relay uses BECN and FECN bits in the Frame Relay header for congestion control.

The use of subinterfaces in Frame Relay configurations helps to alleviate routing protocol split horizon issues.

Practice

The following activities provide practice with the topics introduced in this chapter. The Labs and Class Activities are available in the companion Connecting Networks Lab Manual (978-1-58713-331-2). The Packet Tracer Activity PKA files are found in the online course.

Class Activities

Class Activity 4.0.1.2: Emerging WAN Technologies

Class Activity 4.4.1.1: Frame Relay Budget Proposal

Labs

Lab 4.2.2.7: Configuring Frame Relay and Subinterfaces

Packet Tracer
☐ Activity

Packet Tracer Activities

Packet Tracer Activity 4.2.1.4: Configuring Static Frame Relay Maps

Packet Tracer Activity 4.2.2.6: Configuring Frame Relay Point-to-Point Subinterfaces

Packet Tracer Activity 4.4.1.2: Skills Integration Challenge

Check Your Understanding Questions

Complete all the review questions listed here to test your understanding of the topics and concepts in this chapter. The appendix, "Answers to the 'Check Your Understanding' Questions," lists the answers.

1. What is used to identify the path to the next Frame Relay switch in a Frame Relay network?

   A. CIR

   B. DLCI

   C. FECN

   D. BECN

2. Why are Frame Relay paths referred to as virtual?

   A. There are no dedicated circuits to and from the Frame Relay carrier.

   B. Frame Relay PVCs are created and discarded on demand.

   C. The connections between PVC endpoints act like dialup circuits.

   D. There are no dedicated circuits inside the Frame Relay carrier cloud.

3. Which statement accurately describes the split horizon problem with regard to a multipoint topology?

   A. Split horizon must be disabled for all non-IP protocols.

   B. Split horizon creates IP routing loops in multipoint domains.

   C. Split horizon does not apply to broadcasts, so it does not protect protocols that use broadcast updates.

   D. Split horizon prevents any interface from accepting a valid update and forwarding to all the other interfaces.

4. Why is Frame Relay more cost-effective than leased lines? (Choose two.)

   A. Time-division multiplexing.

   B. It uses less equipment.

   C. Optimized packet routing.

   D. It shares bandwidth across a large customer base.

   E. Dynamic IP addressing.

5. Match each status from the `show frame-relay pvc` command with its meaning:

Active:

Inactive:

Deleted:

A. The DLCI is programmed in the Frame Relay switch, but the other end of the PVC may be down.

B. The DLCI does not exist on the router.

C. The DLCI is programmed in the Frame Relay switch and is usable.

D. The DLCI does not exist on the Frame Relay switch for this router.

E. The DLCI is programmed on the other end of the PVC for this router.

6. What reliability advantage does Frame Relay offer over leased lines?

A. Frame Relay access circuits are higher-grade circuits than leased lines.

B. The pathways for virtual circuits inside the carrier are meshed.

C. From end to end, a single virtual circuit uses a fixed error-checked path.

D. Frame Relay uses more-sophisticated error-detection methods.

7. Refer to Figure 4-36. What is placed in the Address field of a frame that will travel from the Orlando office to the DC office?

Figure 4-36 Network Topology for Question 7

A. MAC address of the Orlando router

B. MAC address of the DC router

C. 192.168.1.25

D. 192.168.1.26

E. DLCI 100

F. DLCI 200

8. Which situation favors a multipoint topology over point to point?

A. When VLSM cannot be used to conserve addresses

B. When using routing protocols other than IP

C. When using a frame mesh topology to save access circuits

D. When using a routing protocol that requires broadcast updates

9. What is an advantage of configuring subinterfaces in a Frame Relay environment?

A. It makes the DLCIs globally significant.

B. It eliminates the need for using Inverse ARP.

C. It solves split horizon issues.

D. It improves flow control and bandwidth usage.

10. Which protocol can provide error correction for data that is transmitted over a Frame Relay link?

A. FECN

B. FTP

C. LMI

D. TCP

E. UDP

11. Match each command with its description:

show interface:
show frame-relay lmi:
show frame-relay pvc:
show frame-relay map:
debug frame-relay lmi:

A. Shows the status of the virtual circuit and FECN/BECN statistics

B. Verifies that the router and Frame Relay switch are sending and receiving LMI packets properly

C. Verifies encapsulation, LMI type, LMI DLCI, and LMI status

D. Verifies LMI statistics

E. Verifies the destination IP address mapping to the DLCI

12. At which rate does a service provider guarantee to transfer data into the Frame Relay network?

A. Baud rate

B. Timing rate

C. Data transfer rate

D. Committed information rate

13. How are DLCI numbers assigned?

    A. They are assigned by a DLCI server.

    B. They are assigned arbitrarily by the user.

    C. They are assigned by the service provider.

    D. They are assigned based on the host IP address.

14. A router can reach multiple networks through a Frame Relay interface. How does the router know which DLCI to assign to the IP address of the destination network?

    A. It consults the Frame Relay map.

    B. It consults the routing table to find the DLCI.

    C. It uses Frame Relay switching tables to map DLCIs to IP addresses.

    D. It uses RARP to find the IP address of the corresponding DLCI.

15. Match each term with its definition:

CIR:

DE:

FECN:

BECN:

    A. A bit that marks the frame to be dropped when congestion is present

    B. A bit set on every frame that a switch places on a congested link

    C. The rate at which the service provider agrees to accept bits on the VC

    D. A bit set on every frame that a switch receives on a congested link

16. Compare and contrast the following terms: DLCI, LMI, and Inverse ARP.

17. Refer to Figure 4-37.

```
interface s0/0/1
ip address 10.1.1.1 255.255.255.252
encapsulation frame-relay
bandwidth 64
```

Figure 4-37   Network Topology for Question 17

The following configuration is for router R1:

```
interface s0/0/1
ip address 10.1.1.1 255.255.255.252
encapsulation frame-relay
bandwidth 64
```

What command on R1 is required to statically configure a Frame Relay connection to R2? Traffic between sites must also support OSPF.

18. Compare and contrast the following terms: access rate, CIR, CBIR, and Be.

19. Refer to Figure 4-38 and the following configuration. R1 cannot establish connectivity with the routers over the Frame Relay cloud. What are the problems with this configuration?

S0/0/0.201 10.1.1.2/30
S0/0/0.203 10.2.2.1/30

S0/0/0.102 10.1.1.1/30
S0/0/0.103 10.3.3.1/30

S0/0/0.302 10.2.2.2/30
S0/0/0.302 10.3.3.2/30

```
hostname R1
interface s/0/0/1
 encapsulation frame-relay
!
interface s/0/0/1.201 point-to-point
 ip address 10.1.1.1 255.255.255.0
 frame-relay interface-dlci 201
!
interface s/0/0/1.301 point-to-point
 ip address 10.3.3.31 255.255.255.0
 frame-relay interface-dlci 301
```

Figure 4-38   Network Topology for Question 19

```
hostname R1

interface s0/0/1

encapsulation frame-relay

!

interface s0/0/1.201 point-to-point

ip address 10.1.1.1 255.255.255.0

frame-relay interface-dlci 201

!

interface s0/0/1.301 point-to-point

ip address 10.3.3.1 255.255.255.0

frame-relay interface-dlci 301

!
```

CHAPTER 5

Network Address Translation for IPv4

Objectives

Upon completion of this chapter

- What are the characteristics of NAT?

- What are the benefits and drawbacks of NAT?

- How do you configure static NAT using the CLI?

- How do you configure dynamic NAT using the CLI?

- How do you configure PAT using the CLI?

- How do you configure port forwarding using the CLI?

- What is NAT64?

- How are the **show** commands used to verify NAT operations?

Key Terms

This chapter uses the following key terms. You can find the definitions in the glossary.

Introduction (5.0.1.1)

All public IPv4 addresses that transverse the Internet must be registered with a Regional Internet Registry (RIR). Organizations can lease public addresses from a service provider (SP), but only the registered holder of a public Internet address can assign that address to a network device. However, with a theoretical maximum of 4.3 billion addresses, IPv4 address space is severely limited. When Bob Kahn and Vint Cerf first developed the suite of TCP/IP protocols including IPv4 in 1981, they never envisioned what the Internet would become. At the time, the personal computer was mostly a curiosity for hobbyists, and the World Wide Web was still more than a decade away.

With the proliferation of personal computing and the advent of the World Wide Web, it soon became obvious that 4.3 billion IPv4 addresses would not be enough. The long-term solution was IPv6, but more immediate solutions to address exhaustion were required. For the short term, several solutions were implemented by the IETF including *Network Address Translation (NAT)* and *RFC 1918 private IPv4 addresses*. The chapter discusses how NAT, combined with the use of private address space, is used to both conserve and more efficiently use IPv4 addresses to provide networks of all sizes access to the Internet. This chapter covers the following:

- NAT characteristics, terminology, and general operations
- The different types of NAT, including static NAT, dynamic NAT, and NAT with overloading
- The benefits and disadvantages of NAT
- The configuration, verification, and analysis of static NAT, dynamic NAT, and NAT with overloading
- How port forwarding can be used to access internal devices from the Internet
- Troubleshooting NAT using **show** and **debug** commands
- How NAT for IPv6 is used to translate between IPv6 addresses and IPv4 addresses

Class Activity 5.0.1.2: Conceptual NAT

You work for a large university or school system.

Because you are the network administrator, many professors, administrative workers, and other network administrators need your assistance with their networks on a daily basis. They call you at all working hours of the day and, because of the number of telephone calls, you cannot complete your regular network administration tasks.

You need to find a way to limit when you take calls and from whom. You also need to mask your telephone number so that when you call someone another number is displayed to the recipient.

This scenario describes a very common problem for most small- to medium-sized businesses. Visit "How Network Address Translation Works," http://computer. howstuffworks.com/nat.htm/printable, to view more information about how the digital world handles these types of workday interruptions.

NAT Operation (5.1)

This section discusses the characteristics, types, and benefits of NAT.

NAT Characteristics (5.1.1)

NAT characteristics include an understanding of IPv4 private address space, NAT terminology, and the basics of how NAT works.

IPv4 Private Address Space (5.1.1.1)

There are not enough public IPv4 addresses to assign a unique address to each device connected to the Internet. Networks are commonly implemented using private IPv4 addresses, as defined in RFC 1918. Table 5-1 shows the range of addresses included in RFC 1918. It is very likely that the computer that you use to view this course is assigned a private address.

Table 5-1   Private IPv4 Addresses

Class	RFC 1918 Internal Address Range	CIDR Prefix
A	10.0.0.0 – 10.255.255.255	10.0.0.0/8
B	172.16.0.0 – 172.31.255.255	172.16.0.0/12
C	192.168.0.0 – 192.168.255.255	192.168.0.0/16

These private addresses are used within an organization or site to allow devices to communicate locally. However, because these addresses do not identify any single company or organization, private IPv4 addresses cannot be routed over the Internet. To allow a device with a private IPv4 address to access devices and resources outside of the local network, the private address must first be translated to a public address.

As shown in Figure 5-1, NAT provides the translation of private addresses to public addresses. This allows a device with a private IPv4 address to access resources outside of their private network, such as those found on the Internet. NAT combined with private IPv4 addresses, has proven to be a useful method of preserving public IPv4 addresses. A single public IPv4 address can be shared by hundreds, even thousands, of devices, each configured with a unique private IPv4 address.

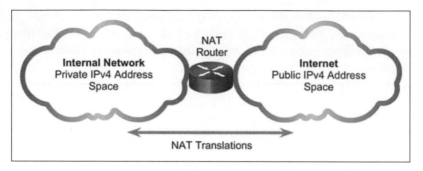

Figure 5-1   Translating Between Private and Public

Without NAT, the exhaustion of the IPv4 address space would have occurred well before the year 2000. However, NAT has certain limitations, which are explored later in this chapter. The solution to the exhaustion of IPv4 address space and the limitations of NAT is the eventual transition to IPv6.

What Is NAT? (5.1.1.2)

NAT has many uses, but its primary use is to conserve public IPv4 addresses. It does this by allowing networks to use private IPv4 addresses internally and providing translation to a public address only when needed. NAT has an added benefit of adding a degree of privacy and security to a network, because it hides internal IPv4 addresses from outside networks.

NAT-enabled routers can be configured with one or more valid public IPv4 addresses. These public addresses are known as the *NAT pool*. When an internal device sends traffic out of the network, the NAT-enabled router translates the internal IPv4 address of the device to a public address from the NAT pool. To outside devices, all traffic entering and exiting the network appears to have a public IPv4 address from the provided pool of addresses.

A NAT router typically operates at the border of a stub network. A stub network is a network that has a single connection to its neighboring network, one way in and one way out of the network. In the example in Figure 5-2, R2 is a border router. As seen from the ISP, R2 forms a stub network.

When a device inside the stub network wants to communicate with a device outside of its network, the packet is forwarded to the border router. The border router performs the NAT process, translating the internal private address of the device to a public, outside, routable address.

Note

The connection to the ISP may use a private address or a public address that is shared among customers. For the purposes of this chapter, a public address is shown.

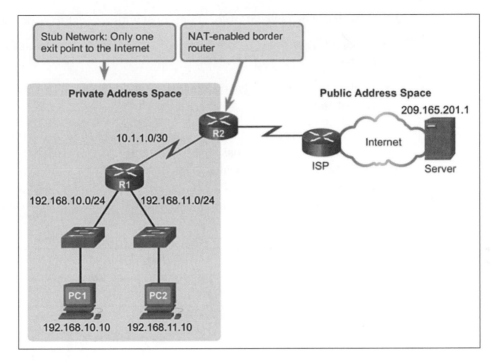

Figure 5-2   NAT Border

NAT Terminology (5.1.1.3)

In NAT terminology, the inside network is the set of networks that is subject to translation. The outside network refers to all other networks.

When using NAT, IPv4 addresses have different designations based on whether they are on the private network or on the public network (Internet) and whether the traffic is incoming or outgoing.

NAT includes four types of addresses:

- *Inside local address*
- *Inside global address*
- *Outside local address*
- *Outside global address*

When determining which type of address is used, it is important to remember that NAT terminology is always applied from the perspective of the device with the translated address:

- **Inside address:** The address of the device that is being translated by NAT.

- **Outside address:** The address of the destination device.

NAT also uses the concept of local or global with respect to addresses:

- **Local address:** A local address is any address that appears on the inside portion of the network.

- **Global address:** A global address is any address that appears on the outside portion of the network.

In Figure 5-3, PC1 has an inside local address of 192.168.10.10. From the perspective of PC1, the web server has an outside address of 209.165.201.1. When packets are sent from PC1 to the global address of the web server, the inside local address of PC1 is translated to 209.165.200.226 (inside global address). The address of the outside device is not typically translated, because that address is usually a public IPv4 address.

Figure 5-3 Types of NAT Addresses

Notice that PC1 has different local and global addresses, whereas the web server has the same public IPv4 address for both. From the perspective of the web server, traffic originating from PC1 appears to have come from 209.165.200.226, the inside global address.

The NAT router, R2 in Figure 5-3, is the demarcation point between the inside and outside networks and between local and global addresses.

The terms *inside* and *outside* are combined with the terms *local* and *global* to refer to specific addresses. In Figure 5-4, router R2 has been configured to provide NAT. It has a pool of public addresses to assign to inside hosts.

- **Inside local address:** The address of the source as seen from inside the network. In Figure 5-4, the IPv4 address 192.168.10.10 is assigned to PC1. This is the inside local address of PC1.

- **Inside global address:** The address of source as seen from the outside network. In Figure 5-4, when traffic from PC1 is sent to the web server at 209.165.201.1, R2 translates the inside local address to an inside global address. In this case, R2 changes the IPv4 source address from 192.168.10.10 to 209.165.200.226. In NAT terminology, the inside local address of 192.168.10.10 is translated to the inside global address of 209.165.200.226.

- **Outside global address:** The address of the destination as seen from the outside network. It is a globally routable IPv4 address assigned to a host on the Internet. For example, the web server is reachable at IPv4 address 209.165.201.1. Most often the outside local and outside global addresses are the same.

- **Outside local address:** The address of the destination as seen from the inside network. In this example, PC1 sends traffic to the web server at the IPv4 address 209.165.201.1. While uncommon, this address could be different than the globally routable address of the destination.

Figure 5-4   NAT Address Example

Figure 5-4 shows how traffic is addressed that is sent from an internal PC to an external web server, across the NAT-enabled router. It also shows how return traffic is initially addressed and translated.

> **Note**
>
> The use of the outside local address is outside the scope of this course.

How NAT Works (5.1.1.5)

In Figure 5-5, PC1 with private address 192.168.10.10 wants to communicate with an outside web server with public address 209.165.201.1:

1. PC1 sends a packet addressed to the web server.

2. The packet is forwarded by R1 to R2.

3. When the packet arrives at R2, the NAT-enabled router for the network, R2 reads the source IPv4 address of the packet to determine if the packet matches the criteria specified for translation. In this case, the source IPv4 address does match the criteria and is translated from 192.168.10.10 (inside local address) to 209.165.200.226 (inside global address). R2 adds this mapping of the local to global address to the NAT table.

4. R2 sends the packet with the translated source address toward the destination.

5. The packet reaches the destination web server.

Figure 5-5 NAT in Action

There is a similar process from the web server back to PC1. The web server responds with a packet addressed to the inside global address of PC1 (209.165.200.226).

R2 receives the packet with destination address 209.165.200.226. R2 checks the NAT table and finds an entry for this mapping. R2 uses this information and translates the inside global address (209.165.200.226) to the inside local address (192.168.10.10), and the packet is forwarded toward PC1.

Activity 5.1.1.6: Identify the NAT Terminology

Go to the course online to perform this practice activity.

Types of NAT (5.1.2)

This section describes the different types of NAT, how each type is used, and a comparison of NAT and PAT.

Static NAT (5.1.2.1)

There are three types of NAT translation:

- **Static address translation (static NAT):** One-to-one address mapping between local and global addresses.

- **Dynamic address translation (dynamic NAT):** Many-to-many address mapping between local and global addresses.

- **Port Address Translation (PAT):** Many-to-one address mapping between local and global addresses. This method is also known as overloading (*NAT overloading*).

Static NAT

Static NAT uses a one-to-one mapping of local and global addresses. These mappings are configured by the network administrator and remain constant.

In Figure 5-6, R2 is configured with static mappings for the inside local addresses of Svr1, PC2, and PC3. When these devices send traffic to the Internet, their inside local addresses are translated to the configured inside global addresses. To outside networks, these devices have public IPv4 addresses.

Static NAT Table	
Inside Local Address	Inside Global Address - Addresses reachable via R2
192.168.10.10	209.165.200.226
192.168.10.11	209.165.200.227
192.168.10.12	209.165.200.228

Figure 5-6   Static NAT

Static NAT is particularly useful for web servers or devices that must have a consistent address that is accessible from the Internet, such as a company web server. It is also useful for devices that must be accessible by authorized personnel when offsite, but not by the general public on the Internet. For example, a network administrator from PC4 can SSH to Svr1's inside global address (209.165.200.226). R2 translates this inside global address to the inside local address and connects the administrator's session to Svr1.

Static NAT requires that enough public addresses are available to satisfy the total number of simultaneous user sessions.

Dynamic NAT (5.1.2.2)

Dynamic NAT uses a pool of public addresses and assigns them on a first-come, first-served basis. When an inside device requests access to an outside network, dynamic NAT assigns an available public IPv4 address from the pool.

In Figure 5-7, PC3 has accessed the Internet using the first available address in the dynamic NAT pool. The other addresses are still available for use. Similar to static NAT, dynamic NAT requires that enough public addresses are available to satisfy the total number of simultaneous user sessions.

IPv4 NAT Pool	
Inside Local Address	Inside Global Address Pool - Addresses reachable via R2
192.168.10.12	209.165.200.226
Available	209.165.200.227
Available	209.165.200.228
Available	209.165.200.229
Available	209.165.200.230

Figure 5-7   Dynamic NAT

Port Address Translation (PAT) (5.1.2.3)

Port Address Translation (PAT), also known as NAT overload, maps multiple private IPv4 addresses to a single public IPv4 address or a few addresses. This is what most home routers do. The ISP assigns one address to the router, yet several members of the household can simultaneously access the Internet. This is the most common form of NAT.

With PAT, multiple addresses can be mapped to one or to a few addresses, because each private address is also tracked by a port number. When a device initiates a TCP/IP session, it generates a TCP or UDP source port value to uniquely identify the session. When the NAT router receives a packet from the client, it uses its source port number to uniquely identify the specific NAT translation.

PAT ensures that devices use a different TCP port number for each session with a server on the Internet. When a response comes back from the server, the source port number, which becomes the destination port number on the return trip, determines to which device the router forwards the packets. The PAT process also validates that the incoming packets were requested, thus adding a degree of security to the session.

Figure 5-8 illustrates the PAT process:

1. PC1 and PC2 send packets destined for the Internet.

2. The packets sent to the NAT router (running PAT), R2, contain the source addresses and their dynamic source port number. PAT uses unique source port numbers on the inside global IP address to distinguish between translations.

3. As R2 processes each packet, it uses a port number (1331 and 1555, in this example) to identify the device from which the packet originated. The source address (SA) is the inside local address with the TCP/IP assigned port number added. The destination address (DA) is the outside local address with the service port number added. In this example, the service port is 80, which is HTTP.

   For the source address, R2 translates the inside local address to an inside global address with the port number added. The destination address is not changed, but is now referred to as the outside global IP address. When the web server replies, the path is reversed.

4. The packets continue the journey to their destinations.

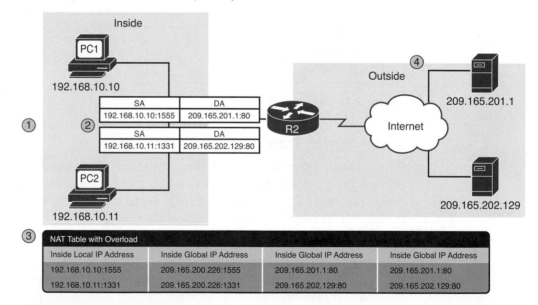

Figure 5-8   PAT Process

Next Available Port (5.1.2.4)

In the previous example, the client port numbers, 1331 and 1555, did not change at the NAT-enabled router. This is not a very likely scenario, because there is a good chance that these port numbers may have already been attached to other active sessions.

PAT attempts to preserve the original source port. However, if the original source port is already used, PAT assigns the first available port number starting from the beginning of the appropriate port group 0–511, 512–1023, or 1024–65,535. When there are no more ports available and there is more than one external address in the address pool, PAT moves to the next address to try to allocate the original source port. This process continues until there are no more available ports or external IP addresses.

Figure 5-9 and the following steps illustrate the PAT process when the same source port is used:

1. PC1 sends a packet destined for the Internet with a source port number of 1444.

2. The NAT router (running PAT), R2, translates the address and assigns it the source port number 1444, as shown in the NAT table.

3. PC2 sends a packet destined for the Internet as well. Coincidently, it also uses the source port number 1444.

4. PC1 and PC2 have chosen the same port number 1444. This is acceptable for the inside address, because the hosts have unique private IP addresses. However, at the NAT router, the port numbers must be changed; otherwise, packets from two different hosts would exit R2 with the same source address. In this example, PAT has assigned the next available port (1445) to the second host address.

Figure 5-9   PAT Process: Same Source Ports

Comparing NAT and PAT (5.1.2.5)

Summarizing the differences between NAT and PAT helps your understanding of each.

As shown in Table 5-2, NAT translates IPv4 addresses on a 1:1 basis between private IPv4 addresses and public IPv4 addresses. However, PAT modifies both the address and the port number.

Table 5-2   Comparing NAT and PAT

NAT

Inside Global Address Pool	Inside Local Pool
209.165.200.226	192.168.10.10
209.165.200.227	192.168.10.11
209.165.200.228	192.168.10.12
209.165.200.229	192.168.10.13

PAT or NAT Overloading

Inside Global Address	Inside Local Pool
209.165.200.226:1444	192.168.10.10:1444
209.165.200.226:1445	192.168.10.11:1444
209.165.200.226:1555	192.168.10.12:1555
209.165.200.226:1556	192.168.10.13:1555

NAT forwards incoming packets to their inside destination by referring to the incoming source IPv4 address given by the host on the public network. With PAT, there is generally only one or a very few publicly exposed IPv4 addresses. Incoming packets from the public network are routed to their destinations on the private network by referring to a table in the NAT router. This table tracks public and private port pairs. This is called connection tracking.

Packets without a Layer 4 Segment

What about IPv4 packets carrying data other than a TCP or UDP segment? These packets do not contain a Layer 4 port number. PAT translates most common protocols carried by IPv4 that do not use TCP or UDP as a transport layer protocol. The most common of these is ICMPv4. Each of these types of protocols is handled differently by PAT. For example, ICMPv4 query messages, echo requests, and echo replies include a Query ID. ICMPv4 uses the Query ID to identify an echo request with its corresponding echo reply. The Query ID is incremented with each echo request sent. PAT uses the Query ID instead of a Layer 4 port number.

Note

Other ICMPv4 messages do not use the Query ID. These messages and other protocols that do not use TCP or UDP port numbers vary and are beyond the scope of this curriculum.

> **Packet Tracer**
> ☐ **Activity**

Packet Tracer Activity 5.1.2.6: Investigating NAT Operation

Background/Scenario

As a frame travels across a network, the MAC addresses may change. IP addresses can also change when a packet is forwarded by a device configured with NAT. In this activity, we will investigate what happens to IP addresses during the NAT process.

Benefits of NAT (5.1.3)

It is important to understand the benefits and disadvantages of NAT. This can become useful when implementing other technologies that might be affected by address translation.

Benefits of NAT (5.1.3.1)

NAT provides many benefits, including the following:

- **Conserves the legally registered addressing scheme:** NAT conserves the legally registered addressing scheme by allowing the privatization of intranets. NAT conserves addresses through application port-level multiplexing. With NAT overload, internal hosts can share a single public IPv4 address for all external communications. In this type of configuration, very few external addresses are required to support many internal hosts.

- **Increases the flexibility of connections to the public network:** Multiple pools, backup pools, and load-balancing pools can be implemented to ensure reliable public network connections.

- **Provides consistency for internal network address schemes:** On a network not using private IPv4 addresses and NAT, changing the public IPv4 address scheme requires the readdressing of all hosts on the existing network. The costs of re-addressing hosts can be significant. NAT allows the existing private IPv4 address scheme to remain while allowing for an easy change to a new public addressing scheme. This means an organization could change ISPs and not need to change any of its inside clients.

- Provides network security: Because private networks do not advertise their addresses or internal topology, they remain reasonably secure when used in conjunction with NAT to gain controlled external access. However, NAT does not replace firewalls.

Disadvantages of NAT (5.1.3.2)

NAT does have some drawbacks. The fact that hosts on the Internet appear to communicate directly with the NAT-enabled device, rather than with the actual host inside the private network, creates a number of issues.

- **Performance is degraded:** One disadvantage of using NAT is related to network performance, particularly for real time protocols such as VoIP. NAT increases switching delays because the translation of each IPv4 address within the packet headers takes time. The first packet is always process-switched going through the slower path. The router must look at every packet to decide whether it needs translation. The router must alter the IPv4 header, and possibly alter the TCP or UDP header. The IPv4 header checksum, along with the TCP or UDP checksum must be recalculated each time a translation is made. Remaining packets go through the fast-switched path if a cache entry exists; otherwise, they too are delayed.

- **End-to-end functionality is degraded:** Another disadvantage of using NAT is that end-to-end addressing is lost. Many Internet protocols and applications depend on end-to-end addressing from the source to the destination. Some applications do not work with NAT. For example, some security applications, such as digital signatures, fail because the source IPv4 address changes before reaching the destination. Applications that use physical addresses, instead of a qualified domain name, do not reach destinations that are translated across the NAT router. Sometimes, this problem can be avoided by implementing static NAT mappings.

- **End-to-end IPv4 traceability is lost:** It becomes much more difficult to trace packets that undergo numerous packet address changes over multiple NAT hops, making troubleshooting challenging.

- **Tunneling becomes more complicated:** Using NAT also complicates tunneling protocols, such as IPsec, because NAT modifies values in the headers that interfere with the integrity checks done by IPsec and other tunneling protocols.

- **Initiating TCP connections can be disrupted:** Services that require the initiation of TCP connections from the outside network, or stateless protocols, such as those using UDP, can be disrupted. Unless the NAT router has been configured to support such protocols, incoming packets cannot reach their destination. Some protocols can accommodate one instance of NAT between participating hosts (passive mode FTP, for example), but fail when both systems are separated from the Internet by NAT.

Configuring NAT (5.2)

This section discusses configuring NAT including static NAT, dynamic NAT, and PAT. Port forwarding and NAT for IPv6 are also discussed.

Configuring Static NAT (5.2.1)

Static NAT is the simplest NAT to configure. We will examine configuring static NAT, analyze how static NAT operates and show how to verify the static NAT configuration.

Configuring Static NAT (5.2.1.1)

Static NAT is a one-to-one mapping between an inside address and an outside address. Static NAT allows external devices to initiate connections to internal devices using the statically assigned public address. For instance, an internal web server may be mapped to a specific inside global address so that it is accessible from outside networks.

Figure 5-10 shows an inside network containing a web server with a private IPv4 address. Router R2 is configured with static NAT to allow devices on the outside network (Internet) to access the web server. The client on the outside network accesses the web server using a public IPv4 address. Static NAT translates the public IPv4 address to the private IPv4 address.

Figure 5-10   Static NAT Topology

There are two basic tasks when configuring static NAT translations.

Step 1.   The first task is to create a mapping between the inside local address and the inside global address. For example, the 192.168.10.254 inside local address and the 209.165.201.5 inside global address in Figure 5-10 are configured as a static NAT translation.

Step 2.   After the mapping is configured, the interfaces participating in the translation are configured as inside or outside relative to NAT. In the example, the Serial 0/0/0 interface of R2 is an inside interface, and Serial 0/1/0 is an outside interface.

Packets arriving on the inside interface of R2 (Serial 0/0/0) from the configured inside local IPv4 address (192.168.10.254) are translated and then forwarded toward the outside network. Packets arriving on the outside interface of R2 (Serial 0/1/0), that are addressed to the configured inside global IPv4 address (209.165.201.5), are translated to the inside local address (192.168.10.254) and then forwarded to the inside network.

Table 5-3 outlines the commands needed to configure static NAT.

Table 5-3   Configuring Static NAT

Step	Action	Notes
1	Establish static translation between an inside local address and an inside global address. Router(config)# **ip nat inside source static** *local-ip global-ip*	Enter the **no ip nat inside source static** global configuration mode command to remove the dynamic source translation.
2	Specify the inside interface. Router(config)# **interface** *type number*	Enter the **interface** command. The CLI prompt changes from (config)# to (config-if)#.
3	Mark the interface as connected to the inside. Router(config-if)# **ip nat inside**	
4	Exit interface configuration mode. Router(config-if)# **exit**	
5	Specify the outside interface. Router(config-if)# **interface** *type number*	
6	Mark the interface as connected to the outside. Router(config-if)# **ip nat outside**	

Using the topology in Figure 5-11, Example 5-1 shows the commands needed on R2 to create a static NAT mapping to the web server in the example topology. With the configuration shown, R2 translates packets from the web server with address 192.168.10.254 to public IPv4 address 209.165.201.5. The Internet client directs web requests to the public IPv4 address 209.165.201.5. R2 forwards that traffic to the web server at 192.168.10.254.

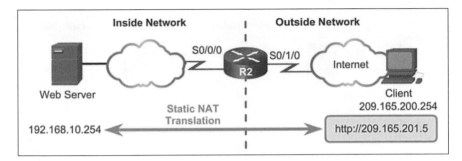

Figure 5-11   Example Static NAT Configuration Topology

Example 5-1   Example Static NAT Configuration Commands

```
Establishes static translation between an inside local address and an inside global
  address.
R2(config)#ip nat inside source static 192.168.10.254 209.165.201.5


R2(config)# interface Serial0/0/0
R2(config-if)# ip address 10.1.1.2 255.255.255.252
Identifies interface Serial 0/0/0 as an inside NAT interface.
R2(config-if)# ip nat inside
R2(config-if)# exit


R2(config)# interface Serial0/1/0
R2(config-if)# ip address 209.165.200.225 255.255.255.224
Identifies interface Serial 0/1/0 as the outside NAT interface.
R2(config-if)# ip nat outside
```

Activity 5.2.1.1: Configuring Static NAT

Go to the course online to use the Syntax Checker to configure an additional static NAT entry on R2.

Analyzing Static NAT (5.2.1.2)

Using the previous configuration, Figure 5-12 illustrates the static NAT translation process between the client and the web server. Usually static translations are used when clients on the outside network (Internet) need to reach servers on the inside (internal) network.

Figure 5-12   Static NAT Process

1. The client wants to open a connection to the web server. The client sends a packet to the web server using the public IPv4 destination address of 209.165.201.5. This is the inside global address of the web server.

2. The first packet that R2 receives from the client on its NAT outside interface causes R2 to check its NAT table. The destination IPv4 address is located in the NAT table and is translated.

3. R2 replaces the inside global address of 209.165.201.5 with the inside local address of 192.168.10.254. R2 then forwards the packet toward the web server.

4. The web server receives the packet and responds to the client using the inside local address, 192.168.10.254.

5a. R2 receives the packet from the web server on its NAT inside interface with the source address of the inside local address of the web server, 192.168.10.254.

5b. R2 checks the NAT table for a translation for the inside local address. The address is found in the NAT table. R2 translates the source address to the inside global address of 209.165.201.5 and forwards the packet out of its serial 0/1/0 interface toward the client.

6. The client receives the packet and continues the conversation. The NAT router performs Steps 2 to 5b for each packet. Step 6 is not shown in Figure 5-12.

Verifying Static NAT (5.2.1.3)

A useful command to verify NAT operation is show **ip nat translations**. This command shows active NAT translations. Static translations, unlike dynamic translations, are always in the NAT table. Example 5-2 shows the output from this command using the previous configuration example. Because the example is a static NAT configuration, the translation is always present in the NAT table regardless of any active communications. If the command is issued during an active session, the output also indicates the address of the outside device as shown in Example 5-2.

Example 5-2   Verifying Static NAT Translations with **show ip nat translations**

```
The static translation is always present in the NAT table.
R2# show ip nat translations
Pro Inside global      Inside local      Outside local       Outside global
--- 209.165.201.5      192.168.10.254    ---                 ---
R2#
The static translation during an active session.
R2# show ip nat translations
Pro Inside global      Inside local      Outside local       Outside global
--- 209.165.201.5      192.168.10.254    209.165.200.254     209.165.200.254
R2#
```

Another useful command is **show ip nat statistics**. As shown in Example 5-3, the **show ip nat statistics** command displays information about the total number of active translations, NAT configuration parameters, the number of addresses in the pool, and the number of addresses that have been allocated.

Example 5-3   Verifying Static NAT Translations with **show ip nat statistics**

```
R2# clear ip nat statistics

R2# show ip nat statistics
Total active translations: 1 (1 static, 0 dynamic; 0 extended)
Peak translations: 0
Outside interfaces:
  Serial0/1/0
Inside interfaces:
  Serial0/0/0
Hits: 0  Misses: 0
<output omitted>
Client PC establishes a session with the web server
 R2# show ip nat statistics
```

```
Total active translations: 1 (1 static, 0 dynamic; 0 extended)
Peak translations: 2, occurred 00:00:14 ago
Outside interfaces:
  Serial0/1/0
Inside interfaces:
  Serial0/0/0
Hits: 5  Misses: 0
<output omitted>
```

To verify that the NAT translation is working, it is best to clear statistics from any past translations using the **clear ip nat statistics** command before testing.

Prior to any communications with the web server, the **show ip nat statistics** command shows no current hits. After the client establishes a session with the web server, the **show ip nat statistics** command has been incremented to five hits. This verifies that the static NAT translation is taking place on R2.

Packet Tracer Activity 5.2.1.4: Configuring Static NAT

Background/Scenario

In IPv4 configured networks, clients and servers use private addressing. Before packets with private addressing can cross the Internet, they need to be translated to public addressing. Servers that are accessed from outside the organization are usually assigned both a public and a private static IP address. In this activity, you will configure static NAT so that outside devices can access an inside server at its public address.

Configuring Dynamic NAT (5.2.2)

Configuring dynamic NAT is similar to configuring static NAT. Instead of specifying a direct one-to-one address mapping, dynamic NAT uses a pool of addresses.

Dynamic NAT Operation (5.2.2.1)

While static NAT provides a permanent mapping between an inside local address and an inside global address, dynamic NAT allows the automatic mapping of inside local addresses to inside global addresses. These inside global addresses are typically public IPv4 addresses. Dynamic NAT uses a group, or pool, of public IPv4 addresses for translation.

Dynamic NAT, like static NAT, requires the configuration of the inside and outside interfaces participating in NAT. However, whereas static NAT creates a permanent mapping to a single address, dynamic NAT uses a pool of addresses.

Note

Translating between public and private IPv4 addresses is by far the most common use of NAT. However, NAT translations can occur between any pair of addresses.

The example topology shown in Figure 5-13 has an inside network using addresses from the RFC 1918 private address space. Attached to router R1 are two LANs, 192.168.10.0/24 and 192.168.11.0/24. Router R2, the border router, is configured for dynamic NAT using a pool of public IPv4 addresses 209.165.200.226 through 209.165.200.240.

Figure 5-13   Dynamic NAT: One-to-One Translation

The pool of public IPv4 addresses (inside global address pool) is available to any device on the inside network on a first-come, first-served basis. With dynamic NAT, a single inside address is translated to a single outside address. With this type of translation, there must be enough addresses in the pool to accommodate all the inside devices needing access to the outside network at the same time. If all the addresses in the pool have been used, a device must wait for an available address before it can access the outside network.

Configuring Dynamic NAT (5.2.2.2)

Table 5-4 shows the steps and the commands used to configure dynamic NAT.

Table 5-4 Configuring Static NAT

Dynamic NAT Configuration Steps

Step 1	Define a pool of global addresses to be used for translation.
	ip nat pool *name start-ip end-ip* {**netmask** *netmask* | **prefix-length** *prefix-length*}
Step 2	Define a standard access list permitting the addresses that should be translated.
	access-list *access-list-number* **permit** *source* [*source-wildcard*]
Step 3	Establish dynamic source translation, specifying the access list and pool defined in prior steps.
	ip nat inside source list *access-list-number* **pool** *name*
Step 4	Identify the inside interface.
	interface *type number*
	ip nat inside
Step 5	Identify the outside interface.
	interface *type number*
	ip nat outside

How To

Step 1. Define the pool of addresses that will be used for translation using the **ip nat pool** command. This pool of addresses is typically a group of public addresses. The addresses are defined by indicating the starting IP address and the ending IP address of the pool. The **netmask** or **prefix-length** keyword indicates which address bits belong to the network and which bits belong to the host for the range of addresses.

Step 2. Configure a standard ACL to identify (permit) only those addresses that are to be translated. An ACL that is too permissive can lead to unpredictable results. Remember there is an implicit **deny all** statement at the end of each ACL.

Step 3. Bind the ACL to the pool. The **ip nat inside source list** *access-list-number* **number pool** *pool name* command is used to bind the ACL to the pool. This configuration is used by the router to identify which devices (**list**) receive which addresses (**pool**).

Step 4. Identify which interfaces are inside, in relation to NAT (that is, any interface that connects to the inside network).

Step 5. Identify which interfaces are outside, in relation to NAT (that is, any interface that connects to the outside network).

Figure 5-14 and Table 5-4 show an example topology and configuration. This configuration allows translation for all hosts on the 192.168.0.0/16 network, which includes the 192.168.10.0 and 192.168.11.0 LANs, when they generate traffic that enters S0/0/0 and exits S0/1/0. These hosts are translated to an available address in the pool in the range 209.165.200.226 - 209.165.200.240.

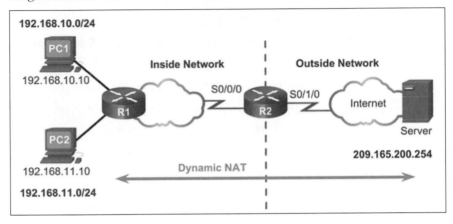

Figure 5-14   Example Dynamic NAT Configuration Topology

Example 5-4   Example Dynamic NAT Configuration Commands

Defines a pool of public IPv4 addresses under the pool name NAT-POOL1.

```
R2(config)# ip nat pool NAT-POOL1 209.165.200.226 209.165.200.240 netmask
  255.255.255.224
```

Defines which addresses are eligible to be translated.

```
R2(config)# access-list 1 permit 192.168.0.0 0.0.255.255
```

Binds NAT-POOL1 with ACL 1.

```
R2(config)# ip nat inside source list 1 pool NAT-POOL1
```

Identifies interface Serial 0/0/0 as an inside NAT interface.

```
R2(config)# interface Serial0/0/0
R2(config-if)# ip nat inside
```

Identifies interface serial 0/1/0 as an outside NAT interface.

```
R2(config)# interface Serial0/1/0
R2(config-if)# ip nat outside
```

Activity 5.2.2.2: Configuring Dynamic NAT

Using Figure 5-14, go to the course online to use the Syntax Checker to configure an additional dynamic NAT on R2.

Analyzing Dynamic NAT (5.2.2.3)

Using the previous configuration, Figures 5-15 and 5-16 illustrate the dynamic NAT translation process between two clients and the web server:

In Figure 5-15, the traffic flow from inside to outside is shown:

1. The hosts with the source IPv4 addresses (192.168.10.10 (PC1) and 192.168.11.10 (PC2)) send packets requesting a connection to the server at the public IPv4 address (209.165.200.254).

2. R2 receives the first packet from host 192.168.10.10. Because this packet was received on an interface configured as an inside NAT interface, R2 checks the NAT configuration to determine if this packet should be translated. The ACL permits this packet, so R2 will translate the packet. R2 checks its NAT table. Because there is no translation entry for this IP address, R2 determines that the source address 192.168.10.10 must be translated dynamically. R2 selects an available global address from the dynamic address pool and creates a translation entry, 209.165.200.226. The original source IPv4 address (192.168.10.10) is the inside local address, and the translated address is the inside global address (209.165.200.226) in the NAT table.

   For the second host, 192.168.11.10, R2 repeats the procedure, selects the next available global address, from the dynamic address pool, and creates a second translation entry, 209.165.200.227.

3. R2 replaces the inside local source address of PC1, 192.168.10.10, with the translated inside global address of 209.165.200.226 and forwards the packet. The same process occurs for the packet from PC2 using the translated address for PC2 (209.165.200.227).

In Figure 5-16, the traffic flow from outside to inside is shown:

Figure 5-15   Dynamic NAT Process: Inside to Outside Address

4. The server receives the packet from PC1 and responds using the IPv4 destination address of 209.165.200.226. When the server receives the second packet, it responds to PC2 using the IPv4 destination address of 209.165.200.227.

5a. When R2 receives the packet with the destination IPv4 address of 209.165.200.226; it performs a NAT table lookup. Using the mapping from the table, R2 translates the address back to the inside local address (192.168.10.10) and forwards the packet toward PC1.

5b. When R2 receives the packet with the destination IPv4 address of 209.165.200.227; it performs a NAT table lookup. Using the mapping from the table, R2 translates the address back to the inside local address (192.168.11.10) and forwards the packet toward PC2.

6. PC1 at 192.168.10.10 and PC2 at 192.168.11.10 receive the packets and continue the conversation. The router performs Steps 2 to 5 for each packet. (Step 6 is not shown in the figures.)

Figure 5-16   Dynamic NAT Process: Outside to Inside Address

Verifying Dynamic NAT (5.2.2.4)

The output of the **show ip nat translations** command shown in Example 5-5 displays the details of the two previous NAT assignments. The command displays all static translations that have been configured and any dynamic translations that have been created by traffic.

Example 5-5   Verifying Dynamic NAT Translations with **show ip nat translations**

```
R2# show ip nat translations
Pro Inside global      Inside local      Outside local      Outside global
--- 209.165.200.226    192.168.10.10     ---                ---
--- 209.165.200.227    192.168.11.10     ---                ---
R2#
R2# show ip nat translations verbose
Pro Inside global      Inside local      Outside local      Outside global
--- 209.165.200.226    192.168.10.10     ---                ---
    create 00:17:25, use 00:01:54 timeout:86400000, left 23:58:05, Map-Id(In): 1,
    flags:
none, use_count: 0, entry-id: 32, lc_entries: 0
--- 209.165.200.227    192.168.11.10     ---                ---
```

```
      create 00:17:22, use 00:01:51 timeout:86400000, left 23:58:08, Map-Id(In): 1,
      flags:
none, use_count: 0, entry-id: 34, lc_entries: 0
R2#
```

Adding the **verbose** keyword displays additional information about each translation, including how long ago the entry was created and used.

By default, translation entries time out after 24 hours, unless the timers have been reconfigured with the **ip nat translation timeout** *timeout-seconds* command in global configuration mode.

To clear dynamic entries before the timeout has expired, use the **clear ip nat translation** global configuration mode command (Example 5-6). It is useful to clear the dynamic entries when testing the NAT configuration. As shown in Table 5-5, this command can be used with keywords and variables to control which entries are cleared. Specific entries can be cleared to avoid disrupting active sessions. Use the **clear ip nat translation** * global configuration command to clear all translations from the table.

Note

Only the dynamic translations are cleared from the table. Static translations cannot be cleared from the translation table.

Example 5-6   Clearing NAT Translations

```
R2# clear ip nat translations
R2# show ip nat translations

R2#
```

Table 5-5   Commands for Clearing NAT Translations

Command	Description
clear ip nat translation *	Clears all dynamic address translation entries form the NAT translation table
clear ip nat translation inside *global-ip local-ip* [**outside** *local-ip global-ip*]	Clears a simple dynamic translation entry containing an inside translation or both inside and outside translation
clear ip nat translation *protocol* **inside** *global-ip global-port local-ip local-port* [**outside** *local-ip local-port global-ip global-port*]	Clears an extended dynamic translation entry

In Example 5-7, the **show ip nat statistics** command displays information about the total number of active translations, NAT configuration parameters, the number of addresses in the pool, and how many of the addresses have been allocated.

Example 5-7   Verifying Dynamic NAT Translations with **show ip nat statistics**

```
R2# clear ip nat statistics


PC1 and PC2 establish sessions with the server


R2# show ip nat statistics
Total active translations: 2 (0 static, 2 dynamic; 0 extended)
Peak translations: 6, occurred 00:27:07 ago
Outside interfaces:
  Serial0/1/0
Inside interfaces:
  Serial0/0/0
Hits: 24  Misses: 0
CEF Translated packets: 24, CEF Punted packets: 0
Expired translations: 4
Dynamic mappings:
-- Inside Source
[Id: 1] access-list 1 pool NAT-POOL1 refcount 2
 pool NAT-POOL1: netmask 255.255.255.224
        start 209.165.200.226 end 209.165.200.240
        type generic, total addresses 15, allocated 2 (13%), misses 0
Total doors: 0
Appl doors: 0
Normal doors: 0
Queued Packets: 0
R2#
```

Alternatively, use the **show running-config** command and look for NAT, ACL, interface, or pool commands with the required values. Examine these carefully and correct any errors discovered.

Packet Tracer Activity 5.2.2.5: Configuring Dynamic NAT

Background/Scenario

- Part 1: Configure Dynamic NAT
- Part 2: Verify NAT Implementation

Lab 5.2.2.6: Configuring Dynamic and Static NAT

In this lab, you will complete the following objectives:

- Part 1: Build the Network and Verify Connectivity

- Part 2: Configure and Verify Static NAT

- Part 3: Configure and Verify Dynamic NAT

Configuring Port Address Translation (PAT) (5.2.3)

Configuring PAT is very similar to configuring dynamic NAT, but is much more scalable. PAT is the most common NAT implementation.

Configuring PAT: Address Pool (5.2.3.1)

PAT (also called NAT overload) conserves addresses in the inside global address pool by allowing the router to use one inside global address for many inside local addresses. In other words, a single public IPv4 address can be used for hundreds, even thousands of internal private IPv4 addresses. When this type of translation is configured, the router maintains enough information from higher-level protocols, TCP or UDP port numbers, for example, to translate the inside global address back into the correct inside local address. When multiple inside local addresses map to one inside global address, the TCP or UDP port numbers of each inside host distinguish between the local addresses.

> **Note**
>
> The total number of internal addresses that can be translated to one external address could theoretically be as high as 65,536 per IP address. However, the number of internal addresses that can be assigned a single IP address is around 4,000.

There are two ways to configure PAT, depending on how the ISP allocates public IPv4 addresses. In the first instance, the ISP allocates more than one public IPv4 address to the organization, and in the other, it allocates a single public IPv4 address that is required for the organization to connect to the ISP.

Configuring PAT for a Pool of Public IP Addresses

If a site has been issued more than one public IPv4 address, these addresses can be part of a pool that is used by PAT. This is similar to dynamic NAT, except that there are not enough public addresses for a one-to-one mapping of inside to outside addresses. The small pool of addresses is shared among a larger number of devices.

Table 5-6 shows the steps to configure PAT to use a pool of addresses. The primary difference between this configuration and the configuration for dynamic, one-to-one NAT is that the **overload** keyword is used. The **overload** keyword enables PAT.

Table 5-6   Configuring PAT for a Pool of Public Addresses

PAT for a Pool of Public Addresses Configuration Steps

Step 1	Define a pool of global addresses to be used for overload translation. **ip nat pool** *name start-ip end-ip* {**netmask** *netmask* | **prefix-length** *prefix-length*}
Step 2	Define a standard access list permitting the addresses that should be translated. **access-list** *access-list-number* **permit** *source* [*source-wildcard*]
Step 3	Establish overload translation, specifying the access list and pool defined in prior steps. **ip nat inside source list** *access-list-number* **pool** *name* **overload**
Step 4	Identify the inside interface. **interface** *type number* **ip nat inside**
Step 5	Identify the outside interface. **interface** *type number* **ip nat outside**

The topology in Figure 5-17, and the example configuration shown in Example 5-8, establishes overload translation for the NAT pool named NAT-POOL2. NAT-POOL2 contains addresses 209.165.200.226 to 209.165.200.240. Hosts in the 192.168.0.0/16 network are subject to translation. The S0/0/0 interface is identified as an inside interface and the S0/1/0 interface is identified as an outside interface.

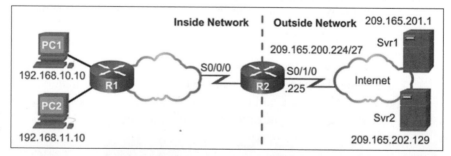

Figure 5-17   Example PAT Topology

Example 5-8   Example PAT with Address Pool Configuration Commands

Define a pool of public IPv4 addresses under the pool name NAT-POOL2.

```
R2(config)#ip nat pool NAT-POOL2 209.165.200.226 209.165.200.240 netmask
  255.255.255.224
```

Define which addresses are eligible to be translated.

```
R2(config)#access-list 1 permit 192.168.0.0 0.0.255.255
```

Bind NAT-POOL2 with ACL 1.

```
R2(config)#ip nat inside source list 1 pool NAT-POOL2 overload
```

Identify interface Serial 0/0/0 as an inside NAT interface.

```
R2(config)#interface Serial0/0/0
R2(config-if)#ip nat inside
```

Identify interface Serial 0/1/0 as the outside NAT interface.

```
R2(config)#interface Serial0/1/0
R2(config-if)#ip nat outside
```

Interactive Graphic

Activity 5.2.3.1: Configuring Dynamic NAT

Go to the course online to use the Syntax Checker to configure PAT using an address pool on R2.

Configuring PAT: Single Address (5.2.3.2)

Figure 5-18 shows the topology of a PAT implementation for a single public IPv4 address translation. In the example, all hosts from network 192.168.0.0/16 (matching ACL 1) that send traffic through router R2 to the Internet will be translated to IPv4 address 209.165.200.225 (IPv4 address of interface S0/1/0). The traffic flows will be identified by port numbers in the NAT table because the **overload** keyword was used.

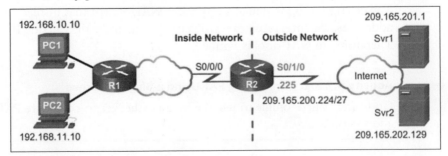

Figure 5-18   PAT with Single Address

Table 5-7 shows the steps to follow to configure PAT with a single IPv4 address. If only a single public IPv4 address is available, the overload configuration typically assigns the public address to the outside interface that connects to the ISP. All inside addresses are translated to the single IPv4 address when leaving the outside interface.

Table 5-7   Configuring PAT with a Single Address

PAT with a Single Address Configuration Steps
Step 1   Define a standard access list permitting the addresses that should be translated.   **access-list** *access-list-number* **permit** *source* [*source-wildcard*]
Step 2   Establish dynamic source translation, specifying the ACL, exit interface, and overload options.   **ip nat inside source list** *access-list-number* **interface** *type number* **overload**
Step 3   Identify the inside interface.   **interface** *type number* **ip nat inside**
Step 4   Identify the outside interface.   **interface** *type number* **ip nat outside**

How To

Step 1.   Define an ACL to permit the traffic to be translated.

Step 2.   Configure source translation using the **interface** and **overload** keywords. The **interface** keyword identifies which interface IP address to use when translating inside addresses. The **overload** keyword directs the router to track port numbers with each NAT entry.

Step 3.   Identify which interfaces are inside in relation to NAT. That is any interface that connects to the inside network.

Step 4.   Identify which interface is outside in relation to NAT. This should be the same interface identified in the source translation statement from Step 2.

The configuration is similar to dynamic NAT, except that instead of a pool of addresses, the **interface** keyword is used to identify the outside IPv4 address. Therefore, no NAT pool is defined.

Interactive Graphic

Activity 5.2.3.2: Configuring PAT Using a Single Address

Go to the course online to use the Syntax Checker to configure PAT using a single address on R2.

Analyzing PAT (5.2.3.3)

The process of NAT overload is the same whether a pool of addresses is used or a single address is used. Continuing with the previous PAT example, using a single public IPv4 address, PC1 wants to communicate with the web server, Svr1. At the same time another client, PC2, wants to establish a similar session with the web server Svr2. Both PC1 and PC2 are configured with private IPv4 addresses, with R2 enabled for PAT.

PC to Server Process

1. Figure 5-19 shows both PC1 and PC2 sending packets to Svr1 and Svr2, respectively. PC1 has the source IPv4 address 192.168.10.10 and is using TCP source port 1444. PC2 has the source IPv4 address 192.168.10.11 and is coincidentally assigned the same source port of 1444.

2. The packet from PC1 reaches R2 first. Using PAT, R2 modifies the source IPv4 address to 209.165.200.225 (inside global address). There are no other devices in the NAT table using port 1444, so PAT maintains the same port number. The packet is then forwarded toward Svr1 at 209.165.201.1.

3. Next, the packet from PC2 arrives at R2. PAT is configured to use a single inside global IPv4 address for all translations, 209.165.200.225. Similar to the translation process for PC1, PAT changes PC2's source IPv4 address to the inside global address 209.165.200.225. However, PC2 has the same source port number as a current PAT entry, the translation for PC1. PAT increments the source port number until it is a unique value in its table. In this instance, the source port entry in the NAT table and the packet for PC2 receives 1445.

Although PC1 and PC2 are using the same translated address, the inside global address of 209.165.200.225, and the same source port number of 1444; the modified port number for PC2 (1445) makes each entry in the NAT table unique. This will become evident with the packets sent from the servers back to the clients.

Figure 5-19 PAT Analysis from PCs to Servers

Server to PC Process

4. As shown in Figure 5-20, in a typical client-server exchange, Svr1 and Svr2 respond to the requests received from PC1 and PC2, respectively. The servers use the source port from the received packet as the destination port, and the source address as the destination address for the return traffic. The servers seem as if they are communicating with the same host at 209.165.200.225; however, this is not the case.

5. As the packets arrive, R2 locates the unique entry in its NAT table using the destination address and the destination port of each packet. In the case of the packet from Svr1, the destination IPv4 address of 209.165.200.225 has multiple entries but only one with the destination port 1444. Using the entry in its table, R2 changes the destination IPv4 address of the packet to 192.168.10.10, with no change required for the destination port. The packet is then forwarded toward PC1.

6. When the packet from Svr2 arrives R2 performs a similar translation. The destination IPv4 address of 209.165.200.225 is located, again with multiple entries. However, using the destination port of 1445, R2 is able to uniquely identify the translation entry. The destination IPv4 address is changed to 192.168.10.11. In this case, the destination port must also be modified back to its original value of 1444, which is stored in the NAT table. The packet is then forwarded toward PC2.

Figure 5-20 PAT Analysis from Servers to PCs

Verifying PAT (5.2.3.4)

Router R2 has been configured to provide PAT to the 192.168.0.0/16 clients. When the internal hosts exit router R2 to the Internet, they are translated to an IPv4 address from the PAT pool with a unique source port number.

The same commands used to verify static and dynamic NAT are used to verify PAT, as shown in Example 5-9. The **show ip nat translations** command displays the translations from two different hosts to different web servers. Notice that two different inside hosts are allocated the same IPv4 address of 209.165.200.226 (inside global address). The source port numbers in the NAT table differentiate the two transactions.

Example 5-9 Verifying PAT Translations

```
R2# show ip nat translations
Pro  Inside global          Inside local        Outside local          Outside global
tcp  209.165.200.226:51839  192.168.10.10:51839  209.165.201.1:80      209.165.201.1:80
tcp  209.165.200.226:42558  192.168.11.10:42558  209.165.202.129:80
     209.165.202.129:80
R2#
```

As shown in Example 5-10, the **show ip nat statistics** command verifies that NAT-POOL2 has allocated a single address for both translations. Included in the output is information about the number and type of active translations, NAT configuration parameters, the number of addresses in the pool, and how many have been allocated.

Example 5-10   Verifying PAT Statistics

```
R2# clear ip nat statistics

R2# show ip nat statistics
Total active translations: 2 (0 static, 2 dynamic; 2 extended)
Peak translations: 2, occurred 00:00:05 ago
Outside interfaces:
  Serial0/1/0
Inside interfaces:
  Serial0/0/0
Hits: 4  Misses: 0
CEF Translated packets: 4, CEF Punted packets: 0
Expired translations: 0
Dynamic mappings:
-- Inside Source
[Id: 3] access-list 1 pool NAT-POOL2 refcount 2
 pool NAT-POOL2: netmask 255.255.255.224
        start 209.165.200.226 end 209.165.200.240
        type generic, total addresses 15, allocated 1 (6%), misses 0
Total doors: 0
Appl doors: 0
Normal doors: 0
Queued Packets: 0
```

Interactive Graphic

Activity 5.2.3.5: Identify the Address Information at Each Hop

Go to the course online to perform this practice activity.

Packet Tracer Activity 5.2.3.6: Implementing Static and Dynamic NAT

Background/Scenario

- Part 1: Configure Dynamic NAT with PAT
- Part 2: Configure Static NAT
- Part 3: Verify NAT Implementation

Lab 5.2.3.7: Configuring Port Address Translation (PAT)

In this lab, you will complete the following objectives:

- Part 1: Build the Network and Verify Connectivity

- Part 2: Configure and Verify NAT Pool Overload

- Part 3: Configure and Verify PAT

Port Forwarding (5.2.4)

One of the disadvantages of NAT is the inability to communicate with devices using a private IPv4 address. In this situation, port forwarding may be an option.

Port Forwarding (5.2.4.1)

Port forwarding (sometimes referred to as tunneling) is the act of forwarding traffic addressed to a specific network port from one network node to another. This technique allows an external user to reach a port on a private IPv4 address (inside a LAN) from the outside, through a NAT-enabled router.

Typically, peer-to-peer file-sharing programs and operations, such as web serving and outgoing FTP, require that router ports be forwarded or opened to allow these applications to work, as shown in Figure 5-21. Because NAT hides internal addresses, peer-to-peer only works from the inside out where NAT can map outgoing requests against incoming replies.

Figure 5-21   TCP and UDP Destination Ports

The problem is that NAT does not allow requests initiated from the outside. This situation can be resolved with manual intervention. Port forwarding can be configured to identify specific ports that can be forwarded to inside hosts.

Recall that Internet software applications interact with user ports that need to be open or available to those applications. Different applications use different ports. This makes it predictable for applications and routers to identify network services. For example, HTTP operates through the well-known port 80. When someone enters the http://cisco.com address, the browser displays the Cisco Systems, Inc. website. Notice that they do not have to specify the HTTP port number for the page request, because the application assumes port 80.

If a different port number is required, it can be appended to the URL separated by a colon (:). For example, if the web server is listening on port 8080, the user would type http://www.example.com:8080.

Port forwarding allows users on the Internet to access internal servers by using the WAN port address of the router and the matched external port number. The internal servers are typically configured with RFC 1918 private IPv4 addresses. When a request is sent to the IPv4 address of the WAN port via the Internet, the router forwards the request to the appropriate server on the LAN. For security reasons, broadband routers do not by default permit any external network request to be forwarded to an inside host.

Figure 5-22 shows a small business owner using a point of sale (PoS) server to track sales and inventories at the store. The server can be accessed within the store, but because it has a private IPv4 address, it is not publicly accessible from the Internet. Enabling the local router for port forwarding allows the owner to access the point of sale server from anywhere on the Internet. Port forwarding on the router is configured using the destination port number and the private IPv4 address of the point of sale server. To access the server, the client software would use the public IPv4 address of the router and the destination port of the server.

Figure 5-22   Port Forwarding

SOHO Example (5.2.4.2)

Figure 5-23 shows the Single Port Forwarding configuration window of a Linksys EA6500 SOHO router. By default, port forwarding is not enabled on the router.

Figure 5-23   Port Forwarding on a SOHO Router

Port forwarding can be enabled for applications by specifying the inside local address that requests should be forwarded to. In the figure, HTTP service requests, coming into this Linksys router, are forwarded to the web server with the inside local address of 192.168.1.254. If the external WAN IPv4 address of the SOHO router is 209.165.200.225, the external user can enter http://www.example.com, and the Linksys router redirects the HTTP request to the internal web server at IPv4 address 192.168.1.254, using the default port number 80.

A port other than the default port 80 can be specified. However, the external user would have to know the specific port number to use. To specify a different port, the value of the External Port in the Single Port Forwarding window would be modified.

The approach taken to configure port forwarding depends on the brand and model of the broadband router in the network. However, there are some generic steps to follow. If the instructions supplied by the ISP, or those that came with the router, do not provide adequate guidance, the website http://www.portforward.com provides guides for several broadband routers. You can follow the instructions to add or delete ports as required to meet the needs of any applications you want to allow or deny.

Configuring Port Forwarding with IOS (5.2.4.3)

Implementing port forwarding with IOS commands is similar to the commands used to configure static NAT. Port forwarding is essentially a static NAT translation with a specified TCP or UDP port number.

The static NAT command used to configure port forwarding using IOS is:

```
ip nat inside source {static {tcp | udp local-ip local-port global-ip global-port}
   [extendable]
```

Table 5-8 shows the static NAT command parameters used when configuring port forwarding using IOS.

Table 5-8   Port Forwarding Using IOS

Parameter	Description
tcp or udp	Indicates if this is a TCP or UDP port number.
local-ip	This is the IPv4 address assigned to the host on the inside network, typically from RFC 1918 private address space.
local-port	Sets the local TCP/UDP port in a range from 1–65535. This is the port number the server is listening on.
global-ip	This is the IPv4 globally unique address of an inside host. This is the IP address the outside clients will use to reach the internal server.
global-port	Sets the local TCP/UDP port in a range from 1–65535. This is the port number the outside client will use to reach the internal server.
extendable	The extendable option is applied automatically. The extendable keyword allows the user to configure several ambiguous static translations, where ambiguous translations are translations with the same local or global address. It allows the router to extend the translation to more than one port if necessary.

Using the topology in Figure 5-24, Example 5-11 shows an example of configuring port forwarding using IOS commands on router R2. 192.168.10.254 is the inside local IPv4 address of the web server listening on port 80. Users will access this internal web server using the global IP address 209.165.200.225, a globally unique public IPv4 address. In this case, it is the address of the Serial 0/1/0 interface of R2. The global port is configured as 8080. This will be the destination port used, along with the global IPv4 address of 209.165.200.225 to access the internal web server. Notice within the NAT configuration, the following command parameters:

```
local-ip = 192.168.10.254
local-port = 80
global-ip = 209.165.200.225
global-port = 8080
```

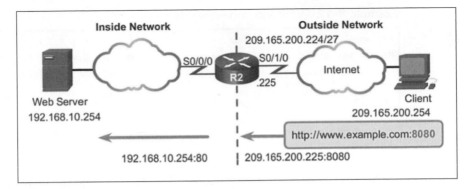

Figure 5-24   Port Forwarding Topology Using IOS

Example 5-11   Port Forwarding Example Using IOS

Establishes static translation between an inside local address and local port and an inside global address and global port.

```
R2(config)# ip nat inside source static tcp 192.168.10.254 80 209.165.200.225 8080
```

Identifies interface Serial 0/0/0 as an inside NAT interface.

```
R2(config)# interface Serial0/0/0
R2(config-if)# ip nat inside
```

Identifies interface Serial 0/1/0 as the outside NAT interface.

```
R2(config)# interface Serial0/1/0
R2(config-if)# ip nat outside
```

When a well-known port number is not being used, the client must specify the port number in the application.

Like other types of NAT, port forwarding requires the configuration of both the inside and outside NAT interfaces.

Similar to static NAT, the **show ip nat translations** command can be used to verify the port forwarding, as shown in Example 5-12.

In the example, when the router receives the packet with the inside global IPv4 address of 209.165.200.225 and a TCP destination port 8080, the router performs a NAT table lookup using the destination IPv4 address and destination port as the key. The router then translates the address to the inside local address of host 192.168.10.254 and destination port 80. R2 then forwards the packet to the web server. For return packets from the web server back to the client, this process is reversed.

Example 5-12 Verifying Port Forwarding

```
R2# show ip nat translations
Pro Inside global       Inside local     Outside local      Outside global
tcp 209.165.200.225:8080 192.168.10.254:80  209.165.200.254:46088
   209.165.200.254:46088
tcp 209.165.200.225:8080 192.168.10.254:80  ---                ---
R2#
```

Packet Tracer Activity 5.2.4.4: Configuring Port Forwarding on a Linksys Router

Your friend wants to play a game with you on your server. Both of you are at your respective homes, connected to the Internet. You need to configure your SOHO (Small Office, Home Office) router to port forward HTTP requests to your server so that your friend can access the game lobby web page.

Configuring NAT and IPv6 (5.2.5)

NAT for IPv6 is typically translation between an IPv6 address and an IPv4 address. Although there are RFCs referring to IPv6-to-IPv6 translations, the current intention by IETF is not to use NAT for IPv6 to hide addresses similar to NAT for IPv4.

NAT for IPv6? (5.2.5.1)

Since the early 1990s, the concern about the depletion of IPv4 address space has been a priority of the IETF. The combination of RFC 1918 private IPv4 addresses and NAT has been instrumental in slowing this depletion. NAT has significant disadvantages, and in January of 2011, IANA allocated the last of its IPv4 addresses to RIRs.

One of the unintentional benefits of NAT for IPv4 is that it hides the private network from the public Internet, as shown in Figure 5-25. NAT has the advantage of providing a perceived level of security by denying computers in the public Internet from accessing internal hosts. However, it should not be considered a substitute for proper network security, such as that provided by a firewall.

Figure 5-25   IPv4 Private Addresses and NAT

In RFC 5902, the Internet Architecture Board (IAB) included the following quote concerning IPv6 network address translation:

> It is commonly perceived that a NAT box provides one level of protection because external hosts cannot directly initiate communication with hosts behind a NAT. However, one should not confuse NAT boxes with firewalls. As discussed in Section 2.2 in RFC4864, the act of translation does not provide security in itself. The stateful filtering function can provide the same level of protection without requiring a translation function.

IPv6, with a 128-bit address, provides 340 undecillion addresses. Therefore, address space is not an issue. IPv6 was developed with the intention of making NAT for IPv4 with its translation between public and private IPv4 addresses unnecessary. However, IPv6 does implement a form of NAT. IPv6 includes both its own IPv6 private address space and NAT, which are implemented differently than they are for IPv4.

IPv6 Unique Local Addresses (5.2.5.2)

IPv6 *unique local addresses* (ULAs) are similar to RFC 1918 private addresses in IPv4, but there are significant differences as well. The intent of ULA is to provide IPv6 address space for communications within a local site; it is not meant to provide additional IPv6 address space, nor is it meant to provide a level of security.

As shown in Figure 5-26, ULAs have the prefix FC00::/7, which results in a first hextet range of FC00 to FDFF. The next 1 bit is set to 1 if the prefix is locally assigned. Set to 0 may be defined in the future. The next 40 bits is a global ID followed by a 16-bit subnet ID. These first 64 bits combine to make the ULA prefix. This leaves the remaining 64 bits for the interface ID, or in IPv4 terms, the host portion of the address.

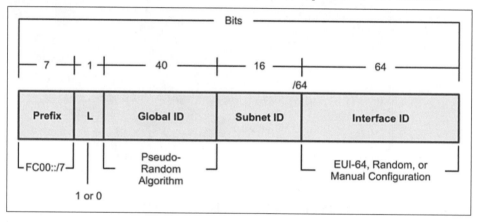

Figure 5-26   IPv6 Unique Local Address

Unique local addresses are defined in RFC 4193. ULAs are also known as local IPv6 addresses (not to be confused with IPv6 link-local addresses) and have several characteristics, including the following:

- Allows sites to be combined or privately interconnected, without creating any address conflicts or requiring renumbering of interfaces that use these prefixes

- Independent of any ISP and can be used for communications within a site without having any Internet connectivity

- Not routable across the Internet, however, if accidentally leaked by routing or DNS, there is no conflict with other addresses

ULA is not quite as straightforward as RFC 1918 addresses. Unlike private IPv4 addresses, it has not been the intention of the IETF to use a form of NAT to translate between unique local addresses and IPv6 global unicast addresses.

The implementation and potential uses for IPv6 unique local addresses are still being examined by the Internet community. For example, the IETF is considering allowing the option to have the ULA prefix created locally using FC00::/8 or to have it assigned automatically by a third-party beginning with FD00::/8.

Note

The original IPv6 specification allocated address space for site-local addresses, defined in RFC 3513. Site-local addresses have been deprecated by the IETF in RFC 3879 because the term *site* was somewhat ambiguous. Site-local addresses had the prefix range of FEC0::/10 and may still be found in some older IPv6 documentation.

NAT for IPv6 (5.2.5.3)

NAT for IPv6 is used in a much different context than NAT for IPv4, as shown in Figure 5-27. The varieties of NAT for IPv6 are used to transparently provide access between IPv6-only and IPv4-only networks. It is not used as a form of private IPv6 to global IPv6 translation.

Figure 5-27 NAT64

Ideally, IPv6 should be run natively wherever possible. This means IPv6 devices communicating with each other over IPv6 networks. However, to aid in the move from IPv4 to IPv6, the IETF has developed several transition techniques to accommodate a variety of IPv4-to-IPv6 scenarios, including dual-stack, tunneling, and translation.

Dual-stack is when the devices are running protocols associated with both the IPv4 and IPv6. Tunneling for IPv6 is the process of encapsulating an IPv6 packet inside an IPv4 packet. This allows the IPv6 packet to be transmitted over an IPv4-only network.

NAT for IPv6 should not be used as a long term strategy, but as a temporary mechanism to assist in the migration from IPv4 to IPv6. Over the years, there have been several types of NAT for IPv6 including Network Address Translation-Protocol Translation (NAT-PT). NAT-PT has been deprecated by IETF in favor of its replacement, *NAT64*. NAT64 is beyond the scope of this curriculum.

Troubleshooting NAT (5.3)

Troubleshooting any technology is an important skill, the same is true for NAT. Having a good understanding of how NAT operates and NAT configuration commands, is important to being able to solve problems related to NAT.

Troubleshooting NAT: show Commands (5.3.1.1)

Figure 5-28 shows R2 enabled for PAT, using the range of addresses 209.165.200.226 to 209.165.200.240.

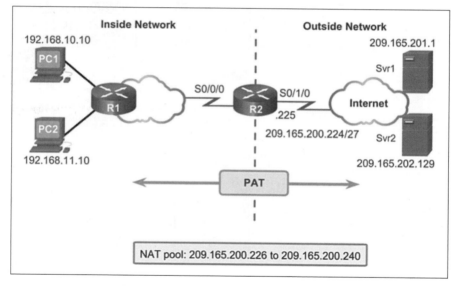

Figure 5-28   Troubleshooting NAT

When there are IPv4 connectivity problems in a NAT environment, it is often difficult to determine the cause of the problem. The first step in solving the problem is to rule out NAT as the cause. Follow these steps to verify that NAT is operating as expected:

Step 1.   Based on the configuration, clearly define what NAT is supposed to achieve. This may reveal a problem with the configuration.

Step 2.   Verify that correct translations exist in the translation table using the **show ip nat translations** command.

Step 3.   Use the **clear** and **debug** commands to verify that NAT is operating as expected. Check to see if dynamic entries are re-created after they are cleared.

Step 4.   Review in detail what is happening to the packet, and verify that routers have the correct routing information to move the packet.

Example 5-13 shows the output of the **show ip nat statistics** and **show ip nat translations** commands. Prior to using the **show** commands, the NAT statistics and entries in the NAT table are cleared with the **clear ip nat statistics** and **clear ip nat translation** * commands. After the host at 192.168.10.10 telnets to the server at 209.165.201.1, the NAT statistics and NAT table are displayed to verify NAT is working as expected.

Example 5-13   Troubleshooting NAT

```
R2# clear ip nat statistics
R2# clear ip nat translation *
R2#


Host 192.168.10.10 telnets to server at 209.165.201.1
R2# show ip nat statistics
Total active translations: 1 (0 static, 1 dynamic; 1 extended)
Peak translations: 1, occurred 00:00:09 ago
Outside interfaces:
  Serial0/0/1
Inside interfaces:
  Serial0/0/0
Hits: 31  Misses: 0
CEF Translated packets: 31, CEF Punted packets: 0
Expired translations: 0
Dynamic mappings:
-- Inside Source
[Id: 5] access-list 1 pool NAT-POOL2 refcount 1
 pool NAT-POOL2: netmask 255.255.255.224
        start 209.165.200.226 end 209.165.200.240
        type generic, total addresses 15, allocated 1 (6%), misses 0
<output omitted>

R2# show ip nat translations
Pro Inside global        Inside local       Outside local      Outside global
tcp 209.165.200.226:19005  192.168.10.10:19005  209.165.201.1:23   209.165.201.1:23
R2#
```

In a simple network environment, it is useful to monitor NAT statistics with the **show ip nat statistics** command. The **show ip nat statistics** command displays information about the total number of active translations, NAT configuration parameters, the number of addresses in the pool, and the number that have been allocated. However, in a more complex NAT environment, with several translations taking place, this command may not clearly identify the issue. It may be necessary to run **debug** commands on the router.

Troubleshooting NAT: debug Command (5.3.1.2)

Use the **debug ip nat** command to verify the operation of the NAT feature by displaying information about every packet that is translated by the router. The **debug ip nat detailed** command generates a description of each packet considered for translation. This command also provides information about certain errors or exception conditions, such as the failure to allocate a global address. The **debug ip nat detailed** command generates more overhead than the **debug ip nat** command, but it can provide the detail that may be needed to troubleshoot the NAT problem. Always turn off debugging when finished.

Example 5-14 shows a sample **debug ip nat** output. The output shows that the inside host (192.168.10.10) initiated traffic to the outside host (209.165.201.1) and the source address was translated to address 209.165.200.226.

Example 5-14   Troubleshooting NAT with **debug ip nat**

```
R2# debug ip nat
IP NAT debugging is on
R2#
*Feb 15 20:01:34.670: NAT*: s=192.168.10.10->209.165.200.226, d=209.165.201.1 [2817]
*Feb 15 20:01:34.682: NAT*: s=209.165.201.1, d=209.165.200.226->192.168.10.10 [4180]
*Feb 15 20:01:34.698: NAT*: s=192.168.10.10->209.165.200.226, d=209.165.201.1 [2818]
*Feb 15 20:01:34.702: NAT*: s=192.168.10.10->209.165.200.226, d=209.165.201.1 [2819]
*Feb 15 20:01:34.710: NAT*: s=192.168.10.10->209.165.200.226, d=209.165.201.1 [2820]
*Feb 15 20:01:34.710: NAT*: s=209.165.201.1, d=209.165.200.226->192.168.10.10 [4181]
*Feb 15 20:01:34.722: NAT*: s=209.165.201.1, d=209.165.200.226->192.168.10.10 [4182]
*Feb 15 20:01:34.726: NAT*: s=192.168.10.10->209.165.200.226, d=209.165.201.1 [2821]
*Feb 15 20:01:34.730: NAT*: s=209.165.201.1, d=209.165.200.226->192.168.10.10 [4183]
*Feb 15 20:01:34.734: NAT*: s=192.168.10.10->209.165.200.226, d=209.165.201.1 [2822]
*Feb 15 20:01:34.734: NAT*: s=209.165.201.1, d=209.165.200.226->192.168.10.10 [4184]
<Output omitted>
```

When decoding the debug output, note what the following symbols and values indicate:

- **(asterisk):** The asterisk next to NAT indicates that the translation is occurring in the fast-switched path. The first packet in a conversation is always process-switched, which is slower. The remaining packets go through the fast-switched path if a cache entry exists.

- **s=:** This symbol refers to the source IP address.

- **a.b.c.d--->w.x.y.z:** This value indicates that source address a.b.c.d is translated to w.x.y.z.

- **d=:** This symbol refers to the destination IP address.

- **[xxxx]:** The value in brackets is the IP identification number. This information may be useful for debugging in that it enables correlation with other packet traces from protocol analyzers.

Note

Verify that the ACL referenced in the NAT command reference is permitting all of the necessary networks. Using the topology in Figure 5-29, the ACL in Example 5-15 shows only 192.168.0.0/16 addresses are eligible to be translated. Packets from the inside network destined for the Internet with source addresses that are not explicitly permitted by ACL 1 are not translated by R2.

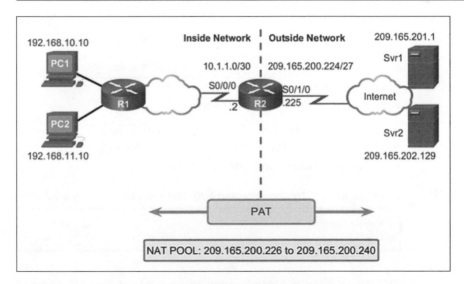

Figure 5-29   Troubleshooting the ACL used with NAT

Example 5-15   Troubleshooting NAT with **show access-lists**

```
R2# show access-lists
Standard IP access list 1
    10 permit 192.168.0.0, wildcard bits 0.0.255.255 (29 matches)
R2#
```

Case Study (5.3.1.3)

Figure 5-30 shows that hosts from the 192.168.0.0/16 LANs, PC1, and PC2 cannot ping servers on the outside network: Svr1 and Svr2.

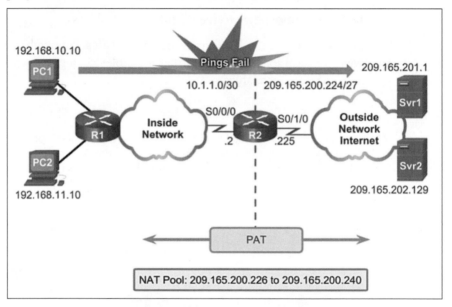

Figure 5-30   PC1 and PC2 Cannot Ping Svr1 and Svr2

To begin troubleshooting the problem, use the **show ip nat translations** command to see if any translations are currently in the NAT table. The output in Example 5-16 shows that no translations are in the table.

Example 5-16   Troubleshooting NAT Case Study with **show ip nat translations**

```
R2# show ip nat translations
R2#
```

The **show ip nat statistics** command is used to determine whether any translations have taken place. It also identifies the interfaces that translation should be occurring between. As shown in the output of Example 5-17, the NAT counters are at 0, verifying that no translation has occurred. By comparing the output with the topology shown in Figure 5-30, notice that the router interfaces are incorrectly defined as NAT inside or NAT outside. The incorrect configuration can also be verified using the **show running-config** command.

Example 5-17   Troubleshooting NAT Case Study with **show ip nat statistics**

```
R2# show ip nat statistics
Total active translations: 0 (0 static, 0 dynamic; 0 extended)
Peak translations: 0
Outside interfaces:
  Serial0/0/0
Inside interfaces:
  Serial0/1/0
Hits: 0  Misses: 0
<Output omitted>

R2(config)# interface serial 0/0/0
R2(config-if)# no ip nat outside
R2(config-if)# ip nat inside
R2(config-if)# exit
R2(config)# interface serial 0/0/1
R2(config-if)# no ip nat inside
R2(config-if)# ip nat outside
```

The current NAT interface configuration must be deleted from the interfaces before applying the correct configuration.

After correctly defining the NAT inside and outside interfaces, another ping from PC1 to Svr1 fails. Using the **show ip nat translations and show ip nat statistics** commands again verifies that translations are still not occurring.

As shown in Example 5-18, the **show access-lists** command is used to determine whether the ACL that the NAT command references is permitting all of the necessary networks. Examining the output indicates that an incorrect wildcard bit mask has been used in the ACL that defines the addresses which need to be translated. The wildcard mask is only permitting the 192.168.0.0/24 subnet. The access list is first removed and then reconfigured using the correct wildcard mask.

Example 5-18   Troubleshooting NAT with **show access-lists**

```
R2# show access-lists
Standard IP access list 1
    10 permit 192.168.0.0, wildcard bits 0.0.0.255
R2#
R2(config)#no access-list 1
R2(config)#access-list 1 permit 192.168.0.0 0.0.255.255
```

After configurations are corrected, another ping is generated from PC1 to Svr1, and this time the ping succeeds. As shown in Example 5-19, the **show ip nat translations** and **show ip nat statistics** commands are used to verify that the NAT translation is occurring.

Example 5-19   Troubleshooting NAT with `show access-lists`

```
R2# show ip nat statistics
Total active translations: 1 (0 static, 1 dynamic; 1 extended)
Peak translations: 1, occurred 00:37:58 ago
Outside interfaces:
  Serial0/0/1
Inside interfaces:
  Serial0/1/0
Hits: 20  Misses: 0
CEF Translated packets: 20, CEF Punted packets: 0
Expired translations: 1
Dynamic mappings:
-- Inside Source
[Id: 5] access-list 1 pool NAT-POOL2 refcount 1
 pool NAT-POOL2: netmask 255.255.255.224
        start 209.165.200.226 end 209.165.200.240
        type generic, total addresses 15, allocated 1 (6%), misses 0
<Output omitted>
R2# show ip nat translations
Pro  Inside global      Inside local     Outside local    Outside global
icmp 209.165.200.226:38 192.168.10.10:38 209.165.201.1:38 209.165.201.1:38
R2#
```

Packet Tracer Activity 5.3.1.4: Verifying and Troubleshooting NAT Configurations

Background/Scenario

A contractor restored an old configuration to a new router running NAT. But the network has changed, and a new subnet was added after the old configuration was backed up. It is your job to get the network working again.

Lab 5.3.1.5: Troubleshooting NAT Configurations

In this lab, you will complete the following objectives:

- Part 1: Build the Network and Configure Basic Device Settings
- Part 2: Troubleshoot Static NAT
- Part 3: Troubleshoot Dynamic NAT

Summary (5.4)

Class Activity 5.4.1.1: NAT Check

Network address translation is not currently included in your company's network design. It has been decided to configure some devices to use NAT services for connecting to the mail server.

Before deploying NAT live on the network, you prototype it using a network simulation program.

Packet Tracer
☐ Activity

Packet Tracer Activity 5.4.1.2: Skills Integration Challenge

This culminating activity includes many of the skills that you have acquired during this course. First, you will complete the documentation for the network. So make sure you have a printed version of the instructions. During implementation, you will configure VLANs, trunking, port security, and SSH remote access on a switch. Then, you will implement inter-VLAN routing and NAT on a router. Finally, you will use your documentation to verify your implementation by testing end-to-end connectivity.

This chapter has outlined how NAT is used to help alleviate the depletion of IPv4 address space. NAT for IPv4 allows network administrators to use RFC 1918 private address space while providing connectivity to the Internet, using a single or limited number of public addresses.

NAT conserves public address space and saves considerable administrative overhead in managing adds, moves, and changes. NAT and PAT can be implemented to conserve public address space and build private secure intranets without affecting the ISP connection. However, NAT has drawbacks in terms of its negative effects on device performance, security, mobility, and end-to-end connectivity and should be considered a short-term implementation for address exhaustion with the long-term solution being IPv6.

This chapter discussed NAT for IPv4, including the following:

- NAT characteristics, terminology, and general operations
- The different types of NAT including static NAT, dynamic NAT, and PAT
- The benefits and disadvantages of NAT
- The configuration, verification, and analysis of static NAT, dynamic NAT, and PAT
- How port forwarding can be used to access internal devices from the Internet
- Troubleshooting NAT using **show** and **debug** commands

Practice

The following activities provide practice with the topics introduced in this chapter. The labs and class activities are available in the companion *Connecting Networks Lab Manual* (978-1-58713-331-2). The Packet Tracer activity PKA files are found in the online course.

Class Activities

Class Activity 5.0.1.2: Conceptual NAT

Class Activity 5.4.1.1: NAT Check

Labs

Lab 5.2.2.6: Configuring Dynamic and Static NAT

Lab 5.2.3.7: Configuring Port Address Translation (PAT)

Lab 5.3.1.5: Troubleshooting NAT Configurations

Packet Tracer Activities

Packet Tracer Activity 5.1.2.6: Investigating NAT Operation

Packet Tracer Activity 5.2.1.4: Configuring Static NAT

Packet Tracer Activity 5.2.2.5: Configuring Dynamic NAT

Packet Tracer Activity 5.2.3.6: Implementing Static and Dynamic NAT

Packet Tracer Activity 5.2.4.4: Configuring Port Forwarding on a Linksys Router

Packet Tracer Activity 5.3.1.4: Verifying and Troubleshooting NAT Configurations

Packet Tracer Activity 5.4.1.2: Skills Integration Challenge

Check Your Understanding Questions

Complete all the review questions listed here to test your understanding of the topics and concepts in this chapter. The appendix, "Answers to the 'Check Your Understanding' Questions," lists the answers.

1. Refer to the following output:

```
NAT1# show ip nat translations
Pro Inside global Inside local Outside local Outside global
udp 198.18.24.211:123 192.168.254.7:123 192.2.182.4:123 192.2.182.4:123
tcp 198.18.24.211:4509 192.168.254.66:4509 192.0.2.184:80 192.0.2.184:80
tcp 198.18.24.211:4643 192.168.254.2:4643 192.0.2.71:5190 192.0.2.71:5190
tcp 198.18.24.211:4630 192.168.254.7:4630 192.0.2.71:5190 192.0.2.71:5190
tcp 198.18.24.211:1026 192.168.254.9:1026 198.18.24.4:53 198.18.24.4:53
```

Based on the output, which statement is true about the NAT configuration?

A. Static NAT is configured.

B. Dynamic NAT is configured.

C. NAT overload (PAT) is configured.

D. NAT is configured incorrectly.

2. If an administrator chooses to avoid using NAT overload, what is the default timeout value for NAT translations?

A. One hour

B. One day

C. One week

D. Indefinite

3. Match each NAT characteristic with its corresponding NAT technique:

Provides one-to-one fixed mappings of local and global addresses:

Assigns the translated addresses of IP hosts from a pool of public addresses:

Can map multiple addresses to a single address of the external interface:

Assigns unique source port numbers of an inside global address on a session-by-session basis:

Allows an external host to establish sessions with an internal host:

A. Dynamic NAT

B. NAT with Overload

C. Static NAT

4. Refer to the following configuration:

```
R1(config)# ip nat inside source static 192.168.0.100 209.165.200.2
R1(config)# interface serial0/0/0
R1(config-if)# ip nat inside
R1(config-if)# no shutdown
R1(config-if)# ip address 10.1.1.2 255.255.255.0
R1(config)# interface serial0/0/2
R1(config-if)# ip address 209.165.200.2 255.255.255.0
R1(config-if)# ip nat outside
R1(config-if)# no shutdown
```

Which host or hosts will have their addresses translated by NAT?

A. 10.1.1.2

B. 192.168.0.100

C. 209.165.200.2

D. All hosts on the 10.1.1.0 network

E. All hosts on the 192.168.0.0 network

5. Based on the following configuration, which addresses will NAT translate?

```
R1(config)# ip nat pool nat-pool1 209.165.200.225 209.165.200.240 netmask
   255.255.255.0
R1(config)# ip nat inside source list 1 pool nat-pool1
R1(config)# interface serial0/0/0
R1(config-if)# ip address 10.1.1.2 255.255.0.0
R1(config-if)# ip nat inside
R1(config-if)# no shutdown
R1(config)# interface serial s0/0/2
R1(config-if)# ip address 209.165.200.1 255.255.255.0
R1(config-if)# ip nat outside
R1(config-if)# no shutdown
R1(config)# access-list 1 permit 192.168.0.0 0.0.0.255
```

A. 10.1.1.2 to 10.1.1.255

B. 192.168.0.0 to 192.168.0.255

C. 209.165.200.240 to 209.165.200.255

D. Only host 10.1.1.2

E. Only host 209.165.200.255

6. Refer to Figure 5-31.

Figure 5-31 NAT Topology for Question 6

Web server 1 is assigned a single IP address of 192.168.14.5/24. For hosts from the Internet to access web server 1, which type of NAT configuration is required on router R1?

A. Static NAT

B. Dynamic NAT

C. NAT overload

D. Port Address Translation (PAT)

7. Which NAT solution allows external users to access an internal FTP server on a private network?

A. Dynamic NAT

B. Port Address Translation (PAT)

C. NAT overload

D. Static NAT

8. Given the following **debug ip nat** router output, what kind of address is 24.74.237.203?

```
s=10.10.10.3->24.74.237.203, d=64.102.252.3 [29854]
s=10.10.10.3->24.74.237.203, d=64.102.252.3 [29855]
s=10.10.10.3->24.74.237.203, d=64.102.252.3 [29856]
s=64.102.252.3, d=24.74.237.203->10.10.10.3 [9935]
s=64.102.252.3, d=24.74.237.203->10.10.10.3 [9937]
s=10.10.10.3->24.74.237.203, d=64.102.252.3 [29857]
s=64.102.252.3, d=24.74.237.203->10.10.10.3 [9969]
s=64.102.252.3, d=24.74.237.203->10.10.10.3 [9972]
s=10.10.10.3->24.74.237.203, d=64.102.252.3 [29858]
```

A. Inside local

B. Inside global

C. Outside local

D. Outside global

9. Describe the differences between static NAT, dynamic NAT, and NAT overload.

10. Refer to the following output:

```
R2# show ip nat translations

Pro Inside global Inside local Outside local
tcp 209.165.200.225:16642 192.168.10.10:16642 209.165.200.254:80
tcp 209.165.200.225:62452 192.168.11.10:62452 209.165.200.254:80
  Outside global
  209.165.200.254:80
  209.165.200.254:80


R2# show ip nat translations verbose
Pro Inside global Inside local Outside local
tcp 209.165.200.225:16642 192.168.10.10:16642 209.165.200.254:80
  Outside global
  209.165.200.254:80
    create 00:01:45, use 00:01:43 timeout:86400000, left 23:58:16, Map-Id(In):
  1,
    flags:
    extended, use_count: 0, entry-id: 4, lc_entries: 0
tcp 209.165.200.225:62452 192.168.11.10:62452 209.165.200.254:80
  209.165.200.254:80
  create 00:00:37, use 00:00:35 timeout:86400000, left 23:59:24, Map-Id(In): 1,
  flags:
  extended, use_count: 0, entry-id: 5, lc_entries: 0
R2#
```

Router R2 has been configured to provide NAT services. On the basis of the information provided, comment on the NAT translations in the output.

11. Refer to Figure 5-32.

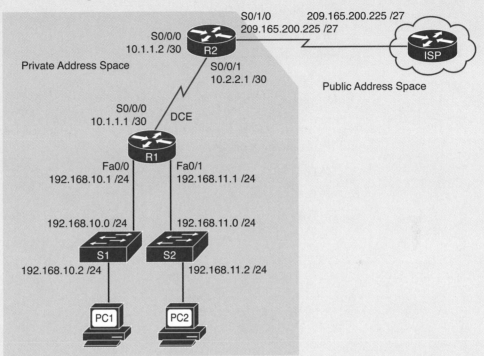

Figure 5-32   Topology for Question 11

The administrator has configured router R2 as a NAT border gateway. Specifically, NAT overload has been configured to translate internal hosts connected to the R1 router to a pool of public addresses in the range of 209.165.200.224/29. The following commands were configured on R2:

```
access-list 1 permit 192.168.0.0 0.0.0.255
ip nat pool NAT-POOL 209.165.200.225 209.165.200.239 netmask 255.255.255.240
ip nat inside source list 1 pool NAT-POOL1
interface serial s0/1/0
ip nat inside
interface serial 0/0/0
ip nat outside
```

The PC1 and PC2 hosts can ping router R2 but cannot get Internet access. On the basis of the information presented, which configuration changes would correctly address the current problem?

12. Which type of IPv6 address is used to provide IPv6 address space for communications within a local site?

    A. Link-local address

    B. Site local address

    C. Unique local address

    D. Loopback address

13. What form of NAT is used to transparently provide access between IPv6-only and IPv4-only networks?

    A. NAT64

    B. NAT66

    C. NATv6

    D. NAT-PT

CHAPTER 6

Broadband Solutions

Objectives

Upon completion of this chapter

- What are the benefits of teleworking?

- What are the requirements for supporting a teleworking solution using broadband?

- Can you describe a cable system and cable broadband access?

- Can you describe a DSL system and DSL broadband access?

- Can you describe wireless broadband access?

- Can you select an appropriate broadband solution for a given network requirement?

- Can you describe the operation of Point-to-Point Protocol over Ethernet (PPPoE)?

- Can you configure a basic PPP over Ethernet connection on a client router?

Key Terms

This chapter uses the following key terms. You can find the definitions in the glossary.

Introduction (6.0.1.1)

Teleworking, or working from a nontraditional workplace such as at home, offers many benefits to the worker and to the business. Broadband solutions provide these workers with high-speed connection options to business locations and to the Internet. Small branch offices can also connect using these same technologies.

This chapter covers commonly used broadband solutions, such as cable, DSL, and wireless. VPN technology provides security options for data running over these connections. This chapter also discusses the factors to consider if more than one broadband solution is available to service a particular location.

Class Activity 6.0.1.2: Broadband Varieties

Telework employment opportunities are expanding in your local area every day. You have been offered employment as a teleworker for a major corporation. The new employer requires teleworkers to have access to the Internet to fulfill their job responsibilities.

Research the following broadband Internet connection types that are available in your geographic area:

- DSL
- Cable
- Satellite

Teleworking (6.1)

More and more companies are finding it beneficial to have teleworkers. With advances in broadband and wireless technologies, working away from the office no longer presents the challenges it did in the past. Workers can work remotely almost as if they were in the next cubicle or office. Organizations can cost-effectively distribute data, voice, video, and real-time applications extended over one common network connection, across their entire workforce, no matter how remote and scattered they might be. This section introduces the benefits of teleworking and the components required.

Benefits of Teleworking (6.1.1)

In this topic, the advantages and disadvantages of teleworking are discussed.

Introducing Teleworking (6.1.1.1)

Teleworking is working away from the traditional workplace, such as working from a home office. The reasons for choosing teleworking are varied and include everything from personal convenience to allowing sick or disabled employees the opportunity to continue working.

Teleworking is a broad term referring to conducting work by connecting to a workplace from a remote location, with the assistance of telecommunications. Efficient teleworking is possible because of broadband Internet connections, virtual private networks (VPNs), Voice over IP (VoIP), and videoconferencing.

Many modern enterprises are offering employment opportunities for people who cannot commute to work every day, or for whom working out of a home office is more practical. These people, called teleworkers, must connect to the company network so that they can work and share information from their home offices.

Broadband solutions are integral to successful teleworking. This chapter details the benefits of teleworking and how broadband solutions enable teleworking as a smarter way to do business.

Employer Benefits of Teleworking (6.1.1.2)

For organizations, there are many benefits of offering a teleworking environment. Some of the most cited benefits include the following:

- **Improved employee productivity:** In general, teleworking allows employees to do more and maintain better quality work, than those workers confined exclusively to an office space. According to a British Telecom Study by the Gartner Group, the average telecommuter works 11 percent more hours than an office counterpart. The Bell Atlantic Corporation (now Verizon) cited that 25 hours spent working at home is the equivalent of 40 office hours.

- **Reduced costs and expenses:** A major expense in many organizations is the cost of real estate. Teleworking means reduced requirements for office space. Savings in real estate cost have the potential of equaling anywhere from 10 percent to 80 percent. Even a 10 percent saving in real estate costs may be the difference between profit and loss. Additional savings include heating, air-conditioning, car parks, lighting, office equipment and supplies, as all these costs, and more, drop as staff take up telework.

- **Easier recruitment and retention:** Being able to offer flexibility can reduce staff turnover by up to 20 percent. With staff replacement costing 75 percent or more of salary, this is a significant saving, even before training and retention costs are considered. Some observers have calculated that the cost of turnover and replacing staff is as high as 250 percent of salary.

- **Reduced absenteeism:** Telework can reduce absenteeism by as much as 80 percent.

- **Improved morale:** Improvements that offer the option of telework are often seen as family-friendly employers.

- **Improved corporate citizenship:** Allowing employees to work from home, and reducing the commuting emissions of a company's employees can be an important part of an organization's plan to become carbon neutral and environmentally responsible. This can have many benefits, including creating marketing opportunities, adding value to products and services, addressing concerns expressed by customers, and responding to supply chain requirements.

- **Improved customer service:** With staff able to start their working day without first commuting to the office, clients and customers will experience improved contact and response times leading to large improvements in client retention and value. Clients and customers report quicker response and better service.

With better response times, better customer service, lower costs, and increased employee productivity, enterprises are better able to compete in rapidly changing markets. Teleworking really is a smart way to do business.

Community and Government Benefits (6.1.1.3)

Teleworking can benefit organizations of all sizes, from small businesses to large corporations. However, those benefits actually expand beyond the organizational level, offering unique advantages to public entities such as communities, and even local and national governments.

Public entities such as communities and governments are businesses that must manage income and expenses. They should be as efficient, accountable, and as transparent as possible because taxpayer money is at stake. For this reason, from the business perspective, all of the employee and cost saving benefits of teleworking apply to these public entities. In addition, public entities benefit from teleworking in the following ways:

- **Helps reduce traffic and infrastructure requirements:** Telework eliminates many contemporary problems at the source. Traffic is only one example. According to a 2004 Washington Post article, traffic delays in the Washington, D.C. region drop 10 percent for every 3 percent of commuters who work from home. In addition, teleworking reduces infrastructure and service delivery costs.

- **Helps reduce urban drift:** Urban drift refers to the movement of individuals from rural locations to city centers and towns in search of better conditions and employment opportunities. Urban drift results in overcrowding and congestion. Teleworking allows individuals to work regardless of physical location, reducing the need for individuals to relocate due to employment.

- **Improved rural and suburban amenities:** More people working in rural or suburban regions could mean better mass transit services and changes to local retail facilities. The post office, doctor, bank, or gas station might be less likely to close up and move somewhere else. With more flexible response, more productive enterprises, and the ability of all individuals to contribute, the regions or nation becomes more competitive and attracts more employment and development.

Individual Benefits of Teleworking (6.1.1.4)

Individuals also gain significant benefits from being able to work remotely, including the following:

- **Productivity:** Over 70 percent of teleworkers claim they are significantly more productive, which means they do more in less time, thus saving time or earning more in the same time.

- **Flexibility:** Teleworkers can better manage when and where work is performed. They have more flexibility to handle many other details of modern life, like getting the car serviced, avoiding the traffic at holiday weekends, and taking children to the doctor.

- **Cost savings:** Employees that must commute to an office spend a significant amount of money adding up vehicle fuel and maintenance, lunches, work clothes, eating out, and all the other costs of traditional work that one can reduce by teleworking.

- **Home and family:** For many people, spending more time with the family or caring for dependent relatives is a major reason for teleworking.

Detriments to Telework (6.1.1.5)

While there are many benefits to teleworking, there are some detriments that must also be considered.

From an employer perspective:

- **Tracking of employee progress:** It may be difficult for some managers to track the work accomplishments of employees that telework. It is necessary to arrange checkpoints and validate task progress in a different manner with employees who work from home.

- **Necessary to implement a new management style:** Managers who oversee employees within an office have the capability to maintain in-person contact with all employees. This means if a problem arises, or there is a misunderstanding of assigned tasks, an unscheduled face-to-face meeting can often resolve the issue quickly. In a telework environment, managers should establish processes for validating understanding and remain flexible to the various needs of the teleworking employee.

From the employee perspective:

- **Feeling of isolation:** For many people, working on their own becomes lonely.

- **Slower connections:** Residential and rural areas do not generally get the kind of technology support and services that inner city offices can receive, and they can be expensive. If the work requires high bandwidth, think carefully about whether a home office is the right choice.

- **Distractions:** Whether it is a neighbor, a spouse, a child, lawn mowing, the laundry, the TV or the refrigerator, there are distractions in the home office. Additionally, many individuals think that telework negates the need for childcare, but this is not necessarily true. With young children especially, it is important to plan for childcare at times when it is necessary to completely focus on work.

Interactive Graphic

Activity 6.1.1.6: Benefits of Teleworking.

Go to the course online to perform this practice activity.

Business Requirements for Teleworker Services (6.1.2)

This topic provides an overview of teleworker solutions and the components required to support teleworkers.

Teleworker Solution (6.1.2.1)

Organizations need secure, reliable, and cost-effective networks to connect corporate headquarters, branch offices, and suppliers. With the growing number of teleworkers, enterprises increasingly need secure, reliable, and cost-effective ways to connect teleworkers with the organizational resources on corporate LAN sites.

Figure 6-1 illustrates the remote connection topologies that modern networks use to connect remote locations. In some cases, the remote locations only connect to the headquarters location, whereas in other cases, remote locations connect to multiple sites. The branch office in the figure connects to the headquarters and partner sites, while the teleworker has a single connection to the headquarters.

Figure 6-1   Remote Connection Options

There are three primary remote connection technologies available to organizations supporting teleworker services:

- *Broadband connections*: The broadband term refers to advanced communications systems capable of providing high-speed transmission of services, such as data, voice, and video, over the Internet and other networks. Transmission is provided by a wide range of technologies, including DSL, fiber-to-the-home, coaxial cable systems, wireless, and satellite. The broadband service data transmission speeds typically exceed 200 Kbps in at least one direction between the ISP and the user.

- *IPsec VPNs*: This is the most common option for teleworkers, combined with remote access over broadband, to establish a secure VPN over the public Internet. This type of WAN connection offers flexible and scalable connectivity. Site-to-site connections can provide a secure, fast, and reliable remote connection to teleworkers.

- **Traditional private WAN Layer 2 technologies:** These types of connections provide many remote connection solutions and include technologies, such as leased lines, Frame Relay, and ATM. The security of these connections is dependent upon the service provider providing them.

Teleworker Connectivity Requirements (6.1.2.2)

Regardless of the remote connection technology used to connect effectively to an organization's networks, teleworkers require both home office components and corporate components:

- **Home office components:** The required home office components are a laptop or desktop computer, broadband access (cable, DSL, or wireless), and a VPN router or VPN client software installed on the computer. Additional components might include a wireless access point. When traveling, teleworkers need an Internet connection and a VPN client to connect to the corporate network over any available dialup, network, or broadband connection.

- **Corporate components:** Corporate components are VPN-capable routers, VPN concentrators, multifunction security appliances, authentication, and central management devices for resilient aggregation and termination of the VPN connections.

Quality of service (QoS)-supported VoIP and videoconferencing components is becoming an integral component of the teleworkers toolkit. QoS refers to the capability of a network to provide better service to selected network traffic, as required by voice and video applications. Providing support for VoIP and videoconferencing requires upgrades to routers and devices that support QoS functionality.

Figure 6-2 shows an encrypted VPN tunnel connecting the teleworker to the corporate network. This is the primary basis of secure and reliable teleworker connections.

Figure 6-2   Teleworker Connectivity Requirements

A VPN is a private data network that uses the public telecommunication infrastructure. VPN security maintains privacy using a tunneling protocol and security procedures. This course presents the IP Security (IPsec) protocol as the favored approach to building secure VPN tunnels. Unlike earlier security approaches that apply security at the application layer of the OSI model, IPsec works at the network layer where packet processing occurs.

As stated, a secure VPN tunnel is used over a public telecommunication infrastructure. This means that prior to initiating a VPN, home users must first be able to connect to Internet services using some form of high-speed, broadband access. The three most common forms of broadband access are as follows:

- Cable

- DSL

- Broadband wireless

Interactive Graphic

Activity 6.1.2.3: Classify Requirements for Teleworker Connectivity.

Go to the course online to perform this practice activity.

Comparing Broadband Solutions (6.2)

Teleworkers typically use diverse applications including email, web-based applications, mission-critical applications, real-time collaboration, voice, video, and videoconferencing that require a high-bandwidth connection. The choice of broadband access network technology and the need to ensure suitable bandwidth are the first considerations to address when connecting teleworkers. This section discusses the various types of broadband solutions.

Cable (6.2.1)

This topic discusses cable broadband services.

What is a Cable System? (6.2.1.1)

Accessing the Internet through a cable network is a popular option used by teleworkers to access their enterprise network. The cable system uses a coaxial cable that carries *radio frequency (RF)* signals across the network. Coaxial cable is the primary medium used to build cable TV systems.

Cable television first began in Pennsylvania in 1948. John Walson, the owner of an appliance store in a small mountain town, needed to solve poor over-the-air reception problems experienced by customers trying to receive TV signals from Philadelphia through the mountains. Walson erected an antenna on a utility pole on a local mountaintop that enabled him to demonstrate the televisions in his store with strong broadcasts coming from the three Philadelphia stations. He connected the antenna to his appliance store via a cable and modified signal boosters. He then connected several of his customers who were located along the cable path. This was the first Community Antenna Television (CATV) system in the United States.

Walson's company grew over the years, and he is recognized as the founder of the cable television industry. He was also the first cable operator to use microwave to import distant television stations, and the first to use coaxial cable to improve picture quality.

Most cable operators use satellite dishes to gather TV signals. Early systems were one way, with cascading amplifiers placed in series along the network to compensate for signal loss. These systems used taps to couple video signals from the main trunks to subscriber homes via drop cables.

Modern cable systems provide two-way communication between subscribers and the cable operator. Cable operators now offer customers advanced telecommunications services, including high-speed Internet access, digital cable television, and residential telephone service. Cable operators typically deploy *hybrid fiber-coaxial (HFC)* networks to enable high-speed transmission of data to cable modems located in a small office/home office (SOHO).

Figure 6-3 displays a sample topology of a typical modern cable system while Table 6-1 summarizes sections in the cable distribution system.

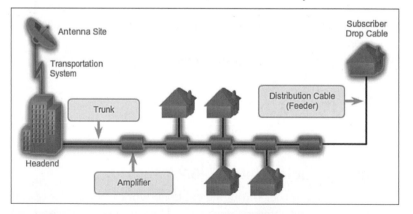

Figure 6-3   Sample Cable System Topology

Table 6-1   Sections of a Cable Distribution System

Section	Description
Antenna site	The location of an antenna site is chosen for optimum reception of over-the-air, satellite, and sometimes point-to-point signals. The main receiving antennas and satellite dishes are located at the antenna site.
Transportation system	A transportation network links a remote antenna site to a headend or a remote headend to the distribution network. The transportation network can be microwave, coaxial supertrunk, or fiber optic.
Headend	This is where signals are first received, processed, formatted, and then distributed downstream to the cable network. The headend facility is usually unmanned, under security fencing, and is similar to a telephone company central office.
Distribution network	In a classic cable system called a tree-and-branch cable system, the distribution network consists of trunk and feeder cables. The trunk is the backbone that distributes signals throughout the community service area to the feeder and typically uses 0.750 inch (19 mm) diameter coaxial cable. The feeder branches flow from a trunk and reach all of the subscribers in the service area via coaxial cables. The feeder cable is usually a 0.50 inch (13 mm) diameter coaxial cable.
Subscriber drop	A subscriber drop connects the subscriber to the cable services. The subscriber drop is a connection between the feeder part of a distribution network and the subscriber terminal device (for example, TV set, Blu-ray players, high-definition TV set-top box, or cable modem). A subscriber drop consists of radio grade (RG) coaxial cabling (usually 59-series or 6-series coaxial cable), grounding and attachment hardware, passive devices, and a set-top box.

Cable and the Electromagnetic Spectrum (6.2.1.2)

The electromagnetic spectrum encompasses a broad range of frequencies.

Frequency is the rate at which current, or voltage, cycles occur. Frequency is computed as the number of waves per second. Wavelength is the distance from the peak of one wave to the peak of the next wave. Wavelength is calculated as the speed of propagation of the electromagnetic signal divided by its frequency in cycles per second.

Radio waves, often called RF, constitute a portion of the electromagnetic spectrum between approximately 1 KHz and 1 THz. When users tune a radio or television to find different radio stations or television channels, they are tuning to different electromagnetic frequencies across that RF spectrum. The same principle applies to the cable system.

The cable TV industry uses a portion of the RF electromagnetic spectrum. Within the cable, different frequencies carry TV channels and data. At the subscriber end, equipment such as TVs, Blu-ray players, DVRs, and HDTV set-top boxes tune to certain frequencies that allow the user to view the channel or use a cable modem to receive high-speed Internet access.

A cable network is capable of transmitting signals on the cable in either direction at the same time. The following frequency scopes are used:

- **Downstream:** The direction of an RF signal transmission, such as TV channels and data, from the source, or headend, to the destination, or subscribers. Transmission from source to destination is called the forward path. Downstream frequencies are in the range of 50 to 860 MHz.

- **Upstream:** The direction of the RF signal transmission from subscribers to the headend. Upstream frequencies are in the range of 5 to 42 MHz.

DOCSIS (6.2.1.3)

The *Data-over-Cable Service Interface Specification (DOCSIS)* is an international standard developed by CableLabs, a non-profit research and development consortium for cable-related technologies. CableLabs tests and certifies cable equipment vendor devices, such as cable modems and cable modem termination systems, and grants DOCSIS-certified or qualified status.

DOCSIS defines the communications and operation support interface requirements for a data-over-cable system, and permits the addition of high-speed data transfer to an existing CATV system. Cable operators employ DOCSIS to provide Internet access over their existing HFC infrastructure.

DOCSIS specifies the OSI Layer 1 and Layer 2 requirements:

- **Physical layer:** For data signals that the cable operator can use, DOCSIS specifies the channel widths, or bandwidths of each channel, as 200 KHz, 400 KHz, 800 KHz, 1.6 MHz, 3.2 MHz, and 6.4 MHz. DOCSIS also specifies modulation technique, which is how to use the RF signal to convey digital data.

- **MAC layer:** Defines a deterministic access method, *time-division multiple access (TDMA)*, or *synchronous code-division multiple access (S-CDMA)* method.

To understand the MAC layer requirements for DOCSIS, an explanation of how various communication technologies divide channel access is helpful. TDMA divides access by time. *Frequency-division multiple access (FDMA)* divides access by frequency. *Code-division multiple access (CDMA)* employs spread-spectrum technology and a special coding scheme in which each transmitter is assigned a specific code.

An analogy that illustrates these concepts starts with a room representing a channel. The room is full of people needing to speak to one another. In other words, each person needs channel access. One solution is for the people to take turns speaking (time division). Another is for each person to speak at different pitches (frequency division). In CDMA, they would speak different languages. People speaking the same language can understand each other, but not other people. In radio CDMA used by many North American cell phone networks, each group of users has a shared code. Many codes occupy the same channel, but only users associated with a particular code can understand each other. S-CDMA is a proprietary version of CDMA developed by Terayon Corporation for data transmission across coaxial cable networks. S-CDMA scatters digital data up and down a wide frequency band and allows multiple subscribers connected to the network to transmit and receive concurrently. S-CDMA is secure and extremely resistant to noise.

Plans for frequency allocation bands differ between North American and European cable systems. Euro-DOCSIS is adapted for use in Europe. The main differences between DOCSIS and Euro-DOCSIS relate to channel bandwidths. TV technical standards vary across the world, which affects the way DOCSIS variants develop. International TV standards include NTSC in North America and parts of Japan; PAL in most of Europe, Asia, Africa, Australia, Brazil, and Argentina; and SECAM in France and some Eastern European countries.

Cable Components (6.2.1.4)

Delivering services over a cable network requires different radio frequencies. Downstream frequencies are in the 50 to 860 MHz range, and the upstream frequencies are in the 5 to 42 MHz range.

Two types of equipment are required to send digital modem signals upstream and downstream on a cable system:

- Cable Modem Termination System (CMTS) at the headend of the cable operator
- Cable Modem (CM) on the subscriber end

Figure 6-4 displays the devices involved in the end-to-end data propagation over cable, and Table 6-2 summarizes the components used.

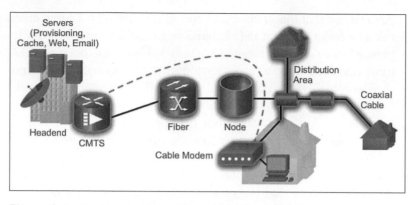

Figure 6-4   End-to-End Data Propagation over Cable

Table 6-2   Components in a Cable System

Component	Description
Cable modem termination system (CMTS)	A CMTS is a component that exchanges digital signals with cable modems on a cable network. A headend CMTS communicates with CMs that are located in subscriber homes.
Fiber	The trunk portion of the cable network is usually fiber-optic cable.
Node	Nodes convert optical signals to RF signals.
Cable modem	A cable modem enables you to receive data at high speeds. Typically, the cable modem attaches to a standard 10BASE-T Ethernet card in the computer.

A headend CMTS communicates with CMs located in subscriber homes. The headend is actually a router with databases for providing Internet services to cable subscribers. The architecture is relatively simple, using a mixed optical-coaxial network in which optical fiber replaces the lower bandwidth coaxial cable.

A web of fiber trunk cables connects the headend to the nodes where optical-to-RF signal conversion takes place. The fiber carries the same broadband content for Internet connections, telephone service, and streaming video as the coaxial cable carries. Coaxial feeder cables connect the node to the subscribers and carry RF signals.

In a modern HFC network, typically 500 to 2,000 active data subscribers are connected to a cable network segment, all sharing the upstream and downstream bandwidth. The actual bandwidth for Internet service over a CATV line can be up to 160 Mbps downstream with the latest iteration of DOCSIS, and up to 120 Mbps upstream.

When high usage causes congestion, the cable operator can add additional bandwidth for data services by allocating an additional TV channel for high-speed data.

This addition may effectively double the downstream bandwidth that is available to subscribers. Another option is to reduce the number of subscribers served by each network segment. To reduce the number of subscribers, the cable operator further subdivides the network by laying the fiber-optic connections deeper into the neighborhoods.

Activity 6.2.1.5: Identify Cable Terminology.

Go to the course online to perform this practice activity.

DSL (6.2.2)

This topic discusses DSL which is another popular broadband technology.

What is DSL? (6.2.2.1)

DSL is a means of providing high-speed connections over installed copper wires. DSL is one of the key teleworker solutions available.

Several years ago, Bell Labs identified that a typical voice conversation over a local loop only required bandwidth of 300 Hz to 3 KHz. For many years, the telephone networks did not use the bandwidth above 3 KHz. Advances in technology allowed DSL to use the additional bandwidth from 3 KHz up to 1 MHz to deliver high-speed data services over ordinary copper lines.

As an example, *asymmetric DSL (ADSL)* uses a frequency range from approximately 20 KHz to 1 MHz. Fortunately, only relatively small changes to existing telephone company infrastructure are required to deliver high-bandwidth data rates to subscribers. Figure 6-5 shows a representation of bandwidth space allocation on a copper wire for ADSL.

Figure 6-5 Asymmetric DSL in the Electromagnetic Spectrum

The area labeled POTS identifies the frequency range used by the voice-grade telephone service. The area labeled ADSL represents the frequency space used by the upstream and downstream DSL signals. The area that encompasses both the POTS area and the ADSL area represents the entire frequency range supported by the copper wire pair.

Another form of DSL technology is *symmetric DSL (SDSL)*. All forms of DSL service are categorized as ADSL or SDSL, and there are several varieties of each type. ADSL provides higher downstream bandwidth to the user than upload bandwidth. SDSL provides the same capacity in both directions.

The different varieties of DSL provide different bandwidths, some with capabilities exceeding 40 Mbps. The transfer rates are dependent on the actual length of the local loop (connecting the subscriber to the central office) and the type and condition of the cabling. For satisfactory ADSL service, the loop must be less than 3.39 miles (5.46 km).

DSL Connections (6.2.2.2)

Service providers deploy DSL connections in the last step of a local telephone network, called the local loop or last mile. The connection is set up between a pair of modems on either end of a copper wire that extends between the customer premises equipment (CPE) and the DSL access multiplexer (DSLAM). A DSLAM is the device located at the central office (CO) of the provider and concentrates connections from multiple DSL subscribers. A DSLAM is often built into an aggregation router.

Figure 6-6 shows the equipment needed to provide a DSL connection to a SOHO.

Figure 6-6 DSL Connections

The two components are the DSL transceiver and the DSLAM:

- **Transceiver:** Connects the computer of the teleworker to the DSL. Usually the transceiver is a DSL modem connected to the computer using a USB or Ethernet cable. Newer DSL transceivers can be built into small routers with multiple 10/100 switch ports suitable for home office use.

- **DSLAM:** Located at the CO of the carrier, the DSLAM combines individual DSL connections from users into one high-capacity link to an ISP and, therefore, to the Internet.

The advantage that DSL has over cable technology is that DSL is not a shared medium. Each user has a separate direct connection to the DSLAM. Adding users does not impede performance, unless the DSLAM Internet connection to the ISP, or the Internet, becomes saturated.

Separating Voice and Data in ADSL (6.2.2.3)

The major benefit of ADSL is the ability to provide data services along with POTS voice services. Transmissions of voice and data signals are propagated along the same wire pair, as shown in Figure 6-7. Data circuits are offloaded from the voice switch.

Figure 6-7   Separating Data from Voice in ADSL

When the service provider puts analog voice and ADSL on the same wire pair, ADSL signals can distort voice transmission. For this reason, the provider splits the POTS channel from the ADSL modem at the customer premises using filters or splitters. This setup guarantees uninterrupted regular phone service even if ADSL fails. When filters or splitters are in place, the user can use the phone line and the ADSL connection simultaneously without adverse effects on either service.

Figure 6-7 shows the local loop terminating on the customer premises at the demarcation point. The demarcation point is the point where the phone line enters the customer premises. The actual device that marks the demarcation point is the *Network Interface Device (NID)*. At this point, a splitter can be attached to the phone line. The splitter forks the phone line; one branch provides the original house telephone wiring for telephones, and the other branch connects to the ADSL modem. The splitter acts as a low-pass filter, allowing only the 0 to 4 KHz frequencies to pass to or from the telephone.

There are two ways to separate ADSL from voice at the customer premises: using a microfilter or using a splitter.

A microfilter is a passive low-pass filter with two ends, as shown in Figure 6-8.

Figure 6-8   Microfilters

One end connects to the telephone, and the other end connects to the telephone wall jack. Figure 6-9 displays images of microfilters. This solution allows the user to use any jack in the house for voice or ADSL service.

Figure 6-9 Examples of Microfilters

A POTS splitter, shown in Figure 6-10, separates the DSL traffic from the POTS traffic. The POTS splitter is a passive device.

Figure 6-10 POTS Splitter

Figure 6-11 displays a diagram of a POTS splitter.

Figure 6-11   Diagram of a POTS Splitter

In the event of a power failure, the voice traffic still travels to the voice switch in the CO of the carrier. Splitters are located at the CO and, in some deployments, at the customer premises. At the CO, the POTS splitter separates the voice traffic, destined for POTS connections, and the data traffic destined for the DSLAM. Installing the POTS splitter at the NID usually means that a technician must go to the customer site.

Interactive Graphic

Activity 6.2.2.4: Identify DSL Terminology.

Go to the course online to perform this practice activity.

Broadband Wireless (6.2.3)

This topic discusses wireless broadband technologies which is a viable option when cable or DSL is not available.

Types of Broadband Wireless Technologies (6.2.3.1, 6.2.3.2)

In place of cable connectivity and DSL, many users are now opting for wireless connectivity.

The reach of wireless connections now includes personal area networks, LANs, and WANs. The number of hotspots has increased access to wireless connections across the world. A hotspot is the area covered by one or more interconnected access points. Public gathering places, like coffee shops, cafes, and libraries, have Wi-Fi hotspots. By overlapping access points, hotspots can cover many square miles.

Developments in broadband wireless technology are increasing wireless availability. Table 6-3 summarizes these wireless technologies:

Table 6-3   Wireless Technologies

Wireless Technology	Description
Municipal Wi-Fi (Mesh)	■ IEEE 802.11 standards commonly called Wi-Fi ■ Implementations employ a mesh topology, with an access point at each node ■ Variations include 802.11a/b/g/n/ac/ad ■ Supports speeds of up to 7 Gbps
WiMAX (Worldwide Interoperability for Microwave Access)	■ IEEE 802.16 standard commonly called WiMAX ■ Uses a point-to-multipoint topology to provide wireless cellular broadband access ■ Supports speeds up to 1 Gbps
Cellular/Mobile	■ Cellular/Mobile broadband access consisting of various standards supporting speeds of up to 5 Mbps ■ Variations such as 2G (using GSM, CDMA, or TDMA), 3G (using UMTS, CDMA2000, EDGE, or HSPA+), and 4G (using WiMAX or LTE)
Satellite Internet	■ Satellite communication using a directional satellite dish aligned with GEO satellite ■ Ideal in situations such as remote areas where no other wireless access is available ■ Support download speeds of up to 10 Mbps

Municipal Wi-Fi

Many municipal governments, often working with service providers, are deploying wireless networks. Some of these networks provide high-speed Internet access at no cost or for substantially less than the price of other broadband services. Other cities reserve their Wi-Fi networks for official use, providing police, firefighters, and city workers remote access to the Internet and municipal networks.

Most municipal wireless networks use a mesh topology rather than a hub-and-spoke model. A mesh is a series of interconnected access points as shown in Figure 6-12.

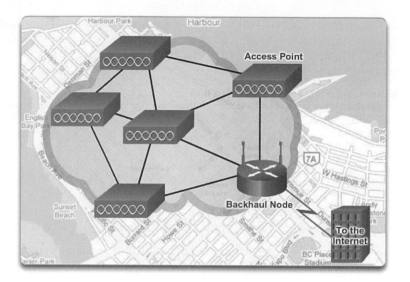

Figure 6-12 Municipal Wi-Fi (Mesh) Implementation

Each access point is in range and can communicate with at least two other access points. The mesh blankets its area with radio signals. Signals travel from access point to access point through this cloud.

A meshed network has several advantages over a singular wireless router hotspot. Installation is easier and can be less expensive because there are fewer wires. Deployment over a large urban area is faster and more reliable. If a node fails, others in the mesh compensate for it.

WiMAX

WiMAX, as shown in Figure 6-13, is a telecommunications technology aimed at providing wireless data over long distances in a variety of ways, from point-to-point links to full mobile cellular type access.

WiMAX operates at higher speeds, over greater distances, and for a greater number of users than Wi-Fi. Because of its higher speed (bandwidth) and falling component prices, it is predicted that WiMAX will soon supplant municipal mesh networks for wireless deployments.

A WiMAX network consists of two main components:

- A tower that is similar in concept to a cellular telephone tower. A single WiMAX tower can provide coverage to an area as large as 3,000 square miles (7,500 square km).

- A WiMAX receiver that is connected to a USB port or is built in to a laptop or other wireless device.

Figure 6-13   WiMAX Implementation

A WiMAX tower station connects directly to the Internet using a high-bandwidth connection, such as a T3 line. A tower can also connect to other WiMAX towers using line-of-sight microwave links. WiMAX is thus able to provide coverage to rural areas out of reach of last mile cable and DSL technologies.

Cellular/Mobile Implementations

Mobile broadband refers to wireless Internet access delivered through mobile phone towers to computers, mobile phones, and other digital devices using portable modems.

Mobile phones use radio waves to communicate through a nearby mobile phone tower. The mobile phone has a small radio antenna. The provider has a much larger antenna that sits at the top of a tower.

Cellular/mobile broadband access consists of various standards supporting speeds of up to 5 Mbps. Variations include 2G using GSM, CDMA, or TDMA; 3G using UMTS, CDMA2000, EDGE, or HSPA+; and 4G, using WiMAX or LTE. A mobile phone subscription does not necessarily include a mobile broadband subscription.

Three common terms that are used when discussing cellular/mobile networks include the following:

- **Wireless Internet:** A general term for Internet services from a mobile phone or from any device that uses the same technology

- **2G/3G/4G Wireless:** Major changes to the mobile phone companies' wireless networks through the evolution of the second, third, and fourth generations of wireless mobile technologies

- **Long Term Evolution (LTE):** A newer and faster technology considered to be part of 4G technology

Satellite Implementations

Satellite Internet services are used in locations where land-based Internet access is not available, or for temporary installations that are mobile. Internet access using satellites is available worldwide, including for providing Internet access to vessels at sea, airplanes in flight, and vehicles moving on land.

There are three ways to connect to the Internet using satellites:

- **One-way multicast:** Satellite Internet systems are used for IP multicast-based data, audio, and video distribution. Even though most IP protocols require two-way communication for Internet content, including web pages; one-way satellite-based Internet services can be used to push pages to local storage at end-user sites. Two-way interactivity is impossible.

- **One-way terrestrial return:** Satellite Internet systems use traditional dialup access to send outbound data through a modem and receive downloads from the satellite.

- **Two-way satellite Internet:** Sends data from remote sites via satellite to a hub, which then sends the data to the Internet. The satellite dish at each location needs precise positioning to avoid interference with other satellites.

Figure 6-14 illustrates a two-way satellite Internet system.

Upload speeds are about one-tenth of the download speed, which is in the range of 500 Kbps.

The primary installation requirement is for the antenna to have a clear view toward the equator, where most orbiting satellites are stationed. Trees and heavy rains can affect reception of the signals.

Two-way satellite Internet uses IP multicasting technology that allows one satellite to serve up to 5,000 communication channels simultaneously. IP multicast sends data from one point to many points at the same time by sending data in a compressed format. Compression reduces the size of the data and the bandwidth requirements.

Figure 6-14   Two-Way Satellite Implementation

A company can create a private WAN using satellite communications and Very Small Aperture Terminals (VSATs). A VSAT is a type of satellite dish similar to the ones used for satellite TV from the home and is usually about 1 meter in width. The VSAT dish sits outside, pointed at a specific satellite, and is cabled to a special router interface, with the router inside the building. Using VSATs creates a private WAN.

Interactive Graphic

Activity 6.2.3.3: Identify Broadband Wireless Terminology.

Go to the course online to perform this practice activity.

Selecting Broadband Solutions (6.2.4)

In this topic, we highlight some of the differences between the various broadband solutions.

Comparing Broadband Solutions (6.2.4.1)

Each broadband solution has advantages and disadvantages. The ideal is to have a fiber optic cable directly connected to the SOHO network. Some locations have only one option, such as cable or DSL. Some locations only have broadband wireless options for Internet connectivity.

If there are multiple broadband solutions available, a cost-versus-benefit analysis should be performed to determine the best solution.

Some factors to consider in making a decision include the following:

- **Cable:** Bandwidth is shared by many users, and upstream data rates are often slow.

- **DSL:** Limited bandwidth that is distance sensitive, and upstream rate is proportionally quite small compared to downstream rate.

- **Fiber-to-the-Home:** Requires fiber installation directly to the home.

- **Cellular/Mobile:** Coverage is often an issue, even within a SOHO, and bandwidth is relatively limited.

- **Wi-Fi Mesh:** Most municipalities do not have a mesh network deployed; if it is available and the SOHO is in range, it is a viable option.

- **WiMAX:** Bit rate is limited to 2 Mbps per subscriber, and cell size is 1 to 2 km (1.25 mi).

- **Satellite:** Expensive, limited capacity per subscriber; often provides access where no other access is possible.

Lab 6.2.4.2: Researching Broadband Internet Access Technologies

In this lab, you will complete the following objectives:

- Part 1: Investigate Broadband Distribution

- Part 2: Research Broadband Access Options for Specific Scenarios

Configuring xDSL Connectivity (6.3)

This section provides an example of how to configure a PPPoE broadband DSL connection.

PPPoE Overview (6.3.1)

This topic introduces PPP over Ethernet (PPPoE).

PPPoE Motivation (6.3.1.1)

In addition to understanding the various technologies available for broadband Internet access, it is also important to understand the underlying data link layer protocol used by the ISP to form a connection.

A commonly used data link layer protocol by ISPs is the Point-to-Point Protocol (PPP). PPP can be used on all serial links including those links created with dialup analog and ISDN modems. To this day, the link from a dialup user to an ISP, using analog modems, likely uses PPP. Figure 6-15 shows a basic representation of that analog dial connection with PPP.

Figure 6-15   PPP Frames over Legacy Dialup Connection

Additionally, ISPs often use PPP as the data link protocol over broadband connections. There are several reasons for this. First, PPP supports the ability to assign IP addresses to remote ends of a PPP link. With PPP enabled, ISPs can use PPP to assign each customer one public IPv4 address. More importantly, PPP supports CHAP authentication. ISPs often want to use CHAP to authenticate customers because during authentication, ISPs can check accounting records to determine whether the customer's bill is paid, prior to letting the customer connect to the Internet.

These technologies came to market in the following order, with varying support for PPP:

- Analog modems for dialup that could use PPP and CHAP

- ISDN for dialup that could use PPP and CHAP

- DSL, which did not create a point-to-point link and could not support PPP and CHAP

ISPs value PPP because of the authentication, accounting, and link management features. Customers appreciate the ease and availability of the Ethernet connection. However, Ethernet links do not natively support PPP. A solution to this problem was created, *PPP over Ethernet (PPPoE)*. As shown in Figure 6-16, PPPoE allows the sending of PPP frames encapsulated inside Ethernet frames.

Figure 6-16   PPP Frames over an Ethernet Connection (PPPoE)

PPPoE Concepts (6.3.1.2)

As shown Figure 6-17, the customer's router is usually connected to a DSL modem using an Ethernet cable.

Figure 6-17   Tunneling to Create a PPP Link over Ethernet

PPPoE creates a PPP tunnel over an Ethernet connection. This allows PPP frames to be sent across the Ethernet cable to the ISP from the customer's router. The modem converts the Ethernet frames to PPP frames by stripping the Ethernet headers. The modem then transmits these PPP frames on the ISP's DSL network.

Configuring PPPoE (6.3.2)

In this topic, a sample PPPoE configuration is examined and discussed.

PPPoE Configuration (6.3.2.1)

With the ability to send and receive PPP frames between the routers, the ISP could continue to use the same authentication model as with analog and ISDN. To make it all work, the client and ISP routers need additional configuration, including PPP configuration. To understand the configuration, consider the following:

1. To create a PPP tunnel, the configuration uses a dialer interface. A dialer interface is a virtual interface. The PPP configuration is placed on the dialer interface, not the physical interface. The dialer interface is created using the interface dialer number command. The client can configure a static IP address, but will more likely be automatically assigned a public IP address by the ISP.

2. The PPP CHAP configuration usually defines one-way authentication; therefore, the ISP authenticates the customer. The hostname and password configured on the customer router must match the hostname and password configured on the ISP router. Notice in Figure 6-18 that the CHAP username and password match the settings on the ISP router.

3. The physical Ethernet interface that connects to the DSL modem is then enabled with the command **pppoe enable** that enables PPPoE and links the physical interface to the dialer interface. The dialer interface is linked to the Ethernet interface with the **dialer pool** and **pppoe-client** commands, using the same number. The dialer interface number does not have to match the dialer pool number.

4. The *maximum transmission unit (MTU)* should be reduced to 1492, versus the default of 1500, to accommodate the PPPoE headers. The default maximum data field of an Ethernet frame is 1500 bytes. However, in PPPoE the Ethernet frame payload includes a PPP frame which also has a header. This reduces the available data MTU to 1492 bytes.

Figure 6-18   Sample PPPoE Configuration

Interactive Graphic

Activity 6.3.2.2: Configuring PPPoE

Go to the course online to use the Syntax Checker in the third graphic to enter OSPF router configuration mode on R2 and list the commands available at the prompt.

Lab 6.3.2.3: Configuring a Router as a PPPoE Client for DSL Connectivity

In this lab, you will complete the following objectives:

- Part 1: Build the Network and Configure Basic Device Settings
- Part 2: Configure and Verify OSPF Routing
- Part 3: Change Router ID Assignments
- Part 4: Configure OSPF Passive Interfaces
- Part 5: Change OSPF Metrics

Summary (6.4)

Class Activity 6.4.1.1: Telework Proposal

Your small- to medium-sized business has just been awarded a large marketing design contract. Because your office space is limited, it has been decided that it would be a good idea to hire teleworkers to help with the contract.

Therefore, a very general teleworking program must be designed for your company due to anticipation of company growth. As more contracts are awarded, you will revise and expand the program to fit your company's needs.

Develop a basic telework proposal outline for your company to consider as groundwork for a telework program.

Broadband transmission is provided by a wide range of technologies, including digital subscriber line (DSL), fiber-to-the-home, coaxial cable systems, wireless, and satellite. This transmission requires additional components at the home end and at the corporate end.

DOCSIS is a CableLabs standard that permits the addition of high-speed data transfer to an existing CATV system. The bandwidth for Internet service over a CATV line can be up to 160 Mbps downstream with the latest iteration of DOCSIS, and up to 120 Mbps upstream, simultaneously. It requires the use of a Cable Modem Termination System (CMTS) at the head-end of the cable operator and a Cable Modem (CM) on the subscriber end.

The two basic types of DSL technologies are asymmetric (ADSL) and symmetric (SDSL). ADSL provides higher downstream bandwidth to the user than upload bandwidth. SDSL provides the same capacity in both directions. DSL can provide bandwidth exceeding 40 Mbps. DSL requires the use of a DSLAM at the carrier CO and a transceiver, often built in to a home router at the customer end.

Broadband wireless solutions include municipal Wi-Fi, WiMAX, cellular/mobile, and satellite Internet. Municipal Wi-Fi mesh networks are not widely deployed. The WiMAX bit rate is limited to 2 Mbps per subscriber. Cellular/mobile coverage can be limited and bandwidth can be an issue. Satellite Internet is relatively expensive and limited, but it may be the only method to provide access.

If multiple broadband connections are available to a particular location, a cost-benefit analysis should be performed to determine the best solution. The best solution may be to connect to multiple service providers to provide redundancy and reliability.

Practice

The following activities provide practice with the topics introduced in this chapter. The labs and class activities are available in the companion *Connecting Networks Lab Manual* (978-1-58713-331-2).

Class Activities

Class Activity 6.0.1.2: Broadband Varieties

Class Activity 6.4.1.1: Telework Proposal

Labs

Lab 6.2.4.2: Researching Broadband Internet Access Technologies

Lab 6.3.2.3: Configuring a Router as a PPPoE Client for DSL Connectivity

Check Your Understanding Questions

Complete all the review questions listed here to test your understanding of the topics and concepts in this chapter. The appendix, "Answers to the 'Check Your Understanding' Questions," lists the answers.

1. A technician is attempting to explain broadband technology to a customer. Which descriptions should he use to educate the customer? (Choose two.)

   A. It includes dialup connections using POTS.

   B. It is incompatible with multiplexing.

   C. It uses a wide band frequency.

   D. It offers sustained speeds of 128 Kbps or more.

   E. It requires line-of-sight connection with the service provider.

2. When accommodating a remote teleworker, which type of connection should be used when broadband options are not available?

   A. Residential cable

   B. DSL

   C. Dialup

   D. Satellite

3. When comparing DOCSIS and Euro-DOCSIS, what is the primary difference between the two specifications?

   A. Flow-control mechanisms

   B. Maximum data rates

   C. Access methods

   D. Channel bandwidths

4. If asked to describe DSL technology, which two statements would help the user develop a better understanding of the technology? (Choose two.)

   A. ADSL can distort voice traffic, therefore a microfilter or splitter is required on phone connections.

   B. ADSL provides higher upstream bandwidth than available downstream bandwidth.

   C. ADSL transfer rates decrease as the local loop length increases.

   D. All varieties of DSL provide the same bandwidth.

   E. DSL is available in any location that has a telephone.

   F. SDSL provides higher download bandwidth than available upload bandwidth.

5. In a typical DSL installation, which devices are installed at the customer site? (Choose two.)

   A. CM

   B. DOCSIS

   C. DSLAM

   D. Microfilter or splitter

   E. DSL transceiver

6. Which two teleworking statements are true? (Choose two.)

   A. Teleworking increases usage of sick or vacation days

   B. Teleworking increases difficulty of tracking task progress

   C. Teleworking increases office expenses

   D. Teleworking requires a need to implement a new management style

   E. Teleworking results in slower customer service response times

7. What type of connection is the most cost-effective to adequately support SOHO teleworker access to the Internet?

   A. A direct T1 link to the Internet

   B. Dialup

   C. A one-way multicast satellite Internet system

   D. DSL to an ISP

8. Which wireless standard operates in both licensed and unlicensed bands of the spectrum from 2 to 6 GHz and allows for transmission rates of 70 Mbps at a range of up to 50 kilometers?

   A. 802.11b

   B. 802.11e

   C. 802.11g

   D. 802.11n

   E. 802.16

9. What do cable providers typically deploy to support high-speed transmissions of data to SOHO cable modems?

   A. 1000BASE-TX

   B. Broadband copper coaxial

   C. High-speed dialup cable modems

   D. Hybrid fiber-coaxial (HFC)

10. Which cable network communication technology is true?

   A. Code-division multiple access (CDMA) divides access by time.

   B. Frequency-division multiple access (FDMA) employs spread-spectrum technology and a special coding scheme.

   C. Synchronous CDMA (S-CDMA) adds a layer of security and noise reduction.

   D. Time-division multiple access (TDMA) divides access by frequency.

11. Which DSL statement is true?

   A. DSL is a good choice when the local loop is over 5 km (3.39 miles).

   B. DSL is faster and uses an HFC infrastructure.

   C. DSL is not a shared medium.

   D. DSL requires the use of the DOCSIS protocol.

   E. DSL upload and download speeds are always the same.

   F. Each DSL modem has a separate connection that terminates at the CMTS.

CHAPTER 7

Securing Site-to-Site Connectivity

Objectives

Upon completion of this chapter

- What are the benefits of VPN technology?

- What are site-to-site and remote-access VPNs?

- What is the purpose and benefit of GRE tunnels?

- How do you configure a site-to-site GRE tunnel?

- What are the characteristics of IPsec?

- How is IPsec implemented using the IPsec protocol framework?

- How does the AnyConnect client and clientless SSL remote-access VPN implementation support business requirements?

- How do IPsec and SSL compare to each other?

Key Terms

This chapter uses the following key terms. You can find the definitions in the glossary.

Introduction (7.0.1.1)

Security is a concern when using the public Internet to conduct business. Virtual private networks (VPNs) are used to ensure the security of data across the Internet. A VPN is used to create a private tunnel over a public network. Data can be secured by using encryption in this tunnel through the Internet and by using authentication to protect data from unauthorized access.

This chapter explains the concepts and processes related to VPNs, as well as the benefits of VPN implementations and the underlying protocols required to configure VPNs.

Class Activity 7.0.1.2: VPNs at a Glance

A small- to medium-sized business is growing and needs customers, teleworkers, and wired/wireless employees to be able to access the main network from any location. As the network administrator for the business, you have decided to implement VPNs for security, network access ease, and cost savings.

It is your job to ensure that all of the network administrators start the VPN planning process with the same knowledge set.

Four basic VPN informational areas need to be researched and presented to the network administrative team:

- Concise definition of VPNs

- Some general VPN facts

- IPsec as a VPN security option

- Ways VPNs use tunneling

VPNs (7.1)

This section examines virtual private network (VPN) technologies, types, components, functional characteristics, and benefits.

Fundamentals of VPNs (7.1.1)

This topic introduces VPNs and highlights the advantages of implementing VPN solutions.

Introducing VPNs (7.1.1.1)

Organizations need secure, reliable, and cost-effective ways to interconnect multiple networks, such as allowing branch offices and suppliers to connect to a corporation's headquarter network. Additionally, with the growing number of teleworkers, enterprises have an increasing need for secure, reliable, and cost-effective ways to connect employees working in small office/home office (SOHO) and other remote locations with resources on corporate sites.

Figure 7-1 illustrates the topologies that modern networks use to connect remote locations. In some cases, the remote locations connect only to the headquarters location; in other cases, remote locations connect to additional sites.

Figure 7-1   VPNs

Organizations use *virtual private networks (VPNs)* to create an end-to-end private network connection over third-party networks such as the Internet or extranets. The tunnel eliminates the distance barrier and enables remote users to access central site network resources. A VPN is a private network created via tunneling over a public network, usually the Internet. A VPN is a communications environment in which access is strictly controlled to permit peer connections within a defined community of interest.

The first VPNs were strictly IP tunnels that did not include authentication or encryption of the data. For example, *generic routing encapsulation (GRE)* is a tunneling protocol developed by Cisco that can encapsulate a wide variety of network layer protocol packet types inside IP tunnels. This creates a virtual point-to-point link to Cisco routers at remote points over an IP internetwork.

Today, a secure implementation of VPN with encryption, such as IPsec VPNs, is what is usually meant by virtual private networking.

To implement VPNs, a VPN gateway is necessary. The VPN gateway could be a router, a firewall, or a *Cisco Adaptive Security Appliance (ASA)*. An ASA is a standalone firewall device that combines firewall, VPN concentrator, and intrusion prevention functionality into one software image.

Benefits of VPNs (7.1.1.2)

As shown in Figure 7-2, a VPN uses virtual connections that are routed through the Internet from the private network of an organization to the remote site or employee host. The information from a private network is securely transported over the public network, to form a virtual network.

Figure 7-2 VPN Internet Connections

The benefits of a VPN include the following:

- **Cost savings:** VPNs enable organizations to use cost-effective, third-party Internet transport to connect remote offices and remote users to the main site (thus eliminating expensive, dedicated WAN links and modem banks). Furthermore, with the advent of cost-effective, high-bandwidth technologies, such as DSL, organizations can use VPNs to reduce their connectivity costs while simultaneously increasing remote connection bandwidth.

- **Scalability:** VPNs enable organizations to use the Internet infrastructure within ISPs and devices, which makes it easy to add new users. Therefore, organizations are able to add large amounts of capacity without adding significant infrastructure.

- **Compatibility with broadband technology:** VPNs allow mobile workers and telecommuters to take advantage of high-speed broadband connectivity, such as DSL and cable, to get access to their organizations' networks. Broadband connectivity provides flexibility and efficiency. High-speed broadband connections also provide a cost-effective solution for connecting remote offices.

- **Security:** VPNs can include security mechanisms that provide the highest level of security by using advanced encryption and authentication protocols that protect data from unauthorized access.

Interactive Graphic

Activity 7.1.1.3: Identify the Benefits of VPNs.

Go to the course online to perform this practice activity.

Types of VPNs (7.1.2)

This topic discusses the two types of VPNs that are commonly deployed in a modern enterprise.

There are two types of VPN networks:

- Site-to-site

- Remote access

Site-to-Site VPNs (7.1.2.1)

A site-to-site VPN is created when devices on both sides of the VPN connection are aware of the VPN configuration in advance, as shown in Figure 7-3.

Figure 7-3   Site-to-Site VPN

The VPN remains static, and internal hosts have no knowledge that a VPN exists. In a site-to-site VPN, end hosts send and receive normal TCP/IP traffic through a VPN "gateway." The VPN gateway is responsible for encapsulating and encrypting outbound traffic for all traffic from a particular site. The VPN gateway then sends it through a VPN tunnel over the Internet to a peer VPN gateway at the target site. Upon receipt, the peer VPN gateway strips the headers, decrypts the content, and relays the packet toward the target host inside its private network.

A site-to-site VPN is an extension of a classic WAN network. Site-to-site VPNs connect entire networks to each other, for example, they can connect a branch office network to a company headquarters network. In the past, a leased line or Frame Relay connection was required to connect sites, but because most corporations now have Internet access, these connections can be replaced with site-to-site VPNs.

Remote-Access VPNs (7.1.2.2)

Where a site-to-site VPN is used to connect entire networks, a remote-access VPN supports the needs of telecommuters, mobile users, and extranet, consumer-to-business traffic. A remote-access VPN is created when VPN information is not statically set up, but instead allows for dynamically changing information, and can be enabled and disabled. Remote-access VPNs support a client/server architecture, where the VPN client (remote host) gains secure access to the enterprise network via a VPN server device at the network edge.

Remote-access VPNs are used to connect individual hosts that must access their company network securely over the Internet. Internet connectivity used by telecommuters is typically a broadband, DSL, wireless, or cable connection, as indicated in Figure 7-4.

Figure 7-4   Remote-Access VPN

VPN client software may need to be installed on the mobile user's end device; for example, each host may have Cisco AnyConnect Secure Mobility Client software installed. When the host tries to send any traffic, the Cisco AnyConnect VPN Client software encapsulates and encrypts this traffic. The encrypted data is then sent over the Internet to the VPN gateway at the edge of the target network. Upon receipt, the VPN gateway behaves as it does for site-to-site VPNs.

> **Note**
>
> The Cisco AnyConnect Secure Mobility Client software builds on prior Cisco AnyConnect VPN Client and Cisco VPN Client offerings to improve the always-on VPN experience across more laptop and smartphone-based mobile devices. This client supports IPv6.

Activity 7.1.2.3: Compare Types of VPNs.

Go to the course online to perform this practice activity.

Packet Tracer Activity 7.1.2.4: Configuring VPNs (Optional)

In this activity, you will configure two routers to support a site-to-site IPsec VPN for traffic flowing from their respective LANs. The IPsec VPN traffic will pass through another router that has no knowledge of the VPN. IPsec provides secure transmission of sensitive information over unprotected networks such as the Internet. IPsec acts at the network layer, protecting and authenticating IP packets between participating IPsec devices (peers), such as Cisco routers.

Site-to-Site GRE Tunnels (7.2)

A disadvantage of IPsec VPNs is that they can only encrypt unicast traffic. To support multicast and broadcast traffic, GRE can be used to encapsulate IPsec traffic between sites. This section discusses the fundamentals of GRE and how to configure a basic GRE tunnel.

Fundamentals of Generic Routing Encapsulation (7.2.1)

This topic introduces generic routing encapsulations (GRE).

Introduction to GRE (7.2.1.1)

Generic routing encapsulation is one example of a basic, nonsecure, site-to-site VPN tunneling protocol. GRE is a tunneling protocol developed by Cisco that can encapsulate a wide variety of protocol packet types inside IP tunnels. GRE creates a virtual point-to-point link to Cisco routers at remote points over an IP internetwork.

GRE is designed to manage the transportation of multiprotocol and IP multicast traffic between two or more sites that may only have IP connectivity. It can encapsulate multiple protocol packet types inside an IP tunnel.

Figure 7-5 displays how GRE is used to encapsulate a packet.

Figure 7-5 GRE Header

As shown in the figure, a tunnel interface supports a header for each of the following:

- An encapsulated protocol (or passenger protocol), such as IPv4, IPv6, AppleTalk, DECnet, or IPX

- An encapsulation protocol (or carrier), such as GRE

- A transport delivery protocol, such as IP, which is the protocol that carries the encapsulated protocol

Characteristics of GRE (7.2.1.2)

GRE is a tunneling protocol developed by Cisco that can encapsulate a wide variety of protocol packet types inside IP tunnels, creating a virtual point-to-point link to Cisco routers at remote points over an IP internetwork. IP tunneling using GRE enables network expansion across a single-protocol backbone environment. It does this by connecting multiprotocol subnetworks in a single-protocol backbone environment.

GRE has these characteristics:

- GRE is defined as an IETF standard (RFC 2784).

- In the outer IP header, 47 is used in the protocol field to indicate that a GRE header will follow.

- GRE encapsulation uses a Protocol Type field in the GRE header to support the encapsulation of any OSI Layer 3 protocol. Protocol types are defined in RFC 1700 as "EtherTypes."

- GRE itself is stateless; by default, it does not include any flow-control mechanisms.

- GRE does not include any strong security mechanisms to protect its payload.

- The GRE header, together with the tunneling IP header indicated in Figure 7-6, creates at least 24 bytes of additional overhead for tunneled packets.

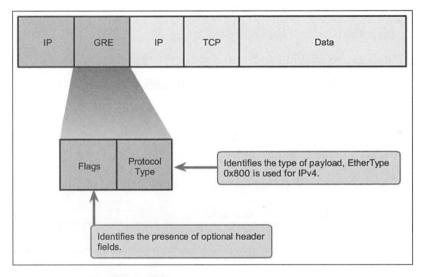

Figure 7-6   IPv4 GRE Header

Activity 7.2.1.3: Identify GRE Characteristics.

Go to the course online to perform this practice activity.

Configuring GRE Tunnels (7.2.2)

This topic explains how to configure a basic GRE tunnel.

GRE Tunnel Configuration (7.2.2.1)

GRE is used to create a VPN tunnel between two sites, as shown in Figure 7-7.

Figure 7-7 GRE Tunnel Topology

To implement a GRE tunnel, the network administrator must first identify the IP addresses of the tunnel endpoints.

There are 5 steps to configure a GRE tunnel:

Step 1. Create a tunnel interface.

Step 2. Configure an IP address for the tunnel interface.

Step 3. Specify the tunnel source IP address (or source interface).

Step 4. Specify the tunnel destination IP address.

Step 5. (Optional) Specify GRE tunnel mode as the tunnel interface mode. (GRE tunnel mode is the default).

The individual GRE tunnel command descriptions are described in Table 7-1.

Table 7-1 GRE Tunnel Commands

Command	Description
interface tunnel *x*	Creates or enters a tunnel interface
ip address *ip_address mask*	Specifies the IP address of the tunnel interface
tunnel source {*ip_address* | *interface number*}	Specifies the tunnel source IP address, in interface tunnel configuration mode
tunnel destination *ip_address*	Specifies the tunnel destination IP address, in interface tunnel configuration mode
tunnel mode gre ip	Specifies GRE tunnel mode as the tunnel interface mode, in interface tunnel configuration mode

Example 7-1 configures a GRE tunnel and enables OSPF on router R1.

Example 7-1   Configure GRE Tunnel and OSPF on R1

```
R1(config)# interface tunnel 0
*Jan  2 13:46:47.391: %LINEPROTO-5-UPDOWN: Line protocol on Interface Tunnel0,
  changed state to down
R1(config-if)# ip address 192.168.2.1 255.255.255.0
R1(config-if)# tunnel source 209.165.201.1
R1(config-if)# tunnel destination 198.133.219.87
R1(config-if)# tunnel mode gre ip
R1(config-if)# exit
R1(config)# router ospf 1
R1(config-router)# network 192.168.2.0 0.0.0.255 area 0
R1(config-router)#
```

Example 7-2 configures a similar GRE tunnel and OSPF on router R2. In this example, the serial interface is used to identify the tunnel source. The tunnel will use the IP address of the source interface.

Example 7-2   Configure GRE Tunnel and OSPF on R2

```
R2(config)# interface tunnel 0
R2(config-if)# ip address 192.168.2.2 255.255.255.0
R2(config-if)# tunnel source serial 0/0/1
R2(config-if)# tunnel destination 209.165.201.1
R2(config-if)# tunnel mode gre ip
R2(config-if)#
*Jan  2 14:14:34.155: %LINEPROTO-5-UPDOWN: Line protocol on Interface Tunnel0,
  changed state to up
R2(config-if)# exit
R2(config)# router ospf 1
R2(config-router)# network 192.168.2.0 0.0.0.255 area 0
R2(config-router)#
*Jan  2 14:14:49.707: %OSPF-5-ADJCHG: Process 1, Nbr 209.165.201.1 on Tunnel0 from
  LOADING to FULL, Loading Done
R2(config-router)#
```

Notice the IOS informational console messages verifying that the tunnel is enabled and routing is occurring over the link.

Note

When configuring GRE tunnels, it can be difficult to remember which IP networks are associated with the physical interfaces and which IP networks are associated with the tunnel interfaces. Remember that before a GRE tunnel is created, the physical interfaces have already been configured. The **tunnel source** and **tunnel destination** commands reference the IP addresses of the preconfigured physical interfaces. The **ip address** command on the tunnel interfaces refers to an IP network specifically manufactured for the purposes of the GRE tunnel.

GRE Tunnel Verification (7.2.2.2)

There are several commands that can be used to monitor and troubleshoot GRE tunnels. To determine whether the tunnel interface is up or down, use the **show ip interface brief** command. The following sample output confirms that the GRE tunnel interface on R1 is enabled:

```
R1# show ip interface brief | include up
Serial0/0/0              209.165.201.1    YES manual up              up
Tunnel0                  192.168.2.1      YES manual up              up
R1#
```

To verify the state of a GRE tunnel, use the **show interface tunnel** command. Example 7-3 confirms GRE tunnel specifics such as the tunnel status, the IP address of the tunnel, the encapsulation, tunnel source and destination addresses, and the tunnel mode.

Example 7-3   Verify the GRE Tunnel on R1

```
R1# show interfaces tunnel 0
Tunnel0 is up, line protocol is up
  Hardware is Tunnel
  Internet address is 192.168.2.1/24
  MTU 17916 bytes, BW 100 Kbit/sec, DLY 50000 usec,
     reliability 255/255, txload 1/255, rxload 1/255
  Encapsulation TUNNEL, loopback not set
  Keepalive not set
  Tunnel source 209.165.201.1, destination 198.133.219.87
  Tunnel protocol/transport GRE/IP
    Key disabled, sequencing disabled
    Checksumming of packets disabled

<Output omitted>
```

The line protocol on a GRE tunnel interface is up as long as there is a route to the tunnel destination. Before implementing a GRE tunnel, IP connectivity must already be in effect between the IP addresses of the physical interfaces on opposite ends of the potential GRE tunnel.

GRE tunnels enable broadcast (and multicast) protocols to operate between sites. In our sample configuration, OSPF has also been enabled between sites. Therefore, use the **show ip ospf neighbor** command to verify that an OSPF adjacency has been established over the tunnel interface. In the following output, the neighbor ID is the router ID of R2, the highest IP address of R2, while the OSPF neighbor peering address is the GRE tunnel IP address.

```
R1# show ip ospf neighbor

Neighbor ID      Pri   State          Dead Time   Address       Interface
198.133.219.87    0    FULL/  -       00:00:37    192.168.2.2   Tunnel0
R1#
```

Interactive Graphic

Activity 7.2.2.2: Configure and Verify GRE

Go to the course online to use the Syntax Checker in the third graphic to configure and verify a GRE tunnel on R2 followed by R1.

GRE is considered a VPN because it is a private network that is created by tunneling over a public network. Using encapsulation, a GRE tunnel creates a virtual point-to-point link to Cisco routers at remote points over an IP internetwork. The advantages of GRE are that it can be used to tunnel non-IP traffic over an IP network, allowing for network expansion by connecting multiprotocol subnetworks across a single-protocol backbone environment. GRE also supports IP multicast tunneling. This means that routing protocols can be used across the tunnel, enabling dynamic exchange of routing information in the virtual network. Finally, it is common practice to create IPv6 over IPv4 GRE tunnels, where IPv6 is the encapsulated protocol and IPv4 is the transport protocol. In the future, these roles will likely be reversed as IPv6 takes over as the standard IP protocol.

However, GRE does not provide encryption or any other security mechanisms. Therefore, data sent across a GRE tunnel is not secure. If secure data communication is needed, IPsec or SSL VPNs should be configured.

Packet Tracer Activity 7.2.2.3: Configuring GRE

In this activity, the IP addressing is already configured. You are the network administrator for a company which wants to set up a GRE tunnel to a remote office. Both networks are locally configured, and need only the tunnel configured.

Packet Tracer Activity 7.2.2.4: Troubleshooting GRE

In this activity, the IP addressing is already configured. A junior network administrator was hired to set up a GRE tunnel between two sites and was unable to complete the task. You have been asked to correct configuration errors in the company network.

Lab 7.2.2.5: Configuring a Point-to-Point GRE VPN Tunnel

In this lab, you will complete the following objectives:

- Part 1: Configure Basic Device Settings
- Part 2: Configure a GRE Tunnel
- Part 3: Enable Routing over the GRE Tunnel

Introducing IPsec (7.3)

IPsec is a protocol suite for securing IP communications that provides encryption, integrity, and authentication. This section introduces the IPsec framework and cryptographic protocols used in site-to-site VPNs.

Internet Protocol Security (7.3.1)

This topic introduces IPsec and discusses the four critical functions that it performs.

IPsec (7.3.1.1)

IPsec VPNs offer flexible and scalable connectivity. Site-to-site connections can provide a secure, fast, and reliable remote connection. With an IPsec VPN, the information from a private network is securely transported over a public network. This forms a virtual network instead of using a dedicated Layer 2 connection, as shown in Figure 7-8. To remain private, the traffic is encrypted to keep the data confidential.

IPsec is an IETF standard that defines how a VPN can be configured in a secure manner using the Internet Protocol.

IPsec is a framework of open standards that spells out the rules for secure communications. IPsec is not bound to any specific encryption, authentication, security algorithms, or keying technology. Rather, IPsec relies on existing algorithms to implement secure communications. IPsec allows newer and better algorithms to be implemented without amending the existing IPsec standards.

IPsec works at the network layer, protecting and authenticating IP packets between participating IPsec devices, also known as peers. IPsec secures a path between a pair of gateways, a pair of hosts, or a gateway and host. As a result, IPsec can protect virtually all application traffic because the protection can be implemented from Layer 4 to Layer 7.

Figure 7-8   IP Security

All implementations of IPsec have a plaintext Layer 3 header, so there are no issues with routing. IPsec functions over all Layer 2 protocols, such as Ethernet, ATM, or Frame Relay.

IPsec characteristics can be summarized as follows:

- IPsec is a framework of open standards that is algorithm independent.

- IPsec provides data confidentiality, data integrity, and origin authentication.

- IPsec acts at the network layer, protecting and authenticating IP packets.

IPsec Security Services (7.3.1.2)

IPsec security services provide four critical functions:

- **Confidentiality (encryption):** In a VPN implementation, private data travels over a public network. For this reason, data confidentiality is vital. It can be attained by encrypting the data before transmitting it across the network. This is the process of taking all the data that one computer is sending to another and encoding it into a form that only the other computer will be able to decode. If the communication is intercepted, it cannot be read by a hacker. IPsec provides enhanced security features, such as strong encryption algorithms.

- **Data integrity:** The receiver can verify that the data was transmitted through the Internet without being changed or altered in any way. While it is important that data is encrypted over a public network, it is just as important to verify that it has not been changed while in transit. IPsec has a mechanism to ensure that the encrypted portion of the packet, or the entire header and data portion of the packet, has not been changed. IPsec ensures data integrity by using checksums, which is a simple redundancy check. If tampering is detected, the packet is dropped.

- **Authentication:** Verify the identity of the source of the data that is sent. This is necessary to guard against a number of attacks that depend on spoofing the identity of the sender. Authentication ensures that the connection is made with the desired communication partner. The receiver can authenticate the source of the packet by certifying the source of the information. IPsec uses *Internet Key Exchange (IKE)* to authenticate users and devices that can carry out communication independently. IKE uses several types of authentication, including username and password, one-time password, biometrics, *pre-shared key (PSK)*, and digital certificates.

- **Anti-Replay Protection:** This is the ability to detect and reject replayed packets and helps prevent spoofing. *Anti-replay protection* verifies that each packet is unique and not duplicated. IPsec packets are protected by comparing the sequence number of the received packets with a sliding window on the destination host or security gateway. A packet that has a sequence number that is before the sliding window is considered to be late or a duplicate packet. Late and duplicate packets are dropped.

The acronym CIA is often used to help remember the first three of these functions: confidentiality, integrity, and authentication.

IPsec Framework (7.3.2)

This topic introduces the concept that IPsec is a framework of protocols interacting together to secure data between sites.

Confidentiality with Encryption (7.3.2.1)

VPN traffic is kept confidential with encryption. Plaintext data that is transported over the Internet can be intercepted and read. Encrypt the data to keep it private. Digitally encrypting the data renders it unreadable until it is unencrypted by the authorized receiver.

For encrypted communication to work, both the sender and the receiver must know the rules that are used to transform the original message into its coded form. Rules are based on algorithms and associated keys. In the context of encryption, an algorithm is a mathematical sequence of steps that combines a message, text, digits, or all three with a string of digits that are called a key. The output is an unreadable cipher string. The encryption algorithm also specifies how an encrypted message is decrypted. Decryption is extremely difficult or impossible without the correct key.

In Figure 7-9, Gail wants to send an electronic funds transfer (EFT) across the Internet to Jeremy.

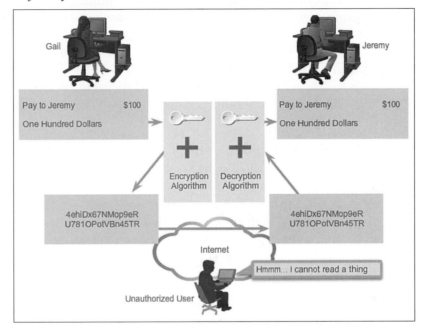

Figure 7-9   Confidentiality with Encryption

At the local end, the document is combined with a key and run through an encryption algorithm. The output is encrypted ciphertext. The ciphertext is then sent through the Internet. At the remote end, the message is recombined with a key and sent back through the encryption algorithm. The output is the original financial document.

Confidentiality is achieved through the encryption of traffic as it travels through a VPN. The degree of security depends on the key length of the encryption algorithm and the sophistication of the algorithm. If a hacker tries to hack the key through a brute-force attack, the number of possibilities to try is a function of the key length. The time to process all of the possibilities is a function of the computer power of the attacking device. The shorter the key, the easier it is to break. For example, where a relatively sophisticated computer may take approximately one year to break a 64-bit long key, the same computer may take anywhere from 10 to 19 years to decrypt a 128-bit long key.

Encryption Algorithms (7.3.2.2)

The degree of security depends on the key length of the encryption algorithm. As key length increases, it becomes more difficult to break the encryption. However, a longer key requires more processor resources when encrypting and decrypting data.

Encryption algorithms include *Data Encryption Standard (DES)* and *Triple Data Encryption Algorithm (3DES)*. DES and 3DES are no longer considered secure; therefore, it is recommended that *Advanced Encryption Standard (AES)* be used for IPsec encryption. The greatest security for IPsec encryption of VPNs between Cisco devices is provided by the 256-bit option of AES. In addition, 512-bit and 768-bit *Rivest-Shamir-Adleman (RSA)* keys have been cracked and Cisco recommends using 2048-bit keys with the RSA option, if used during the authentication phase of IKE.

Symmetric Encryption

Encryption algorithms, such as AES, require a shared secret key to perform encryption and decryption. Each of the two networking devices must know the key to decode the information. With *symmetric encryption*, also called secret-key encryption, each device encrypts the information before sending it over the network to the other device. Symmetric key encryption requires knowledge of which devices talk to each other so that the same key can be configured on each device, as depicted in Figure 7-10.

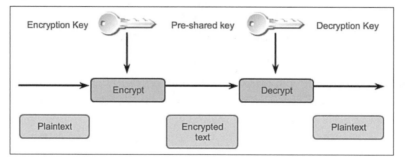

Figure 7-10 Symmetric Encryption

For example, a sender creates a coded message where each letter is substituted with the letter that is two letters down in the alphabet; *A* becomes *C*, *B* becomes *D*, and so on. In this case, the word SECRET becomes UGETGV. The sender has already told the recipient that the secret key is shift by 2. When the recipient receives the message UGETGV, the recipient computer decodes the message by shifting back two letters and calculating SECRET. Anyone else who sees the message sees only the encrypted message, which looks like nonsense, unless the person knows how it was encrypted and the secret key.

Here is a synopsis for symmetric algorithms:

- Uses symmetric key cryptography

- Encryption and decryption use the same key

- Typically used to encrypt the content of the message

- Examples: DES, 3DES, and AES

How do the encrypting and decrypting devices both have a shared secret key? One could use email, courier, or overnight express to send the shared secret keys to the administrators of the devices. Another, more secure method is asymmetric encryption.

Asymmetric Encryption

Asymmetric encryption uses different keys for encryption and decryption. Knowing one of the keys does not allow a hacker to deduce the second key and decode the information. One key encrypts the message, while a second key decrypts the message, as depicted in Figure 7-11. It is not possible to encrypt and decrypt with the same key.

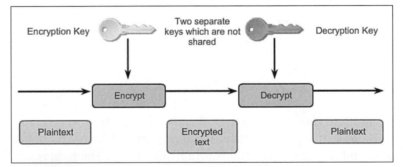

Figure 7-11   Asymmetric Encryption

Public key encryption is a variant of asymmetric encryption that uses a combination of a private key and a public key. The recipient gives a public key to any sender with whom the recipient wants to communicate. The sender uses a private key that is combined with the public key of the recipient to encrypt the message. Also, the sender must share its public key with the recipient. To decrypt a message, the recipient will use the public key of the sender with its own private key.

Here is a synopsis for asymmetric algorithms:

- Uses public key cryptography.

- Encryption and decryption use a different key.

- Typically used in digital certification and key management.

- Examples: RSA.

Diffie-Hellman Key Exchange (7.3.2.3)

Diffie-Hellman (DH) algorithm is not an encryption mechanism and is not typically used to encrypt data. Instead, it is a method to securely exchange the keys that encrypt data. (DH) algorithms allow two parties to establish a shared secret key that is used by encryption and hash algorithms.

Introduced by Whitfield Diffie and Martin Hellman in 1976, DH was the first system to utilize public key or asymmetric cryptographic keys. Today, DH is part of the IPsec standard. Also, a protocol known as OAKLEY uses a DH algorithm. OAKLEY is used by the IKE protocol, which is part of the overall framework called Internet Security Association and Key Management Protocol (ISAKMP).

Encryption algorithms such as DES, 3DES, and AES, as well as the MD5 and SHA-1 hashing algorithms require a symmetric, shared secret key to perform encryption and decryption. How do the encrypting and decrypting devices get the shared secret key? The easiest key exchange method is a public key exchange method between the encrypting and decrypting devices.

The DH algorithm specifies a public key exchange method that provides a way for two peers to establish a shared secret key that only they know, although they are communicating over an insecure channel. Like all cryptographic algorithms, DH key exchange is based on a mathematical sequence of steps.

Integrity with Hash Algorithms (7.3.2.4)

The integrity and authentication of VPN traffic is handled by hash algorithms. Hashes provide data integrity and authentication by ensuring that unauthorized persons do not tamper with transmitted messages. A hash, also called a message digest, is a number that is generated from a string of text. The hash is smaller than the text itself. It is generated by using a formula in such a way that it is extremely unlikely that some other text will produce the same hash value.

The original sender generates a hash of the message and sends it with the message itself. The recipient parses the message and the hash, produces another hash from the received message, and compares the two hashes. If they are the same, the recipient can be reasonably sure of the integrity of the original message.

In Figure 7-12, Gail sent Alex an EFT of $100. Jeremy has intercepted and altered this EFT to show himself as the recipient and the amount as $1,000. In this case, if a data integrity algorithm were used, the hashes would not match, and the transaction would be invalid.

Figure 7-12   Hash Algorithms Ensure Integrity

VPN data is transported over the public Internet. As shown, there is potential for this data to be intercepted and modified. To guard against this threat, hosts can add a hash to the message. If the transmitted hash matches the received hash, the integrity of the message has been preserved. However, if there is no match, the message was altered.

VPNs use a message authentication code to verify the integrity and the authenticity of a message, without using any additional mechanisms.

Hash-based Message Authentication Code (HMAC) is a mechanism for message authentication using hash functions. A keyed HMAC is a data integrity algorithm that guarantees the integrity of a message. An HMAC has two parameters, a message input and a secret key that is known only to the message originator and intended receivers. The message sender uses an HMAC function to produce a value (the message authentication code) that is formed by condensing the secret key and the message input. The message authentication code is sent along with the message. The receiver computes the message authentication code on the received message using the same key and HMAC function as the sender used. Then the receiver compares the result that is computed with the received message authentication code. If the two values match, the message has been correctly received and the receiver is assured that the sender is a member of the community of users that share the key. The cryptographic strength of the HMAC depends upon the cryptographic strength of the underlying hash function, on the size and quality of the key, and on the size of the hash output length in bits.

There are two common HMAC algorithms:

- **MD5 message-digest algorithm:** Uses a 128-bit shared secret key. The variable-length message and 128-bit shared secret key are combined and run through the HMAC-MD5 hash algorithm. The output is a 128-bit hash. The hash is appended to the original message and forwarded to the remote end.

- *Secure Hashing Algorithm (SHA)*: SHA-1 uses a 160-bit secret key. The variable-length message and the 160-bit shared secret key are combined and run through the HMAC-SHA1 hash algorithm. The output is a 160-bit hash. The hash is appended to the original message and forwarded to the remote end.

> **Note**
>
> Cisco IOS also supports, 256-bit, 384-bit, and 512-bit SHA implementations.

IPsec Authentication (7.3.2.5)

IPsec VPNs support authentication. When conducting business long distance, it is necessary to know who is at the other end of the phone, email, or fax. The same is true of VPN networks. The device on the other end of the VPN tunnel must be authenticated before the communication path is considered secure, as indicated in Figure 7-13.

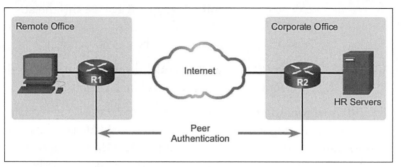

Figure 7-13   IPsec Authentication

There are two peer authentication methods:

- **PSK:** A secret key that is shared between the two parties using a secure channel before it needs to be used. Pre-shared keys (PSKs) use symmetric key cryptographic algorithms. A PSK is entered into each peer manually and is used to authenticate the peer. At each end, the PSK is combined with other information to form the authentication key.

- *RSA signatures*: Digital certificates are exchanged to authenticate peers. The local device derives a hash and encrypts it with its private key. The encrypted hash, or digital signature, is attached to the message and forwarded to the remote end. At the remote end, the encrypted hash is decrypted using the public key of the local end. If the decrypted hash matches the recomputed hash, the signature is genuine.

IPsec uses RSA (public-key cryptosystem) for authentication in the context of IKE. The RSA signature method uses a digital signature setup in which each device digitally signs a set of data and sends it to the other party. RSA signatures use a certificate authority (CA) to generate a unique-identity digital certificate that is assigned to each peer for authentication. The identity digital certificate is similar in function to a

PSK, but provides much stronger security. Each initiator and responder to an IKE session using RSA signatures sends its own ID value, its identity digital certificate, and an RSA signature value consisting of a variety of IKE values, all encrypted by the negotiated IKE encryption method (such as AES).

The Digital Signature Algorithm (DSA) is another option for authentication.

IPsec Protocol Framework (7.3.2.6)

As stated earlier, the IPsec protocol framework describes the messaging to secure the communications, but it relies on existing algorithms.

There are two main IPsec protocols:

- *Authentication Header (AH)*: As shown in Figure 7-14, AH is the appropriate protocol to use when confidentiality is not required or permitted. It provides data authentication and integrity for IP packets that are passed between two systems. However, AH does not provide data confidentiality (encryption) of packets. All text is transported in plaintext. Used alone, the AH protocol provides weak protection.

Figure 7-14   Authentication Header

- *Encapsulating Security Payload (ESP)*: A security protocol that provides confidentiality and authentication by encrypting the IP packet. IP packet encryption conceals the data and the identities of the source and destination. As shown in Figure 7-15, ESP authenticates the inner IP packet and ESP header. Authentication provides data origin authentication and data integrity. Although both encryption and authentication are optional in ESP, at a minimum, one of them must be selected.

Figure 7-15   Encapsulation Security Payload Header

There are five basic building blocks of the IPsec framework that must be selected.

- **IPsec protocol:** When configuring an IPsec gateway to provide security services, an IPsec protocol must be selected. The choices are some combination of ESP and AH. Realistically, the ESP or ESP+AH options are almost always selected because AH itself does not provide encryption.

- **Confidentiality (if IPsec is implemented with ESP):** The encryption algorithm chosen should best meet the desired level of security: DES, 3DES, or AES. AES is strongly recommended, with AES-GCM providing the greatest security.

- **Integrity:** Guarantees that the content has not been altered in transit and is implemented through the use of hash algorithms. Choices include MD5 and SHA.

- **Authentication:** Represents how devices on either end of the VPN tunnel are authenticated. The two methods are PSK or RSA.

- **DH algorithm group:** Represents how a shared secret key is established between peers. There are several options, but DH24 provides the greatest security.

Figure 7-16 identifies the choices of protocols for each building block in the IPsec framework.

Figure 7-16 IPsec Protocol Framework

It is the combination of these building blocks that provides the confidentiality, integrity, and authentication options for IPsec VPNs.

Note

This section introduced IPsec to provide an understanding of how IPsec secures VPN tunnels. Configuring IPsec VPNs is beyond the scope of this course.

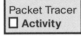

Activity 7.3.2.7: Identify IPsec Terminology and Concepts.

Go to the course online to perform this practice activity.

Packet Tracer Activity 7.3.2.8: Configuring. GRE over IPsec (Optional)

In this activity, the IP addressing is already configured. You are the network administrator for a company which wants to set up a GRE tunnel over IPsec to remote offices. All networks are locally configured, and need only the tunnel and the encryption configured.

Remote Access (7.4)

Teleworkers and travelling users demand access to corporate resources. This section introduces the two types of remote-access VPNs: IPsec and SSL based VPNs.

Remote-Access VPN Solutions (7.4.1)

This topic introduces the two types of remote-access VPNs.

Types of Remote-Access VPNs (7.4.1.1)

VPNs have become the logical solution for remote-access connectivity for many reasons. VPNs provide secure communications with access rights tailored to individual users, such as employees, contractors, and partners. As shown in Figure 7-17, remote-access VPNs also enhance productivity by extending the corporate network and applications securely while reducing communication costs and increasing flexibility.

Using VPN technology, employees can essentially take their office with them, including access to emails and network applications. VPNs can also allow contractors and partners to have limited access to the specific servers, web pages, or files required. This network access allows them to contribute to business productivity without compromising network security.

Figure 7-17 Remote Access with VPNs

There are two primary methods for deploying remote-access VPNs:

- *Secure Sockets Layer (SSL)*
- IP Security (IPsec)

The type of VPN method implemented is based on the access requirements of the users and the organization's IT processes.

Both IPsec and SSL VPN technologies offer access to virtually any network application or resource. SSL VPNs offer such features as easy connectivity from non-company-managed desktops, little or no desktop software maintenance, and user-customized web portals upon login.

Cisco SSL VPN (7.4.1.2)

Cisco IOS SSL VPN is the industry's first router-based SSL VPN solution. It offers "anywhere" connectivity not only from company-managed resource, but also from employee-owned PCs, contractor or business partner desktops, and Internet kiosks.

The SSL protocol supports various cryptographic algorithms for operations, such as authenticating the server and client to each other, transmitting certificates, and establishing session keys. Cisco SSL VPN solutions can be customized for businesses of any size. These solutions deliver many remote-access connectivity features and benefits, including the following:

- Web-based, clientless access and complete network access without preinstalled desktop software. This facilitates customized remote access based on user and security requirements, and it minimizes desktop support costs.

- Protection against viruses, worms, spyware, and hackers on a VPN connection by integrating network and endpoint security in the Cisco SSL VPN platform. This reduces cost and management complexity by eliminating the need for additional security equipment and management infrastructure.

- Use of a single device for both SSL VPN and IPsec VPN. This reduces cost and management complexity by facilitating robust remote-access and site-to-site VPN services from a single platform with unified management.

Cisco IOS SSL VPN is a technology that provides remote access by using a web browser and the web browser's native SSL encryption. Alternatively, it can provide remote access using the Cisco AnyConnect Secure Mobility Client software.

The Cisco ASA provides two main deployment modes that are found in Cisco SSL VPN solutions, as shown in Figure 7-18:

- **Cisco AnyConnect Secure Mobility Client with SSL:** Requires the Cisco AnyConnect Client

- **Cisco Secure Mobility Clientless SSL VPN:** Requires an Internet browser

Figure 7-18   Cisco SSL VPN Solutions

The Cisco ASA must be configured to support the SSL VPN connection.

Cisco SSL VPN Solutions (7.4.1.3)

Client-based SSL VPNs provide authenticated users with LAN-like full network access to corporate resources. However, the remote devices require a client application, such as the Cisco VPN Client or the newer AnyConnect client to be installed on the end-user device.

In a basic Cisco ASA configured for full tunneling and a remote-access SSL VPN solution, remote users use the Cisco AnyConnect Secure Mobility Client, shown in Figure 7-19, to establish an SSL tunnel with the Cisco ASA.

Figure 7-19 Cisco AnyConnect Secure Mobility Client

After the Cisco ASA establishes the VPN with the remote user, the remote user can forward IP traffic into the SSL tunnel. The Cisco AnyConnect Secure Mobility Client creates a virtual network interface to provide this functionality. The client can use any application to access any resource, subject to access rules, behind the Cisco ASA VPN gateway.

The clientless SSL VPN deployment model enables corporations to provide access to corporate resources even when the remote device is not corporately-managed. In this deployment model, the Cisco ASA is used as a proxy device to network resources. It provides a web portal interface for remote devices to navigate the network using port-forwarding capabilities.

In a basic Cisco ASA clientless SSL VPN solution, remote users employ a standard web browser to establish an SSL session with the Cisco ASA, as shown in Figure 7-20.

Figure 7-20   Establishing an SSL Connection with an ASA

The Cisco ASA presents the user with a web portal over which the user can access internal resources. In the basic clientless solution, the user can access only some services, such as internal web applications and browser-based file-sharing resources, as shown in Figure 7-21.

Figure 7-21   Cisco ASA Web Portal

Interactive Graphic

Activity 7.4.1.4: Compare Cisco SSL VPN Solutions.

Go to the course online to perform this practice activity.

IPsec Remote-Access VPNs (7.4.2)

This topic discusses the Cisco Easy VPN remote-access solution.

IPsec Remote Access (7.4.2.1)

Many applications require the security of an IPsec remote-access VPN connection for authentication and encryption of data. When deploying VPNs for telecommuters and small branch offices, ease of deployment is critical if technical resources are not available for VPN configuration on a remote site router.

The Cisco Easy VPN solution feature offers flexibility, scalability, and ease of use for both site-to-site and remote-access IPsec VPNs. The Cisco Easy VPN solution consists of three components:

- *Cisco Easy VPN Server*: A Cisco IOS router or Cisco ASA Firewall acting as the VPN head-end device in site-to-site or remote-access VPNs

- *Cisco Easy VPN Remote*: A Cisco IOS router or Cisco ASA Firewall acting as a remote VPN client

- *Cisco VPN Client*: An application supported on a PC used to access a Cisco VPN server

Using the Cisco Easy VPN server makes it possible for mobile and remote workers using a VPN Client on their PCs, or using Cisco Easy VPN Remote on an edge router, to create secure IPsec tunnels to access a headquarter's intranet, as shown in Figure 7-22.

Figure 7-22   Cisco Easy VPN

Cisco Easy VPN Server and Remote (7.4.2.2)

The Cisco Easy VPN Server makes it possible for mobile and remote workers using VPN Client software on their PCs to create secure IPsec tunnels to access a headquarter's intranet where critical data and applications exist. It enables Cisco IOS routers and Cisco ASA Firewalls to act as VPN headend devices in site-to-site or remote-access VPNs. Remote office devices use the Cisco Easy VPN Remote feature or the Cisco VPN Client application to connect to the server, which then pushes defined security policies to the remote VPN device. This ensures that those connections have up-to-date policies in place before the connection is established.

The Cisco Easy VPN Remote enables Cisco IOS routers or software clients to act as remote VPN clients. These devices can receive security policies from a Cisco Easy VPN Server, minimizing VPN configuration requirements at the remote location. This cost-effective solution is ideal for remote offices with little IT support or for large customer premises equipment (CPE) deployments where it is impractical to individually configure multiple remote devices.

Figure 7-23 shows three network devices with Easy VPN Remote enabled, all connecting to an Easy VPN Server for configuration parameters.

Figure 7-23   Easy VPN Remote Enabled Sites Connect to an Easy VPN Server

Cisco Easy VPN Client (7.4.2.3)

The Cisco VPN Client is a simple to use application that allows organizations to establish end-to-end encrypted VPN tunnels for secure connectivity for mobile employees or telecommuters.

To initiate an IPsec connection using the Cisco VPN client, all the user must do is open the Cisco VPN client window, as shown in Figure 7-24.

The Cisco VPN client application lists the available preconfigured sites. The user double-clicks a site to select it and the VPN client initiates the IPsec connection. In the user authentication dialog box, the user is authenticated with a username and password, as shown in Figure 7-25. After authentication, the Cisco VPN Client displays a connected status.

Figure 7-24 Cisco VPN Client Software

Figure 7-25 Connecting to an Easy VPN Server

Most of the VPN parameters are defined on the Cisco IOS Easy VPN Server to simplify deployment. After a remote client initiates a VPN tunnel connection, the Cisco Easy VPN Server pushes the IPsec policies to the client, minimizing configuration requirements at the remote location.

This simple and highly scalable solution is ideal for large remote-access deployments where it is impractical to configure policies individually for multiple remote PCs. This architecture also ensures that those connections are using up-to-date security policies and eliminates the operational costs associated with maintaining a consistent policy and key management method.

Note

Configuring the Cisco VPN client is beyond the scope of this course. Check http://www.cisco.com for more information.

Comparing IPsec and SSL (7.4.2.4)

Both IPsec and SSL VPN technologies offer access to virtually any network application or resource, as shown in Table 7-2. SSL VPNs offer such features as easy connectivity from non-company-managed desktops, little or no desktop software maintenance, and user-customized web portals upon login.

IPsec exceeds SSL in many significant ways:

- Number of applications that are supported
- Strength of encryption
- Strength of authentication
- Overall security

When security is an issue, IPsec is the superior choice. If support and ease of deployment are the primary issues, consider SSL.

IPsec and SSL VPN are complementary because they solve different problems. Depending on its needs, an organization can implement one or both. This complementary approach allows a single device such as an ISR router or an ASA firewall appliance to address all remote-access user requirements. While many solutions offer either IPsec or SSL, Cisco remote-access VPN solutions offer both technologies integrated on a single platform with unified management. Offering both IPsec and SSL technologies enables organizations to customize their remote-access VPN without any additional hardware or management complexity.

Table 7-2 highlights the differences between SSL and IPsec VPNs.

Table 7-2   Differences Between SSL and IPsec VPNs

	SSL	IPsec
Applications	Web-enabled applications, file sharing, email.	All IP-based applications.
Encryption	**Moderate to strong** Key lengths from 40 bits to 256 bits.	**Strong** Key lengths from 56 bits to 256 bits.
Authentication	**Moderate** One-way or two-way authentication.	**Strong** Two-way authentication using shared secrets or digital certificates.
Connection Complexity	**Low** Requires a web browser.	**Medium** Can be challenging to nontechnical users.
Connection Options	Any device with a browser and Internet access can connect.	Only specific devices with specific configurations can connect.

Interactive Graphic

Activity 7.4.2.5: Identify Remote-Access Characteristics.

Go to the course online to perform this practice activity.

Summary (7.5)

Class Activity 7.5.1.1: VPN Planning Design

Your small- to medium-sized business has received quite a few new contracts lately. This has increased the need for teleworkers and workload outsourcing. The new contract vendors and clients will also need access to your network as the projects progress.

As network administrator for the business, you recognize that VPNs must be incorporated as a part of your network strategy to support secure access by the teleworkers, employees, and vendors or clients.

To prepare for implementation of VPNs on the network, you devise a planning checklist to bring to the next department meeting for discussion.

Packet Tracer Activity 7.5.1.2: Skills Integration Challenge

This activity allows you to practice a variety of skills, including configuring Frame Relay, PPP with CHAP, NAT overloading (PAT), and GRE tunnels. The routers are partially configured for you.

VPNs are used to create a secure end-to-end private network connection over a third party network, such as the Internet. A site-to-site VPN uses a VPN gateway device at the edge of both sites. The end hosts are unaware of the VPN and have no additional supporting software.

A remote-access VPN requires software to be installed on the individual host device that accesses the network from a remote location. The two types of remote-access VPNs are SSL and IPsec. SSL technology can provide remote access using a client's web browser and the browser's native SSL encryption. Using Cisco AnyConnect software on the client, users can have LAN-like full network access using SSL.

GRE is a basic, nonsecure site-to-site VPN tunneling protocol that can encapsulate a wide variety of protocol packet types inside IP tunnels, thus allowing an organization to deliver other protocols through an IP-based WAN. Today it is primarily used to deliver IP multicast traffic or IPv6 traffic over an IPv4 unicast-only connection.

IPsec, an IETF standard, is a secure tunnel operating at Layer 3 of the OSI model that can protect and authenticate IP packets between IPsec peers. It can provide confidentiality by using encryption, data integrity, authentication, and anti-replay protection. Data integrity is provided by using a hash algorithm, such as MD5 or SHA. Authentication is provided by the PSK or RSA peer authentication method.

The level of confidentiality provided by encryption depends on the algorithm used and the key length. Encryption can be symmetrical or asymmetrical. DH is a method used to securely exchange the keys to encrypt data.

Practice

The following activities provide practice with the topics introduced in this chapter. The labs and class activities are available in the companion *Connecting Networks Lab Manual* (978-1-58713-331-2). The Packet Tracer activity PKA files are found in the online course.

Class Activities

Class Activity 7.0.1.2: VPNs at a Glance

Class Activity 7.5.1.1: VPN Planning Design

Labs

Lab 7.2.2.5: Configuring a Point-to-Point GRE VPN Tunnel

Packet Tracer
☐ Activity

Packet Tracer Activities

Packet Tracer Activity 7.1.2.4: Configuring VPNs (Optional)

Packet Tracer Activity 7.2.2.3: Configuring GRE

Packet Tracer Activity 7.2.2.4: Troubleshooting GRE

Packet Tracer Activity 7.3.2.8: Configuring. GRE over IPsec (Optional)

Packet Tracer Activity 7.5.1.2: Skills Integration Challenge

Check Your Understanding Questions

Complete all the review questions listed here to test your understanding of the topics and concepts in this chapter. The appendix, "Answers to the 'Check Your Understanding' Questions," lists the answers.

1. Which techniques can be used to secure the traffic sent over an IPsec VPN connection? (Choose two.)

    A. Data labeling, used to mark and separate the VPN traffic to different customers

    B. Data encapsulation, used to transmit data transparently from network to network through a shared network infrastructure

    C. Data encryption, used to code data into a different format using a secret key

    D. Use of a second routing protocol to transport the traffic over the VPN tunnel

    E. Use of a dedicated connection over the company private leased line

2. Which of the following network security statements are true?

   A. Authentication prevents tampering and alterations to data while data travels between the source and destination.

   B. Data integrity ensures that the communicating peers are who they say they are.

   C. Data integrity is the use of passwords, digital certificates, smart cards, and biometrics.

   D. Encryption protects the contents of messages from interception by unauthenticated or unauthorized sources.

3. Which is an example of a tunneling protocol developed by Cisco?

   A. AES

   B. DES

   C. ESP

   D. GRE

   E. RSA

4. What two components does a teleworker require to establish a secure connection to a corporate site? (Choose two.)

   A. ASA security appliance

   B. Authentication server

   C. Broadband Internet connection

   D. VPN server or concentrator

   E. VPN client software or VPN-enabled router

5. A sales agent connecting to the company network using a browser on a hotel computer and an employee connecting from home using VPN client software are examples of which type of network?

   A. GRE VPNs

   B. Layer 2 VPNs

   C. Remote-access VPNs

   D. Site-to-site IPsec VPNs

   E. Site-to-site SSL VPNs

6. Which statement regarding site-to-site VPNs is true?

   A. Individual hosts can enable and disable the VPN connection.

   B. Internal hosts send normal unencapsulated packets.

   C. The VPN connection is not statically defined.

   D. VPN client software is installed on each host.

7. Which Cisco remote-access VPN solution allows remote users access using a browser and Internet connection?

A. Clientless SSL VPN

B. Client-based SSL VPN

C. SSL

D. IPsec

8. Which of the following ensures that the data has not changed while in transit?

A. Authentication protocols

B. Diffie-Hellman (DH) algorithms

C. Encryption protocols

D. Message hashes

9. Which of the following allow two parties to establish a shared secret key that is used by encryption and hash algorithms?

A. Authentication protocols

B. Diffie-Hellman (DH) algorithms

C. Encryption protocols

D. Message hashes

10. Which two of the following would provide message confidentiality? (Choose two.)

A. 3DES

B. AES

C. Diffie-Hellman (DH) algorithms

D. MD5

E. SHA

11. Which two of the following would provide message integrity? (Choose two.)

A. 3DES

B. AES

C. Diffie-Hellman (DH) algorithms

D. MD5

E. SHA

CHAPTER 8

Monitoring the Network

Objectives

Upon completion of this chapter

- How can you explain syslog operation?

- How do you configure syslog to compile messages on a small- to medium-sized business network management device?

- How can you explain SNMP operation?

- How do you configure SNMP to compile messages on a small- to medium-sized business network?

- How can you describe NetFlow operation?

- How do you configure NetFlow to monitor traffic on a small- to medium-sized business network?

- How is NetFlow data used to examine traffic patterns?

Key Terms

This chapter uses the following key terms. You can find the definitions in the glossary.

Introduction (8.0.1.1)

Monitoring an operational network can provide a network administrator with information to proactively manage the network and to report network usage statistics to others. Link activity, error rates, and link status are a few of the factors that help a network administrator determine the health and usage of a network. Collecting and reviewing this information over time enables a network administrator to see and project growth and may enable the administrator to detect and replace a failing part before it completely fails.

This chapter covers three protocols that a network administrator can use to monitor the network. Syslog, SNMP, and NetFlow are popular protocols with different strengths and weaknesses. Together, they provide a good toolset for understanding what is happening on a network. The *Network Time Protocol* (NTP) is used to synchronize time across devices, which is especially important when trying to compare log files from different devices.

Class Activity 8.0.1.2: Network Maintenance Development

Currently, there are no formal policies or procedures for recording problems experienced on your company's network. Furthermore, when network problems occur, you must try many methods to find the causes, and this approach takes time.

You know there must be a better way to resolve these issues. You decide to create a network maintenance plan to keep repair records and pinpoint the causes of errors on the network.

Syslog (8.1)

Syslog is a standard, well-known protocol for logging computer and network device messages.

Syslog Operation (8.1.1)

Syslog is used on network devices, servers, and other devices that require event monitoring of any events that occur on those devices. Various applications can be used to display these messages and if necessary alert the network administrator.

Introduction to Syslog (8.1.1.1)

When certain events occur on a network, networking devices have trusted mechanisms to notify the administrator with detailed system messages. These messages can be either noncritical or significant. Network administrators have a variety of options for storing, interpreting, and displaying these messages, and for being alerted to those messages that could have the greatest impact on the network infrastructure.

The most common method of accessing system messages that networking devices provide is to use a protocol called *syslog*.

Syslog is a term used to describe a standard. It is also used to describe the protocol developed for that standard. The syslog protocol was developed for UNIX systems in the 1980s, but was first documented as RFC 3164 by IETF in 2001. Syslog uses UDP port 514 to send event notification messages across IP networks to event message collectors, as illustrated in Figure 8-1.

Many networking devices support syslog, including routers, switches, application servers, firewalls, and other network appliances. As shown in Figure 8-1, the syslog protocol allows networking devices to send their system messages across the network to syslog servers. It is possible to build a special out-of-band (OOB) network for this purpose.

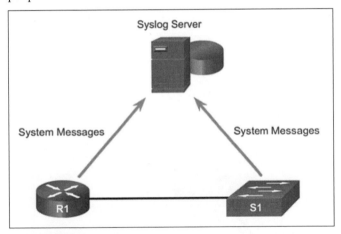

Figure 8-1   Syslog

There are several different syslog server software packages for Windows and UNIX. Many of them are freeware.

The syslog logging service provides three primary functions:

1. The ability to gather logging information for monitoring and troubleshooting

2. The ability to select the type of logging information that is captured

3. The ability to specify the destinations of captured syslog messages

Syslog Operation (8.1.1.2)

On Cisco network devices, the syslog protocol starts by sending system messages and **debug** output to a local logging process internal to the device. How the logging process manages these messages and outputs is based on device configurations. For example, syslog messages may be sent across the network to an external syslog server. These messages can be retrieved without the need for accessing the actual device. Log messages and outputs stored on the external server can be pulled into various reports for easier reading.

Alternatively, syslog messages may be sent to an internal buffer. Messages sent to the internal buffer are only viewable through the CLI of the device.

Finally, the network administrator may specify that only certain types of system messages are sent to various destinations. For example, the device may be configured to forward all system messages to an external syslog server. However, debug-level messages are forwarded to the internal buffer and are only accessible by the administrator from the CLI.

As shown in Figure 8-2, popular destinations for syslog messages include the following:

- Logging buffer (RAM inside a router or switch)

- Console line

- Terminal line

- Syslog server

Figure 8-2   Syslog Destination Message Options

It is possible to remotely monitor system messages by viewing the logs on a syslog server, or by accessing the device through Telnet, SSH, or through the console port.

Syslog Message Format (8.1.1.3)

Cisco devices produce syslog messages as a result of network events. Every syslog message contains a severity level and a facility.

The smaller numerical levels are the more critical syslog alarms. The severity level of the messages can be set to control where each type of message is displayed (that is, on the console or the other destinations). The complete list of syslog levels is shown in Table 8-1.

Table 8-1 Syslog Severity Level

Severity Name	Severity Level	Explanation
Emergency	Level 0	System unusable
Alert	Level 1	Immediate action needed
Critical	Level 2	Critical condition
Error	Level 3	Error condition
Warning	Level 4	Warning condition
Notification	Level 5	Normal but significant condition
Informational	Level 6	Informational message
Debugging	Level 7	Debugging message

Each syslog level has its own meaning:

- **Warning level - emergency level:** These messages are error messages about software or hardware malfunctions; these types of messages mean that the functionality of the device is affected. The severity of the issue determines the actual syslog level applied.

- **Debugging level:** This level indicates that the messages are output generated from issuing various **debug** commands.

- **Notification Level:** The notification level is only for information; device functionality is not affected. Interface up or down transitions and system restart messages are displayed at the notification level.

In addition to specifying the severity, syslog messages also contain information on the facility. Syslog facilities are service identifiers that identify and categorize system state data for error and event message reporting. The logging facility options that are available are specific to the networking device. For example, Cisco 2960 series switches running Cisco IOS Release 15.0(2) and Cisco 1941 routers running Cisco IOS Release 15.2(4) support 24 facility options that are categorized into 12 facility types.

Some common syslog message facilities reported on Cisco IOS routers include the following:

- IP
- OSPF protocol
- SYS operating system
- IP security (IPsec)
- Interface IP (IF)

By default, the format of syslog messages on the Cisco IOS Software is as follows:

```
seq no: timestamp: %facility-severity-MNEMONIC: description
```

The fields contained in the Cisco IOS Software syslog message are explained in Table 8-2.

Table 8-2   Syslog Message Format

Field	Explanation
seq no	Stamps log messages with a sequence number only if the **service sequence-numbers** global configuration command is configured
Timestamp	Date and time of the message or event, which appears only if the **service timestamps** global configuration command is configured
Facility	The facility to which the message refers
Severity	Single-digit code from 0 to 7 that is the severity of the message
MNEMONIC	Text string that uniquely describes the message
Description	Text string containing detailed information about the event being reported

For example, sample output on a Cisco switch for an EtherChannel link changing state to up is as follows:

```
00:00:46: %LINK-3-UPDOWN: Interface Port-channel1, changed state to up
```

Here the facility is LINK, and the severity level is 3, with a mnemonic of UPDOWN.

The most common messages are link up and down messages, and messages that a device produces when it exits from configuration mode. If ACL logging is configured, the device generates syslog messages when packets match a parameter condition.

Service Timestamp (8.1.1.4)

Log messages can be time-stamped and the source address of syslog messages can be set. This enhances real-time debugging and management.

When the **service timestamps log uptime** global configuration mode command is entered, the amount of time since the switch last booted is displayed on logged events. A more useful version of this command applies the **datetime** keyword in place of the **uptime** keyword; this forces each logged event to display the date and time associated with the event.

When using the **datetime** keyword, the clock on the networking device must be set. This can be accomplished in one of two ways:

1. Manually set, using the **clock set** command

2. Automatically set, using the Network Time Protocol (NTP)

Recall that NTP is a protocol that is used to allow network devices to synchronize their time settings with an NTP server.

To allow the software clock to be synchronized by an NTP time server, use the **ntp server** *ip-address* command in global configuration mode. A sample topology is shown in Figure 8-3. In Example 8-1, R1 is configured as an NTP client, while router R2 serves as an authoritative NTP server. A network device can be configured as either an NTP server, thereby allowing other devices to synchronize off of its time, or as an NTP client.

Figure 8-3   NTP Topology

Example 8-1   Configuring NTP

```
R2(config)# ntp master 1
R2(config)# ntp server 10.1.1.1
```

For the remainder of the chapter, it is assumed that the clock has been set and that the **service timestamps log datetime** command has been configured on all devices.

Activity 8.1.1.5: Interpret Syslog Output.

Go to the course online to perform this practice activity.

Configuring Syslog (8.1.2)

To use the basic functionality of syslog, most syslog server applications require very little configuration.

Syslog Server (8.1.2.1)

To view syslog messages, a *syslog server* must be installed on a workstation in the network. There are several freeware and shareware versions of syslog, as well as enterprise versions for purchase. In Figure 8-4, an evaluation version of the Kiwi Syslog Daemon is displayed on a Windows 7 machine.

Figure 8-4 Kiwi Syslog Server

The syslog server provides a relatively user-friendly interface for viewing syslog output. The server parses the output and places the messages into predefined columns for easy interpretation. If timestamps are configured on the networking device sourcing the syslog messages, then the date and time of each message displays in the syslog server output, as shown in Figure 8-5.

Figure 8-5   Syslog Message Displayed on Syslog Server

Network administrators can easily navigate the large amount of data compiled on a syslog server. One advantage of viewing syslog messages on a syslog server is the ability to perform granular searches through the data. Also, a network administrator can quickly delete unimportant syslog messages from the database.

Default Logging (8.1.2.2)

By default, Cisco routers and switches send log messages for all severity levels to the console. On some IOS versions, the device also buffers log messages by default. To enable these two settings, use the **logging console** and **logging buffered** global configuration commands, respectively.

The **show logging** command displays the default logging service settings on a Cisco router, as shown in Example 8-2. The first lines of output list information about the logging process, with the end of the output listing log messages.

Example 8-2   Default Logging Service Settings

```
R1# show logging
Syslog logging: enabled (0 messages dropped, 2 messages rate-limited, 0 flushes, 0
  overruns, xml disabled, filtering disabled)
No Active Message Discriminator.
No Inactive Message Discriminator.
    Console logging: level debugging, 32 messages logged, xml disabled,
                    filtering disabled
    Monitor logging: level debugging, 0 messages logged, xml disabled,
                    filtering disabled
    Buffer logging: level debugging, 32 messages logged, xml disabled,
                    filtering disabled
    Exception Logging: size (4096 bytes)
```

```
        Count and timestamp logging messages: disabled
        Persistent logging: disabled
No active filter modules.
    Trap logging: level informational, 34 message lines logged
        Logging Source-Interface:       VRF Name:
Log Buffer (8192 bytes):
*Jan  2 00:00:02.527: %LICENSE-6-EULA_ACCEPT_ALL: The Right to Use End User License
  Agreement is accepted
*Jan  2 00:00:02.631: %IOS_LICENSE_IMAGE_APPLICATION-6-LICENSE_LEVEL: Module name =
  c1900 Next reboot level = ipbasek9 and License = ipbasek9
*Jan  2 00:00:02.851: %IOS_LICENSE_IMAGE_APPLICATION-6-LICENSE_LEVEL: Module name =
  c1900 Next reboot level = securityk9 and License = securityk9
*Jun 12 17:46:01.619: %IFMGR-7-NO_IFINDEX_FILE: Unable to open nvram:/ifIndex-table No
  such file or directory
<output omitted>
```

The first highlighted line states that this router logs to the console and includes debug messages. This actually means that all debug level messages, as well as any lower level messages (such as notification level messages), are logged to the console. The output also notes that 32 such messages have been logged.

The second highlighted line states that this router logs to an internal buffer. Because this router has enabled logging to an internal buffer, the **show logging** command also lists the messages in that buffer. You can view some of the system messages that have been logged at the end of the output.

Router and Switch Commands for Syslog Clients (8.1.2.3)

There are three steps to configuring the router to send system messages to a syslog server where they can be stored, filtered, and analyzed:

Step 1.   Configure the destination hostname or IP address of the syslog server in global configuration mode:

```
R1(config)# logging 192.168.1.3
```

Step 2.   Control the messages that will be sent to the syslog server with the **logging trap** *level* global configuration mode command. For example, to limit the messages to levels 4 and lower (0 to 4), use one of the two equivalent commands:

```
R1(config)# logging trap 4
R1(config)# logging trap warning
```

Step 3. Optionally, configure the source interface with the **logging source-interface** *interface-type interface number* global configuration mode command. This specifies that syslog packets contain the IPv4 or IPv6 address of a specific interface, regardless of which interface the packet uses to exit the router. For example, to set the source interface to g0/0, use the following command:

```
R1(config)# logging source-interface g0/0
```

In Example 8-3, R1 is configured to send log messages of levels 4 and lower to the syslog server at 192.168.1.3. The source interface is set as the G0/0 interface. A loopback interface is created, then shut down, and then brought back up. The console output reflects these actions.

Example 8-3   Syslog Configuration

```
R1(config)# logging 192.168.1.3
R1(config)# logging trap 4
R1(config)# logging source-interface gigabitEthernet 0/0
R1(config)# interface loopback 0
R1(config-if)#
*Jun 12 22:06:02.902: %LINK-3-UPDOWN: Interface Loopback0, changed state to up
*Jun 12 22:06:03.902: %LINEPROTO-5-UPDOWN: Line protocol on Interface Loopback0,
  changed state to up
*Jun 12 22:06:03.902: %SYS-6-LOGGINGHOST_STARTSTOP: Logging to host 192.168.1.3 port
  514 started - CLI initiated
R1(config-if)# shutdown
R1(config-if)#
*Jun 12 22:06:49.642: %LINK-5-CHANGED: Interface Loopback0, changed state to
  administratively down
*Jun 12 22:06:50.642: %LINEPROTO-5-UPDOWN: Line protocol on Interface Loopback0,
  changed state to down
R1(config-if)# no shutdown
R1(config-if)#
*Jun 12 22:09:18.210: %LINK-3-UPDOWN: Interface Loopback0, changed state to up
*Jun 12 22:09:19.210: %LINEPROTO-5-UPDOWN: Line protocol on Interface Loopback0,
  changed state to up
R1(config-if)#
```

Shown in Figure 8-6, the Tftpd32 syslog server has been set up on a Windows 7 machine with IP address 192.168.1.3. As you can see, the only messages that appear on the syslog server are those with severity level of 4 or lower (more severe). The messages with severity level of 5 or higher (less severe) appear on the router console output, but do not appear on the syslog server output, because the **logging trap** limits the syslog messages sent to the syslog server based on severity.

Figure 8-6   Syslog Server Output

Verifying Syslog (8.1.2.4)

You can use the **show logging** command to view any messages that are logged. When the logging buffer is large, it is helpful to use the pipe option (|) with the **show logging** command. The pipe option allows the administrator to specifically state which messages should be displayed.

For example, issuing the **show logging | include changed state to up** command, as shown in Example 8-4, ensures that only interface notifications stating that the interface has "changed to state up" will be displayed.

Example 8-3   Syslog Configuration

```
R1# show logging | include changed state to up
*Jun 12 17:46:26.143: %LINK-3-UPDOWN: Interface GigabitEthernet0/1, changed state to
  up
*Jun 12 17:46:26.143: %LINK-3-UPDOWN: Interface Serial0/0/1, changed state to up
*Jun 12 17:46:27.263: %LINEPROTO-5-UPDOWN: Line protocol on Interface
  GigabitEthernet0/1, changed state to up
*Jun 12 17:46:27.263: %LINEPROTO-5-UPDOWN: Line protocol on Interface Serial0/0/1,
  changed state to up
*Jun 12 20:28:43.427: %LINK-3-UPDOWN: Interface GigabitEthernet0/0, changed state to
  up
*Jun 12 20:28:44.427: %LINEPROTO-5-UPDOWN: Line protocol on Interface
  GigabitEthernet0/0, changed state to up
*Jun 12 22:04:11.862: %LINEPROTO-5-UPDOWN: Line protocol on Interface Loopback0,
  changed state to up
*Jun 12 22:06:02.902: %LINK-3-UPDOWN: Interface Loopback0, changed state to up
*Jun 12 22:06:03.902: %LINEPROTO-5-UPDOWN: Line protocol on Interface Loopback0,
```

```
                     changed state to up
*Jun 12 22:09:18.210: %LINK-3-UPDOWN: Interface Loopback0, changed state to up
*Jun 12 22:09:19.210: %LINEPROTO-5-UPDOWN: Line protocol on Interface Loopback0,
  changed state to up
*Jun 12 22:35:55.926: %LINK-3-UPDOWN: Interface Loopback0, changed state to up
*Jun 12 22:35:56.926: %LINEPROTO-5-UPDOWN: Line protocol on Interface Loopback0,
  changed state to up
R1# show logging | begin Jun 12 22:35
*Jun 12 22:35:46.206: %LINK-5-CHANGED: Interface Loopback0, changed state to
  administratively down
*Jun 12 22:35:47.206: %LINEPROTO-5-UPDOWN: Line protocol on Interface Loopback0,
  changed state to down
*Jun 12 22:35:55.926: %LINK-3-UPDOWN: Interface Loopback0, changed state to up
*Jun 12 22:35:56.926: %LINEPROTO-5-UPDOWN: Line protocol on Interface Loopback0,
  changed state to up
*Jun 12 22:49:52.122: %SYS-5-CONFIG_I: Configured from console by console
*Jun 12 23:15:48.418: %SYS-5-CONFIG_I: Configured from console by console
R1#
```

Also shown in Example 8-4, issuing the **show logging | begin June 12 22:35** command displays the contents of the logging buffer that occurred on or after June 12.

Activity 8.1.2.4: Configuring and Verifying Syslog

Go to the course online to use the Syntax Checker to configure and verify the syslog on R1.

Packet Tracer Activity 8.1.2.5: Configuring Syslog and NTP

In this activity, you will enable and use the Syslog service and the NTP service so that the network administrator is able to monitor the network more effectively.

Lab 8.1.2.6: Configuring Syslog and NTP

In this lab, you will complete the following objectives:

- Part 1: Configure Basic Device Settings
- Part 2: Configure NTP
- Part 3: Configure Syslog

SNMP (8.2)

Simple Network Management (SNMP) is a standard, well-known protocol for managing devices on IP networks.

SNMP Operation (8.2.1)

SNMP operations are configured on SNMP servers and agents using Management Information Base (MIB) variables used to store information about devices.

Introduction to SNMP (8.2.1.1)

SNMP was developed to allow administrators to manage nodes, such as servers, workstations, routers, switches, and security appliances, on an IP network. It enables network administrators to manage network performance, find and solve network problems, and plan for network growth.

SNMP is an application layer protocol that provides a message format for communication between managers and agents. The SNMP system consists of three elements:

1. *SNMP manager*

2. *SNMP agents* (managed node)

3. *Management Information Base (MIB)*

To configure SNMP on a networking device, it is first necessary to define the relationship between the manager and the agent.

The SNMP manager is part of a network management system (NMS). The SNMP manager runs SNMP management software. As shown in Figure 8-7, the SNMP manager can collect information from an SNMP agent using the "get" action and can change configurations on an agent using the "set" action. In addition, SNMP agents can forward information directly to an NMS using "traps."

The SNMP agent and MIB reside on networking device clients. Network devices that must be managed, such as switches, routers, servers, firewalls, and workstations, are equipped with an SMNP agent software module. MIBs store data about the device operation and are meant to be available to authenticated remote users. The SNMP agent is responsible for providing access to the local MIB of objects that reflects resources and activity.

SNMP defines how management information is exchanged between network management applications and management agents. SNMP uses UDP, port number 162, to retrieve and send management information.

Figure 8-7   Simple Network Management Protocol

SNMP Operation (8.2.1.2)

SNMP agents that reside on managed devices collect and store information about the device and its operation. This information is stored by the agent locally in the MIB. The SNMP manager then uses the SNMP agent to access information within the MIB.

There are two primary SNMP manager requests, get and set. A get request is used by the NMS to query the device for data. A set request is used by the NMS to change configuration variables in the agent device. A set request can also initiate actions within a device. For example, a set can cause a router to reboot, send a configuration file, or receive a configuration file. The SNMP manager uses the get and set actions to perform the operations described in Table 8-3.

Table 8-3   Syslog Message Format

Operation	Description
get-request	Retrieves a value from a specific variable.
get-next-request	Retrieves a value from a variable within a table. The SNMP manager does not need to know the exact variable name; a sequential search is performed to find the needed variable from within a table.

Operation	Description
get-bulk-request	Retrieves large blocks of data, such as multiple rows in a table, that would otherwise require the transmission of many small blocks of data; only works with SNMPv2 or later.
get-response	Replies to a get-request, get-next-request, and set-request sent by an NMS.
set-request	Stores a value in a specific variable.

The SNMP agent responds to SNMP manager requests as follows:

- **Get an MIB variable:** The SNMP agent performs this function in response to a GetRequest-PDU from the NMS. The agent retrieves the value of the requested MIB variable and responds to the NMS with that value.

- **Set an MIB variable:** The SNMP agent performs this function in response to a SetRequest-PDU from the NMS. The SNMP agent changes the value of the MIB variable to the value specified by the NMS. An SNMP agent reply to a set request includes the new settings in the device.

Figure 8-8 illustrates the use of an SNMP GetRequest to determine if interface G0/0 is up/up.

Figure 8-8   SNMP Get Request

SNMP Agent Traps (8.2.1.3)

An NMS periodically polls the SNMP agents residing on managed devices, by querying the device for data using the get request. Using this process, a network management application can collect information to monitor traffic loads and to verify device configurations of managed devices. The information can be displayed via GUI on the NMS. Averages, minimums, or maximums can be calculated, the data can be graphed, or thresholds can be set to trigger a notification process when the thresholds are exceeded. For example, an NMS can monitor CPU utilization of a Cisco router. The SNMP manager samples the value periodically and presents this information in a graph for the network administrator to use in creating a baseline.

Periodic SNMP polling does have disadvantages. First, there is a delay between the time that an event occurs and the time that it is noticed (via polling) by the NMS. Second, there is a trade-off between polling frequency and bandwidth usage.

To mitigate these disadvantages, it is possible for SNMP agents to generate and send traps to inform the NMS immediately of certain events. Traps are unsolicited messages alerting the SNMP manager to a condition or event on the network. Examples of trap conditions include, but are not limited to, improper user authentication, restarts, link status (up or down), MAC address tracking, closing of a TCP connection, loss of connection to a neighbor, or other significant events. Trap-directed notifications reduce network and agent resources, by eliminating the need for some of the SNMP polling requests.

Figure 8-9 illustrates the use of an SNMP trap to alert the network administrator that interface G0/0 has failed. The NMS software can send the network administrator a text message, pop up a window on the NMS software, or turn the router icon red in the NMS GUI.

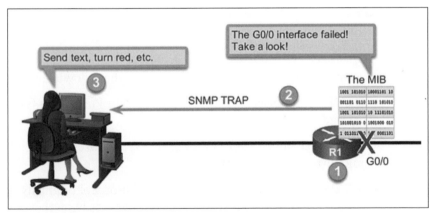

Figure 8-9 SNMP Trap

The exchange of all SNMP messages is illustrated in Figure 8-10.

Figure 8-10   SNMP Operations

SNMP Versions (8.2.1.4)

There are several versions of SNMP, including the following:

- **SNMPv1:** The Simple Network Management Protocol, a full Internet standard, defined in RFC 1157.

- **SNMPv2c:** Defined in RFCs 1901 to 1908; utilizes community-string-based administrative framework.

- **SNMPv3:** Interoperable standards-based protocol originally defined in RFCs 2273 to 2275; provides secure access to devices by authenticating and encrypting packets over the network. It includes these security features: message integrity to ensure that a packet was not tampered with in transit, authentication to determine that the message is from a valid source, and encryption to prevent the contents of a message from being read by an unauthorized source.

All versions use SNMP managers, agents, and MIBs. Cisco IOS Software supports the above three versions. Version 1 is a legacy solution and not often encountered in networks today; therefore, this course focuses on Versions 2c and 3.

Both SNMPv1 and SNMPv2c use a community-based form of security. The community of managers able to access the agent's MIB is defined by an ACL and password.

Unlike SNMPv1, SNMPv2c includes a bulk retrieval mechanism and more detailed error message reporting to management stations. The bulk retrieval mechanism retrieves tables and large quantities of information, minimizing the number of round trips required. The SNMPv2c improved error-handling includes expanded error codes that distinguish different kinds of error conditions. These conditions are reported through a single error code in SNMPv1. Error return codes in SNMPv2c include the error type.

Note

SNMPv1 and SNMPv2c offer minimal security features. Specifically, SNMPv1 and SNMPv2c can neither authenticate the source of a management message nor provide encryption. SNMPv3 is most currently described in RFCs 3410 to 3415. It adds methods to ensure the secure transmission of critical data between managed devices.

SNMPv3 provides for both security models and security levels. A security model is an authentication strategy set up for a user and the group within which the user resides. A security level is the permitted level of security within a security model. A combination of the security level and the security model determine which security mechanism is used when handling an SNMP packet. Available security models are SNMPv1, SNMPv2c, and SNMPv3.

Table 8-4 identifies the characteristics of the different combinations of security models and levels.

Table 8-4   SNMP Security Models and Levels

Model	Level	Authentication	Encryption	Result
SNMPv1	noAuthNoPriv	Community string	No	Uses a community string match for authentication
SNMPv2c	noAuthNoPriv	Community string	No	Uses a community string match for authentication
SNMPv3	noAuthNoPriv	Username	No	Uses a username match for authentication (an improvement over SNMPv2c)
SNMPv3	authNoPriv	Message digest 5 (MD5) or Secure Hash Algorithm (SHA)	No	Provides authentication based on the HMAC-MD5 or HMAC-SHA algorithms

Model	Level	Authentication	Encryption	Result
SNMPv3	authPriv (Requires the cryptographic software image)	MD5 or SHA	Data Encryption Standard (DES) or Advanced Encryption Standard (AES)	Provides authentication based on the HMAC-MD5 or HMAC-SHA algorithms. Allows specifying the User-based Security Model (USM) with these encryption algorithms: ■ DES 56-bit encryption in addition to authentication based on the CBC-DES (DES-56) standard. ■ 3DES 168-bit encryption ■ AES 128-bit, 192-bit, or 256-bit encryption

A network administrator must configure the SNMP agent to use the SNMP version supported by the management station. Because an agent can communicate with multiple SNMP managers, it is possible to configure the software to support communications using SNMPv1, SNMPv2c, or SNMPv3.

Community Strings (8.2.1.5)

For SNMP to operate, the NMS must have access to the MIB. To ensure that access requests are valid, some form of authentication must be in place.

SNMPv1 and SNMPv2c use *community strings* that control access to the MIB. Community strings are plaintext passwords. SNMP community strings authenticate access to MIB objects.

There are two types of community strings:

- **Read-only (ro):** Provides access to the MIB variables, but does not allow these variables to be changed, only read. Because security is minimal in Version 2c, many organizations use SNMPv2c in read-only mode.

- **Read-write (rw):** Provides read and write access to all objects in the MIB.

To view or set MIB variables, the user must specify the appropriate community string for read or write access.

Note

Plaintext passwords are not considered a security mechanism. This is because plaintext passwords are highly vulnerable to man-in-the-middle attacks, in which they are compromised through the capture of packets.

Management Information Base Object ID (8.2.1.6)

The MIB organizes variables hierarchically. MIB variables enable the management software to monitor and control the network device. Formally, the MIB defines each variable as an object ID (OID). OIDs uniquely identify managed objects in the MIB hierarchy. The MIB organizes the OIDs based on RFC standards into a hierarchy of OIDs, usually shown as a tree.

The MIB tree for any given device includes some branches with variables common to many networking devices and some branches with variables specific to that device or vendor.

RFCs define some common public variables. Most devices implement these MIB variables. In addition, networking equipment vendors, like Cisco, can define their own private branches of the tree to accommodate new variables specific to their devices. Figure 8-11 shows portions of the MIB structure defined by Cisco Systems, Inc. Note how the OID can be described in words or numbers to help locate a particular variable in the tree. OIDs belonging to Cisco, as shown in Figure 8-11, are numbered as follows: .iso (1).org (3).dod (6).internet (1).private (4).enterprises (1).cisco (9). This is displayed as 1.3.6.1.4.1.9.

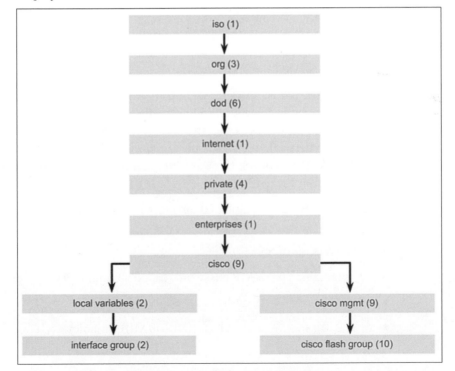

Figure 8-11   Management Information Base Object ID

Because the CPU is one of the key resources, it should be measured continuously. CPU statistics should be compiled on the NMS and graphed. Observing CPU utilization over an extended time period allows the administrator to establish a baseline estimate for CPU utilization. Threshold values can then be set relative to this baseline. When CPU utilization exceeds this threshold, notifications are sent. An SNMP graphing tool can periodically poll SNMP agents, such as a router, and graph the gathered values. Figure 8-12 illustrates 5-minute samples of router CPU utilization over the period of a few weeks.

Figure 8-12   SNMP Graphing Tool

The data is retrieved via the snmpget utility, issued on the NMS. Using the snmpget utility, one can manually obtain values for the average of the CPU busy percentage. The snmpget utility requires that the SNMP version, the correct community, the IP address of the network device to query, and the OID number are set. Figure 8-13 demonstrates the use of the freeware snmpget utility, which allows quick retrieval of information from the MIB.

Figure 8-13 shows a rather long command with several parameters, including the following:

- `-v2c` (version of SNMP)

- `-c community` (SNMP password, called a community string)

- `10.250.250.14` (IP address of monitored device)

- `1.3.6.1.4.1.9.2.1.58.0` (OID of MIB variable)

Figure 8-13   snmpget Utility

The last line shows the response. The output shows a shortened version of the MIB variable. It then lists the actual value in the MIB location. In this case, the 5-minute exponential moving average of the CPU busy percentage is 11 percent. The utility gives some insight into the basic mechanics of how SNMP works. However, working with long MIB variable names like 1.3.6.1.4.1.9.2.1.58.0 can be problematic for the average user. More commonly, the network operations staff uses a network management product with an easy-to-use GUI, with the entire MIB data variable naming transparent to the user.

The Cisco SNMP Navigator website allows a network administrator to research details about a particular OID. Figure 8-14 displays an example associated with a configuration change on a Cisco 2960 switch.

Interactive Graphic

Activity 8.2.1.7: Identify Characteristics of SNMP Versions.

Go to the course online to perform this practice activity.

Lab 8.2.1.8: Researching Network Monitoring Software

In this lab, you will complete the following objectives:

- Part 1: Survey Your Understanding of Network Monitoring

- Part 2: Research Network Monitoring Tools

- Part 3: Select a Network Monitoring Tool

Figure 8-14   Cisco SNMP Navigator

Configuring SNMP (8.2.2)

Configuring and verifying SNMP is fairly straightforward. Most of the complexity arrives from using the tools to analyze the information received.

Steps for Configuring SNMP (8.2.2.1)

A network administrator can configure SNMPv2 to obtain network information from network devices. As shown in Example 8-5, the basic steps to configuring SNMP are all in global configuration mode.

How To

Step 1.   (Required) Configure the community string and access level (read-only or read-write) with the **snmp-server community** *string* **ro | rw** command.

Step 2.   (Optional) Document the location of the device using the **snmp-server location** *text* command.

Step 3.   (Optional) Document the system contact using the **snmp-server contact** *text* command.

Step 4.   (Optional) Restrict SNMP access to NMS hosts (SNMP managers) that are permitted by an ACL: define the ACL and then reference the ACL with the **snmp-server community** *string access-list-number-or-name* command. This command can be used both to specify a community string and to restrict SNMP access via ACLs. Step 1 and Step 4 can be combined into one step, if desired; the Cisco networking device combines the two commands into one if they are entered separately.

Step 5.   (Optional) Specify the recipient of the SNMP trap operations with the **snmp-server host** *host-id* [**version**{**1**| **2c** | **3** [**auth** | **noauth** | **priv**]}] *community-string* command. By default, no trap manager is defined.

Step 6.   (Optional) Enable traps on an SNMP agent with the **snmp-server enable traps** *notification-types* command. If no trap notification types are specified in this command, then all trap types are sent. Repeated use of this command is required if a particular subset of trap types is desired.

Note

By default, SNMP does not have any traps set. Without this command, SNMP managers must poll for all relevant information.

Example 8-5   SNMP Configuration Example

```
R1(config)# snmp-server community batonaug ro SNMP_ACL
R1(config)# snmp-server location NOC_SNMP_MANAGER
R1(config)# snmp-server contact Wayne World
R1(config)# snmp-server host 192.168.1.3 version 2c batonaug
R1(config)# snmp-server enable traps
R1(config)# ip access-list standard SNMP_ACL
R1(config-std-nacl)# permit 192.168.1.3
```

Verifying SNMP Configuration (8.2.2.2)

There are several software solutions for viewing SNMP output. For our purposes, the Kiwi Syslog Server displays SNMP messages associated with SNMP traps.

PC1 and R1 are configured to demonstrate output on an SNMP Manager as related to SNMP traps.

As shown in Example 8-5, PC1 is assigned the IP address 192.168.1.3/24. The Kiwi Syslog Server is installed on PC1.

After R1 is configured, whenever an event occurs which qualifies as a trap, the SNMP traps are sent to the SNMP manager. For instance, if an interface comes up, a trap is sent to the server. Configuration changes on the router also trigger SNMP traps to be sent to the SNMP manager. A list of over 60 trap notification types can be seen with the **snmp-server enable traps ?** command. In the configuration of R1, no trap notification types are specified in the **snmp-server enable traps** *notification-types* command, so all traps are sent.

In Figure 8-15, a check box is checked in the Setup menu to indicate that the network administrator wants SNMP manager software to listen for SNMP traps on UDP port 162.

Figure 8-15   SNMP Manager Setup

In Figure 8-16, the top row of the displayed SNMP trap output indicates that interface GigabitEthernet0/0 changed state to up. Also, each time the global configuration mode is entered from privileged EXEC mode, a trap is received by the SNMP manager, as shown in the highlighted row.

To verify the SNMP configuration, use any of the variations of the **show snmp** privileged EXEC mode command. The most useful command is simply the **show snmp** command, as it displays the information that is commonly of interest when examining the SNMP configuration. Unless there is an involved SNMPv3 configuration, for the most part the other command options only display selected portions of the output of the **show snmp** command. Example 8-6 provides an example of **show snmp** output.

Figure 8-16   SNMP Manager Message Display

Example 8-6   Verifying SNMP Configuration

```
R1# show snmp
Chassis: FTX1636848Z
Contact: Wayne World
Location: NOC_SNMP_MANAGER
0 SNMP packets input
    0 Bad SNMP version errors
    0 Unknown community name
    0 Illegal operation for community name supplied
    0 Encoding errors
    0 Number of requested variables
    0 Number of altered variables
    0 Get-request PDUs
    0 Get-next PDUs
    0 Set-request PDUs
    0 Input queue packet drops (Maximum queue size 1000)
19 SNMP packets output
    0 Too big errors (Maximum packet size 1500)
    0 No such name errors
    0 Bad values errors
    0 General errors
    0 Response PDUs
    19 Trap PDUs
SNMP Dispatcher:
   queue 0/75 (current/max), 0 dropped
SNMP Engine:
   queue 0/1000 (current/max), 0 dropped
SNMP logging: enabled
    Logging to 192.168.1.3.162, 0/10, 19 sent, 0 dropped.
```

The **show snmp** command output does not display information relating to the SNMP community string or, if applicable, the associated ACL. Example 8-7 displays the SNMP community string and ACL information, using the **show snmp community** command.

Example 8-7   SNMP Community Service

```
R1# show snmp community
Community name: ILMI
Community Index: cisco0
Community SecurityName: ILMI
storage-type: read-only          active

Community name: batonaug
Community Index: cisco7
Community SecurityName: batonaug
storage-type: nonvolatile        active         access-list: SNMP_ACL

Community name: batonaug@1
Community Index: cisco8
Community SecurityName: batonaug@1
storage-type: nonvolatile        active         access-list: SNMP_ACL
```

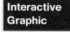

Activity 8.2.2.2: Configure and Verify SNMP

Go to the course online to use the Syntax Checker to configure and verify SNMP on R1.

Security Best Practices (8.2.2.3)

While SNMP is very useful for monitoring and troubleshooting, like the one shown in Figure 8-17, it can also create security vulnerabilities. For this reason, prior to implementing SNMP, be mindful of security best practices.

Both SNMPv1 and SNMPv2c rely on SNMP community strings in plaintext to authenticate access to MIB objects. These community strings, as with all passwords, should be carefully chosen to ensure that they are not too easy to crack. Additionally, community strings should be changed at regular intervals and in accordance with network security policies. For example, the strings should be changed when a network administrator changes roles or leaves the company. If SNMP is used only to monitor devices, use read-only communities.

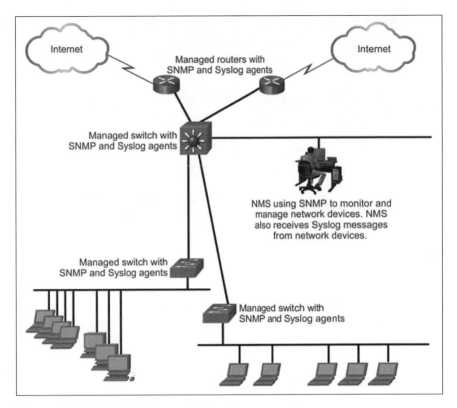

Figure 8-17   SNMP Managed Network

Ensure that SNMP messages do not spread beyond the management consoles. ACLs should be used to prevent SNMP messages from going beyond the required devices. ACL should also be used on the monitored devices to limit access for management systems only.

SNMPv3 is recommended because it provides security authentication and encryption. There are a number of other global configuration mode commands that a network administrator can implement to take advantage of the authentication and encryption support in SNMPv3:

- The **snmp-server group** *groupname* {**v1** | **v2c** | **v3** {**auth** | **noauth** | **priv**}} command creates a new SNMP group on the device.

- The **snmp-server user** *username groupname* **v3** [**encrypted**] [**auth** {**md5** | **sha**} auth-password] [*priv* {**des** | **3des** | **aes** {**128** | **192** | **256**}} priv-password] command is used to add a new user to the SNMP group specified in the **snmp-server group** *groupname* command.

> **Note**
>
> SNMPv3 configuration is beyond the scope of the CCNA curricula.

Lab 8.2.2.4: Configuring SNMP

In this lab, you will complete the following objectives:

- Part 1: Build the Network and Configure Basic Device Settings
- Part 2: Configure an SNMP Manager and Agents
- Part 3: Convert OID Codes with the Cisco SNMP Object Navigator

NetFlow (8.3)

High-speed router and switch hardware forwards traffic without use of operating system software. In 1996, Cisco created a method where routing decisions were decided by flows.

NetFlow Operation (8.3.1)

The value of the information in theses flows can be made accessible to network administrators, using a Cisco feature known as NetFlow.

Introducing NetFlow (8.3.1.1)

NetFlow is a Cisco IOS technology that provides statistics on packets flowing through a Cisco router or multilayer switch. NetFlow is the standard for collecting IP operational data from IP networks.

Historically, NetFlow technology was developed because networking professionals needed a simple and efficient method for tracking TCP/IP flows in the network, and SNMP was not sufficient for these purposes. While SNMP attempts to provide a very wide range of network management features and options, NetFlow is focused on providing statistics on IP packets flowing through network devices.

NetFlow provides data to enable network and security monitoring, network planning, traffic analysis to include identification of network bottlenecks, and IP accounting for billing purposes. For example, in Figure 8-18, PC 1 connects to PC 2 using an application such as HTTPS. NetFlow can monitor that application connection, tracking byte and packet counts for that individual application flow. It then pushes the statistics over to an external server called a NetFlow collector.

Figure 8-18   NetFlow in the Network

NetFlow has become a monitoring standard, and is now widely supported in the networking industry.

Flexible NetFlow is the latest NetFlow technology. Flexible NetFlow improves on "original NetFlow" by adding the capability to customize the traffic analysis parameters for the specific requirements of a network administrator. Flexible NetFlow facilitates the creation of more complex configurations for traffic analysis and data export through the use of reusable configuration components.

Flexible NetFlow uses the Version 9 export format. The distinguishing feature of the NetFlow Version 9 export format is that it is template-based. Templates provide an extensible design to the record format, a feature that allows future enhancements to NetFlow services without requiring concurrent changes to the basic flow-record format. It is important to note that many useful Flexible NetFlow commands were introduced with Cisco IOS Release 15.1.

Understanding NetFlow (8.3.1.2)

There are many potential uses of the statistics that NetFlow provides; however, most organizations use NetFlow for some or all of the following important data collection purposes:

- Measuring who is using what network resources for what purpose

- Accounting and charging back according to the resource utilization level

- Using the measured information to do more effective network planning so that resource allocation and deployment is well aligned with customer requirements

- Using the information to better structure and customize the set of available applications and services to meet user needs and customer service requirements

When comparing the functionality of SNMP to NetFlow, an analogy for SNMP might be remote-control software for an unmanned vehicle; whereas an analogy for NetFlow is a simple, yet detailed phone bill. Phone records provide call-by-call and aggregated statistics that enable the person paying the bill to track long calls, frequent calls, or calls that should not have been made.

In contrast to SNMP, NetFlow uses a "push-based" model. The collector simply listens for NetFlow traffic, and the networking devices are in charge of sending NetFlow data to the collector, based on changes in their flow cache. Another difference between NetFlow and SNMP is that NetFlow only gathers traffic statistics, as shown in Figure 8-19, whereas SNMP can also collect many other performance indicators, such as interface errors, CPU usage, and memory usage. However, the traffic statistics collected using NetFlow have a lot more granularity than the traffic statistics that can be collected using SNMP.

Figure 8-19   Gathering Traffic Data with NetFlow

Note

Do not confuse NetFlow's purpose and results with that of packet capture hardware and software. Whereas packet captures record all possible information exiting or entering a network device for later analysis, NetFlow targets specific statistical information.

When Cisco sought out to create NetFlow, two key criteria provided guidance in its creation:

- NetFlow should be completely transparent to the applications and devices in the network.

- NetFlow should not have to be supported and running on all devices in the network to function.

Achieving these design criteria ensured that NetFlow is very easy to implement in the most complex modern networks.

Note

Although NetFlow is simple to implement and transparent to the network, it does consume additional memory on the Cisco device, because NetFlow stores record information in "cache" on the device. The default size of this cache varies based on the platform, and the administrator can adjust this value.

Network Flows (8.3.1.3)

NetFlow breaks down TCP/IP communications for statistical record keeping using the concept of a flow. A flow is a unidirectional stream of packets between a specific source system and a specific destination. The figure demonstrates the flow concept.

For NetFlow, which is built around TCP/IP, the source and destination are defined by their network layer IP addresses and their transport layer source and destination port numbers.

NetFlow technology has seen several generations that provide more sophistication in defining traffic flows, but "original NetFlow" distinguished flows using a combination of seven fields. Should one of these fields vary in value from another packet, the packets could be safely determined to be from different flows:

- Source IP address

- Destination IP address

- Source port number

- Destination port number

- Layer 3 protocol type

- Type of Service (ToS) marking

- Input logical interface

The first four of the fields NetFlow uses to identify a flow should be familiar. The source and destination IP addresses, plus the source and destination ports, identify the connection between source and destination application. The Layer 3 protocol type identifies the type of header that follows the IP header (usually TCP or UDP, but other options include ICMP). The ToS byte in the IPv4 header holds information about how devices should apply quality of service (QoS) rules to the packets in that flow.

Flexible NetFlow supports more options with flow data records. Flexible NetFlow enables an administrator to define records for a Flexible NetFlow flow monitor cache by specifying the user-defined optional and required fields to customize the data collection to suit specific requirements. When defining records for a Flexible NetFlow flow monitor cache, they are referred to as user-defined records. The values in optional fields are added to flows to provide additional information about the traffic in the flows. A change in the value of an optional field does not create a new flow.

Interactive Graphic

Activity 8.3.1.4: Compare SNMP and NetFlow.

Go to the course online to perform this practice activity.

Configuring NetFlow (8.3.2)

To implement NetFlow on a router, complete these steps:

How To

Step 1. Configure NetFlow data capture. NetFlow captures data from ingress (incoming) and egress (outgoing) packets.

Step 2. Configure NetFlow data export. The IP address or hostname of the NetFlow collector must be specified, and the UDP port to which the NetFlow collector listens.

Step 3. Verify NetFlow, its operation, and statistics. After configuring NetFlow, the exported data can be analyzed on a workstation running an application, such as SolarWinds NetFlow Traffic Analyzer, Plixer Scrutinizer, or Cisco NetFlow Collector (NFC). Minimally, one can rely on the output from a number of **show** commands on the router itself.

Some NetFlow configuration considerations include the following:

- Newer Cisco routers, such as the ISR G2 series, support both NetFlow and Flexible NetFlow.

- Newer Cisco switches, such as the 3560-X series switches, support Flexible NetFlow; however, some Cisco switches, such as Cisco 2960 series switches, do not support NetFlow or Flexible NetFlow.

- NetFlow consumes additional memory. If a Cisco networking device has memory constraints, the size of the NetFlow cache can be pre-set so that it contains a smaller number of entries. The default cache size depends on the platform.

- NetFlow software requirements for the NetFlow collector vary. For example, the Scrutinizer NetFlow software on a Windows host requires 4 GB of RAM and 50 GB of drive space.

Note

The focus here is on Cisco router configuration of the original NetFlow (referred to simply as NetFlow in the Cisco documentation). The configuration of Flexible Netflow is beyond the scope of this course.

A NetFlow flow is unidirectional. This means that one user connection to an application exists as two NetFlow flows, one for each direction. To define the data to be captured for NetFlow in interface configuration mode:

- Capture NetFlow data for monitoring incoming packets on the interface using the **ip flow ingress** command.

- Capture NetFlow data for monitoring outgoing packets on the interface using the **ip flow egress** command.

To enable the NetFlow data to be sent to the NetFlow collector, there are several items to configure on the router in global configuration mode:

- **NetFlow collector's IP address and UDP port number:** Use the **ip flow-export destination** *ip-address udp-port* command. The collector has one or more ports, by default, for NetFlow data capture. The software allows the administrator to specify which port or ports to accept for NetFlow capture. Some common UDP ports allocated are 99, 2055, and 9996.

- **(Optional) NetFlow version to follow when formatting the NetFlow records sent to the collector:** Use the **ip flow-export version** *version* command. NetFlow exports data in UDP in one of five formats (1, 5, 7, 8, and 9). Version 9 is the most versatile export data format, but it is not backward compatible with previous versions. Version 1 is the default version if the version is not specified with Version 5. Version 1 should be used only when it is the only NetFlow data export format version that is supported by the NetFlow collector software.

- **(Optional) Source interface to use as the source of the packets sent to the collector:** Use the **ip flow-export source** *typenumber* command.

Using the topology in Figure 8-20, Example 8-8 shows a basic NetFlow configuration. Router R1 has IP address 192.168.1.1 on the G0/1 interface. The NetFlow collector has the IP address of 192.168.1.3 and is configured to capture the data on UDP port 2055. Ingress and egress traffic through G0/1 is monitored. NetFlow data is sent in Version 5 format.

Figure 8-20   Network Topology Using NetFlow

Example 8-8   NetFlow Router Configuration

```
R1(config)# interface GigabitEthernet 0/1
R1(config-if)# ip flow ingress
R1(config-if)# ip flow egress
R1(config-if)# exit
R1(config)# ip flow-export destination 192.168.1.3 2055
R1(config)# ip flow-export version 5
```

Verifying NetFlow (8.3.2.2)

After it is verified that NetFlow is working properly, data collection can begin on the NetFlow collector. Netflow verification is done by examining the information stored on the NetFlow collector. At a minimum, check the local NetFlow cache on a router to ensure that the router is collecting the data.

NetFlow was configured on router R1 as follows:

- IP address 192.168.1.1/24 on G0/1

- Ingress and egress traffic monitored by NetFlow

- NetFlow collector at 192.168.1.3/24

- NetFlow UDP capture port 2055

- NetFlow Version 5 export format

To display a summary of the NetFlow accounting statistics, as well as which protocol uses the highest volume of the traffic, and to see between which hosts this traffic flows, use the **show ip cache flow** command in user EXEC or privileged EXEC mode. This command is entered on R1 to verify the NetFlow configuration, as seen in Example 8-9. The command output details which protocol uses the highest volume of the traffic and between which hosts this traffic flows. The table in Example 8-9 describes the significant fields shown in the flow switching cache lines of the display.

Example 8-9   Verifying NetFlow Configuration

```
R1# show ip cache flow
IP packet size distribution (178617 total packets):
   1-32   64    96   128   160   192   224   256   288   320   352   384   416   448   480
   .002  .080  .008  .005  .001  .000  .001  .001  .000  .000  .000  .000  .000  .000  .000

   512   544   576  1024  1536  2048  2560  3072  3584  4096  4608
   .000  .000  .000  .000  .895  .000  .000  .000  .000  .000  .000
IP Flow Switching Cache, 278544 bytes
  5 active, 4091 inactive, 1573 added
  18467 ager polls, 0 flow alloc failures
```

```
   Active flows timeout in 1 minutes
   Inactive flows timeout in 15 seconds
IP Sub Flow Cache, 34056 bytes
   5 active, 1019 inactive, 1569 added, 1569 added to flow
   0 alloc failures, 0 force free
   1 chunk, 1 chunk added
   last clearing of statistics never
Protocol        Total        Flows   Packets  Bytes   Packets Active(Sec) Idle(Sec)
--------        Flows        /Sec    /Flow    /Pkt    /Sec    /Flow       /Flow
TCP-Telnet          3         0.0       3       50     0.0      1.0        15.0
TCP-WWW           245         0.0       6       93     0.0      0.3         2.4
TCP-other         529         0.0      27       57     0.2      0.7         6.2
UDP-other         328         0.0       6      107     0.0      2.4        15.3
ICMP              711         0.0     226     1261     2.4      0.2        15.4
Total:           1816         0.0      98     1137     2.7      0.8        11.0


SrcIf           SrcIPaddress  DstIf        DstIPaddress    Pr   SrcP DstP      Pkts
UDP-other           253         0.0       6      105     0.0      2.6        15.3
ICMP                560         0.0     286     1262     2.6      0.2        15.5
Total:             1568         0.0     113     1142     2.9      0.8        10.4
SrcIf           SrcIPaddress  DstIf        DstIPaddress    Pr   SrcP DstP      Pkts
Gi0/1           192.168.1.3   Local        192.168.1.1     06   100B 01BB        1
Gi0/1           192.168.1.3   Local        192.168.1.1     01   0000 0303        1
Gi0/1           192.168.1.3   Local        192.168.1.1     01   0000 0800        1
```

The output at the top of the display confirms that the router is collecting data. The first highlighted entry lists a count of 178,617 packets monitored by NetFlow. The end of the output shows statistics about three flows, the highlighted one corresponding to an active HTTPS connection between the NetFlow collector and R1. It also shows the source port (SrcP) and destination port (DstP) in hexadecimal.

Note

Hexadecimal 01BB is equal to decimal 443, the well-known TCP port for HTTPS.

Table 8-5 describes the significant fields in the flow switching cache lines of the **show ip cache flow** command output.

Table 8-5 *show ip cache flow* Switch Cache Descriptors

Field	Description
bytes	Number of bytes of memory used by the NetFlow cache
active	Number of active flows in the NetFlow cache at the time this command was entered
inactive	Number of flow buffers that are allocated in the NetFlow cache, but were not currently assigned to a specific flow at the time this command was entered

Table 8-6 describes the significant fields in the activity by protocol lines of the **show ip cache flow** command output.

Table 8-6 *show ip cache flow* Protocol Output Descriptors

Operation	Description
Protocol	IP protocol and the well-known port number
Total Flows	Number of flows in the cache for this protocol since the last time the statistics were cleared
Flows/Sec	Average number of flows for this protocol per second; equal to the total flows divided by the number of seconds for this summary period
Packets/Flow	Average number of packets for the flows for this protocol; equal to the total packets for this protocol divided by the number of flows for this protocol for this summary period
Bytes/Pkt	Average number of bytes for the packets for this protocol; equal to the total bytes for this protocol divided by the total number of packets for this protocol for this summary period
Packets/Sec	Average number of packets for this protocol per second; equal to the total packets for this protocol divided by the total number of seconds for this summary period
Active(Sec)/Flow	Number of seconds from the first packet to the last packet of an expired flow divided by the number of total flows for this protocol for this summary period
Idle(Sec)/Flow	Number of seconds observed from the last packet in each non-expired flow for this protocol until the time at which the **show ip cache verbose flow** command was entered divided by the total number of flows for this protocol for this summary period

Table 8-7 describes the significant fields in the NetFlow record lines of the **show ip cache flow** command output.

Table 8-7 SNMP Security Models and Levels

Operation	Description
SrcIf	Interface on which the packet was received
SrcIPaddress	IP address of the device that transmitted the packet
DstIf	Interface from which the packet was transmitted; if an asterisk (*) immediately follows the DstIf field, the flow being shown is an egress flow
DstIPaddress	IP address of the destination device
Pr	IP protocol "well-known" port number, displayed in hexadecimal format
SrcP	The source protocol port number in hexadecimal
DstP	The destination protocol port number in hexadecimal
Pkts	Number of packets switched through this flow

Although the output of the **show ip cache flow** command confirms that the router is collecting data, to ensure that NetFlow is configured on the correct interfaces in the correct directions, use the **show ip flow interface** command, as shown in Example 8-10.

Example 8-10 Verifying NetFlow Configuration

```
R1# show ip flow interface
GigabitEthernet0/1
  ip flow ingress
  ip flow egress
R1# show ip flow export
Flow export v5 is enabled for main cache
  Export source and destination details :
  VRF ID : Default
    Destination(1)  192.168.1.3 (2055)
  Version 5 flow records
  1764 flows exported in 532 udp datagrams
  0 flows failed due to lack of export packet
  0 export packets were sent up to process level
  0 export packets were dropped due to no fib
  0 export packets were dropped due to adjacency issues
  0 export packets were dropped due to fragmentation failures
  0 export packets were dropped due to encapsulation fixup failures
```

To check the configuration of the export parameters, use the **show ip flow export** command, shown in Example 8-10. The first highlighted line shows that NetFlow is enabled with Version 5 export format. The last highlighted lines in Example 8-10 show that 1,764 flows have been exported in the form of 532 UDP datagrams to the NetFlow collector at 192.168.1.3 via port 2055.

Activity 8.3.2.2: Configuring and Verifying NetFlow

Go to the course online to use the Syntax Checker to configure and verify the NetFlow on R1.

Examining Traffic Patterns (8.3.3)

Using special application software, NetFlow data can be examined and analyzed to display traffic patterns, reveal unauthorized traffic and used for network performance monitoring.

Identifying NetFlow Collector Functions (8.3.3.1)

A NetFlow collector is a host that is running application software. This software is specialized for handling raw NetFlow data. This collector can be configured to receive NetFlow information from many networking devices. NetFlow collectors aggregate and organize NetFlow data as prescribed by the network administrator within the constraints of the software.

On a NetFlow collector, the NetFlow data is written to a drive, at specified intervals. The administrator may run multiple collection schemes or threads concurrently. For example, different cuts of data can be stored to support planning versus billing; a NetFlow collector can easily produce the appropriate aggregation schemes.

Figure 8-21 illustrates a NetFlow collector passively listening for exported NetFlow datagrams. A NetFlow collector application provides a high-performance, easy-to-use, scalable solution to accommodate consumption of NetFlow export data from multiple devices. The intended use by an organization varies, but often the purpose is to support critical flows associated with consumer applications. These include accounting, billing, and network planning and monitoring.

There are several NetFlow collectors on the market. These tools enable traffic analysis on the network by showing the top (or most active) hosts, most used applications, and other means of measuring the traffic data, as shown in Figure 8-22. A NetFlow collector displays the kinds of traffic (web, mail, FTP, peer-to-peer, and so on) on the network, as well as the devices that send and receive most of the traffic. Collecting data provides a network administrator with data on top talkers, top hosts, and top listeners. Because data is preserved over time, after-the-fact network traffic analyses can determine network use trends.

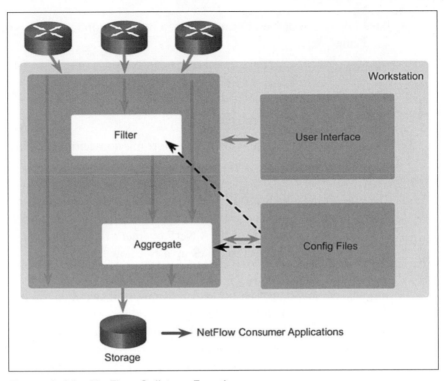

Figure 8-21   NetFlow Collector Functions

CONVERSATION	INGRESS BYTES	EGRESS BYTES	INGRESS PACKETS	EGRESS PACKETS	PERCENT
Between KJOHNSTONXP and rapidshare.com (198.18.131.7)	354.4 Kbytes	10.7 Mbytes	621	30.47 k	21.82%
Between mbishopwks and rapidshare.com (198.18.131.7)	243.0 Kbytes	9.0 Mbytes	445	18.77 k	18.16%

Figure 8-22   NetFlow Collector Top Talkers

Based on usage of NetFlow analyzers, a network administrator is able to identify the following:

- Who are the top talkers and to whom are they talking?

- What websites are routinely visited and what is downloaded?

- Who is generating the most traffic?

- Is there enough bandwidth to support mission-critical activity?

- Who is monopolizing the bandwidth?

The amount of information that can be analyzed by a NetFlow collector varies based on the NetFlow version used, because different NetFlow export formats consist of distinct NetFlow record types. A NetFlow record contains the specific information about the actual traffic that makes up a NetFlow flow.

A NetFlow collector provides real-time visualization and analysis of recorded and aggregated flow data. The routers and supported switches can be specified, as well as the aggregation scheme and the time interval to store data prior to the next periodic analysis. One can sort and visualize the data in a manner which makes sense for the users: bar charts, pie charts, or histograms of the sorted reports. The data can then be exported to spreadsheets, such as Microsoft Excel, for more detailed analysis, trending, and reporting.

NetFlow Analysis with a NetFlow Collector (8.3.3.2)

Plixer International developed the Scrutinizer NetFlow Analyzer software. Scrutinizer is one of many options for capturing and analyzing NetFlow data on a NetFlow collector.

Recall the configuration from the previous topic:

- IP address 192.168.1.1/24 on G0/1

- Ingress and egress traffic monitored for NetFlow

- NetFlow collector at 192.168.1.3/24

- NetFlow UDP capture port 2055

- NetFlow Version 5 export format

The Scrutinizer software has been installed on the NetFlow collector at 192.168.1.3/24.

Figure 8-23 displays the software interface upon opening the Scrutinizer application.

Figure 8-23   NetFlow Analysis: Opening the Scrutinizer Application

Figure 8-24 displays the result of clicking the Status tab after the application is running. The software displays a message: Flows detected, please wait while Scrutinizer prepares the initial reports.

Figure 8-24   NetFlow Analysis: Scrutinizer Status Tab

Figure 8-25 displays the Status screen after a few minutes. Router R1 has been configured with the cisco.com domain name.

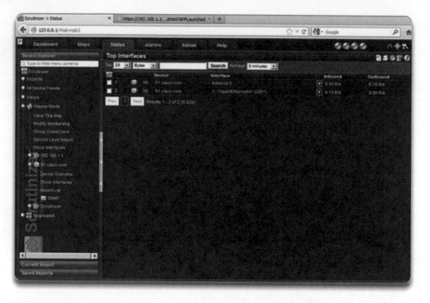

Figure 8-25 NetFlow Analysis: Scrutinizer Status Screen

The SNMP configuration from the previous section is still active on R1. The Scrutinizer software was configured with the SNMP community batonaug in the Admin Settings tab. When the SNMP link under R1.cisco.com in the left panel is clicked, the display in Figure 8-26 appears. This shows a basic traffic analysis for R1 communicated to the NetFlow collector via SNMPv2c. The Multi Router Traffic Grapher (MRTG) is free software that many network administrators use for basic traffic analysis. The Scrutinizer application integrates MRTG, and the graphs in Figure 8-26 are produced by MRTG. The top graph reflects ingress traffic, and the bottom graph reflects egress traffic for interface G0/1 on R1.

Finally, in Figure 8-27 the Dashboard tab displays actual NetFlow data reported for Top Hosts and Top Applications. The Scrutinizer software has dozens of these gadgets available for displaying various categorizations of data. In Figure 8-27, the top host is R1, with the greatest amount of traffic between R1 and the NetFlow collector. The top application is HTTPS, followed by SNMP, HTTP, SSH, ICMP, and NetBIOS.

Figure 8-26   NetFlow Analysis: MRTG

Figure 8-27   NetFlow Analysis: Scrutinizer Dashboard

Lab 8.3.3.3: Collecting and Analyzing NetFlow Data

In this lab, you will complete the following objectives:

- Part 1: Configure Basic Device Settings
- Part 2: Configure NetFlow on a Router
- Part 3: Analyze NetFlow Using the CLI
- Part 4: Explore NetFlow Collector and Analyzer Software

Summary (8.4)

Class Activity 8.4.1.1: A Network Administrator's Toolbox for Monitoring

As the network administrator for a small- to medium-sized business, you have just started using CLI network monitoring on the company routers, switches, and servers.

You decide to create a situational listing explaining when to use each method. Network monitoring methods to include are:

- Syslog
- SNMP
- NetFlow

The time on Cisco network devices can be synchronized using NTP.

Cisco network devices can log syslog messages to an internal buffer, the console, a terminal line, or an external syslog server. A network administrator can configure the types of messages to be collected and where to send the time-stamped messages.

The SNMP protocol has three elements: the manager, the agent, and the MIB. The SNMP manager resides on the NMS, while the agent and the MIB are on the client devices. The SNMP manager can poll the client devices for information, or it can use a trap message that tells a client to report immediately if the client reaches a particular threshold. SNMP can also be used to change the configuration of a device. SNMPv3 is the recommended version because it provides security. SNMP is a comprehensive and powerful remote management tool. Nearly every item available in a **show** command is available through SNMP.

NetFlow is a Cisco IOS technology that is the standard for collecting IP operational data from IP networks. NetFlow efficiently measures what network resources are being used and for what purposes. NetFlow uses header fields to distinguish between data flows. NetFlow is a "push" technology, where the client device initiates the sending of data to a configured server.

Practice

The following activities provide practice with the topics introduced in this chapter. The labs and class activities are available in the companion *Connecting Networks Lab Manual* (978-1-58713-331-2). The Packet Tracer activity PKA files are found in the online course.

Class Activities

Class Activity 8.0.1.2: Network Maintenance Development

Class Activity 8.4.1.1: A Network Administrator's Toolbox for Monitoring of SNMP Versions.

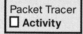

Labs

Lab 8.1.2.6: Configuring Syslog and NTP

Lab 8.2.1.8: Researching Network Monitoring Software

Lab 8.2.2.4: Configuring SNMP

Lab 8.3.3.3: Collecting and Analyzing NetFlow Data

Packet Tracer
☐ Activity

Packet Tracer Activities

Packet Tracer Activity 8.1.2.5: Configuring Syslog and NTP

Check Your Understanding Questions

Complete all the review questions listed here to test your understanding of the topics and concepts in this chapter. The appendix, "Answers to the 'Check Your Understanding' Questions," lists the answers.

1. Match the network management service with its description:

   Network Time Protocol (NTP)

   NetFlow

   Simple Network Management Protocol (SNMP)

   A. An application layer protocol that provides a facility for retrieving and posting data for monitoring and managing devices in a network using TCP port 161

   B. A protocol designed to synchronize the time on a network of machines and that runs over UDP using port 123

   C. A protocol that provides statistics on packets flowing through a Cisco router or multilayer switch

2. Which of the following destinations can receive syslog messages? Choose all that apply.

   A. Logging buffer (RAM inside a router or switch)

   B. Console line

   C. Terminal line

   D. Syslog server

3. Which command is used to allow the software clock to be synchronized with an NTP time server with the IP address 192.168.1.10?

   A. Router(config)# `ntp master 192.168.1.10`

   B. Router(config)# `ntp synchronize 192.168.1.10`

   C. Router(config)# `ntp address 192.168.1.10`

   D. Router(config)# `ntp server 192.168.1.10`

4. Which syslog severity level would be used to indicate that an interface is down?

   A. Level 0

   B. Level 1

   C. Level 2

   D. Level 3

   E. Level 4

   F. Level 5

   G. Level 6

   H. Level 7

   Use the following configuration to answer questions 5 through 7.

   ```
   R1(config)# logging 10.1.1.1
   R1(config)# logging trap 5
   R1(config)# logging source-interface GigabitEthernet 0/1
   R1(config)# interface loopback 0
   ```

5. What is the IP address of the syslog server?

6. What are the severity levels of the messages sent to the syslog sever?

7. What will be the source IP address of the syslog packets?

8. SNMP consists of what three elements?

9. Which version of SNMP provides secure access to devices by authenticating and encrypting packets over the network?

A. SNMPv1

B. SNMPv2

C. SNMPv3

Use the following configuration to answer questions 10 through 12.

```
R1(config)# snmp-server community steamerlane ro SNMP_ACCESS
R1(config)# snmp-server location NOC_HQ
R1(config)# snmp-server contact Enrico
R1(config)# snmp-server host 10.1.1.2 version 2c steamerlane
R1(config)# snmp-server enable traps
R1(config)# ip access-list standard SNMP_ACCESS
R1(config-std-nacl)# permit 10.1.1.2
```

10. What is the SNMP community string?

11. What is the IP address of the device that will receive the SNMP trap messages?

12. What is the version of SNMP used?

13. Which seven fields combine to create a flow in NetFlow?

14. Which two router commands are used to capture data from the incoming and outgoing packets on an interface?

A. ```
Router(config)# ip netflow ingress
Router(config)# ip netflow egress
```

B. ```
Router(config)# ip flow ingress
Router(config)# ip flow egress
```

C. ```
Router(config-if)# ip netflow ingress
Router(config-if)# ip netflow egress
```

D. ```
Router(config-if)# ip flow ingress
Router(config-if)# ip flow egress
```

15. What command is used to verify that NetFlow is working properly on a router?

A. **show ip cache flow**

B. **show ip interface**

C. **show interface**

D. **show ip cache**

CHAPTER 9

Troubleshooting the Network

Objectives

Upon completion of this chapter

- How is network documentation developed and how is it used to troubleshoot network issues?

- What is the general troubleshooting process?

- How do you compare the troubleshooting methods that use a systematic layered approach?

- What are the troubleshooting tools used to gather and analyze symptoms of network problems?

- What are the symptoms and causes of network problems using a layered model?

- How do you troubleshoot a network using the layered model?

Key Terms

This chapter uses the following key terms. You can find the definitions in the Glossary.

Introduction (9.0.1.1)

If a network or a portion of a network goes down, it can have a severe negative impact on the business. Network administrators must use a systematic approach to troubleshooting when network problems occur to bring the network back to full production as quickly as possible.

The ability for a network administrator to be able to resolve network problems quickly and efficiently is one of the most sought after skills in IT. Enterprises need individuals with strong network troubleshooting skills, and the only way to gain these skills is through hands-on experience and by using systematic troubleshooting approaches.

This chapter describes the network documentation that should be maintained and general troubleshooting procedures, methods, and tools. Typical symptoms and causes at several layers of the OSI model are also discussed. This chapter also includes some information about troubleshooting path and access control list (ACL) issues.

Class Activity 9.0.1.2: Network Breakdown

You have just moved in to your new office, and your network is very small. After a long weekend of setting up the new network, you discover that it is not working correctly.

Some of the devices cannot access each other and some cannot access the router which connects to the ISP.

It is your responsibility to troubleshoot and fix the problems. You decide to start with basic commands to identify possible troubleshooting areas.

Troubleshooting with a Systematic Approach (9.1)

This section discusses the systematic troubleshooting methodology. The systematic troubleshooting process is introduced along with how to use the layered model and the guidelines for selecting a troubleshooting method.

Network Documentation (9.1.1)

Network documentation is a key component to proper network administration and an important asset during network troubleshooting.

Documenting the Network (9.1.1.1)

For network administrators to be able to monitor and troubleshoot a network, they must have a complete set of accurate and current network documentation. This documentation includes the following:

- Configuration files, including network configuration files and end-system configuration files
- Physical and logical topology diagrams
- A baseline performance level

Network documentation allows network administrators to efficiently diagnose and correct network problems, based on the network design and the expected performance of the network under normal operating conditions. All network documentation information should be kept in a single location, either as hard copy or on the network on a protected server. Backup documentation should be maintained and kept in a separate location.

Network Configuration Files

Network configuration files contain accurate, up-to-date records of the hardware and software used in a network. Within the network configuration files, a table should exist for each network device used on the network, containing all relevant information about that device. Table 9-1 shows sample network configuration tables for two routers. Table 9-2 is a similar table for a LAN switch.

Table 9-1   pRouter Documentation

Device Name, Model	Interface Name	MAC Address	IPv4 Address	IPv6 Addresses	IP Routing Protocols
R1, Cisco 1941, c1900-univseralk9-mz. SPA152-4.M1	Gig0/0	0007.8580.a159	192.168.10.1 /24	2001:db8:cafe:10::1/64 fe80::1	EIGRPv4 10 EIGRPv6 20
	Gig0/1	0007.8580.a160	192.168.11.1 /24	2001:db8:cafe:11::1/64 fe80::1	EIGRPv4 10 EIGRPv6 20
	Serial 0/0/0	N/A	10.1.1.1/30	2001:db8:cafe:20::1/64 fe80::1	EIGRPv4 10 EIGRPv6 20
	Serial 0/0/1	N/A	None	None	None
R2, Cisco 1941, c1900-univseralk9-mz. SPA152-4.M1	Serial 0/0/0	N/A	10.1.1.2/30	2001:db8:acad:20::2/64 fe80::2	EIGRPv4 10 EIGRPv6 20

Table 9-2   Switch Documentation

Switch Name, Model, Management IP Addresses	Port	Speed	Duplex	STP	PortFast	Trunk Status	Ether Channel L2 or L3	VLANs	Key
S1, Cisco WS-2960-24TT	Fa0/1	100	Auto	Fwd	No	On	None	1	Connects to R1
192.168.10.2/24, 2001:db8:acad:99::2,	Fa0/2	100	Auto	Fwd	Yes	No	None	1	Connects to PC1
c2960-lanbasek9-mz.150-2.SE	Fa0/3								Not Connected

Information that could be captured within a device table includes the following:

- Type of device, model designation
- IOS image name
- Device network hostname
- Location of the device (building, floor, room, rack, panel)
- If it is a modular device, include all module types and in which module slot they are located
- Data link layer addresses
- Network layer addresses
- Any additional important information about physical aspects of the device

End-System Configuration Files

End-system configuration files focus on the hardware and software used in end-system devices, such as servers, network management consoles, and user workstations. An incorrectly configured end system can have a negative impact on the overall performance of a network. For this reason, having a sample baseline record of the hardware and software used on devices and recorded in end-system documentation as shown in Table 9-3 can be very useful when troubleshooting.

Table 9-3   End-System Documentation

Device Name, Purpose	Operating System	MAC Address	IP Address	Default Gateway	DNS Server	Network Applications	High-Bandwidth Applications
PC2	Windows 8	5475.D08E.9AD8	192.168.11.10 /24	192.168.11.1 /24	192.168.11.11 /24	HTTP FTP	VoIP
			2001:DB8: ACAD:11:5075: D0FF:FE8E:9AD8 /64	2001:DB8: ACAD:11::1	2001:DB8: ACAD:11::99		
SRV1	Linux	000C.D991.A138	192.168.20.254 /24	192.168.20.1 /24	192.168.20.1 /24	FTP, HTTP	
			2001:DB8: ACAD:4::100 /64	2001:DB8: ACAD:4::1	2001:DB8: ACAD:1::99		

For troubleshooting purposes, the following information could be documented within the end-system configuration table:

- Device name (purpose)
- Operating system and version
- IPv4 and IPv6 addresses
- Subnet mask and prefix length
- Default gateway, DNS server, and WINS server addresses
- Any high-bandwidth network applications that the end system runs

Network Topology Diagrams (9.1.1.2)

Network topology diagrams are an essential component to network documentation. This is helpful when configuring and troubleshooting network operations.

Network Topology Diagrams

Network topology diagrams keep track of the location, function, and status of devices on the network. There are two types of network topology diagrams: the physical topology and the logical topology.

Physical Topology

A *physical network* topology shows the physical layout of the devices connected to the network. It is necessary to know how devices are physically connected to troubleshoot physical layer problems. Information recorded on the diagram typically includes the following:

- Device type
- Model and manufacturer
- Operating system version
- Cable type and identifier
- Cable specification
- Connector type
- Cabling endpoints

Figure 9-1 shows a sample physical network topology diagram.

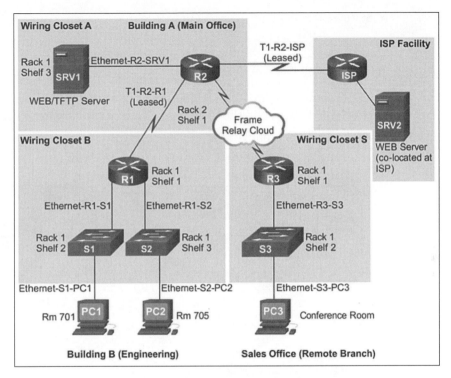

Figure 9-1 Physical Network Topology

Logical Topology

A *logical network topology* illustrates how devices are logically connected to the network, meaning how devices actually transfer data across the network when communicating with other devices. Symbols are used to represent network elements, such as routers, servers, hosts, virtual private network (VPN) concentrators, and security devices. Additionally, connections between multiple sites may be shown, but do not represent actual physical locations. Information recorded on a logical network diagram may include the following:

- Device identifiers
- IP address and prefix lengths
- Interface identifiers
- Connection type
- DLCI for virtual circuits
- Site-to-site VPNs
- Routing protocols

- Static routes

- Data-link protocols

- WAN technologies used

Figure 9-2 shows a sample logical IPv4 network topology. Although IPv6 addresses could also be displayed in the same topology, it may be clearer to create a separate logical IPv6 network topology diagram.

Figure 9-2 Logical IPv4 Network Topology

Network Baseline Performance Level (9.1.1.3)

The purpose of network monitoring is to watch network performance in comparison to a predetermined baseline. A *network baseline* is used to establish normal network or system performance. Establishing a network performance baseline requires collecting performance data from the ports and devices that are essential to network operation. Figure 9-3 shows several questions that a baseline is used to answer.

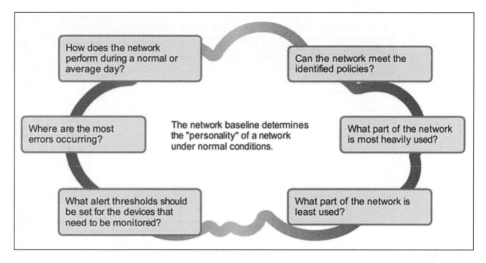

Figure 9-3   Questions That a Network Baseline Answers

Measuring the initial performance and availability of critical network devices and links allows a network administrator to determine the difference between abnormal behavior and proper network performance as the network grows or traffic patterns change. The baseline also provides insight into whether the current network design can meet business requirements. Without a baseline, no standard exists to measure the optimum nature of network traffic and congestion levels.

Analysis after an initial baseline also tends to reveal hidden problems. The collected data shows the true nature of congestion or potential congestion in a network. It may also reveal areas in the network that are underutilized and quite often can lead to network redesign efforts, based on quality and capacity observations.

Establishing a Network Baseline (9.1.1.4)

Because the initial network performance baseline sets the stage for measuring the effects of network changes and subsequent troubleshooting efforts, it is important to plan for it carefully.

How To

To plan the first baseline, perform the following steps:

Step 1.   Determine what types of data to collect. When conducting the initial baseline, start by selecting a few variables that represent the defined policies. If too many data points are selected, the amount of data can be overwhelming, making analysis of the collected data difficult. Start out simply and fine-tune along the way. Some good starting measures are interface utilization and CPU utilization. Figure 9-4 shows screenshots of CPU usage data, as displayed by the Cisco Wide Area Application Services (WAAS) software.

Figure 9-4   Collecting Data

Step 2.   Identify devices and ports of interest.

Use the network topology to identify those devices and ports for which performance data should be measured. Devices and ports of interest include the following:

- Network device ports that connect to other network devices
- Servers
- Key users
- Anything else considered critical to operations

A logical network topology diagram can be useful in identifying key devices and ports to monitor. For example, in Figure 9-5 the network administrator has highlighted the devices and ports of interest to monitor during the baseline test. The devices of interest include PC1 (the Admin terminal) and SRV1 (the Web/TFTP server). The ports of interest include those ports on R1, R2, and R3 that connect to the other routers or to switches, and on R2, the port that connects to SRV1 (G0/0).

By shortening the list of ports that are polled, the results are concise, and the network management load is minimized. Remember that an interface on a router or switch can be a virtual interface, such as a switch virtual interface (SVI).

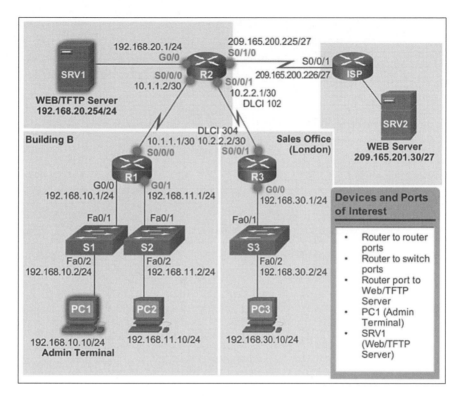

Figure 9-5   Planning for the First Baseline

Step 3.   Determine the baseline duration. The length of time and the baseline information being gathered must be sufficient for establishing a typical picture of the network. It is important that daily trends of network traffic are monitored. It is also important to monitor for trends that occur over a longer period of time, such as weekly or monthly. For this reason, when capturing data for analysis, the period specified should be, at a minimum, seven days long. Figure 9-6 shows examples of several screenshots of CPU utilization trends captured over a daily, weekly, monthly, and yearly period. In this example, notice that the work week trends are too short to reveal the recurring utilization surge every weekend on Saturday evening, when a database backup operation consumes network bandwidth. This recurring pattern is revealed in the monthly trend. A yearly trend, as shown in the example, may be too long of a duration to provide meaningful baseline performance details. However, it may help identify long term patterns which should be analyzed further. Typically, a baseline needs to last no more than six weeks, unless specific long-term trends need to be measured. Generally, a two- to four-week baseline is adequate. Baseline measurements should not be performed during times of unique traffic patterns, because the data would provide an inaccurate picture of normal network operations. Baseline analysis of the network should be conducted on a regular basis. Perform an annual analysis of the entire network or baseline different sections of the network on a rotating basis. Analysis must be conducted regularly to understand how the network is affected by growth and other changes.

Figure 9-6 Data Trends

Measuring Data (9.1.1.5)

When documenting the network, it is often necessary to gather information directly from routers and switches. Obvious useful network documentation commands include **ping**, **traceroute**, and **telnet** as well as the following **show** commands:

- The **show ip interface brief** and **show ipv6 interface brief** commands are used to display the up or down status and IP address of all interfaces on a device.

- The **show ip route** and **show ipv6 route** commands are used to display the routing table in a router to learn the directly connected neighbors, more remote devices (through learned routes), and the routing protocols that have been configured.

- The **show cdp neighbor detail** command is used to obtain detailed information about directly connected Cisco neighbor devices.

Table 9-4 lists some of the most common Cisco IOS commands used for data collection.

Table 9-4   End-System Documentation

Command	Description
show version	Shows uptime, version information for device software and hardware.
show ip interface [brief] show ipv6 interface [brief]	Shows all the configuration options that are set on an interface. Use the **brief** keyword to only show up/down status of IP interfaces and the IP address is of each interface.
show interface [*interface_type interface_num*]	Shows detailed output for each interface. To show detailed output for only a single interface, include the interface type and number in the command (for example, gigabitethernet 0/0).
show ip route show ipv6 route	Shows the contents of the routing table.
show arp show neighbors	Shows the contents of the ARP table (IPv4) and the neighbor table (IPv6).
show running-config	Shows current configuration.
show port	Shows the status of ports on a switch.
show vlan	Shows the status of VLANs on a switch.
show tech-support	This command is useful for collecting a large amount of information about the device for troubleshooting purposes. It executes multiple **show** commands, which can be provided to technical support representatives when reporting a problem.
show ip cache flow	Displays a summary of the NetFlow accounting statistics.

Manual data collection using **show** commands on individual network devices is extremely time-consuming and is not a scalable solution. Manual collection of data should be reserved for smaller networks or limited to mission-critical network devices. For simpler network designs, baseline tasks typically use a combination of manual data collection and simple network protocol inspectors.

Sophisticated network management software is often used to baseline large and complex networks. For example, as shown in Figure 9-7, the Fluke Network SuperAgent module enables administrators to automatically create and review reports using its Intelligent Baselines feature. This feature compares current performance levels with historical observations and can automatically identify performance problems and applications that do not provide expected levels of service.

Figure 9-7   Fluke Network SuperAgent Baseline Detail Report

Establishing an initial baseline or conducting a performance-monitoring analysis may require many hours or days to accurately reflect network performance. Network management software or protocol inspectors and sniffers often run continuously over the course of the data collection process.

Interactive Graphic

Activity 9.1.1.6: Identify Benefits for Establishing a Network Baseline

Go to the course online to perform this practice activity.

Interactive Graphic

Activity 9.1.1.7: Identify Commands Used for Measuring Data

Go to the course online to perform this practice activity.

Packet Tracer □ Activity

Packet Tracer Activity 9.1.1.8: Troubleshooting Challenge - Documenting the Network

Background/Scenario

This activity covers the steps to take to discover a network using primarily the **telnet, show cdp neighbors detail**, and **show ip route commands.** This is Part I of a two-part activity. Part II is Packet Tracer - Troubleshooting Challenge - Using Documentation to Solve Issues, which comes later in the chapter.

The topology you see when you open the Packet Tracer activity does not reveal all of the details of the network. The details have been hidden using the cluster function of Packet Tracer. The network infrastructure has been collapsed, and the topology in the file shows only the end devices. Your task is to use your knowledge of networking and discovery commands to learn about the full network topology and document it.

Troubleshooting Process (9.1.2)

The troubleshooting process involves general troubleshooting procedures, gathering symptoms, and questioning users.

General Troubleshooting Procedures (9.1.2.1)

Troubleshooting takes a large portion of network administrators' and support personnel's time. Using efficient troubleshooting techniques shortens overall troubleshooting time when working in a production environment. As shown in Figure 9-8, there are three major stages to the troubleshooting process:

Stage 1.   **Gather symptoms.** Troubleshooting begins with gathering and documenting symptoms from the network, end systems, and users. In addition, the network administrator determines which network components have been affected and how the functionality of the network has changed compared to the baseline. Symptoms may appear in many different forms, including alerts from the network management system, console messages, and user complaints. While gathering symptoms, it is important that the network administrator ask questions and investigate the issue to localize the problem to a smaller range of possibilities. For example, is the problem restricted to a single device, a group of devices, or an entire subnet or network of devices?

Stage 2.   **Isolate the problem.** Isolating is the process of eliminating variables until a single problem, or a set of related problems, has been identified as the cause. To do this, the network administrator examines the characteristics of the problems at the logical layers of the network so that the most likely cause can be selected. At this stage, the network administrator may gather and document more symptoms, depending on the characteristics that are identified.

Stage 3.   **Implement corrective action.** Having identified the cause of the problem, the network administrator works to correct the problem by implementing, testing, and documenting possible solutions. After finding the problem and determining a solution, the network administrator may need to decide if the solution can be implemented immediately or if it must be postponed. This depends on the impact of the changes on the users and the network. The severity of the problem should be weighed against the impact of the solution. For example, if a critical server or router must be offline for a significant amount of time, it may be better to wait until the end of the workday to implement the fix. Sometimes, a workaround can be created until the actual problem is resolved. This is typically part of a network's change control procedures.

If the corrective action creates another problem or does not solve the problem, the attempted solution is documented, the changes are removed, and the network administrator returns to gathering symptoms and isolating the issue.

These stages are not mutually exclusive. At any point in the process, it may be necessary to return to previous stages. For instance, the network administrator may need to gather more symptoms while isolating a problem. Additionally, when attempting to correct a problem, another problem could be created. In this instance, remove changes and begin troubleshooting again.

A troubleshooting policy, including change control procedures, should be established for each stage. A policy provides a consistent manner in which to perform each stage. Part of the policy should include documenting every important piece of information.

Note

Communicate to the users and anyone involved in the troubleshooting process that the problem has been resolved. Other IT team members should be informed of the solution. Appropriate documentation of the cause and the fix will assist other support technicians in preventing and solving similar problems in the future.

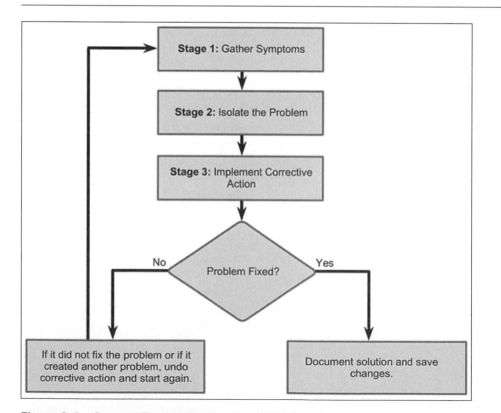

Figure 9-8   General Troubleshooting Procedures

Gathering Symptoms (9.1.2.2)

When gathering symptoms, it is important that the administrator gather facts and evidence to progressively eliminate possible causes and eventually identify the root cause of the issue. By analyzing the information, the network administrator formulates a hypothesis to propose possible causes and solutions while eliminating others.

There are five steps to gathering information:

Step 1. **Gather information.** Gather information from the trouble ticket, users, or end systems affected by the problem to form a definition of the problem.

Step 2. **Determine ownership.** If the problem is within the control of the organization, move on to the next stage. If the problem is outside the boundary of the organization's control (for example, lost Internet connectivity outside of the autonomous system), contact an administrator for the external system before gathering additional network symptoms.

Step 3. **Narrow the scope.** Determine if the problem is at the core, distribution, or access layer of the network. At the identified layer, analyze the existing symptoms and use your knowledge of the network topology to determine which piece of equipment is the most likely cause.

Step 4. **Gather symptoms from suspect devices.** Using a layered troubleshooting approach, gather hardware and software symptoms from the suspect devices. Start with the most likely possibility and use knowledge and experience to determine if the problem is more likely a hardware or software configuration problem.

Step 5. **Document symptoms.** Sometimes the problem can be solved using the documented symptoms. If not, begin the isolating stage of the general troubleshooting process.

Use Cisco IOS commands and other tools to gather symptoms about the network, such as the following:

- **ping**, **traceroute**, and **telnet** commands
- **show** and **debug** commands
- Packet captures
- Device logs

Table 9-5 describes the common Cisco IOS commands used to gather the symptoms of a network problem.

Table 9-5   Commands for Gathering Symptoms

Command	Description
traceroute {*destination*}	Identifies the path a packet takes through the networks. The destination variable is the hostname or IP address of the target system.
telnet {*host* | *ip-address*}	Connects to an IP address using the Telnet application.
show ip interface brief show ipv6 interface brief	Displays a summary of the status of all interfaces on a device.
show ip route show ipv6 route	Displays contents of currently running configuration file.
show running-config	Displays a list of options for enabling or disabling debugging events on a device.
[no] debug ?	Displays a list of options for enabling or disabling debugging events on a device.
show protocols	Displays the configured protocols and shows the global and interface-specific status of any configured Layer 3 protocol.

Note

Although the **debug** command is an important tool for gathering symptoms, it generates a large amount of console message traffic and the performance of a network device can be noticeably affected. If the **debug** must be performed during normal working hours, warn network users that a troubleshooting effort is underway and that network performance may be affected. Remember to disable debugging when you are done.

Questioning End Users (9.1.2.3)

In many cases, the problem is reported by an end user. The information may often be vague or misleading, such as, "The network is down" or "I cannot access my email." In these cases, the problem must be better defined. This may require asking questions of the end users.

Use effective questioning techniques when asking the end users about a network problem they may be experiencing. This will help you to get the information required to document the symptoms of a problem. Table 9-6 provides some guidelines and end-user example questions.

Table 9-6   Questioning End Users

Guidelines	Examples of End-User Questions
Ask questions that are pertinent to the problem.	What does not work?
Use each question as a means to either eliminate or discover possible problems.	Are the things that do work and the things that do not work related?
Speak at a technical level that the user can understand.	Has the thing that does not work ever worked?
Ask the user when the problem was first noticed.	When was the problem first noticed?
Has anything unusual happened since the last time it worked?	What has changed sing the last time it worked?
Ask the user to re-create the problem, if possible.	Can you reproduce the problem?
Determine the sequence of events that took place before the problem happened.	When exactly does the problem occur?

Interactive
Graphic

Activity 9.1.2.4: Identify Commands for Gathering Symptoms

Go to the course online to perform this practice activity.

Isolating the Issue Using Layered Models (9.1.3)

Using a layered reference model, either the OSI model or TCP/IP model, provides a method to isolate and resolve troubleshooting issues.

Using Layered Models for Troubleshooting (9.1.3.1)

After all symptoms are gathered, if no solution is identified, the network administrator compares the characteristics of the problem to the logical layers of the network to isolate and solve the issue.

Logical networking models, such as the OSI and TCP/IP models, separate network functionality into modular layers. These layered models can be applied to the physical network to isolate network problems when troubleshooting. For example, if the symptoms suggest a physical connection problem, the network technician can focus on troubleshooting the circuit that operates at the physical layer. If that circuit functions as expected, the technician looks at areas within another layer that could be causing the problem.

OSI Reference Model

The OSI reference model provides a common language for network administrators and is commonly used in troubleshooting networks. Problems are typically described in terms of a given OSI model layer.

The OSI reference model describes how information from a software application in one computer moves through a network medium to a software application in another computer.

The upper layers (5 to 7) of the OSI model deal with application issues and generally are implemented only in software. The application layer is closest to the end user. Both users and application layer processes interact with software applications that contain a communications component.

The lower layers (1 to 4) of the OSI model handle data-transport issues. Layers 3 and 4 are generally implemented only in software. The physical layer (Layer 1) and data link layer (Layer 2) are implemented in hardware and software. The physical layer is closest to the physical network medium, such as the network cabling, and is responsible for actually placing information on the medium.

Figure 9-9 shows some common devices and the OSI layers that must be examined during the troubleshooting process for that device. Notice that routers and multilayer switches are shown at Layer 4, the transport layer. Although routers and multilayer switches usually make forwarding decisions at Layer 3, ACLs on these devices can be used to make filtering decisions using Layer 4 information.

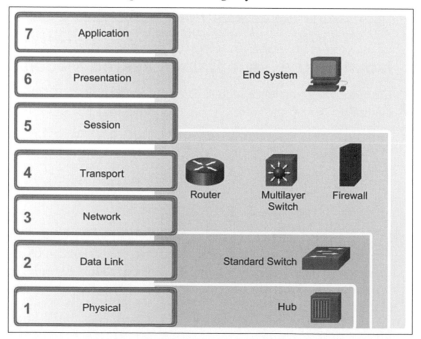

Figure 9-9   OSI Reference Model

TCP/IP Model

Similar to the OSI networking model, the TCP/IP networking model also divides networking architecture into modular layers. Figure 9-10 shows how the TCP/IP networking model maps to the layers of the OSI networking model. It is this close mapping that allows the TCP/IP suite of protocols to successfully communicate with so many networking technologies.

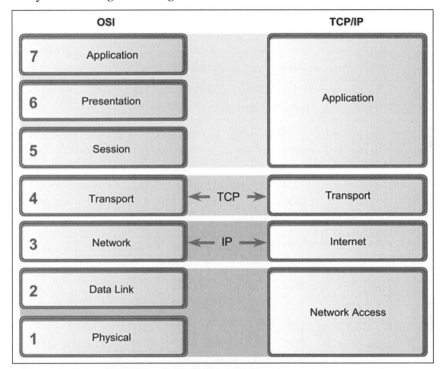

Figure 9-10 Comparing OSI Model TCP/IP Model

The application layer in the TCP/IP suite actually combines the functions of the three OSI model layers: session, presentation, and application. The application layer provides communication between applications, such as FTP, HTTP, and SMTP on separate hosts.

The transport layers of TCP/IP and OSI directly correspond in function. The transport layer is responsible for exchanging segments between devices on a TCP/IP network.

The TCP/IP Internet layer relates to the OSI network layer. The Internet layer is responsible for placing messages in a fixed format that allows devices to handle them.

The TCP/IP network access layer corresponds to the OSI physical and data link layers. The network access layer communicates directly with the network media and provides an interface between the architecture of the network and the Internet layer.

Troubleshooting Methods (9.1.3.2, 9.1.3.3)

Using the layered models, there are three primary methods for troubleshooting networks:

- Bottom-up
- Top-down
- Divide-and-conquer

Each approach has its advantages and disadvantages. This topic describes the three methods and provides guidelines for choosing the best method for a specific situation.

Bottom-Up Troubleshooting Method

In *bottom-up troubleshooting*, you start with the physical components of the network and move up through the layers of the OSI model until the cause of the problem is identified, as shown in Figure 9-11. Bottom-up troubleshooting is a good approach to use when the problem is suspected to be a physical one. Most networking problems reside at the lower levels, so implementing the bottom-up approach is often effective.

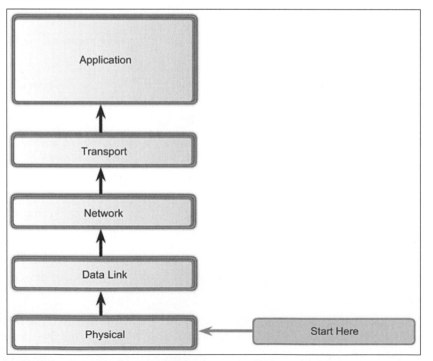

Figure 9-11   Bottom-Up Method

The disadvantage with the bottom-up troubleshooting approach is it requires that you check every device and interface on the network until the possible cause of the problem is found. Remember that each conclusion and possibility must be documented so there can be a lot of paperwork associated with this approach. A further challenge is to determine which devices to start examining first.

Top-Down Troubleshooting Method

In Figure 9-12, *top-down troubleshooting* starts with the end-user applications and moves down through the layers of the OSI model until the cause of the problem has been identified. End-user applications of an end system are tested before tackling the more specific networking pieces. Use this approach for simpler problems, or when you think the problem is with a piece of software.

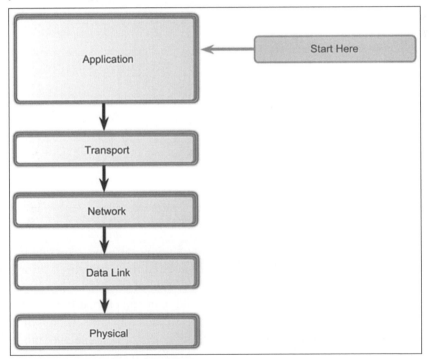

Figure 9-12   Top-Down Method

The disadvantage with the top-down approach is it requires checking every network application until the possible cause of the problem is found. Each conclusion and possibility must be documented. The challenge is to determine which application to start examining first.

Divide-and-Conquer Troubleshooting Method

Figure 9-13 shows the *divide-and-conquer approach* to troubleshooting a networking problem. The network administrator selects a layer and tests in both directions from that layer.

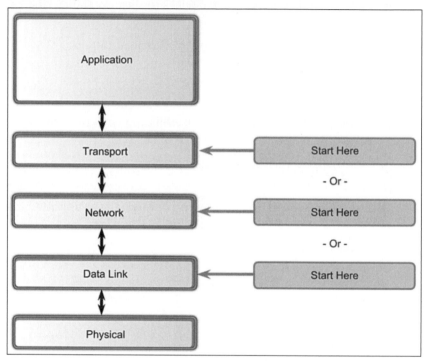

Figure 9-13   Divide-And-Conquer Method

In divide-and-conquer troubleshooting, you start by collecting user experiences of the problem, document the symptoms, and then, using that information, make an informed guess as to which OSI layer to start your investigation. When a layer is verified to be functioning properly, it can be assumed that the layers below it are functioning. The administrator can work up the OSI layers. If an OSI layer is not functioning properly, the administrator can work down the OSI layer model.

For example, if users cannot access the web server, but they can ping the server, then the problem is above Layer 3. If pinging the server is unsuccessful, then the problem is likely at a lower OSI layer.

In addition to the *systematic layered approach* to troubleshooting, there are also less-structured troubleshooting approaches.

One troubleshooting approach is based on an educated guess by the network administrator, based on the symptoms of the problem. This method is more successfully implemented by seasoned network administrators because seasoned network administrators rely on their extensive knowledge and experience to decisively isolate and solve network issues. With a less-experienced network administrator, this troubleshooting method may be more like random troubleshooting.

Another approach involves comparing a working and nonworking situation and spotting significant differences, including the following:

- Configurations

- Software versions

- Hardware and other device properties

Using this method may lead to a working solution, but without clearly revealing the cause of the problem. This method can be helpful when the network administrator is lacking an area of expertise or when the problem needs to be resolved quickly. After the fix has been implemented, the network administrator can do further research on the actual cause of the problem.

Substitution is another quick troubleshooting methodology. It involves swapping the problematic device with a known working one. If the problem is fixed, the network administrator knows the problem is with the removed device. If the problem remains, then the cause may be elsewhere. In specific situations, this can be an ideal method for quick problem resolution, such as when a critical single point of failure, like a border router, goes down. It may be more beneficial to simply replace the device and restore service rather than troubleshoot the issue.

Guidelines for Selecting a Troubleshooting Method (9.1.3.4)

To quickly resolve network problems, take the time to select the most effective network troubleshooting method. Figure 9-14 illustrates this process.

The following is an example of how to choose a troubleshooting method based on a specific problem:

Two IP routers are not exchanging routing information. The last time this type of problem occurred it was a protocol issue. Therefore, choose the divide-and-conquer troubleshooting method. Analysis reveals that there is connectivity between the routers. Start the troubleshooting process at the physical or data link layer. Confirm connectivity and begin testing the TCP/IP-related functions at next layer up in the OSI model, the network layer.

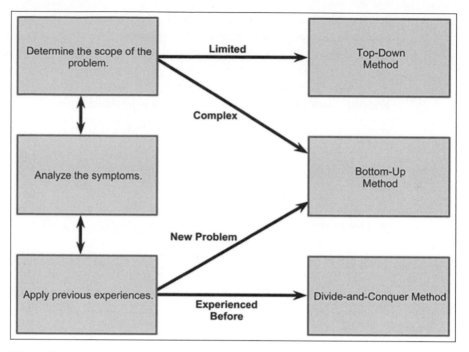

Figure 9-14   Guidelines for Selecting a Troubleshooting Method

Activity 9.1.3.5: Troubleshooting Methods

Go to the course online to perform this practice activity.

Network Troubleshooting (9.2)

In this section, network troubleshooting tools, along with the symptoms and causes of network problems, are examined.

Troubleshooting Tools (9.2.1)

Troubleshooting tools involve both software tools and hardware tools. Depending upon the symptoms, one or both of these may be used.

Software Troubleshooting Tools (9.2.1.1, 9.2.1.2)

A wide variety of software and hardware tools is available to make troubleshooting easier. These tools may be used to gather and analyze symptoms of network problems. They often provide monitoring and reporting functions that can be used to establish the network baseline.

Common software troubleshooting tools include those discussed in the following subsections.

Network Management System Tools

Network management system (NMS) tools include device-level monitoring, configuration, and fault-management tools. Figure 9-15 shows an example display from the WhatsUp Gold NMS software. These tools can be used to investigate and correct network problems. Network monitoring software graphically displays a physical view of network devices, allowing network managers to monitor remote devices without actually physically checking them. Device management software provides dynamic status, statistics, and configuration information for switched products. Examples of other commonly used network management tools are CiscoView, HPBTO Software (formerly OpenView), and SolarWinds.

Figure 9-15   Network Management System

Knowledge Bases

Online network device vendor *knowledge bases* have become indispensable sources of information. When vendor-based knowledge bases are combined with Internet search engines like Google, a network administrator has access to a vast pool of experience-based information.

Figure 9-16 shows the Cisco *Tools & Resources* page found at http://www.cisco.com. This is a free tool providing information on Cisco-related hardware and software. It contains troubleshooting procedures, implementation guides, and original white papers on most aspects of networking technology.

Figure 9-16   Tools and Resources

Baselining Tools

Many tools for automating the network documentation and baselining process are available. These tools are available for Windows, Linux, and AUX operating systems. Figure 9-17 shows a screen capture of the SolarWinds LANsurveyor and CyberGauge software. Baselining tools help with common documentation tasks. For example, they can draw network diagrams, help keep network software and hardware documentation up-to-date, and help to cost-effectively measure baseline network bandwidth use.

SolarWinds LANsurveyor (Automated Network Mapping Tool)

SolarWinds CyberGauge (Bandwidth Monitoring Tool)

Figure 9-17   Baselining Tools

A common software troubleshooting tool is a protocol analyzer. These can include the following:

- Host-based protocol analyzer
- Cisco IOS Embedded Packet Capture

Host-Based Protocol Analyzers

A *protocol analyzer* decodes the various protocol layers in a recorded frame and presents this information in a relatively easy-to-use format. The figure shows a screen capture of the Wireshark protocol analyzer. The information displayed by a protocol analyzer includes the physical, data link, protocol, and descriptions for each frame. Most protocol analyzers can filter traffic that meets certain criteria so that, for example, all traffic to and from a particular device can be captured. Protocol analyzers such as Wireshark in Figure 9-18 can help troubleshoot network performance problems. It is important to have both a good understanding of how to use the protocol analyzer and TCP/IP. To become more knowledgeable and skillful using Wireshark, an excellent resource is http://www.wiresharkbook.com.

Figure 9-18 Wireshark Protocol Analyzer

Cisco IOS Embedded Packet Capture

The Cisco IOS Embedded Packet Capture (EPC) delivers a powerful troubleshooting and tracing tool. The feature allows for network administrators to capture IPv4 and IPv6 packets flowing through, to, and from, a Cisco router. The Cisco IOS EPC function is mainly used in troubleshooting scenarios where it is helpful to see the actual data being sent through, from, or to the network device.

For example, support desk personnel need to determine why a particular device cannot access the network or some application. It might be necessary to capture IP data packets and examine the data to discover the problem. Another example would be determining an attack signature for a network threat or server system security breach. The Cisco IOS EPC can help capture packets flowing into the network at the origin or perimeter.

The Cisco IOS EPC is useful whenever a network protocol analyzer might be useful in debugging a problem but when it is not practical to install such a device.

For more information on using and configuring Cisco EPC, consult the Embedded Packet Capture Configuration Guide.

Hardware Troubleshooting Tools (9.2.1.3)

Common hardware troubleshooting tools include the following:

- **Network analysis module:** As shown in Figure 9-19, a *network analysis module (NAM)* can be installed in Cisco Catalyst 6500 series switches and Cisco 7600 series routers. NAMs provide a graphical representation of traffic from local and remote switches and routers. The NAM is an embedded browser-based interface that generates reports on the traffic that consumes critical network resources. In addition, the NAM can capture and decode packets and track response times to pinpoint an application problem to the network or the server.

Figure 9-19 Network Analysis Module

- **Digital Multimeters (DMMs):** *Digital multimeters*, such as the Fluke 179 shown in Figure 9-20, are test instruments that are used to directly measure electrical values of voltage, current, and resistance. In network troubleshooting, most of the multimedia tests involve checking power-supply voltage levels and verifying that network devices are receiving power.

Fluke 179 Digital Multimeter

Figure 9-20   Digital Multimeter

■ **Cable testers:** *Cable testers* are specialized, handheld devices designed for testing the various types of data communication cabling. Figure 9-21 shows two different Fluke cable testers. Cabling testers can be used to detect broken wires, crossed-over wiring, shorted connections, and improperly paired connections. These devices can be inexpensive continuity testers, moderately priced data cabling testers, or expensive time-domain reflectometers (TDRs). TDRs are used to pinpoint the distance to a break in a cable. These devices send signals along the cable and wait for them to be reflected. The time between sending the signal and receiving it back is converted into a distance measurement. The TDR function is normally packaged with data cabling testers. TDRs used to test fiber optic cables are known as *optical time-domain reflectometers (OTDRs).*

Fluke Networks LinkRunner Pro Tester

Fluke Networks CableIQ
Qualification Tester

Figure 9-21 Cable Testers

■ **Cable analyzers:** *Cable analyzers*, such as the Fluke DTX Cable Analyzer in
   Figure 9-22, are multifunctional handheld devices that are used to test and certify copper and fiber cables for different services and standards. The more sophisticated tools include advanced troubleshooting diagnostics that measure distance
   to performance defect (NEXT, RL), identify corrective actions, and graphically
   display crosstalk and impedance behavior. Cable analyzers also typically include
   PC-based software. After field data is collected, the handheld device can upload
   its data to create up-to-date reports.

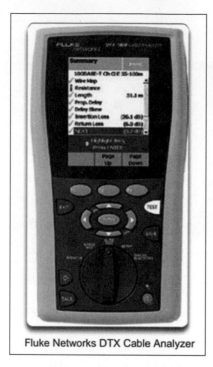

Fluke Networks DTX Cable Analyzer

Figure 9-22   Cable Analyzer

■ **Portable network analyzers:** Portable devices, like the Fluke OptiView in Figure 9-23, are used for troubleshooting switched networks and VLANs. By plugging the network analyzer in anywhere on the network, a network engineer can see the switch port to which the device is connected and the average and peak utilization. The *portable network analyzer* can also be used to discover VLAN configuration, identify top network talkers, analyze network traffic, and view interface details. The device can typically output to a PC that has network monitoring software installed for further analysis and troubleshooting.

Fluke Networks OptiView™ Series III Integrated Network Analyzer

Figure 9-23   Network Analyzer

Using a Syslog Server for Troubleshooting (9.2.1.4)

Syslog is a simple protocol used by an IP device known as a syslog client to send text-based log messages to another IP device, the syslog server. Syslog is currently defined in RFC 5424.

Implementing a logging facility is an important part of network security and for network troubleshooting. Cisco devices can log information regarding configuration changes, ACL violations, interface status, and many other types of events. Cisco devices can send log messages to several different facilities. Event messages can be sent to one or more of the following:

- **Console:** Console logging is on by default. Messages log to the console and can be viewed when modifying or testing the router or switch using terminal emulation software while connected to the console port of the router.

- **Terminal lines:** Enabled EXEC sessions can be configured to receive log messages on any terminal lines. Similar to console logging, this type of logging is not stored by the router and, therefore, is only valuable to the user on that line.

- **Buffered logging:** Buffered logging is a little more useful as a troubleshooting tool because log messages are stored in memory for a time. However, log messages are cleared when the device is rebooted.

- **SNMP traps:** Certain thresholds can be preconfigured on routers and other devices. Router events, such as exceeding a threshold, can be processed by the router and forwarded as SNMP traps to an external SNMP server. SNMP traps are a viable security logging facility, but require the configuration and maintenance of an SNMP system.

- **Syslog:** Cisco routers and switches can be configured to forward log messages to an external syslog service. This service can reside on any number of servers or workstations, including Microsoft Windows and Linux-based systems. Syslog is the most popular message logging facility because it provides long-term log storage capabilities and a central location for all router messages.

Cisco IOS log messages fall into one of eight levels, shown in Table 9-7. The lower the level number, the higher the severity level. By default, all messages from level 0 to 7 are logged to the console. While the ability to view logs on a central syslog server is helpful in troubleshooting, sifting through a large amount of data can be an overwhelming task. The **logging trap** *level* command limits messages logged to the syslog server based on severity. The level is the name or number of the severity *level*. Only messages equal to or numerically lower than the specified *level* are logged.

Table 9-7   Severity Levels

	Level	Keyword	Description	Definition
Highest Level	0	Emergencies	System is unusable.	LOG_EMERG
	1	Alerts	Immediate action is needed.	LOG_ALERT
	2	Critical	Critical conditions exist.	LOG_CRIT
	3	Errors	Error conditions exist.	LOG_ERR
	4	Warnings	Warning conditions exist.	LOG_WARNING
	5	Notifications	Normal but significant condition.	LOG_NOTICE
	6	Informational	Informational messages only.	LOG_INFO
Lowest Level	7	Debugging	Debugging messages.	LOG_DEBUG

In Example 9-1, system messages from level 0 (emergencies) to 5 (notifications) are sent to the syslog server at 209.165.200.225.

Example 9-1   Limiting Messages Sent to the Syslog Server

```
R1(config)# logging host 209.165.200.225
R1(config)# logging trap notifications
R1(config)# logging on
```

**Interactive
Graphic**

Activity 9.2.1.5: Identify Common Troubleshooting Tools

Go to the course online to perform this practice activity.

Symptoms and Causes of Network Troubleshooting (9.2.2)

Using a layered approach, the different symptoms and causes of networking troubleshooting will be examined. Using a layered approach helps you isolate, understand, and solve network problems.

Physical Layer Troubleshooting (9.2.2.1)

The physical layer transmits bits from one computer to another and regulates the transmission of a stream of bits over the physical medium. The physical layer is the only layer with physically tangible properties, such as wires, cards, and antennas.

Issues on a network often present as performance problems. Performance problems mean that there is a difference between the expected behavior and the observed behavior and that the system is not functioning as could be reasonably expected. Failures and suboptimal conditions at the physical layer not only inconvenience users but can also impact the productivity of the entire company. Networks that experience these kinds of conditions usually shut down. Because the upper layers of the OSI model depend on the physical layer to function, a network administrator must have the ability to effectively isolate and correct problems at this layer.

Common symptoms of network problems at the physical layer include the following:

- **Performance lower than baseline:** The most common reasons for slow or poor performance include overloaded or underpowered servers, unsuitable switch or router configurations, traffic congestion on a low-capacity link, and chronic frame loss.

- **Loss of connectivity:** If a cable or device fails, the most obvious symptom is a loss of connectivity between the devices that communicate over that link or with the failed device or interface. This is indicated by a simple ping test. Intermittent loss of connectivity can indicate a loose or oxidized connection.

- **Network bottlenecks or congestion:** If a router, interface, or cable fails, routing protocols may redirect traffic to other routes that are not designed to carry the extra capacity. This can result in congestion or bottlenecks in those parts of the network.

- **High CPU utilization rates:** High CPU utilization rates are a symptom that a device, such as a router, switch, or server, is operating at or exceeding its design limits. If not addressed quickly, CPU overloading can cause a device to shut down or fail.

- **Console error messages:** Error messages reported on the device console indicate a physical layer problem.

Issues that commonly cause network problems at the physical layer include the following:

- **Power related:** Power-related issues are the most fundamental reason for network failure. Also, check the operation of the fans, and ensure that the chassis intake and exhaust vents are clear. If other nearby units have also powered down, suspect a power failure at the main power supply.

- **Hardware faults:** Faulty network interface cards (NICs) can be the cause of network transmission errors due to late collisions, short frames, and jabber. *Jabber* is often defined as the condition in which a network device continually transmits random, meaningless data onto the network. Other likely causes of jabber are faulty or corrupt NIC driver files, bad cabling, or grounding problems.

- **Cabling faults:** Many problems can be corrected by simply reseating cables that have become partially disconnected. When performing a physical inspection, look for damaged cables, improper cable types, and poorly crimped RJ-45s. Suspect cables should be tested or exchanged with a known functioning cable.

- **Attenuation:** Attenuation can be caused if a cable length exceeds the design limit for the media or when there is a poor connection resulting from a loose cable or dirty or oxidized contacts. If attenuation is severe, the receiving device cannot always successfully distinguish the component bits of the stream from each other.

- **Noise:** Local electromagnetic interference (EMI) is commonly known as noise. Noise can be generated by many sources, such as FM radio stations, police radio, building security, and avionics for automated landing, crosstalk (noise induced by other cables in the same pathway or adjacent cables), nearby electric cables, devices with large electric motors, or anything that includes a transmitter more powerful than a cell phone.

- **Interface configuration errors:** Many things can be misconfigured on an interface to cause it to go down, such as incorrect clock rate, incorrect clock source, and interface not being turned on. This causes a loss of connectivity with attached network segments.

- **Exceeding design limits:** A component may be operating suboptimally at the physical layer because it is being utilized at a higher average rate than it is configured to operate. When troubleshooting this type of problem, it becomes evident that resources for the device are operating at or near the maximum capacity and there is an increase in the number of interface errors.

- **CPU overload:** Symptoms include processes with high CPU utilization percentages, input queue drops, slow performance, router services such as Telnet and ping are slow or fail to respond, or there are no routing updates. One of the causes of CPU overload in a router is high traffic. If some interfaces are regularly overloaded with traffic, consider redesigning the traffic flow in the network or upgrading the hardware.

The symptoms and causes associated with the physical layer are summarized in Figure 9-24.

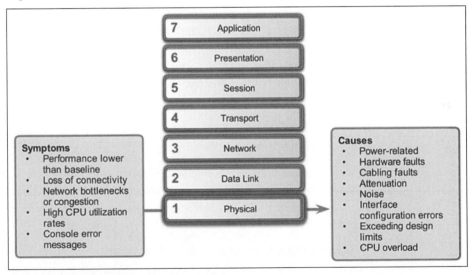

Figure 9-24 Physical Layer Symptoms and Causes

Data Link Layer Troubleshooting (9.2.2.2)

Troubleshooting Layer 2 problems can be a challenging process. The configuration and operation of these protocols are critical to creating a functional, well-tuned network. Layer 2 problems cause specific symptoms that, when recognized, will help identify the problem quickly.

Common symptoms of network problems at the data link layer include the following:

- **No functionality or connectivity at the network layer or above:** Some Layer 2 problems can stop the exchange of frames across a link, while others only cause network performance to degrade.

- **Network is operating below baseline performance levels:** There are two distinct types of suboptimal Layer 2 operation that can occur in a network. First, the frames take a suboptimal path to their destination but do arrive. In this case, the network might experience high-bandwidth usage on links that should not have that level of traffic. Second, some frames are dropped. These problems can be identified through error counter statistics and console error messages that appear on the switch or router. In an Ethernet environment, an extended or continuous ping also reveals if frames are being dropped.

- **Excessive broadcasts:** Operating systems use broadcasts and multicasts extensively to discover network services and other hosts. Generally, excessive broadcasts result from one of the following situations: poorly programmed or configured applications, large Layer 2 broadcast domains, or underlying network problems, such as STP loops or route flapping.

- **Console messages:** In some instances, a router recognizes that a Layer 2 problem has occurred and sends alert messages to the console. Typically, a router does this when it detects a problem with interpreting incoming frames (encapsulation or framing problems) or when keepalives are expected but do not arrive. The most common console message that indicates a Layer 2 problem is a line protocol down message.

Issues at the data link layer that commonly result in network connectivity or performance problems include the following:

- **Encapsulation errors:** An encapsulation error occurs because the bits placed in a particular field by the sender are not what the receiver expects to see. This condition occurs when the encapsulation at one end of a WAN link is configured differently from the encapsulation used at the other end.

- **Address mapping errors:** In topologies, such as point to multipoint, Frame Relay, or broadcast Ethernet, it is essential that an appropriate Layer 2 destination address be given to the frame. This ensures its arrival at the correct destination. To achieve this, the network device must match a destination Layer 3 address with the correct Layer 2 address using either static or dynamic maps. In a dynamic environment, the mapping of Layer 2 and Layer 3 information can fail because devices may have been specifically configured not to respond to ARP or Inverse-ARP requests, the Layer 2 or Layer 3 information that is cached may have physically changed, or invalid ARP replies are received because of a misconfiguration or a security attack.

- **Framing errors:** Frames usually work in groups of 8-bit bytes. A framing error occurs when a frame does not end on an 8-bit byte boundary. When this happens, the receiver may have problems determining where one frame ends and another frame starts. Too many invalid frames may prevent valid keepalives from being exchanged. Framing errors can be caused by a noisy serial line, an improperly designed cable (too long or not properly shielded), or an incorrectly configured channel service unit (CSU) line clock.

- **STP failures or loops:** The purpose of the Spanning Tree Protocol (STP) is to resolve a redundant physical topology into a tree-like topology by blocking redundant ports. Most STP problems are related to forwarding loops that occur when no ports in a redundant topology are blocked and traffic is forwarded in circles indefinitely, causing excessive flooding because of a high rate of STP topology changes. A topology change should be a rare event in a well-configured network. When a link between two switches goes up or down, there is eventually a topology change when the STP state of the port is changing to or from forwarding. However, when a port is flapping (oscillating between up and down states), this causes repetitive topology changes and flooding, or slow STP convergence or re-convergence. This can be caused by a mismatch between the real and documented topology, a configuration error, such as an inconsistent configuration of STP timers, an overloaded switch CPU during convergence, or a software defect.

The symptoms and causes associated with the data layer are summarized in Figure 9-25.

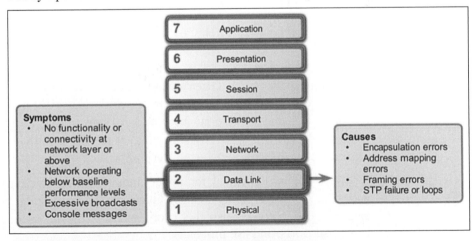

Figure 9-25   Data Link Layer Symptoms and Causes

Network Layer Troubleshooting (9.2.2.3)

Network layer problems include any problem that involves a Layer 3 protocol, both routed protocols (such as IPv4 or IPv6) and routing protocols (such as EIGRP, OSPF, and so on).

Common symptoms of network problems at the network layer include the following:

- **Network failure:** Network failure is when the network is nearly or completely non-functional, affecting all users and applications on the network. These failures are usually noticed quickly by users and network administrators, and are obviously critical to the productivity of a company.

- **Suboptimal performance:** Network optimization problems usually involve a subset of users, applications, destinations, or a particular type of traffic. Optimization issues can be difficult to detect and even harder to isolate and diagnose. This is because they usually involve multiple layers, or even the host computer itself. Determining that the problem is a network layer problem can take time.

In most networks, static routes are used in combination with dynamic routing protocols. Improper configuration of static routes can lead to less-than-optimal routing. In some cases, improperly configured static routes can create routing loops which make parts of the network unreachable.

Troubleshooting dynamic routing protocols requires a thorough understanding of how the specific routing protocol functions. Some problems are common to all routing protocols, while other problems are particular to the individual routing protocol.

There is no single template for solving Layer 3 problems. Routing problems are solved with a methodical process, using a series of commands to isolate and diagnose the problem.

Here are some areas to explore when diagnosing a possible problem involving routing protocols:

- **General network issues:** Often a change in the topology, such as a down link, may have effects on other areas of the network that might not be obvious at the time. This may include the installation of new routes, static or dynamic, or removal of other routes. Determine whether anything in the network has recently changed, and if there is anyone currently working on the network infrastructure.

- **Connectivity issues:** Check for any equipment and connectivity problems, including power problems such as outages and environmental problems (for example, overheating). Also check for Layer 1 problems, such as cabling problems, bad ports, and ISP problems.

- **Neighbor issues:** If the routing protocol establishes an adjacency with a neighbor, check to see if there are any problems with the routers forming neighbor adjacencies.

- **Topology database:** If the routing protocol uses a topology table or database, check the table for anything unexpected, such as missing entries or unexpected entries.

- **Routing table:** Check the routing table for anything unexpected, such as missing routes or unexpected routes. Use **debug** commands to view routing updates and routing table maintenance.

The symptoms and causes associated with the network layer are summarized in Figure 9-26.

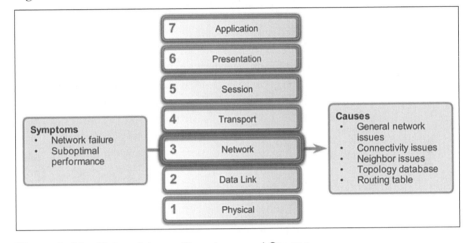

Figure 9-26   Network Layer Symptoms and Causes

Transport Layer Troubleshooting – ACLs (9.2.2.4)

Network problems can arise from transport layer problems on the router, particularly at the edge of the network where traffic is examined and modified. Two of the most commonly implemented transport layer technologies are access control lists (ACLs) and Network Address Translation (NAT), as shown in Figure 9-27.

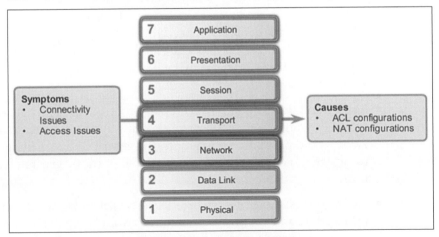

Figure 9-27   Transport Layer Symptoms and Causes

The most common issues with ACLs are caused by improper configuration, as shown in Figure 9-28. Problems with ACLs may cause otherwise working systems to fail. There are several areas where misconfigurations commonly occur:

- **Selection of traffic flow:** The most common router misconfiguration is applying the ACL to incorrect traffic. Traffic is defined by both the router interface through which the traffic is traveling and the direction in which this traffic is traveling. An ACL must be applied to the correct interface, and the correct traffic direction must be selected to function properly.

- **Order of access control entries:** The entries in an ACL should be from specific to general. Although an ACL may have an entry to specifically permit a particular traffic flow, packets never match that entry if they are being denied by another entry earlier in the list. If the router is running both ACLs and NAT, the order in which each of these technologies is applied to a traffic flow is important. Inbound traffic is processed by the inbound ACL before being processed by outside-to-inside NAT. Outbound traffic is processed by the outbound ACL after being processed by inside-to-outside NAT.

- **Implicit deny all:** When high security is not required on the ACL, this implicit access control element can be the cause of an ACL misconfiguration.

- **Addresses and IPv4 wildcard masks:** Complex IPv4 wildcard masks provide significant improvements in efficiency, but are more subject to configuration errors. An example of a complex wildcard mask is using the IPv4 address 10.0.32.0 and wildcard mask 0.0.32.15 to select the first 15 host addresses in either the 10.0.0.0 network or the 10.0.32.0 network.

- **Selection of transport layer protocol:** When configuring ACLs, it is important that only the correct transport layer protocols be specified. Many network administrators, when unsure whether a particular traffic flow uses a TCP port or a UDP port, configure both. Specifying both opens a hole through the firewall, possibly giving intruders an avenue into the network. It also introduces an extra element into the ACL, so the ACL takes longer to process, introducing more latency into network communications.

- **Source and destination ports:** Properly controlling the traffic between two hosts requires symmetric access control elements for inbound and outbound ACLs. Address and port information for traffic generated by a replying host is the mirror image of address and port information for traffic generated by the initiating host.

- **Use of the established keyword:** The **established** keyword increases the security provided by an ACL. However, if the keyword is applied incorrectly, unexpected results may occur.

- **Uncommon protocols:** Misconfigured ACLs often cause problems for protocols other than TCP and UDP. Uncommon protocols that are gaining popularity are VPN and encryption protocols.

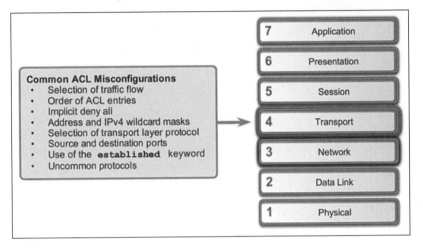

Figure 9-28   Common ACL Misconfigurations

The **log** keyword is a useful command for viewing ACL operation on ACL entries. This keyword instructs the router to place an entry in the system log whenever that entry condition is matched. The logged event includes details of the packet that matched the ACL element. The **log** keyword is especially useful for troubleshooting and also provides information on intrusion attempts being blocked by the ACL.

Transport Layer Troubleshooting – NAT for IPv4 (9.2.2.5)

There are a number of problems with NAT such as not interacting with services like DHCP and tunneling. These can include misconfigured NAT inside, NAT outside, or ACL. Other issues include interoperability with other network technologies, especially those that contain or derive information from host network addressing in the packet. Some of these technologies include the following:

- **BOOTP and DHCP:** Both protocols manage the automatic assignment of IPv4 addresses to clients. Recall that the first packet that a new client sends is a DHCP-Request broadcast IPv4 packet. The DHCP-Request packet has a source IPv4 address of 0.0.0.0. Because NAT requires both a valid destination and source IPv4 address, BOOTP and DHCP can have difficulty operating over a router running either static or dynamic NAT. Configuring the IPv4 helper feature can help solve this problem.

- **DNS and WINS:** Because a router running dynamic NAT is changing the relationship between inside and outside addresses regularly as table entries expire and are recreated, a DNS or WINS server outside the NAT router does not have an accurate representation of the network inside the router. Configuring the IPv4 helper feature can help solve this problem.

- **SNMP:** Similar to DNS packets, NAT is unable to alter the addressing information stored in the data payload of the packet. Because of this, an SNMP management station on one side of a NAT router may not be able to contact SNMP agents on the other side of the NAT router. Configuring the IPv4 helper feature can help solve this problem.

- **Tunneling and encryption protocols:** Encryption and tunneling protocols often require that traffic be sourced from a specific UDP or TCP port, or use a protocol at the transport layer that cannot be processed by NAT. For example, IPsec tunneling protocols and generic routing encapsulation protocols used by VPN implementations cannot be processed by NAT.

Note

DHCPv6 from an IPv6 client can be forwarded by the router using the **ipv6 dhcp relay** command.

- The common interoperability areas with NAT are summarized in Figure 9-29.

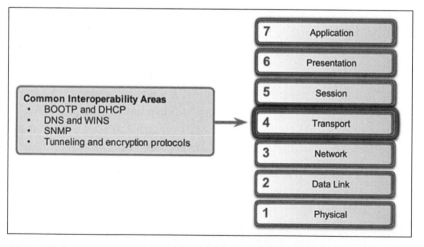

Figure 9-29   Common Interoperability with NAT

Application Layer Troubleshooting (9.2.2.6)

Most of the application layer protocols provide user services. Application layer protocols are typically used for network management, file transfer, distributed file services, terminal emulation, and email. New user services are often added, such as VPNs and VoIP.

Figure 9-30 shows the most widely known and implemented TCP/IP application layer protocols including the following:

- **SSH/Telnet:** Enables users to establish terminal session connections with remote hosts.

- **HTTP:** Supports the exchanging of text, graphic images, sound, video, and other multimedia files on the Web.

- **FTP:** Performs interactive file transfers between hosts.

- **TFTP:** Performs basic interactive file transfers typically between hosts and networking devices.

- **SMTP:** Supports basic message delivery services.

- **POP:** Connects to mail servers and downloads email.

- **Simple Network Management Protocol (SNMP):** Collects management information from network devices.

- **DNS:** Maps IP addresses to the names assigned to network devices.

- **Network File System (NFS):** Enables computers to mount drives on remote hosts and operate them as if they were local drives. Originally developed by Sun Microsystems, it combines with two other application layer protocols, eXternal Data Representation (XDR) and Remote Procedure Call (RPC), to allow transparent access to remote network resources.

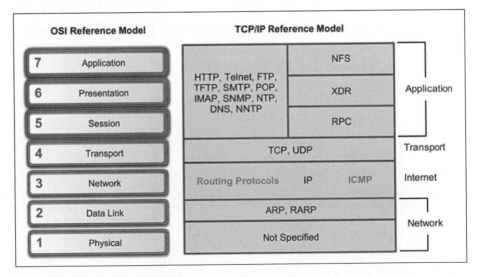

Figure 9-30 Application Layer

The types of symptoms and causes depend upon the actual application itself.

Application layer problems prevent services from being provided to application programs. A problem at the application layer can result in unreachable or unusable resources when the physical, data link, network, and transport layers are functional. It is possible to have full network connectivity, but the application simply cannot provide data.

Another type of problem at the application layer occurs when the physical, data link, network, and transport layers are functional, but the data transfer and requests for network services from a single network service or application do not meet the normal expectations of a user.

A problem at the application layer may cause users to complain that the network or the particular application that they are working with is sluggish or slower than usual when transferring data or requesting network services.

Interactive Graphic

Activity 9.2.2.7: Identify the OSI Layer Associated with a Network Issue

Go to the course online to perform this practice activity.

Troubleshooting IP Connectivity (9.2.3)

Using the systematic layered approach, the components of troubleshooting end-to-end connectivity are discussed.

Components of Troubleshooting End-to-End Connectivity (9.2.3.1)

Diagnosing and solving problems is an essential skill for network administrators. There is no single recipe for troubleshooting, and a particular problem can be diagnosed in many different ways. However, by employing a structured approach to the troubleshooting process, an administrator can reduce the time it takes to diagnose and solve a problem.

Using the topology in Figure 9-31, throughout this topic, the following scenario is used. The client host PC1 is unable to access applications on Server SRV1 or Server SRV2. The figure shows the topology of this network. PC1 uses SLAAC with EUI-64 to create its IPv6 global unicast address. EUI-64 creates the interface ID using the Ethernet MAC address, inserting FFFE in the middle, and flipping the seventh bit.

Figure 9-31   Topology used for the Components of End-to-End Troubleshooting

When there is no end-to-end connectivity, and the administrator chooses to troubleshoot with a bottom-up approach, these are common steps the administrator can take:

Step 1. Check physical connectivity at the point where network communication stops. This includes cables and hardware. The problem might be with a faulty cable or interface, or involve misconfigured or faulty hardware.

Step 2. Check for duplex mismatches.

Step 3. Check data link and network layer addressing on the local network. This includes IPv4 ARP tables, IPv6 neighbor tables, MAC address tables, and VLAN assignments.

Step 4. Verify that the default gateway is correct.

Step 5. Ensure that devices are determining the correct path from the source to the destination. Manipulate the routing information if necessary.

Step 6. Verify the transport layer is functioning properly. Telnet can also be used to test transport layer connections from the command line.

Step 7. Verify that there are no ACLs blocking traffic.

Step 8. Ensure that DNS settings are correct. There should be a DNS server that is accessible.

The outcome of this process is operational end-to-end connectivity. If all of the steps have been performed without any resolution, the network administrator may either want to repeat the previous steps or escalate the problem to a senior administrator.

End-to-End Connectivity Problem Initiates Troubleshooting (9.2.3.2)

Usually what initiates a troubleshooting effort is the discovery that there is a problem with end-to-end connectivity. Two of the most common utilities used to verify a problem with end-to-end connectivity are **ping** and **traceroute**, as shown in Figure 9-32.

Figure 9-32 Verification of End-to-End Troubleshooting

ping is probably the most widely known connectivity-testing utility in networking and has always been part of Cisco IOS Software. It sends out requests for responses from a specified host address. The **ping** command uses a Layer 3 protocol that is a part of the TCP/IP suite called ICMP. **ping** uses the ICMP echo request and ICMP echo reply packets. If the host at the specified address receives the ICMP echo request, it responds with an ICMP echo reply packet. **ping** can be used to verify end-to-end connectivity for both IPv4 and IPv6. Example 9-2 shows a successful **ping** from PC1 to SRV1, at address 172.16.1.100.

Example 9-2   Successful IPv4 **ping** from PCS1 to SVR1

```
PC1> ping 172.16.1.100
Pinging 172.16.1.100 with 32 bytes of data:
Reply from 172.16.1.100: bytes=32 time=8ms TTL=254
Reply from 172.16.1.100: bytes=32 time=1ms TTL=254
Reply from 172.16.1.100: bytes=32 time=1ms TTL=254
Reply from 172.16.1.100: bytes=32 time=1ms TTL=254
Ping statistics for 172.16.1.100:
Packets: Sent = 4, Received = 4, Lost = 0 (0% loss),
Approximate round-trip times in milliseconds:
Minimum = 1ms, Maximum = 8ms, Average = 2ms
```

The **traceroute** command in Example 9-3 illustrates the path the IPv4 packets take to reach their destination. Similar to the **ping** command, the Cisco IOS **traceroute** command can be used for both IPv4 and IPv6. The **tracert** command is used with Windows operating system. The trace generates a list of hops, router IP addresses and the final destination IP address that are successfully reached along the path. This list provides important verification and troubleshooting information. If the data reaches the destination, the trace lists the interface on every router in the path. If the data fails at some hop along the way, the address of the last router that responded to the trace is known. This address is an indication of where the problem or security restrictions reside.

Example 9-3   Successful IPv4 **tracert** from PCS1 to SVR1

```
C:\Windows\system32> tracert 172.16.1.100
Tracing route to 172.16.1.100 over a maximum of 30 hops
1    1 ms    <1 ms    <1 ms     10.1.10.1
2    2 ms    2 ms     1 ms      192.168.1.2
3    2 ms    2 ms     1 ms      192.168.1.6
4    2 ms    2 ms     1 ms      172.16.1.100
Trace complete.
```

As stated, the **ping** and **traceroute** utilities can be used to test and diagnose end-to-end IPv6 connectivity by providing the IPv6 address as the destination address. When using these utilities, the Cisco IOS utility recognizes whether the address is an IPv4 or IPv6 address and uses the appropriate protocol to test connectivity. Example 9-4 shows the **ping** and **traceroute** commands on router R1 used to test IPv6 connectivity.

Example 9-4   Successful IPv6 **ping** and **traceroute** from PCS1 to SVR1

```
R1# ping 2001:db8:acad:4::100
Type escape sequence to abort.
Sending 5, 100-byte ICMP Echos to 2001:DB8:ACAD:4::100, timeout is 2 seconds:
!!!!!
Success rate is 100 percent (5/5), round-trip min/avg/max = 56/56/56 ms
R1# traceroute 2001:db8:acad:4::100
Type escape sequence to abort.
Tracing the route to 2001:DB8:ACAD:4::100
  1 2001:DB8:ACAD:2::2 20 msec 20 msec 20 msec
  2 2001:DB8:ACAD:3::2 44 msec 40 msec 40 msec
R1#
```

Step 1 - Verify the Physical Layer (9.2.3.3)

All network devices are specialized computer systems. At a minimum, these devices consist of a CPU, RAM, and storage space, allowing the device to boot and run the operating system and interfaces. This allows for the reception and transmission of network traffic. When a network administrator determines that a problem exists on a given device, and that problem might be hardware related, it is worthwhile to verify the operation of these generic components. The most commonly used Cisco IOS commands for this purpose are **show processes cpu, show memory**, and **show interfaces**. This topic discusses the **show interfaces** command.

When troubleshooting performance-related issues and hardware is suspected to be at fault, the **show interfaces** command can be used to verify the interfaces through which the traffic passes.

The output of the **show interfaces** command in Example 9-5 lists a number of important statistics that can be checked:

- **Input queue drops:** Input queue drops (and the related ignored and throttle counters) signify that at some point, more traffic was delivered to the router than it could process. This does not necessarily indicate a problem. That could be normal during traffic peaks. However, it could be an indication that the CPU cannot process packets in time, so if this number is consistently high, it is worth trying to spot at which moments these counters are increasing and how this relates to CPU usage.

- **Output queue drops:** Output queue drops indicate that packets were dropped due to congestion on the interface. Seeing output drops is normal for any point where the aggregate input traffic is higher than the output traffic. During traffic peaks, packets are dropped if traffic is delivered to the interface faster than it can be sent out. However, even if this is considered normal behavior, it leads to packet drops and queuing delays, so applications that are sensitive to those, such as VoIP, might suffer from performance issues. Consistently seeing output drops can be an indicator that you need to implement an advanced queuing mechanism to provide good QoS to each application.

- **Input errors:** Input errors indicate errors that are experienced during the reception of the frame, such as CRC errors. High numbers of CRC errors could indicate cabling problems, interface hardware problems, or, in an Ethernet-based network, duplex mismatches.

- **Output errors:** Output errors indicate errors, such as collisions, during the transmission of a frame. In most Ethernet-based networks today, full-duplex transmission is the norm, and half-duplex transmission is the exception. In full-duplex transmission, operation collisions cannot occur; therefore, collisions and especially late collisions often indicate duplex mismatches.

Example 9-5   Examining Input and Output Statistics on R1

```
R1# show interfaces GigabitEthernet 0/0
GigabitEthernet0/0 is up, line protocol is up
  Hardware is CN Gigabit Ethernet, address is d48c.b5ce.a0c0 (bia d48c.b5ce.a0c0)
  Internet address is 10.1.10.1/24
  <Output Omitted>
  Input queue: 0/75/0/0 (size/max/drops/flushes); Total output drops: 0
  Queueing strategy: fifo
  Output queue: 0/40 (size/max)
  5 minute input rate 0 bits/sec, 0 packets/sec
  5 minute output rate 0 bits/sec, 0 packets/sec
     85 packets input, 7711 bytes, 0 no buffer
     Received 25 broadcasts (0 IP multicasts)
     0 runts, 0 giants, 0 throttles
     0 input errors, 0 CRC, 0 frame, 0 overrun, 0 ignored
     0 watchdog, 5 multicast, 0 pause input
     10112 packets output, 922864 bytes, 0 underruns
     0 output errors, 0 collisions, 1 interface resets
     11 unknown protocol drops
     0 babbles, 0 late collision, 0 deferred
     0 lost carrier, 0 no carrier, 0 pause output
     0 output buffer failures, 0 output buffers swapped out
R1#
```

Step 2 - Check for Duplex Mismatches (9.2.3.4)

Another common cause for interface errors is a mismatched duplex mode between two ends of an Ethernet link. In many Ethernet-based networks, point-to-point connections are now the norm, and the use of hubs and the associated half-duplex operation is becoming less common. This means that most Ethernet links today operate in full-duplex mode, and while collisions were seen as normal for an Ethernet link, collisions today often indicate that duplex negotiation has failed and that the link is not operating in the correct duplex mode.

The IEEE 802.3ab Gigabit Ethernet standard mandates the use of autonegotiation for speed and duplex. In addition, although it is not strictly mandatory, practically all Fast Ethernet NICs also use autonegotiation by default. The use of autonegotiation for speed and duplex is the current recommended practice. The guidelines are described in the following bulleted list. However, if duplex negotiation fails for some reason, it might be necessary to set the speed and duplex manually on both ends. Typically, this would mean setting the duplex mode to full-duplex on both ends of the connection. However, if this does not work, running half-duplex on both ends is preferred over a duplex mismatch.

General duplex configuration guidelines are as follows:

- Point-to-point Ethernet links should always run in full-duplex mode.

- Half-duplex Ethernet is not common anymore and mostly encountered if hubs are used.

- Autonegotiation of speed and duplex is recommended.

- If autonegotiation does not work, manually set the speed and duplex on both ends.

- Half-duplex on both ends performs better than duplex mismatch.

Note

Most 802.11 wireless protocols operate in half-duplex.

Troubleshooting Example

In the previous scenario, the network administrator needed to add additional users to the network. To incorporate these new users, the network administrator installed a second switch and connected it to the first. Soon after, S2 was added to the network, users on both switches began experiencing significant performance problems connecting with devices on the other switch, as shown in Figure 9-33.

Figure 9-33   Duplex Mismatch

The network administrator notices a console message on switch S2:

```
*Mar  1 00:45:08.756: %CDP-4-DUPLEX_MISMATCH: duplex mismatch discovered
on FastEthernet0/20 (not half duplex), with Switch FastEthernet0/20 (half
duplex).
```

Using the **show interfaces fa 0/20** command, the network administrator examines the interface on S1 used to connect to S2 and notices it is set to full-duplex, as shown in Example 9-6. The network administrator now examines the other side of the connection, the port on S2. Example 9-7 shows that this side of the connection has been configured for half-duplex. The network administrator corrects the setting to `duplex auto` to automatically negotiate the duplex. Because the port on S1 is set to full-duplex, S2 also uses full-duplex.

The users report that there are no longer any performance problems.

Example 9-6   S1 Port Operating in Full-Duplex

```
S1# show interface fa 0/20
FastEthernet0/20 is up, line protocol is up (connected)
  Hardware is Fast Ethernet, address is 0cd9.96e8.8a01 (bia 0cd9.96e8.8a01)
  MTU 1500 bytes, BW 10000 Kbit/sec, DLY 1000 usec,
     reliability 255/255, txload 1/255, rxload 1/255
  Encapsulation ARPA, loopback not set
  Keepalive set (10 sec)
  Full-duplex, Auto-speed, media type is 10/100BaseTX
<Output omitted>
```

Example 9-7   S2 Port Operating in Half-Duplex

```
S2# show interface fa 0/20
FastEthernet0/20 is up, line protocol is up (connected)
  Hardware is Fast Ethernet, address is 0cd9.96d2.4001 (bia 0cd9.96d2.4001)
  MTU 1500 bytes, BW 100000 Kbit/sec, DLY 100 usec,
     reliability 255/255, txload 1/255, rxload 1/255
  Encapsulation ARPA, loopback not set
  Keepalive set (10 sec)
  Half-duplex, Auto-speed, media type is 10/100BaseTX
<Output omitted>
Switch(config)# interface fa 0/20
Switch(config-if)# duplex auto
Switch(config-if)#
```

Step 3 - Verify Layer 2 and Layer 3 Addressing on the Local Network (9.2.3.5)

When troubleshooting end-to-end connectivity, it is useful to verify mappings between destination IP addresses and Layer 2 Ethernet addresses on individual segments. In IPv4, this functionality is provided by ARP. In IPv6, the ARP functionality is replaced by the neighbor discovery process and ICMPv6. The neighbor table caches IPv6 addresses and their resolved Ethernet physical (MAC) addresses.

IPv4 ARP Table

The **arp** Windows command displays and modifies entries in the ARP cache that are used to store IPv4 addresses and their resolved Ethernet physical (MAC) addresses. As shown in Example 9-8, the **arp** Windows command lists all devices that are currently in the ARP cache. The information that is displayed for each device includes the IPv4 address, physical (MAC) address, and the type of addressing (static or dynamic).

Example 9-8   ARP Table on PC1

```
PC1> arp -a
Interface: 10.1.10.100 --- 0xd
Internet        Address Physical  Address Type
10.1.10.1       d4-8c-b5-ce-a0-c0  dynamic
224.0.0.22      01-00-5e-00-00-16  static
224.0.0.252     01-00-5e-00-00-fc  static
255.255.255.255 ff-ff-ff-ff-ff-ff  static
```

The cache can be cleared by using the **arp -d** Windows command if the network administrator wants to repopulate the cache with updated information.

Note

The **arp** commands in Linux and MAC OS X have a similar syntax.

IPv6 Neighbor Table

As shown in Example 9-9, the **netsh interface ipv6 show neighbor** Windows command lists all devices that are currently in the neighbor table. The information that is displayed for each device includes the IPv6 address, physical (MAC) address, and the type of addressing. By examining the neighbor table, the network administrator can verify that destination IPv6 addresses map to correct Ethernet addresses. The IPv6 link-local addresses on all of R1's interfaces have been manually configured to FE80::1. Similarly, R2 has been configured with the link-local address of FE80::2 on its interfaces, and R3 has been configured with the link-local address of FE80::3 on its interfaces. Remember, link-local addresses only have to be unique on the link or network.

Example 9-9   Neighbor Table on PC1

```
PC1> netsh interface ipv6 show neighbor
Interface 13: LAB
Internet Address                            Physical Address      Type
---------------------------------------     -----------------     ----------
fe80::9c5a:e957:a865:bde9                   00-0c-29-36-fd-f7     Stale
fe80::1                                     d4-8c-b5-ce-a0-c0     Reachable (Router)
ff02::2                                     33-33-00-00-00-02     Permanent
ff02::16                                    33-33-00-00-00-16     Permanent
ff02::1:2                                   33-33-00-01-00-02     Permanent
ff02::1:3                                   33-33-00-01-00-03     Permanent
ff02::1:ff05:f9fb                           33-33-ff-05-f9-fb     Permanent
ff02::1:ffce:a0c0                           33-33-ff-ce-a0-c0     Permanent
ff02::1:ff65:bde9                           33-33-ff-65-bd-e9     Permanent
ff02::1:ff67:bae4
```

Note

The neighbor table for Linux and MAC OS X can be displayed using **ip neigh show** command.

Example 9-10 shows an example of the neighbor table on the Cisco IOS router, using the **show ipv6 neighbors** command.

Example 9-10   Neighbor Table on R1

```
R1# show ipv6 neighbors
IPv6 Address                          Age   Link-layer Addr   State    Interface
FE80::21E:7AFF:FE79:7A81               8    001e.7a79.7a81    STALE    Gi0/0
2001:DB8:ACAD:1:5075:D0FF:FE8E:9AD8    0    5475.d08e.9ad8    REACH    Gi0/0
```

Note

The neighbor states for IPv6 are more complex than the ARP table states in IPv4. Additional information is contained in RFC 4861.

Switch MAC Address Table

A switch forwards a frame only to the port where the destination is connected. To do this, the switch consults its MAC address table. The MAC address table lists the MAC address connected to each port. Use the **show mac address-table** command to display the MAC address table on the switch. An example of PC1's local switch is shown in Example 9-11. Remember, a switch's MAC address table only contains Layer 2 information, including the Ethernet MAC address and the port number. IP address information is not included.

Example 9-11   MAC Address Table on Local LAN Switch

```
S1# show mac address-table
            Mac Address Table
-------------------------------------------

Vlan    Mac Address      Type       Ports
All     0100.0ccc.cccc   STATIC     CPU
All     0100.0ccc.cccd   STATIC     CPU
 10     d48c.b5ce.a0c0   DYNAMIC    Fa0/4
 10     000f.34f9.9201   DYNAMIC    Fa0/5
 10     5475.d08e.9ad8   DYNAMIC    Fa0/13
Total Mac Addresses for this criterion: 5
```

VLAN Assignment

Another issue to consider when troubleshooting end-to-end connectivity is VLAN assignment. In the switched network, each port in a switch belongs to a VLAN. Each VLAN is considered a separate logical network, and packets destined for stations that do not belong to the VLAN must be forwarded through a device that supports routing. If a host in one VLAN sends a broadcast Ethernet frame, such as an ARP request, all hosts in the same VLAN receive the frame; hosts in other VLANs do not. Even if two hosts are in the same IP network, they will not be able to communicate if they are connected to ports assigned to two separate VLANs. Additionally, if the VLAN to which the port belongs is deleted, the port becomes inactive. All hosts attached to ports belonging to the VLAN that was deleted are unable to communicate with the rest of the network. Commands such as show vlan can be used to validate VLAN assignments on a switch.

Troubleshooting Example

Refer to the topology in Figure 9-34. To improve the wire management in the wiring closet, the cables connecting to S1 were reorganized. Almost immediately afterward, users started calling the support desk stating that they could no longer reach devices outside their own network. An examination of PC1's ARP table using the **arp** Windows command shows that the ARP table no longer contains an entry for the default gateway 10.1.10.1, as shown in Example 9-12. There were no configuration changes on the router, so S1 is the focus of the troubleshooting.

Figure 9-34   Troubleshooting Example

Example 9-12   S1 ARP Table on PC1

```
PC1> arp -a
Interface: 10.1.10.100 --- 0xd
Internet         Address Physical    Address Type
224.0.0.22       01-00-5e-00-00-16   static
224.0.0.252      01-00-5e-00-00-fc   static
255.255.255.255  ff-ff-ff-ff-ff-ff   static
```

The MAC address table for S1, as shown in Example 9-13, shows that the MAC address for R1 is on a different VLAN than the rest of the 10.1.10.0/24 devices including PC1. During the recabling, R1's patch cable was moved from Fa 0/4 on VLAN 10 to Fa 0/1 on VLAN 1. After the network administrator configured S1's Fa 0/1 port to be on VLAN 10, as shown in Example 9-14, the problem was resolved. As shown in Example 9-15, the MAC address table now shows VLAN 10 for the MAC address of R1 on port Fa 0/1.

Example 9-13   MAC Address Table Reveals Wrong VLAN for Fa0/1

```
S1# show mac address-table
            Mac Address Table
-------------------------------------------
Vlan     Mac Address       Type      Ports
All      0100.0ccc.cccc    STATIC    CPU
All      0100.0ccc.cccd    STATIC    CPU
  1      d48c.b5ce.a0c0    DYNAMIC   Fa0/1    ! R1
 10      000f.34f9.9201    DYNAMIC   Fa0/5
 10      5475.d08e.9ad8    DYNAMIC   Fa0/13   ! PC1
Total Mac Addresses for this criterion: 5
```

Example 9-14   Configuring the Correct VLAN

```
S1(config)# interface fa 0/1
S1(config-if)# switchport mode access
S1(config-if)# switchport access vlan 10
S1(config-if)#
```

Example 9-15   S1 MAC Address Table on Local LAN Switch

```
S1# show mac address-table
          Mac Address Table
-------------------------------------------
Vlan     Mac Address      Type      Ports
All      0100.0ccc.cccc   STATIC    CPU
All      0100.0ccc.cccd   STATIC    CPU
 10      d48c.b5ce.a0c0   DYNAMIC   Fa0/1    ! R1
 10      000f.34f9.9201   DYNAMIC   Fa0/5
 10      5475.d08e.9ad8   DYNAMIC   Fa0/13   ! PC1
Total Mac Addresses for this criterion: 5
```

Step 4 - Verify Default Gateway (9.2.3.6)

If there is no detailed route on the router or if the host is configured with the wrong default gateway, then communication between two endpoints in different networks does not work. Figure 9-35 illustrates that PC1 uses R1 as its default gateway. Similarly, R1 uses R2 as its default gateway or gateway of last resort.

Figure 9-35   Identification of Current and Desired Path: Default Gateway

If a host needs access to resources beyond the local network, the default gateway must be configured. The default gateway is the first router on the path to destinations beyond the local network.

Troubleshooting Example 1

Example 9-16 shows the **show ip route** Cisco IOS command and the **route print** Windows command to verify the presence of the IPv4 default gateway.

Example 9-16   Verify the IPv4 Default Gateway

```
R1# show ip route
<Output omitted>


Gateway of last resort is 192.168.1.2 to network 0.0.0.0


S*    0.0.0.0/0 [1/0] via 192.168.1.2


C:\Windows\system32> route print
<Output omitted>
Network  Destination  Netmask    Gateway     Interface     Metric
         0.0.0.0      0.0.0.0    10.1.10.2   10.1.10.100   11
```

In this example, the R1 router has the correct default gateway, which is the IPv4 address of the R2 router. However, PC1 has the wrong default gateway. PC1 should have the default gateway of R1 router 10.1.10.1. This must be configured manually if the IPv4 addressing information was manually configured on PC1. If the IPv4 addressing information was obtained automatically from a DHCPv4 server, then the configuring on the DHCP server must be examined. A configuration problem on a DHCP server is usually seen by multiple clients.

Troubleshooting Example 2

In IPv6, the default gateway can be configured manually or by using stateless autoconfiguration (SLAAC) or DHCPv6. With SLAAC, the default gateway is advertised by the router to hosts using ICMPv6 router advertisement (RA) messages. The default gateway in the RA message is the link-local IPv6 address of a router interface. If the default gateway is configured manually on the host, which is very unlikely, the default gateway can be set either to the global IPv6 address or to the link-local IPv6 address.

As shown in Example 9-17, the **show ipv6 route** Cisco IOS command displays the IPv6 default route on R1, and the **ipconfig** Windows command is used to verify the presence of the IPv6 default gateway.

Example 9-17   Missing IPv6 Default Gateway

```
R1# show ipv6 route
<Output omitted>
S    ::/0 [1/0]
     via 2001:DB8:ACAD:2::2

C:\Windows\system32> ipconfig
Windows IP Configuration
   Connection-specific DNS Suffix . :
   Link-local IPv6 Address . . . . . : fe80::5075:d0ff:fe8e:9ad8%13
   IPv4 Address. . . . . . . . . . . : 10.1.1.100
   Subnet Mask . . . . . . . . . . . : 255.255.255.0
   Default Gateway . . . . . . . . . : 10.1.10.1
```

R1 has a default route via router R2, but notice the **ipconfig** command reveals the absence of an IPv6 global unicast address and an IPv6 default gateway. PC1 is enabled for IPv6 because it has an IPv6 link-local address. The link-local address is automatically created by the device. Checking the network documentation, the network administrator confirms that hosts on this LAN should be receiving their IPv6 address information from the router using SLAAC.

Note

In this example, other devices on the same LAN using SLAAC would also experience the same problem receiving IPv6 address information.

Using the **show ipv6 interface GigabitEthernet 0/0** command in Example 9-18, it can be seen that although the interface has an IPv6 address, it is not a member of the All-IPv6-Routers multicast group FF02::2. This means the router is not sending out ICMPv6 RAs on this interface. In Example 9-19, R1 is enabled as an IPv6 router using the **ipv6 unicast-routing** command. The **show ipv6 interface GigabitEthernet 0/0** command now reveals that R1 is a member of FF02::2, the All-IPv6-Routers multicast group.

Example 9-18   R1 Not Configured as an IPv6 Router

```
R1# show ipv6 interface GigabitEthernet 0/0
GigabitEthernet0/0 is up, line protocol is up
  IPv6 is enabled, link-local address is FE80::1
  No Virtual link-local address(es):
  Global unicast address(es):
    2001:DB8:ACAD:1::1, subnet is 2001:DB8:ACAD:1::/64
  Joined group address(es):
    FF02::1
    FF02::1:FF00:1
<Output Omitted>
```

Example 9-19 R1 Configured as an IPv6 Router

```
R1(config)# ipv6 unicast-routing
R1(config)# end
R1# show ipv6 interface GigabitEthernet 0/0
GigabitEthernet0/0 is up, line protocol is up
  IPv6 is enabled, link-local address is FE80::1
  No Virtual link-local address(es):
  Global unicast address(es):
    2001:DB8:ACAD:1::1, subnet is 2001:DB8:ACAD:1::/64
  Joined group address(es):
    FF02::1
    FF02::2
    FF02::1:FF00:1
<Output Omitted>
```

To verify that PC1 has the default gateway set, use the **ipconfig** command on the Microsoft Windows PC or the **ifconfig** command on Linux and Mac OS X. In Example 9-20, PC1 has an IPv6 global unicast address and an IPv6 default gateway. The default-gateway is set to the link-local address of router R1, FE80::1.

Example 9-20 Verify the IPv6 Default Gateway

```
PC1> ipconfig
Windows IP Configuration
   Connection-specific DNS Suffix . :
   IPv6 Address. . . . . . . . . . . : 2001:db8:acad:1:5075:d0ff:fe8e:9ad8
   Link-local IPv6 Address . . . . . : fe80::5075:d0ff:fe8e:9ad8
   IPv4 Address. . . . . . . . . . . : 10.1.1.100
   Subnet Mask . . . . . . . . . . . : 255.255.255.0
   Default Gateway . . . . . . . . . : fe80::1
                                        10.1.10.1
```

Step 5 - Verify Correct Path (9.2.3.7)

Understanding the process of packet forwarding is an essential element in verifying the correct path to the destination.

Troubleshooting the Network Layer

When troubleshooting, it is often necessary to verify the path to the destination network. Figure 9-36 shows the reference topology indicating the intended path for packets from PC1 to SRV1.

Figure 9-36   Identification of Current and Desired Path: Network Layer

In Example 9-21, the **show ip route** command is used to examine the IPv4 routing table.

The IPv4 and IPv6 routing tables can be populated by the following methods:

- Directly connected networks

- Local host or local routes

- Static routes

- Dynamic routes

- Default routes

Example 9-21   Examining the IPv4 Routing Table on R1

```
R1# show ip route
Codes: L - local, C - connected, S - static, R - RIP, M - mobile, B - BGP
       D - EIGRP, EX - EIGRP external, O - OSPF, IA - OSPF inter area
       N1 - OSPF NSSA external type 1, N2 - OSPF NSSA external type 2
       E1 - OSPF external type 1, E2 - OSPF external type 2
       i - IS-IS, su - IS-IS summary, L1 - IS-IS level-1, L2 - IS-IS level-2
       ia - IS-IS inter area, * - candidate default, U - per-user static route
       o - ODR, P - periodic downloaded static route, H - NHRP, l - LISP
       + - replicated route, % - next hop override
```

```
Gateway of last resort is 192.168.1.2 to network 0.0.0.0
S*    0.0.0.0/0 [1/0] via 192.168.1.2
      10.0.0.0/8 is variably subnetted, 2 subnets, 2 masks
C        10.1.10.0/24 is directly connected, GigabitEthernet0/0
L        10.1.10.1/32 is directly connected, GigabitEthernet0/0
      172.16.0.0/24 is subnetted, 1 subnets
D        172.16.1.0 [90/41024256] via 192.168.1.2, 05:32:46, Serial0/0/0
      192.168.1.0/24 is variably subnetted, 3 subnets, 2 masks
C        192.168.1.0/30 is directly connected, Serial0/0/0
L        192.168.1.1/32 is directly connected, Serial0/0/0
D        192.168.1.4/30 [90/41024000] via 192.168.1.2, 05:32:46, Serial0/0/0
R1#
```

The process of forwarding IPv4 and IPv6 packets is based on the longest bit match or longest prefix match. The routing table process will attempt to forward the packet using an entry in the routing table with the greatest number of far left matching bits. The number of matching bits is indicated by the route's prefix length.

Example 9-22 shows a similar scenario with IPv6. To verify that the current IPv6 path matches the desired path to reach destinations, use the **show ipv6 route** command on a router to examine the routing table. After examining the IPv6 routing table, R1 does have a path to 2001:DB8:ACAD:4::/64 via R2 at FE80::2.

Example 9-22   Examining the IPv6 Routing Table on R1

```
R1# show ipv6 route
IPv6 Routing Table - default - 7 entries
Codes: C - Connected, L - Local, S - Static, U - Per-user Static route
       B - BGP, R - RIP, I1 - ISIS L1, I2 - ISIS L2
       IA - ISIS interarea, IS - ISIS summary, D - EIGRP, EX - EIGRP external
       ND - ND Default, NDp - ND Prefix, DCE - Destination, NDr - Redirect
       O - OSPF Intra, OI - OSPF Inter, OE1 - OSPF ext 1, OE2 - OSPF ext 2
       ON1 - OSPF NSSA ext 1, ON2 - OSPF NSSA ext 2
S   ::/0 [1/0]
     via 2001:DB8:ACAD:2::2
C   2001:DB8:ACAD:1::/64 [0/0]
     via GigabitEthernet0/0, directly connected
L   2001:DB8:ACAD:1::1/128 [0/0]
     via GigabitEthernet0/0, receive
C   2001:DB8:ACAD:2::/64 [0/0]
     via Serial0/0/0, directly connected
L   2001:DB8:ACAD:2::1/128 [0/0]
     via Serial0/0/0, receive
D   2001:DB8:ACAD:3::/64 [90/41024000]
     via FE80::2, Serial0/0/0
D   2001:DB8:ACAD:4::/64 [90/41024256]
```

```
     via FE80::2, Serial0/0/0
L   FF00::/8 [0/0]
     via Null0, receive
R1#
```

The following list, along with Figure 9-37, describes the process for both the IPv4 and IPv6 routing tables. If the destination address in a packet

- Does not match an entry in the routing table, then the default route is used. If there is not a default route that is configured, the packet is discarded.

- Matches a single entry in the routing table, then the packet is forwarded through the interface that is defined in this route.

- Matches more than one entry in the routing table and the routing entries have the same prefix length, then the packets for this destination can be distributed among the routes that are defined in the routing table.

- Matches more than one entry in the routing table and the routing entries have different prefix lengths, then the packets for this destination are forwarded out of the interface that is associated with the route that has the longer prefix match.

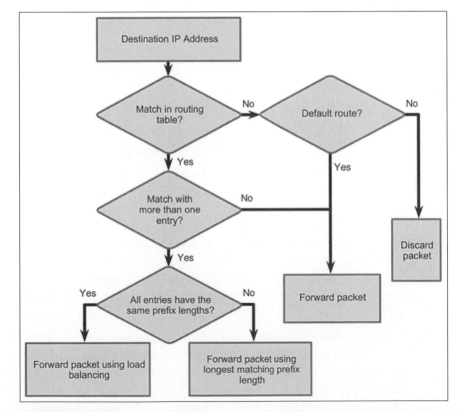

Figure 9-37   Routing Table Process

Troubleshooting Example

Devices are unable to connect to the server SRV1 at 172.16.1.100. Using the **show ip route** command, the administrator should check to see if a routing entry exists to network 172.16.1.0/24. If the routing table does not have a specific route to SRV1's network, the network administrator must then check for the existence of a default or summary route entry in the direction of the 172.16.1.0/24 network. If none exists, then the problem may be with routing and the administrator must verify that the network is included within the dynamic routing protocol configuration, or add a static route.

Step 6 - Verify the Transport Layer (9.2.3.8)

If the network layer appears to be functioning as expected, but users are still unable to access resources, then the network administrator must begin troubleshooting the upper layers. Two of the most common issues that affect transport layer connectivity include ACL configurations and NAT configurations. A common tool for testing transport layer functionality is the Telnet utility.

Caution

While Telnet can be used to test the transport layer, for security reasons, SSH should be used to remotely manage and configure devices.

A network administrator is troubleshooting a problem where someone cannot send email through a particular SMTP server. The administrator pings the server, and it responds. This means that the network layer, and all layers below the network layer, between the user and the server is operational. The administrator knows the issue is with Layer 4 or up and must start troubleshooting those layers.

Although the Telnet server application runs on its own well-known port number 23 and Telnet clients connect to this port by default, a different port number can be specified on the client to connect to any TCP port that must be tested. This indicates whether the connection is accepted (as indicated by the word Open in the output), refused, or times out. From any of those responses, further conclusions can be made concerning the connectivity. Certain applications, if they use an ASCII-based session protocol, might even display an application banner, it may be possible to trigger some responses from the server by typing in certain keywords, such as with SMTP, FTP, and HTTP.

Given the previous scenario, the administrator Telnets from PC1 to the server HQ, using IPv6, and the Telnet session is successful, as shown in Example 9-23. In Example 9-24 the administrator attempts to Telnet to the same server, using port 80. The output verifies that the transport layer is connecting successfully from PC1 to HQ. However, the server is not accepting connections on port 80.

Example 9-23   Successful Telnet Connection Over IPv4

```
PC1> telnet 2001:DB8:172:16::100
HQ#
```

Example 9-24   Testing the Transport Layer over IPv4 Using Port 80 (HTTP)

```
PC1> telnet 2001:DB8:172:16::100 80
HTTP/1.1 400 Bad Request
Date: Wed, 26 Sep 2012 07:27:10 GMT
Server: cisco-IOS
Accept-Ranges: none
400 Bad Request
Connection to host lost.
```

The example in Example 9-25 shows a successful Telnet connection from R1 to R3, over IPv6. Example 9-26 is a similar Telnet attempt using port 80. Again, the output verifies a success transport layer connection, but R3 is refusing the connection using port 80.

Example 9-25   Successful Telnet Connection over IPv6

```
R1# telnet 2001:db8:acad:3::2
Trying 2001:DB8:ACAD:3::2 ... Open

User Access Verification

Password:
R3>
```

Example 9-26   Testing the Transport Layer over IPv6 Using Port 80 (HTTP)

```
R1# telnet 2001:db8:acad:3::2 80
Trying 2001:DB8:ACAD:3::2, 80 ...
% Connection refused by remote host

R1#
```

Step 7 - Verify ACLs (9.2.3.9)

On routers, there may be ACLs configured that prohibit protocols from passing through the interface in the inbound or outbound direction.

Use the **show ip access-lists** command to display the contents of all IPv4 ACLs and the **show ipv6 access-list** command to show the contents of all IPv6 ACLs configured on a router. The specific ACL can be displayed by entering the ACL name or number as an option for this command; you can display a specific ACL. The **show ip interfaces and show ipv6 interfaces** commands display IPv4 and IPv6 interface information that indicates whether any IP ACLs are set on the interface.

Troubleshooting Example

To prevent spoofing attacks, the network administrator decided to implement an ACL preventing device with a source network address of 172.16.1.0/24 from entering the inbound S0/0/1 interface on R3, as shown in Figure 9-38. All other IP traffic should be allowed.

Figure 9-38   ACL Issues

However, shortly after implementing the ACL, users on the 10.1.10.0/24 network were unable to connect to devices on the 172.16.1.0/24 network, including SRV1. The **show ip access-lists** command shows that the ACL is configured correctly, as shown in Example 9-27. However, the **show ip interfaces serial 0/0/1** command reveals that the ACL was never applied to the inbound interface on s0/0/1. Further investigation reveals that the ACL was accidentally applied to the G0/0 interface, blocking all outbound traffic from the 172.16.1.0/24 network.

Example 9-27   Display ACLs and ACL Placement on R1

```
R3# show ip access-lists
Extended IP access list 100
    deny ip 172.16.1.0 0.0.0.255 any (3 match(es))
    permit ip any any


R3# show ip interface Serial 0/0/1 | include access list
  Outgoing access list is not set
  Inbound access list is not set
R3# show ip interface gigabitethernet 0/0 | include access list
  Outgoing access list is not set
  Inbound  access list is 100
```

After correctly placing the IPv4 ACL on the s0/0/1 inbound interface, as shown in Example 9-28, devices are able to successfully connect to the server.

Example 9-28   Changing ACL Placement

```
R3(config)# interface gigabitethernet 0/0
R3(config-if)# no ip access-group 100 in
R3(config-if)# interface serial 0/0/1
R3(config-if)# ip access-group 100 in
```

Step 8 - Verify DNS (9.2.3.10)

The DNS protocol controls the DNS, a distributed database with which you can map hostnames to IP addresses. When you configure DNS on the device, you can substitute the hostname for the IP address with all IP commands, such as **ping** or **telnet**.

To display the DNS configuration information on the switch or router, use the **show running-config** command. When there is no DNS server installed, it is possible to enter names to IP mappings directly into the switch or router configuration. Use the **ip host** command to enter names to IPv4 mapping to the switch or router. The **ipv6 host** command is used for the same mappings using IPv6. These commands are demonstrated in Example 9-29. Because IPv6 network numbers are long and difficult to remember, DNS is even more important for IPv6 than for IPv4.

Example 9-29   Creating Name-to-IP Mappings

```
R1(config)# ip host ipv4-server 172.16.1.100
R1# ping ipv4-server
Type escape sequence to abort.
Sending 5, 100-byte ICMP Echos to 172.16.1.100, timeout is 2 seconds:
```

```
!!!!!
Success rate is 100 percent (5/5), round-trip min/avg/max = 52/56/64 ms
R1#
R1(config)# ipv6 host ipv6-server 2001:db8:acad:4::100
R1# ping ipv6-server
Type escape sequence to abort.
Sending 5, 100-byte ICMP Echos to 2001:DB8:ACAD:4::100, timeout is 2 seconds:
!!!!!
Success rate is 100 percent (5/5), round-trip min/avg/max = 52/54/56 ms
R1#
```

To display the name-to-IP-address mapping information on the Windows-based PC, use the **nslookup** command.

Troubleshooting Example

The output in Example 9-30 indicates that either the client was unable to reach the DNS server or the DNS service on the 10.1.1.1 was not running. At this point, the troubleshooting needs to focus on communications with the DNS server, or to verify the DNS server is running properly.

Example 9-30   Unable to Reach DNS Server

```
PC1> nslookup Server
*** Request to 10.1.1.1 timed-out
```

To display the DNS configuration information on a Microsoft Windows PC, use the **nslookup** command. There should be DNS configured for IPv4, IPv6, or both. DNS can provide IPv4 and IPv6 addresses at the same time, regardless of the protocol that is used to access the DNS server.

Because domain names and DNS are a vital component of accessing servers on the network, many times the user thinks the "network is down" when the problem is actually with the DNS server.

Interactive Graphic

Activity 9.2.3.11: Identify Commands to Troubleshoot a Network Issue

Go to the course online to perform this practice activity.

Packet Tracer Activity 9.2.3.12: Troubleshooting Enterprise Networks 1

Background/Scenario

This activity uses a variety of technologies you have encountered during your CCNA studies including VLANs, STP, routing, inter-VLAN routing, DHCP, NAT, PPP, and Frame Relay. Your task is to review the requirements, isolate and resolve any issues, and then document the steps you took to verify the requirements.

Packet Tracer Activity 9.2.3.13: Troubleshooting Enterprise Networks 2

Background/Scenario

This activity uses IPv6 configurations including DHCPv6, EIGRPv6, and IPv6 default routing. Your task is to review the requirements, isolate and resolve any issues, and then document the steps you took to verify the requirements.

Packet Tracer Activity 9.2.3.14: Troubleshooting Enterprise Networks 3

Background/Scenario

This activity uses a variety of technologies you have encountered during your CCNA studies including routing, port security, EtherChannel, DHCP, NAT, PPP, and Frame Relay. Your task is to review the requirements, isolate and resolve any issues, and then document the steps you took to verify the requirements.

Packet Tracer Activity 9.2.3.15: Troubleshooting Challenge - Using Documentation to Solve Issues

Background/Scenario

This is Part II of a two-part activity. Part I is Packet Tracer - Troubleshooting Challenge - Documenting the Network, which you should have completed earlier in the chapter. In Part II, you will use your troubleshooting skills and documentation from Part I to solve connectivity issues between PCs.

Summary (9.3)

Class Activity 9.3.1.1: Documentation Development

As the network administrator for a small business, you want to implement a documentation system to use with troubleshooting network-based problems.

After much thought, you decide to compile simple network documentation information into a file to be used when network problems arise. You also know that if the company gets larger in the future, this file can be used to export the information to a computerized network software system.

To start the network documentation process, you include the following:

- A physical diagram of your small business network

- A logical diagram of your small business network

- Network configuration information for major devices, including routers and switches

For network administrators to be able to monitor and troubleshoot a network, they must have a complete set of accurate and current network documentation, including configuration files, physical and logical topology diagrams, and a baseline performance level.

The three major stages to troubleshooting problems are gather symptoms, isolate the problem, and then correct the problem. It is sometimes necessary to temporarily implement a workaround to the problem. If the intended corrective action does not fix the problem, the change should be removed. In all process steps, the network administrator should document the process. A troubleshooting policy, including change control procedures, should be established for each stage. After the problem is resolved, it is important to communicate this to the users, anyone involved in the troubleshooting process, and to other IT team members.

The OSI model or the TCP/IP model can be applied to a network problem. A network administrator can use the bottom-up method, the top-down method, or the divide-and-conquer method. Less-structured methods include shoot-from-the-hip, spot-the-differences, and move-the-problem.

Common software tools that can help with troubleshooting include network management system tools, knowledge bases, baselining tools, host-based protocol analyzers, and Cisco IOS EPC. Hardware troubleshooting tools include a NAM, digital multimeters, cable testers, cable analyzers, and portable network analyzers. Cisco IOS log information can also be used to identify potential problems.

There are characteristic physical layer, data link layer, network layer, transport layer, and application layer symptoms and problems of which the network administrator should be aware. The administrator may need to pay particular attention to physical connectivity, default gateways, MAC address tables, NAT, and routing information.

Practice

The following activities provide practice with the topics introduced in this chapter. The Labs and Class Activities are available in the companion Connecting Networks Lab Manual (978-1-58713-331-2). The Packet Tracer activity PKA files are found in the online course.

Class Activities

Class Activity 9.0.1.2: Network Breakdown

Class Activity 9.3.1.1: Documentation Development

Packet Tracer
☐ Activity

Packet Tracer Activities

Packet Tracer Activity 9.1.1.8: Troubleshooting Challenge - Documenting the Network

Packet Tracer Activity 9.2.3.12: Troubleshooting Enterprise Networks 1

Packet Tracer Activity 9.2.3.13: Troubleshooting Enterprise Networks 2

Packet Tracer Activity 9.2.3.14: Troubleshooting Enterprise Networks 3

Packet Tracer Activity 9.2.3.15: Troubleshooting Challenge - Using Documentation to Solve Issues

Check Your Understanding Questions

Complete all the review questions listed here to test your understanding of the topics and concepts in this chapter. The appendix, "Answers to the 'Check Your Understanding' Questions," lists the answers.

1. Match each item with its appropriate diagram type:

   Cable type:

   IPv6 address and prefix length:

   Connection type:

   Device ID:

   Operating system version:

   Device type and model:

   Routing protocols:

   Connector type:

   A. Physical diagram

   B. Logical diagram

2. What is one symptom of a physical layer problem?

   A. High CPU utilization

   B. Excessive broadcasts

   C. Slow STP convergence

   D. Routing loops

3. A network administrator receives the output "Serial0/0/0 is up, line protocol is down" from the **show interface serial 0/0/0** command. At what layer is this problem most likely being caused?

   A. Physical layer

   B. Data link layer

   C. Network layer

   D. Transport layer

4. Which protocols can be involved in network layer problems? (Choose three.)

   A. DNS

   B. EIGRP

   C. IPv6

   D. OSPF

   E. TCP

   F. UDP

5. Match the application layer protocol with the port number it is commonly associated with.

FTP:

HTTP:

POP3:

SMTP:

SNMP:

Telnet:

A. 20 and 21

B. 23

C. 25

D. 80

E. 110

F. 161

6. A technician has been asked to troubleshoot a simple network problem that seems to be caused by software. Which troubleshooting approach would you suggest?

A. Bottom-up

B. Top-down

C. Divide-and-conquer

D. Middle-out

7. Which questions are appropriate to ask when gathering information from a user? (Choose three.)

A. What does work?

B. Who did you call after the problem appeared?

C. When did you first notice the problem?

D. When does the problem occur?

E. What is your password?

F. What did you do after the problem occurred?

8. Which network troubleshooting tool can you use to test the physical medium for defects, such as near-end crosstalk (NEXT)?

A. Cable analyzer

B. Cable tester

C. Digital multimeter

D. Baselining tool

9. Which documents are needed to efficiently diagnose and correct network problems? (Choose three.)

   A. Network management command reference

   B. Network configuration tables

   C. Network device installation guide

   D. Network topology diagrams

   E. End-system documentation

   F. Service provider documentation

10. What are the steps for establishing a network baseline? (Choose three.)

   A. Determine the type of network management traffic to be collected and evaluated.

   B. Determine the types of data to be collected and evaluated.

   C. Identify devices and ports to be monitored.

   D. Identify the virtual interfaces, VLANs, and virtual routing tables to be monitored.

   E. Determine the number of baseline tests to establish a typical picture of the network.

   F. Determine the duration for baseline testing to establish a typical picture of the network.

11. Explain the function and contents of network documentation, including router, switch, and end-user documentation, as well as network topology diagrams.

12. Explain the recommended steps for planning the first network baseline.

13. Explain the three stages of the general troubleshooting process.

14. Explain the three main troubleshooting methods.

15. List at least three things to check when troubleshooting Layer 1 problems.

Answers to the "Check Your Understanding" Questions

Chapter 1

1. Explanation: C. The critical network design principles are hierarchy, modularity, resiliency, and flexibility.

2. Explanation: B. The core layer is often referred to as the backbone.

3. Explanation: A. The Cisco Collaboration Architecture helps increase productivity through the use of individual components that work together to provide a comprehensive solution that encourages cooperation and innovation.

4. Explanation: A. The access layer provides connectivity to end users.

5. Explanation: A, F. Cisco AnyConnect software allows most smartphones, tablets, and other devices to connect securely, reliably, seamlessly, and persistently according to a policy-based connection.

6. Explanation: B, E, F. While some designs do route at the access layer, the two devices that should always be placed at the access layer of the hierarchical design model are an access point and a Layer 2 switch. A modular switch is commonly used at the core layer. Routing by a Layer 3 device is commonly used in the distribution layer. The firewall is a device in the Internet edge network design.

7. Explanation: A, E. To reduce cost in a medium-size network, the functions of the core and distribution layers can be combined into a two-tier network design named collapsed core.

8. Explanation: B. The enterprise teleworker module is responsible for providing secure connectivity to staff so that they can securely log in to the network over the VPN and gain access to authorized applications and services from a single cost-effective platform.

9. Explanation: D. Access security, type of applications, and protocols used on the network are only considered after the size of the network is identified.

10. Explanation: A. The Cisco Borderless Network Architecture allows multiple technologies including wired, wireless, routing, switching, security, and application optimization devices to work together.

11. Explanation: C. The application and devices layer of the Cisco Collaboration Architecture contains the software that allows users to collaborate.

Chapter 2

1. Explanation: A. For a small office, an appropriate connection to the Internet would be through DSL available from a local service provider. With so few employees, bandwidth is not a significant problem.

2. Explanation: E. A router is a DTE.

3. Explanation: B, C. Digital leased lines require a channel service unit (CSU) and a data service unit (DSU). An access server concentrates dialup modem dial-in and dial-out user communications. Dialup modems are used to temporarily enable the use of analog telephone lines for digital data communications. A Layer 2 switch is used to connect a LAN.

4. Explanation: A, B, F. A connection-oriented system predetermines the network path, creates a virtual circuit for the duration of the packet delivery, and requires that each packet only carry an identifier. A connectionless packet-switched network, such as the Internet, requires each data packet to carry addressing information.

5. Explanation: C. ATM (Asynchronous Transfer Mode), Frame Relay, ISDN (Integrated Services Digital Network), and MPLS (Multiprotocol Label Switching) do not describe optic fiber technologies. DWDM assigns incoming signals specific wavelengths of light and enables bidirectional communications over one strand of fiber. SONET and SDH are common high-bandwidth fiber-optic media standards. WiMAX provides high-speed broadband service with wireless access and provides broad coverage. Municipal Wi-Fi is used for emergency services such as fire and police. DSL is a wired solution. 802.11 is a wireless LAN solution.

6. Explanation: A. ATM is cell-based architecture. The small and fixed cells are well suited for carrying voice and video traffic because this traffic is intolerant of delay. Video and voice traffic do not have to wait for larger data packets to be transmitted. ISDN is circuit switched. Frame Relay and VSAT are packet switched.

7. Explanation: C. PRI delivers 23 B channels with 64 Kbps and 1 D channel with 64 Kbps for a total bit rate of up to 1.544 Mbps.

8. Explanation: G. A VPN is a recommended technology to use when a branch office is connected to the corporate site over a public WAN infrastructure.

9. Explanation: D. The local loop is the actual copper or fiber cable that connects the CPE to the CO of the service provider. The local loop is also sometimes called the "last- mile."

10. Explanation: A, B. The setting up of a dedicated circuit through the service provider network between each pair of communicating nodes and fewer delays in the data communications processes are advantages of circuit-switched networks. Packet-switched networks have multiple pairs of nodes that communicate over the same network channel, and the communication costs are lower than in circuit-switched networks.

Chapter 3

1. Step 1: C

   Step 2: D

   Step 3: A

   Step 4: B

   Step 5: E, F

2. Explanation: B. This is the state of the interface when the local or remote router is misconfigured with a different Layer 2 encapsulation. In our labs, a missing clock rate would also cause this message to appear.

3. Explanation: A. Cisco HDLC is the default encapsulation method used by Cisco devices on synchronous serial lines.

4. Explanation: D. The protocol field in a PPP frame indicates the type of Layer 3 information that is carried in the frame's Data field.

5. Error control: B

   Authentication protocols: D

   Allows load balancing: C

   Compression protocols: A

6. Explanation: A, D, E. TDM is inefficient when traffic is intermittent, because the time slot is still allocated even when the channel has no data to transmit. STDM was developed to overcome this inefficiency. STDM uses a variable time slot length allowing channels to compete for any free slot space. STDM uses multiple data streams that can share a single channel. The sources of data alternate during transmission and are reconstructed at the receiving end.

7. Explanation: B. HDLC is a bit-oriented synchronous data link layer protocol developed by the International Organization for Standardization (ISO). HDLC was developed from the Synchronous Data Link Control (SDLC) standard proposed in the 1970s. HDLC provides both connection-oriented and connectionless service.

8. Explanation: C. Authentication takes place after link establishment and before any network layer protocol configuration.

9. Explanation: D. PPP uses the Network Control Protocol (NCP) process to negotiate the Layer 3 protocols to operate over the link. IPCP is an example of an NCP for IP.

10. Explanation: B. PAP uses a two-way handshake, whereas CHAP uses a three-way handshake. The other three possible answers are features of CHAP.

11. Explanation: B, F. This state can be caused by the router's not sensing a CD signal, which means that the CD is not active. This state can also be caused by faulty or incorrect cabling. Other causes include a WAN carrier service provider problem, which means that the line is down or is not connected to the CSU/DSU, or a hardware failure (CSU/DSU).

12. Configure the username and password: A

Enter interface configuration mode: C

Specify the encapsulation type: D

Configure authentication: G

13. Explanation: E. With CHAP authentication, the hostname on one router must match the username the other router has configured. The passwords must also match on both routers.

14. Two-way handshake: PAP

Three-way handshake: CHAP

Open to trial-and-error attacks: PAP

Password sent in cleartext: PAP

Periodic verification: CHAP

Uses a one-way hash function: CHAP

15. Negotiates link establishment parameters: LCP

Negotiates Layer 3 protocol parameters: NCP

Maintains/debugs a link: LCP

Can negotiate multiple Layer 3 protocols: NCP

Terminates a link: LCP

16. Explanation: Sits on top of the physical layer and has a role in establishing, configuring, and testing the data-link connection.

Link Control Protocol (LCP) layer

- Establishes the point-to-point link.

- Provides automatic configuration of the interfaces at each end. This includes handling varying limits on packet size, detecting common misconfiguration errors, terminating the link, and determining when a link is functioning properly or when it is failing.

- Is also used to negotiate authentication, compression, error detection, multilink, and PPP callback after the link is established.

- Negotiates and sets up control options on the WAN data link, which are handled by the NCPs.

Network Control Protocol (NCP) layer

- Includes functional fields containing standardized codes to indicate the network layer protocol that PPP encapsulates.

- Handles the assignment and management of IP addresses in IPCP.

- Encapsulates and negotiates options for multiple network layer protocols.

17. Explanation:

Authentication using PAP or CHAP

- If all you need is password authentication, configure PAP using the **ppp authentication pap** command.

- If you want a challenge handshake, configure CHAP using the **ppp authentication chap** command (it's more secure).

Compression

- Increases the effective throughput by reducing the amount of data in the PPP frame that must travel across the link.

- To configure Stacker, use the **compress stac** command. To configure Predictor, use the **compress predictor** command.

Error detection

- Identifies fault conditions to help ensure a reliable, loop-free data link.

- Configured using the **ppp quality** *percentage* command.

Multilink

- Provides load balancing over the router interfaces that PPP uses using the command **ppp multilink**.

PPP callback

- Enhances security by making a Cisco router a callback client. It makes the initial call, requests that the other Cisco router configured as a server call it back, and terminates its initial call.

- The command is **ppp callback** [accept | request].

18. Explanation: The username command has two errors. The router name should be R3, and the password should be cisco. Therefore, the correct command is **username R3 password cisco**.

   ■ The third error is in the **ppp authentication** command. It should be **ppp authentication chap**.

Chapter 4

1. Explanation: B. VCs are identified by DLCIs. DLCI values typically are assigned by the Frame Relay service provider (for example, the telephone company).

2. Explanation: D. Unlike leased lines, there are no dedicated circuits in the carrier's Frame Relay network for end-to-end customer connectivity. Most providers use PVCs (some use SVCs) to create and discard circuits as customers purchase them without needing to deploy additional cabling.

3. Explanation: D. Whether using a single physical interface, or an interface configured as a multipoint subinterface, when the remote ends of the virtual circuits are on the same subnet, it is subject to split horizon. If point-to-point subinterfaces are used with each virtual circuit on a separate subnet, split horizon is no longer an issue.

4. Explanation: B, D. Frame Relay requires a single access line or circuit to the provider's frame network cloud, regardless of the number of remote networks. A router with a single WAN interface and CSU/DSU is needed, along with a single access circuit. Frame Relay allows a provider to efficiently share the bandwidth within its cloud instead of deploying a large number of individual dedicated point-to-point links.

5. Active: C

   Inactive: A

   Deleted: D

6. Explanation: B. A Frame Relay cloud typically is a meshed network of circuits and Layer 2 switches (usually ATM). This allows for redundancy within the provider's network that does not exist with a dedicated leased line.

7. Explanation: E. The Layer 2 encapsulation is Frame Relay, with the local DLCI used as the address.

8. Explanation: A. Point-to-point topologies typically require a separate subnet for each point-to-point connection. In many networks, VLSM is used to subnet one of the subnets as /30 networks. If this is not an option, multipoint topology can be used. Multipoint topology means that all the VCs share the same subnet address. (Note: In today's modern networks, VLSM usually is an option.)

9. Explanation: C. When point-to-point subinterfaces are used, each VC is on a separate subnet; therefore, split horizon is not an issue. From the perspective of the router, each VC is on a separate (logical) interface. This eliminates split horizon as an issue.

10. Explanation: D. Frame Relay does not provide any error correction. Only the upper-layer protocol TCP, used by the host, provides any error detection when Frame Relay is used as the Layer 2 transport.

11. `show interface:` C

    `show frame-relay lmi:` D

    `show frame-relay pvc:` A

    `show frame-relay map:` E

    `debug frame-relay lmi:` B

12. Explanation: D. The CIR is the amount of data that the network receives from the access circuit. The service provider guarantees that the customer can send data at the CIR. All frames received at or below the CIR are accepted.

13. Explanation: C. The DLCI numbers are assigned by the service provider. Most providers allow the customer to choose its own DLCI numbers as long as they are valid numbers.

14. Explanation: A. Frame Relay maps are used to map the remote network address to the local DLCI.

15. CIR: C

    DE: A

    FECN: B

    BECN: D

16. Explanation:

    DLCI: Data-link connection identifier

    - VCs are identified by DLCIs, and the DLCI values are assigned by the Frame Relay service provider.
    - Frame Relay DLCIs have local significance and no significance beyond the single link.
    - A DLCI identifies a VC to the equipment at an endpoint.

    LMI: Local Management Interface

    - LMI is a keepalive mechanism that provides status information about Frame Relay connections between the router (DTE) and the Frame Relay switch (DCE).
    - Cisco routers support three types of LMIs: Cisco, ANSI, and q933a.

Inverse ARP

- Inverse Address Resolution Protocol (ARP) obtains Layer 3 addresses of other stations from Layer 2 addresses, such as the DLCI in Frame Relay networks (which is the reverse of what ARP does).

- It is primarily used in Frame Relay and ATM networks, where Layer 2 addresses of VCs are sometimes obtained from Layer 2 signaling, and the corresponding Layer 3 addresses must be available before these VCs can be used.

17. Explanation: **frame-relay map ip 10.1.1.2 102 broadcast**

18. Explanation:

Access rate (or port speed)

- The capacity of the local loop.

- This line is charged based on the port speed between the DTE and the DCE (customer to service provider).

CIR: Committed information rate

- The capacity through the local loop guaranteed by the provider.

- Customers normally choose a CIR lower than the access rate to allow them to take advantage of bursts.

CBIR: Committed burst information rate

- The maximum number of frames allowed in a burst.

- It cannot exceed the CIR for the link.

Be: Excess Burst

- The amount of data above the CBIR that the network tries to deliver, up to the maximum speed of the access link.

- Packets over CIR are marked Discard Eligible (DE), indicating that they may be dropped if the network does not have capacity.

19. Explanation: On router R1

- The main serial interface and subinterfaces should be Serial 0/0/0, Serial 0/0/0.102, and Serial 0/0/0.103, respectively.

- The wrong subnet mask is applied to the subinterfaces. The subnet mask should be 255.255.255.252.

- The DLCIs in the **frame-relay interface-dlci** command should be 102 and 103, respectively.

Chapter 5

1. Explanation: C. The output lists port numbers. This occurs only when NAT overload is configured.

2. Explanation: B. By default, translation entries time out after 24 hours, unless the timers have been reconfigured with the **ip nat translation timeout timeout_ seconds** command in global configuration mode.

3. Provides one-to-one fixed mappings of local and global addresses: C

   Assigns the translated addresses of IP hosts from a pool of public addresses: A

   Can map multiple addresses to a single address of the external interface: B

   Assigns unique source port numbers of an inside global address on a session-by-session basis: B

   Allows an external host to establish sessions with an internal host: C

4. Explanation: B. IP address 192.168.0.100 is the inside local address and will be translated into 209.165.200.2.

5. Explanation: B. NAT will translate the internal addresses 192.168.0.0 to 192.168.0.255 as identified by access list 1.

6. Explanation: A. IP address 192.168.14.5 is a private address. Therefore, static NAT must be configured, because it would enable an outside host to contact the inside global address of web server 1.

7. Explanation: D. An FTP server requires a reachable public Internet address to be statically assigned to its internal address.

8. Explanation: B. The inside local address 10.10.10.3 is being translated into the inside global address 24.74.237.203.

9. Explanation:

   Static NAT:

   - Static NAT uses a one-to-one mapping of local and global addresses, and these mappings remain constant.
   - Static NAT is particularly useful for web servers or in general hosts that must have a consistent address that is accessible from the Internet.

   Dynamic NAT:

   - Dynamic NAT uses a pool of public addresses and assigns them on a first-come, first-served basis.
   - When a host requests access to the Internet, dynamic NAT chooses an IP address from the public pool and temporarily binds it with the internal local address.

NAT overload:

- NAT overloading (sometimes called Port Address Translation or PAT) maps inside local IP addresses to a combination of a global IP address and a unique port number.

- When a response returns to the NAT router, the router examines the source port number and forwards the packet to the originating inside local address.

- It also validates that the incoming packets were requested, thus adding a degree of security to the session.

10. Explanation: Router R2 was configured to provide NAT overload translation to hosts on the 192.168.10.0 and 192.168.11.0 networks. The host with the inside local IP address 192.168.10.10 was translated into the overloaded inside global IP address 209.165.200.225 using the unique port number 16642 when accessing the web server located at 209.165.200.254.

The host with the inside local IP address 192.168.11.10 was translated into the overloaded inside global IP address 209.165.200.225 using the unique port number 62452 when accessing the web server located at 209.165.200.254.

11. Explanation: The configurations have several problems:

- ACL 1 has an incorrect subnet mask and is too restrictive. It permits only hosts on nonexistent subnet 192.168.0.0/24. This excludes hosts on the 192.168.10.0 and 192.168.11.0 networks. ACL 1 should be **access-list 1 permit 192.168.0.0 0.0.255.255**.

- The NAT pool is incorrectly identified. The router interface should not be included in the pool. The pool should be configured to a 255.255.255.248 (/29), not a 255.255.255.224 (/27). The command should be **ip nat pool NAT-POOL 209.165.200.226 209.165.200.230 netmask 255.255.255.248**.

- In the **ip nat inside** command, the pool name should be NAT-POOL, not NAT-POOL1. Also, the **overload** keyword is missing at the end of the command. The command should be **ip nat inside source list 1 pool NAT-POOL overload**.

- The inside and outside NAT interfaces are incorrectly identified. Interface serial s0/1/0 should be configured with the **ip nat outside** interface command, and serial 0/0/0 with the **ip nat inside** interface command.

The correct configuration is as follows:

access-list 1 permit 192.168.0.0 0.0.255.255

ip nat pool NAT-POOL 209.165.200.226 209.165.200.230 netmask 255.255.255.248

ip nat inside source list 1 pool NAT-POOL overload

interface serial s0/1/0

ip nat outside

interface fastethernet 0/0

ip nat inside

12. Explanation: C. Unique local addresses (ULAs) are used for this purpose. The intent of ULA is to provide IPv6 address space for communications within a local site; it is not meant to provide additional IPv6 address space, nor is it meant to provide a level of security. The original IPv6 RFC specified site-local addresses, which have since been deprecated.

13. Explanation: A. NAT64 is used to provide IPv6-to-IPv4 address translation. NAT-PT has been deprecated by IETF in favor of its replacement, NAT64.

Chapter 6

1. Explanation: C, D. Broadband refers to the capability to provide high-speed transmission (128 Kbps or higher) of services (for example, data, voice, and video) using technologies such as DSL, cable, satellite, and broadband wireless. These technologies use a wide range of frequencies and multiplexing techniques.

2. Explanation: C. With a maximum speed of 56 Kbps (throughput is actually lower), dialup connections are not considered a broadband technology like DSL, cable, satellite, and broadband wireless.

3. Explanation: D. DOCSIS defines the Layer 1 channel bandwidth and modulation technique for a cable Internet connection. Euro-DOCSIS is adapted for use in Europe. The main differences between DOCSIS and Euro-DOCSIS relate to channel bandwidths.

4. Explanation: A, C. The different varieties of DSL provide different bandwidths, some with capabilities exceeding those of a T1 or E1 leased line. Within the variety of DSL, transfer rates are less as the distance from the central office increases. ADSL is asymmetric DSL, which provides higher download bandwidth than

upload bandwidth. SDSL (symmetric DSL) provides the same capacity in both directions. ADSL and voice signals use the same wire pair, and ADSL signals can distort voice transmissions. For this reason, a microfilter or splitter is used to separate them. This also ensures that voice communication can continue when the ADSL service fails.

5. Explanation: D, E. The customer site may include devices such as a microfilter and a DSL transceiver, which usually is a DSL modem.

6. Explanation: B, D. An organization that supports teleworkers will generally find it harder to track employee progress and maintain a management style that allows interaction among employees. Organizations that support teleworkers will generally have a reduction in office expenses, faster customer service response times, and less absenteeism.

7. Explanation: D. Given these choices, DSL is the most cost-effective method for broadband teleworker access to the Internet. Cable is another cost-effective technology that competes with DSL. Broadband wireless and two-way satellite Internet are becoming more common and more competitive.

8. Explanation: E. The 802.16 (or WiMAX) standard allows transmissions up to 70 Mbps. 802.16 has a range of up to 30 miles (50 km). It can operate in the licensed or unlicensed bands of the spectrum from 2 to 6 GHz. WiMax towers connect to other WiMax towers by means of line-of-sight microwave links or they can provide cellular access to devices.

9. Explanation: Cable operators typically deploy HFC networks to enable high-speed transmission of data to cable modems located in a SOHO. The trunks typically are fiber with coaxial distribution cable to the homes (feeders).

10. Explanation: C. Time-division multiple access (TDMA) divides access by time, whereas frequency-division multiple access (FDMA) divides access by frequency. Code-division multiple access (CDMA) employs spread-spectrum technology and a special coding scheme in which each transmitter is assigned a specific code. Synchronous code-division multiple access (S-CDMA) adds a layer of security and noise reduction by scattering digital data up and down a wide frequency band and allows multiple subscribers who are connected to the network to transmit and receive concurrently.

11. Explanation: C. Unlike cable technology, DSL is not a shared medium. DSL delivers high-speed connections over existing copper wires (PSTN). Each user has a separate connection to the DSLAM. Different varieties of DSL provide both symmetrical and asymmetrical connections. Generally, the local loop is limited to 3.39 miles using DSL.

Chapter 7

1. Explanation: B, C. VPNs secure data by encapsulating, creating a tunnel, or encrypting the data. Most VPNs can do both. VPN tunnels are typically IPsec or SSL based. IPsec is a Layer 3 protocol suite to secure network data.

2. Explanation: D. Encryption protects the contents of messages from interception by unauthenticated or unauthorized sources. Authentication refers to password management and ensuring authenticity that the peer is who they say they are. Data integrity ensures that the original message is intact and has not been altered.

3. Explanation: D. GRE is a tunneling protocol developed by Cisco Systems. It can encapsulate a variety of Layer 3 packets inside IP tunnels, creating a virtual point-to-point link to Cisco routers at remote points over an IP internetwork.

4. Explanation: C, E. To enable the secure management of teleworkers who connect to the corporate network via VPN, a VPN server or concentrator, an authentication server, and multifunction security appliances are necessary components at the corporate end. They are not client requirements.

5. Explanation: C. Remote-access VPNs connect individual users to another network via a VPN client that is installed on the user device. Site-to-site VPNs are "always-on" connections that use VPN gateways to connect two sites together. Users at each site can access the network on the other site without having to use any special clients or configurations on their individual devices.

6. Explanation: B. Site-to-site VPNs are statically defined VPN connections between two sites that use VPN gateways. The internal hosts do not require VPN client software and send normal unencapsulated packets onto the network where they are encapsulated by the VPN gateway.

7. Explanation: A. Cisco clientless SSL VPN provides limited access to internal network resources by utilizing a Cisco ASA and provides browser-based access only.

8. Explanation: D. Message hashes provide data integrity by ensuring that the data in the packet was not changed between the source and destination nodes. The hash value is generated by running the data through a hash algorithm. This hash is then appended to the data before it is sent across the link. The receiving node calculates a hash on the received data, and if the received hash does not match the hash attached to the data then the data has been altered in transit. MD5 and SHA are both hashing algorithms that can be used to protect the integrity of messages that are traversing a VPN. MD5 uses a 128-bit secret key, whereas SHA-1 uses a 160-bit secret key. Both MD5 and SHA-1 have cryptographic weaknesses, and it is now recommended to use the SHA algorithms with 256-bit or 512-bit secret keys..

9. Explanation: B. The DH algorithm specifies a public key exchange method that provides a way for two peers to establish a shared secret key that only they know, although they are communicating over an insecure channel.

10. Explanation: A, B. DES, 3DES, and AES are encryption algorithms that provide message confidentiality.

11. Explanation: D, E. MD5 and SHA both use Hash-based Message Authentication Code for message authentication.

Chapter 8

1. Network Time Protocol (NTP) B

   NetFlow C

   Simple Network Management Protocol (SNMP) A

2. Explanation: A, B, C, and D. The logging buffer, console line, terminal line, and a syslog server can all receive syslog messages.

3. Explanation: D. The correct command to synchronize the clock with an NTP server is the global configuration command **Router(config)# ntp server ip-address**.

4. Explanation: D. Severity level 3, also known as the error level, is used to display changes in the state of interfaces.

5. Explanation: The syslog server is 10.1.1.1.

6. Explanation: The messages sent to the syslog server will be 0 through 5.

7. Explanation: The syslog packets will have the IP address of the GigabitEthernet 0/1 interface.

8. Explanation: SNMP consists of an SNMP manager, SNMP agents (managed node), and Management Information Base (MIB).

9. Explanation: C. SNMPv3 introduced authentication based on HMAC-MD5 or HMAC-SHA, and encryption services use CBC-DES, 3DES, and AES 128, 192, or 256 bits.

10. Explanation: The community string is steamerlane.

11. Explanation: SNMP trap messages will be sent to 10.1.1.2.

12. Explanation: SNMP version is 2c.

13. Explanation: The seven fields are as follows:

Source IP address

Destination IP address

Source port number

Destination port number

Layer 3 protocol type

Type of Service (ToS) marking

Input logical interface

14. Explanation: D. To capture data on an interface, the NetFlow interface commands **ip flow ingress** and **ip flow egress** are used.

15. Explanation: A. The command **show ip cache flow** will display a summary of the NetFlow accounting statistics, as well as which protocol uses the highest volume of the traffic, and traffic flows between hosts.

Chapter 9

1. Cable type: A

   IPv6 address and prefix length: B

   Connection type: B

   Device ID: B

   Operating system version: A

   Device type and model: A

   Routing protocols: A

   Connector type: A

2. Explanation: A. Common symptoms of physical layer problems include performance less than the baseline; loss of connectivity; high collision counts; network bottlenecks or congestion; high CPU utilization rates on routers, switches, and servers; and console error messages.

3. Explanation: B. The first part, "Serial0/0/0 is up," indicates that the physical layer is operational. The second part, "line protocol is down," indicates a Layer 2 problem.

4. Explanation: B, C, D. Only EIGRP, IPv6, and OSPF operate at Layer 3. TCP and UDP operate at Layer 4. DNS operates at Layer 7.

5. FTP: A

   HTTP: D

   POP3: E

   SMTP: C

   SNMP: F

   Telnet: B

6. Explanation: B. Software interacts with Layer 7. Therefore, the top-down approach is the most logical place to start.

7. Explanation: A, C, D. These are logical questions that will help you narrow down the specific problem. Options B, E, and F do not add any value and are not pertinent.

8. Explanation: A. The only tool listed that detects near-end crosstalk is a cable analyzer. Cable testers, digital multimeters, and baselining tools do not detect NEXT.

9. Explanation: B, D, E. Although the documents listed in options A, C, and F could be of help, documents B, D, and E are required.

10. Explanation: B, C, F. Option A would be trivial to collect. Option D does not make sense. Option E is incorrect because you should conduct the baseline over a period of time and not have multiple baseline tests.

11. Explanation:

    Router documentation:

    - The router documentation should include the router names, model designation, location in the enterprise (building, floor, room, rack, panel), configured interfaces, data link layer addresses, network layer addresses, routing protocols configured, and any additional important information about the device.

    Switch documentation:

    - The switch documentation should include the switch names, model designation, location in the enterprise (building, floor, room, rack, panel), management IP address, port names and status, speed, duplex, STP state, PortFast setting, trunk status, Layer 2 or Layer 3 EtherChannel, VLAN IDs, and any additional important information about the device.

    End-system documentation:

    - The end-system documentation should include the server names and functions, operating system version, IP address, gateways, DNS server, network application, and any additional important information about the device.

Topology diagrams should be available in a physical and logical variation.

Physical network topology diagram:

- A graphical representation that identifies the physical location of the networking device.

- Also details the types of cabling between them and the cable identification numbers.

Logical network topology diagram:

- A graphical representation that uses symbols to identify each network device and how it is interconnected.

- Also, details the logical architecture, including interface types and numbers, IP addresses, subnet masks, routing protocols, autonomous system domains, and any additional important information, such as DLCI numbers and Layer 2 protocol.

12. Explanation:

Step 1: Determine what types of data to collect:

- Start simply, by selecting a few variables that represent the defined policies, and fine-tune along the way.

- Generally, some good starting measures are interface utilization and CPU utilization.

Step 2: Identify devices and ports of interest:

- Devices and ports of interest must be identified, such as network device ports that connect to other network devices, servers, key users, and anything else considered critical to the operation.

Step 3: Determine the baseline duration:

- This period should be at least seven days to capture daily or weekly trends and should last two to four weeks.

- Do not perform a baseline measurement during times of unique traffic patterns.

- Should be conducted on a regular basis, such as an annual analysis of the entire network or a baseline of different sections of the network on a rotating basis.

13. Explanation:

Stage 1: Gather symptoms:

- Symptoms may appear in many different forms, including alerts from the network management system, console messages, and user complaints.

- Gather and document symptoms from the network, end systems, and users.

- In addition, determine which network components have been affected and how the network's functionality has changed compared to the baseline.

Stage 2: Isolate the problem:

- The problem is not truly isolated until a single problem, or a set of related problems, is identified.

- Examine the characteristics of problems at the logical layers of the network so that the most likely cause can be selected.

- Depending on the problem characteristics identified, gather and document more symptoms.

Stage 3: Correct the problem:

- Work to correct the problem by implementing, testing, and documenting a solution.

14. Explanation:

Bottom-up troubleshooting method:

- Start with the network's physical components, and work up through the layers of the OSI or TCP/IP model until you identify the cause of the problem.

- This is a good approach to use when you suspect that the problem is physical.

Top-down troubleshooting method:

- Examine the end-user application first.

- The analysis continues downward from the upper layers of the layered model until the cause of the problem is identified.

Divide-and-conquer troubleshooting method:

- Select a layer, and test in both directions from the starting layer.

- If you can verify that a layer is functioning properly, typically it is safe to assume that the layers below it are functioning.

- If a layer is not functioning properly, gather symptoms of the problem at that layer, and work your way down.

15. Explanation:

Check for bad cables or connections:

- Use a cable tester to verify that the cable from the source interface is properly connected and is in good condition.

- When you doubt a cable's integrity, swap the suspect cable with a known working cable.

Make sure that the correct cabling standard is adhered to throughout the network:

- Verify that the proper cable is being used for the connection.

Check that devices are cabled correctly:

- Verify that all cables are connected to their correct ports or interfaces.

Verify proper interface configurations:

- Check that all switch ports are set in the correct VLAN and that spanning-tree, speed, and duplex settings are correctly configured.

- Confirm that any active ports or interfaces are not shut down.

This glossary defines many of the terms and abbreviations related to networking. It includes all the key terms used throughout the book. As with any growing technical field, some terms evolve and take on several meanings. Where necessary, multiple definitions and abbreviation expansions are presented.

Numbers/Symbols

3G/4G Wireless   Cellular/mobile broadband standards supporting speeds of up to 5 Mbps.

A

access layer   The access layer is where end users connect to the network.

access server   A communications processor that connects asynchronous devices to a LAN or WAN through network and terminal emulation software. Performs both synchronous and asynchronous routing of supported protocols. Sometimes called a network access server.

Advanced Encryption Standard (AES)   An encryption standard used to ensure confidentiality of the packet. AES is considered to be more secure than DES or 3DES.

Anti-replay protection   Feature that is used to stop hackers from making changes to captured packets and resending to the destination.

asymmetric DSL (ADSL)   Type of DSL broadband communications technology used for connecting to the Internet. ADSL allows more data to be sent over existing copper telephone lines (POTS). Specifically, ADSL has higher download speeds compared to upload speeds.

Asymmetric encryption   Also known as public-key cryptography, this is a cryptographic algorithm that requires two separate keys. One key is private while the other is public.

Asynchronous Transfer Mode (ATM)   An international standard for cell relay in which multiple service types (such as voice, video, or data) are conveyed in fixed-length (53-byte) cells. Fixed-length cells allow cell processing to occur in hardware, thereby reducing transit delays.

Authentication Header (AH) This is an IPsec packet encapsulation method that guarantees connectionless integrity and data origin authentication of IP packets. However, unlike ESP, it does not encrypt the payload.

B

Backward Explicit Congestion Notification (BECN)   A bit set by a Frame Relay network in frames traveling in the opposite direction of frames encountering a congested path. The DTE receiving frames with the BECN bit set can request that higher-level protocols take flow control action as appropriate.

Basic Rate Interface (BRI)   An ISDN interface composed of two 64-Kbps B channels and one D 16-bit channel for circuit-switched communication of voice, video, and data.

bit-oriented   A class of data link layer communication protocols that can transmit frames regardless of frame content. Compared with byte-oriented protocols, bit-oriented protocols provide full-duplex operation and are more efficient and reliable.

bottom-up troubleshooting   You start with the physical components of the network and move up through the layers of the OSI model until you find the cause of the problem. Bottom-up troubleshooting is a good approach to use when you suspect a physical problem.

broadband connections   A broadband connection typically refers to the wide bandwidth characteristics of a transmission medium and its ability to transport multiple signals and traffic types simultaneously. The medium can be coax, optical fiber, twisted pair, or wireless.

broadband modem   A broadband modem is a type of digital modem used with broadband communications such as DSL or cable Internet service.

C

cable   A transmission medium of copper wire or optical fiber wrapped in a protective cover.

cable analyzer   A multifunctional handheld device that is used to test and certify copper and fiber cables for different services and standards. The more sophisticated tools include advanced troubleshooting diagnostics that measure distance to performance defect (NEXT, RL),

identify corrective actions, and graphically display crosstalk and impedance behavior.

cable modem (CM)   Device located at the customer premise and is used to convert an Ethernet signal from the user device to broadband cable frequencies, which is transmitted to the central office.

cable modem termination system (CMTS)   A component that exchanges digital signals with cable modems on a cable network. A headend CMTS communicates with cable modems that are located in the subscriber homes.

cable testers   A specialized handheld device designed to test the various types of data communication cabling. Cabling testers can be used to detect broken wires, crossed-over wiring, shorted connections, and improperly paired connections.

central office (CO)   A local telephone company office to which all local loops in a given area connect and in which circuit switching of subscriber lines occurs.

Challenge Handshake Authentication Protocol (CHAP)   A security feature supported on lines using PPP encapsulation that prevents unauthorized access. CHAP does not itself prevent unauthorized access; it merely identifies the remote end. The router or access server then determines whether that user is allowed access.

channel service unit/data service unit (CSU/DSU)   A digital interface device that connects end-user equipment to the local digital telephone loop. Often mentioned with DSU as CSU/DSU.

circuit-switched network   A type of communication where two network nodes establish a dedicated communications channel (circuit) through the network before the nodes may communicate.

Cisco 7000 Any of the Cisco 7000 series of routers. A high-end router platform that supports a wide range of network interface and media types and is designed for use in enterprise networks.

Cisco Adaptive Security Appliance (ASA) This is a security device from Cisco that provides proactive threat defense to stop attacks by combining firewall, antivirus, intrusion prevention, and virtual private network (VPN) capabilities in one device.

Cisco Borderless Network Architecture Cisco Borderless Networks are designed to help IT balance demanding business challenges and changing business models promoted by the influx of consumer devices into the business world. Cisco Borderless Networks can help IT evolve its infrastructure to deliver secure, reliable, and seamless user experiences in a world with many new and shifting borders.

Cisco Collaboration Architecture Cisco Collaboration Architecture enables network administrators to address trends such as mobility, "bring-your-own-device," and video, and create a flexible platform for collaboration.

Cisco Data Center/Virtualization Architecture Cisco Data Center/Virtualization Architecture is a unified data center architecture that combines computer, storage, network, and management into a platform designed to automate IT as a service across physical and virtual environments, resulting in increased budget efficiency, more agile business responsiveness, and simplified IT operations.

Cisco Easy VPN Remote A Cisco IOS router or Cisco ASA Firewall acting as a remote VPN client.

Cisco Easy VPN Server A Cisco IOS router or Cisco ASA Firewall acting as the VPN headend device in site-to-site or remote-access VPNs.

Cisco Enterprise Architecture model The model separates the enterprise network into functional areas; the enterprise campus module, the enterprise edge module, and the service provider edge module. The modularity that is built into the architecture allows flexibility in network design and facilitates implementation and troubleshooting.

Cisco VPN Client An application supported on a PC used to access a Cisco VPN Server.

clock skew A clock's frequency difference, or the first derivative of its offset with respect to time.

code-division multiple access (CDMA) This is a channel access method used by various radio communication technologies that allows several transmitters to send information simultaneously over a single communication channel.

collapsed core The distribution layer and core layer functions are implemented by a single device.

committed information rate (CIR) The rate at which a Frame Relay network agrees to transfer information under normal conditions, averaged over a minimum increment of time. CIR, measured in bits per second, is one of the key negotiated tariff metrics.

community string A text string that acts as a password and is used to authenticate messages sent between a management station and a router containing an SNMP agent. The community string is sent in every packet between the manager and the agent.

congestion   Traffic in excess of network capacity.

core layer   Provides fast transport between distribution switches within the enterprise campus.

customer premises equipment (CPE)   Terminating equipment, such as terminals, telephones, and modems, supplied by the telephone company, installed at customer sites, and connected to the telephone company network.

D

data communications equipment (DCE)   Data communications equipment is the EIA expansion. Data circuit-terminating equipment is the ITU-T expansion. The devices and connections of a communications network that comprise the network end of the user-to-network interface. The DCE provides a physical connection to the network, forwards traffic, and provides a clocking signal used to synchronize data transmission between DCE and DTE devices. Modems and interface cards are examples of DCE.

Data Encryption Standard (DES) Older encryption standard used for IPsec VPNs. It is considered the weakest of encryption algorithms. Contrast with 3DES and AES.

data-link connection identifier (DLCI)   A value that specifies a PVC or SVC in a Frame Relay network. In the basic Frame Relay specification, DLCIs are locally significant (connected devices might use different values to specify the same connection). In the LMI extended specification, DLCIs are globally significant (DLCIs specify individual end devices).

Data-Over-Cable Service Interface Specification (DOCSIS)   An international standard developed by CableLabs, a nonprofit research and development consortium for cable-related technologies. CableLabs tests and certifies cable equipment vendor devices, such as cable modems and cable modem termination systems, and grants DOCSIS-certified or qualified status.

data stream   All data transmitted through a communications line in a single read or write operation.

data terminal equipment (DTE)   A device at the user end of a user-network interface that serves as a data source, destination, or both. DTE connects to a data network through a DCE device (such as a modem) and typically uses clocking signals generated by the DCE. DTE includes such devices as computers, protocol translators, and multiplexers.

dedicated line   A communications line that is indefinitely reserved for transmissions, rather than switched as transmission is required.

demarcation point   The point where the service provider or telephone company network ends and connects with the customer's equipment at the customer's site.

dense wavelength-division multiplexing (DWDM)   An optical technology used to increase bandwidth over existing fiber optic backbones. DWDM works by combining and transmitting multiple signals simultaneously at different wavelengths on the same fiber.

dialup modem   An older type of Modem that connects a computer to the Internet via a standard telephone line.

Diffie-Hellman (DH) algorithm   Used by various encryption algorithms, this is a method to securely exchange the keys that encrypt data without having a pre-shared secret.

digital multimeter (DMM)   A test instrument that directly measures electrical values of voltage, current, and resistance. In network troubleshooting, most multimedia tests involve checking power-supply voltage levels and verifying that network devices are receiving power.

Digital signal level (DS) A term for the series of standard digital transmission rates or levels based on DS0, a transmission rate of 64 Kbps. This originated from the bandwidth normally used for one telephone voice channel.

digital subscriber line (DSL)   An always-on connection technology that uses existing twisted-pair telephone lines to transport high-bandwidth data and that provides IP services to subscribers. A DSL modem converts an Ethernet signal from the user device into a DSL signal, which is transmitted to the central office.

Discard Eligible (DE)   Also known as tagged traffic. If the network is congested, tagged traffic can be dropped to ensure delivery of higher-priority traffic.

distribution layer   The distribution layer is where policy-based connectivity is applied, such as access control lists and QoS. The distribution layer includes routers and multilayer switches.

divide-and-conquer troubleshooting   You start by collecting users' experiences with the problem and document the symptoms. Then, using that information, you make an informed guess about the OSI layer at which to start your investigation. After you verify that a layer is functioning properly, assume that the layers below it are functioning, and work up the OSI layers. If an OSI layer is not functioning properly, work your way down the OSI layer model.

DSL access multiplexer (DSLAM)   The device located at the provider's central office (CO). Concentrates connections from multiple DSL subscribers.

DSL modem   Device located at the customer premise and is used to convert an Ethernet signal from the user device to a DSL signal, which is transmitted to the central office.

dynamic NAT   Dynamic NAT is a form of Network Address Translation that creates a many-to-many address mapping between local and global addresses.

E

E1   A wide-area digital transmission scheme used predominantly in Europe that carries data at a rate of 2.048 Mbps. E1 lines can be leased for private use from common carriers.

E3   A wide-area digital transmission scheme used predominantly in Europe that carries data at a rate of 34.368 Mbps. E3 lines can be leased for private use from common carriers.

Encapsulating Security Payload (ESP)   This is an IPsec encapsulation protocol that provides data authentication, integrity, and confidentiality for IP packets exchanged between two systems. Contrast with Encapsulating Security Payload (ESP).

end-system configuration table   Contains baseline records of the hardware and software used in end-system devices such as servers, network management consoles, and desktop workstations. An incorrectly configured end system can have a negative impact on a network's overall performance.

enterprise branch module   The enterprise branch module includes remote branches that allow employees to work at non-campus locations. These locations are typically responsible for providing security, telephony, and mobility options to these employees, as well as general connectivity into the campus and the different components located inside the enterprise campus.

enterprise campus module   The enterprise campus module is separated out into a number of different layers that include the different parts of the network.

enterprise data center module   The enterprise data center module includes a data center that includes all of the same functionality options as the campus data center, but existing at a remote location. This provides an added layer of security when done correctly, as this remote location can provide backup options should something happen to the campus data center location.

enterprise edge module   The enterprise edge functional area is responsible for the aggregation of several different off-campus elements as well as the routing of this traffic into the campus core module within the Enterprise Campus Functional area.

enterprise teleworker module   The enterprise teleworker module is responsible for the connectivity of providing connectivity for workers who operate out of different geographically dispersed locations, including home offices, hotels or customer/client sites. Cisco Virtual Office is used to support these workers; Virtual Office provides an ability to provide productivity, security, and business resiliency. This solution requires a remote and central equipment presence that is used to provide connectivity back into the central campus location.

enterprise network   A large and diverse network connecting most major points in a company or other organization. Differs from a WAN in that it is privately owned and maintained.

Ethernet over MPLS (EoMPLS)   Type of Ethernet WAN service that works by encapsulating Ethernet PDUs in MPLS packets and forwarding them across the MPLS network. Each PDU is transported as a single packet.

Excess Burst Size (Be)   A negotiated tariff metric in Frame Relay internetworks. The number of bits that a Frame Relay internetwork attempts to transmit after the committed burst (BC) is accommodated. In general, Be data is delivered with a lower probability than BC data, because Be data can be marked as DE by the network.

F

firewall   A router or access server designated as a buffer between any connected public network and a private network. A firewall router uses access lists and other methods to ensure the security of the private network.

Flexible NetFlow   Flexible NetFlow is the next-generation in flow technology. It optimizes the network infrastructure, reducing operation costs and improving capacity planning and security incident detection with increased flexibility and scalability.

Forward Explicit Congestion Notification (FECN)   A bit set by a Frame Relay network to inform the DTE receiving the frame that congestion occurred in the path from source to destination. DTE receiving frames with the FECN bit set can request that higher-level protocols take flow-control action as appropriate.

Frame Relay   An industry-standard WAN Layer 2 protocol that handles multiple virtual circuits between connected devices.

frequency-division multiple access (FDMA)   Frequency Division Multiple Access or FDMA is a channel access method used in multiple-access protocols as a channelization protocol. FDMA gives users an individual allocation of one or several frequency bands, or channels. It is particularly commonplace in satellite communication.

full-mesh topology   A network in which each network node has either a physical circuit or a virtual circuit connecting it to every other network node. A full mesh provides a great deal of redundancy, but because it can be prohibitively expensive to implement, it is usually reserved for network backbones.

G

generic routing encapsulation (GRE)   GRE is a tunneling protocol developed by Cisco that can encapsulate a wide variety of protocol packet types inside IP tunnels. GRE creates a virtual point-to-point link to Cisco routers at remote points, over an IP internetwork. GRE is designed to manage the transportation of multiprotocol and IP multicast traffic between two or more sites, that may only have IP connectivity. It can encapsulate multiple protocol packet types inside an IP tunnel.

H

Hash-based Message Authentication Code (HMAC)   This is a data integrity algorithm that guarantees the integrity of a message.

headend   The endpoint of a broadband cable network. All stations transmit toward the headend; the headend then transmits toward the destination stations.

High-Level Data Link Control (HDLC)   A bit-oriented synchronous data link layer protocol developed by ISO. HDLC specifies a data encapsulation method on synchronous serial links using frame characters and checksums.

hub   Generally, a term used to describe a device that serves as the center of a star topology network.

Hybrid fiber-coaxial (HFC)   A telecommunications industry term for a broadband network that combines optical fiber and coaxial cable. It is commonly used by cable television operators.

I

inside global address   Used with NAT, a valid public address that the inside host is given when it exits the NAT router.

inside local address   Used with NAT, this usually is not an IP address assigned by a RIR or service provider and is most likely an RFC 1918 private address.

Integrated Services Digital Network (ISDN)   A communication protocol, offered by telephone companies, that permits telephone networks to carry data, voice, and other source traffic.

Internet Key Exchange (IKE)   Defines how two peers authenticate each other. IKE uses several types of authentication, including username and password, one-time password, biometrics, pre-shared key (PSK), and digital certificates.

Inverse Address Resolution Protocol (InARP)   A method of building dynamic routes in a network. Allows an access server to discover the network address of a device associated with a virtual circuit.

IPsec   IPsec is a framework of open standards that spells out the rules for secure communications. IPsec works at the network layer, protecting and authenticating IP packets between participating IPsec peers.

IPsec VPNs   Network security technologies that provide high levels of security through encryption and authentication, protecting data from unauthorized access.

J

jabber   The condition in which a network device continually transmits random, meaningless data onto the network.

K

keepalive interval   The amount of time between each keepalive message sent by a network device.

knowledge bases   An information database used to assist in the use or troubleshooting of a product. Online network device vendor knowledge bases have become indispensable sources of information. When vendor-based knowledge bases are combined with Internet search engines such as Google, a network administrator has access to a vast pool of experience-based information.

L

large network   Provides services for 1000+ devices.

leased lines   A transmission line reserved by a communications carrier for a customer's private use. A leased line is a type of dedicated line.

light-emitting diodes (LEDs)   A semiconductor light source. LEDs are used as indicator lamps in many devices and are increasingly used for general lighting.

Link Access Procedure for Frame Relay (LAPF)   As defined in the ITU Q.922, specifies Frame Mode Services in the Frame Relay network.

Link Control Protocol (LCP)   A protocol that establishes, configures, and tests data-link connections for use by PPP.

local loop   A line from the premises of a telephone subscriber to the telephone company CO.

Local Management Interface (LMI)   A keepalive mechanism that provides status information about Frame Relay connections between the router (DTE) and the Frame Relay switch (DCE).

logical network topology   Describes the arrangement of devices on a network and how they communicate with one another.

Long Term Evolution (LTE)   This is usually marketed as 4G LTE and is a standard for wireless communication of high-speed data for mobile phones and data terminals.

M

Management Information Base   A MIB (Management Information Base) is a database of the objects that can be managed on a device. The managed objects, or variables, can be set or read to provide information on the network devices and interfaces.

maximum transmission unit (MTU)   Maximum transmission unit (MTU) defines the largest size of packets that an interface can transmit without the need to fragment.

medium-size network   Provides services for 200 to 1,000 devices.

mesh   A network topology in which devices are organized in a manageable, segmented manner with many, often redundant, interconnections strategically placed between network nodes.

message digest 5 (MD5)   This is a popular cryptographic hash function producing a 128-bit (16-byte) hash value, typically expressed in text format as a 32 digit hexadecimal number. MD5 has been utilized in a wide variety of cryptographic applications, and is also commonly used to verify data integrity. Contrast with SHA message-digest algorithm.

Metropolitan Ethernet (MetroE)   Also called Ethernet MAN or metro Ethernet. It is a metropolitan area network (MAN) that is based on Ethernet standards. It is commonly used to connect subscribers to a larger service network or the Internet.

modular network design   Modular network design separates the network into various functional network modules, each targeting a specific place or purpose in the network. The modules represent areas that have different physical or logical connectivity.

Multiprotocol Label Switching (MPLS)   MPLS is a packet-forwarding technology which uses labels to make data forwarding decisions. With MPLS, the Layer 3 header analysis is done just once (when the packet enters the MPLS domain). Label inspection drives subsequent packet forwarding.

Municipal Wi-Fi   Cities that provide wireless Internet access for free or for a nominal fee. Most implementations use a mesh topology which is a series of interconnected access points located throughout a city.

N

NAT overloading   Sometimes called Port Address Translation (PAT). Maps multiple private IP addresses to a single public IP address or a few addresses.

NAT pool   A list of public IP addresses used in NAT.

NAT64   Network Address Translation IPv6 to IPv4, or NAT64, technology facilitates communication between IPv6-only and IPv4-only hosts and networks (whether in a transit, an access, or an edge network). This solution allows both enterprises and ISPs to accelerate IPv6 adoption while simultaneously handling IPv4 address depletion.

NetFlow   NetFlow efficiently provides a key set of services for IP applications, including network traffic accounting, usage-based network billing, network planning, security, Denial of Service monitoring capabilities, and network monitoring. NetFlow creates an environment where administrators have the tools to understand who, what, when, where, and how network traffic is flowing.

Network Address Translation (NAT)   Only globally unique in terms of the public Internet. A mechanism for translating private addresses into publicly usable addresses to be used within the public Internet. An effective means of hiding actual device addressing within a private network.

network analysis module (NAM)   Can be installed in Cisco Catalyst 6500 series switches and Cisco 7600 series routers to provide a graphical representation of traffic from local and remote switches and routers. The NAM is an embedded browser-based interface that generates reports on the traffic that consumes critical network resources. In addition, the NAM can capture and decode packets and track response times to pinpoint an application problem to the network or server.

network baseline   Used to efficiently diagnose and correct network problems. A network baseline documents what the network's expected performance should be under normal operating conditions. This information is captured in documentation such as configuration tables and topology diagrams.

network configuration files   Files that contain accurate, up-to-date records of the hardware and software used in a network. Within the network configuration files a table should exist for each network device used on the network, containing all relevant information about that device.

Network Control Protocols (NCPs)   Used to establish and configure different network layer protocols.

network documentation   Provides a logical diagram of the network and detailed information about each component. This information should be kept in a single location, either as hard copy or on the network on a protected website.

Network documentation should include a network configuration table, an end-system configuration table, and a network topology diagram.

Network Interface Device (NID)   Connects the customer premises to the local loop at the demarcation point.

network management system (NMS)   Responsible for managing at least part of a network. An NMS is generally a reasonably powerful and well-equipped computer, such as an engineering workstation. NMSs communicate with agents to help keep track of network statistics and resources.

Network Time Protocol   Network Time Protocol (NTP) synchronizes the time of day among a set of distributed time servers and clients so that you can correlate events when you receive system logs and other time-specific events from multiple network devices. NTP uses the User Datagram Protocol (UDP) as its transport protocol. All NTP communications use coordinated universal time (UTC).

network topology diagrams   A graphical representation of a network that illustrates how each device is connected and its logical architecture. A topology diagram has many of the same components as the network configuration table. Each network device should be represented on the diagram with consistent notation or a graphical symbol. Also, each logical and physical connection should be represented using a simple line or other appropriate symbol. Routing protocols also can be shown.

nonbroadcast multiaccess (NBMA)   A term describing a multiaccess network that does not support broadcasting (such as X.25) or in which broadcasting is not feasible (for example, an SMDS broadcast group or an extended Ethernet that is too large).

null modem   A small box or cable used to join computing devices directly, rather than over a network.

O

OSPF   The OSPF protocol was developed due to a need in the Internet community to introduce a high-functionality nonproprietary internal gateway protocol (IGP) for the TCP/IP protocol family. The discussion of the creation of a common interoperable IGP for the Internet started in 1988 and did not get formalized until 1991. The OSPF protocol is based on link-state technology, which is a departure from the Bellman-Ford vector based algorithms used in traditional Internet routing protocols such as RIP. OSPF introduced new concepts such as authentication of routing updates, variable-length subnet masks (VLSMs) and route summarization.

optical time-domain reflectometers (OTDRs)   An OTDR pinpoints the distance to a break in a fiber-optic cable. An OTDR device sends signals along the cable and waits for them to be reflected. The time between sending the signal and getting it back is converted into a distance measurement. The TDR function normally is packaged with data cabling testers.

outside global address   A reachable IP address used in NAT and assigned to hosts on the Internet.

outside local address   The address of the destination as seen from the inside network. Although uncommon, this address could be different than the globally routable address of the destination.

P

packet-switched network (PSN)   Packet switching splits traffic data into packets that are routed over a shared network. Routers determine the links that packets must be sent over based on the addressing information in each packet. Packet-switching networks do not require a circuit to be established, and they allow many pairs of nodes to communicate over the same channel.

partial-mesh topology   A network in which some network nodes are organized in a full mesh and others are connected to only one or two other nodes in the network. A partial mesh does not provide the level of redundancy of a full-mesh topology, but it is less expensive to implement. Partial-mesh topologies generally are used in the peripheral networks that connect to a fully meshed backbone.

Password Authentication Protocol (PAP)   An authentication protocol that allows PPP peers to authenticate one another. The remote router attempting to connect to the local router is required to send an authentication request. Unlike CHAP, PAP passes the password and username in the clear (unencrypted). PAP does not itself prevent unauthorized access, but merely identifies the remote end. The router or access server then determines if that user is allowed access. PAP is supported only on PPP lines.

physical topology   The mapping of a network that shows the physical layout of equipment, cables, and interconnections.

point of presence (POP)   A point of interconnection between the communications facilities provided by the telephone company and the building's main distribution facility.

point-to-point connections Connections used to connect LANs to service provider WANs and to connect LAN segments within an enterprise network.

Point-to-Point Protocol (PPP) A Layer 2 WAN protocol that provides router-to-router and host-to-network connections over synchronous and asynchronous circuits.

Port Address Translation (PAT) Sometimes called NAT overloading. Maps multiple private IP addresses to a single public IP address or a few addresses.

portable network analyzers A portable device that is used to troubleshoot switched networks and VLANs. By plugging in the network analyzer anywhere on the network, a network engineer can see the switch port to which the device is connected and the average and peak utilization.

port forwarding Sometimes called tunneling. The act of forwarding a network port from one network node to another. This technique can allow an external user to reach a port on a private IP address (inside a LAN) from the outside through a NAT-enabled router.

PPP over Ethernet (PPPoE) PPPoE combines two widely accepted standards, Ethernet and PPP, to provide an authenticated method of assigning IP addresses to client systems. PPPoE clients are typically personal computers connected to an ISP over a remote broadband connection, such as DSL or cable service. ISPs deploy PPPoE because it supports high-speed broadband access using their existing remote access infrastructure and because it is easier for customers to use.

pre-shared key (PSK) IPsec authentication method in which two parties have previously exchanged passwords.

Primary Rate Interface (PRI) An ISDN interface to primary rate access. Primary rate access consists of a single 64-Kbps D channel plus 23 (T1) or 30 (E1) B channels for voice or data.

primary station In bit-synchronous data link layer protocols such as HDLC and SDLC, a station that controls the transmission activity of secondary stations. Also performs other management functions such as error control through polling or other means. Primary stations send commands to secondary stations and receive responses.

private WAN infrastructure Dedicated point-to-point leased lines, circuit-switched links, such as PSTN or ISDN, and packet-switched links, such as Ethernet WAN, ATM, or Frame Relay.

protocol analyzer Decodes the various protocol layers in a recorded frame and presents this information in a relatively easy-to-use format.

public key encryption This is a type of asymmetric encryption in which the recipient gives a public key to any sender with whom the recipient wants to communicate. The sender uses a private key that is combined with the public key of the recipient to encrypt the message. Also, the sender must share its public key with the recipient. To decrypt a message, the recipient will use the public key of the sender with its own private key.

public switched telephone network (PSTN) A general term referring to the variety of telephone networks and services in place worldwide. Also called the plain old telephone service (POTS).

public WAN infrastructure   Broadband Internet access using digital subscriber line (DSL), cable, and satellite access. Broadband connection options are typically used to connect small offices and telecommuting employees to a corporate site over the Internet. Data traveling between corporate sites over the public WAN infrastructure should be protected using VPNs.

R

radio frequency (RF)   A generic term referring to frequencies that correspond to radio transmissions. Cable TV and broadband networks use RF technology.

remote-access VPNs   Created when VPN information is not statically set up, but instead allows for dynamically changing information, and can be enabled and disabled. Remote-access VPNs support a client/server architecture, where the VPN client (remote host) gains secure access to the enterprise network via a VPN server device at the network edge.

RFC 1918 private IPv4 addresses   Private IP addresses that are a reserved block of numbers that can be used by anyone. ISPs typically configure their border routers to prevent privately addressed traffic from being forwarded over the Internet.

Rivest-Shamir-Adleman (RSA)   Hashing algorithm used mostly for public-key infrastructures and in IPsec VPNs as an alternative to PSKs.

RSA signatures   These are digital certificates that are exchanged to authenticate peers.

S

satellite Internet   Typically used by rural users where cable and DSL are not available. A VSAT provides two-way (upload and download) data communications. The upload speed is about one-tenth of the 500-Kbps download speed. Cable and DSL have higher download speeds, but satellite systems are about ten times faster than an analog modem. To access satellite Internet services, subscribers need a satellite dish, two modems (uplink and downlink), and coaxial cables between the dish and the modem.

Secure Hashing Algorithm (SHA) This is a popular cryptographic hash function producing a 160-bit (16-byte) hash value.   SHA actually consists of several variations including, from weakest to strongest, SHA-1, SHA2, and SHA-3. Cisco IOS also supports, 256-bit, 384-bit, and 512-bit SHA implementations.   SHA is considered to be cryptographically stronger than MD5. Contrast with MD5 message-digest algorithm.

Secure Sockets Layer (SSL)   This is a cryptographic protocol designed to provide communication security over the Internet. It has since been replaced by Transport Layer Security (TLS).

service provider   A company that provides access to other networks or the Internet to its subscribers.

site-to-site VPNs   Site-to-site VPNs connect entire networks to each other; for example, they can connect a branch office network to a company headquarters network.

small network   Provides services for up to 200 devices.

SNA Control Protocol   The SNA Control Protocol is responsible for configuring, enabling, and disabling SNA on both ends of the point-to-point link.

SNMP agents   SNMP agents reside on managed devices. SNMP agents collect and store information about the device and its operation.

SNMP manager   The SNMP manager is part of a network management system (NMS). The SNMP manager runs SNMP management software.

SP edge module   The SP edge module provides connectivity between the enterprise campus module to the remote enterprise data center, enterprise branch, and enterprise teleworker modules.

star topology   A LAN topology in which endpoints on a network are connected to a common central switch by point-to-point links.

static NAT   Uses a one-to-one mapping of local and global addresses, and these mappings remain constant. Static NAT is particularly useful for web servers or hosts that must have a consistent address that is accessible from the Internet. These internal hosts may be enterprise servers or networking devices.

statistical time-division multiplexing (STDM)   A technique whereby information from multiple logical channels can be transmitted across a single physical channel. Statistical multiplexing dynamically allocates bandwidth only to active input channels, making better use of available bandwidth and allowing more devices to be connected than with other multiplexing techniques.

symmetric DSL (SDSL)   A type of DSL connection similar to ADSL, but provides the same download and upload speeds.

symmetric encryption   Also called secret-key encryption. It uses the same key to encrypt and decrypt the data. This is when each device encrypts the information using a known shared password before sending it over the network to the other device. Contrast with asymmetric key encryption.

synchronous code-division multiple access (S-CDMA)   S-CDMA is a proprietary version of CDMA developed by Terayon Corporation for data transmission across coaxial cable networks. S-CDMA scatters digital data up and down a wide frequency band and allows multiple subscribers connected to the network to transmit and receive concurrently. S-CDMA is secure and extremely resistant to noise.

Synchronous Data Link Control (SDLC)   An SNA data link layer communications protocol. A bit-oriented, full-duplex protocol that has spawned numerous similar protocols, including HDLC and LAPB.

Synchronous Digital Hierarchy (SDH)
Synchronous Digital Hierarchy (SDH) is a standard that defines how to transfer multiple data, voice, and video traffic over optical fiber using lasers or light-emitting diodes (LEDs) over great distances. SDH is a European-based ETSI and ITU standard while SONET is an American-based ANSI standard. Both are essentially the same and, therefore, often listed as SONET/SDH.

Synchronous Optical Networking (SONET)   A high-speed (up to 2.5 Gbps) synchronous network specification developed by Bellcore and designed to run on optical fiber. STS-1 is the basic building block of SONET. Approved as an international standard in 1988, SONET is an American-based ANSI standard, while SDH is a European-based ETSI and ITU standard. Both are essentially the same and, therefore, often listed as SONET/SDH.

syslog The syslog protocol was developed for UNIX systems in the 1980s, but was first documented as RFC 3164 by IETF in 2001. Syslog uses UDP port 514 to send event notification messages across IP networks to event message collectors.

syslog server A server that receives and stores syslog messages that can be displayed with a syslog application.

systematic layered approach A troubleshooting method that analyzes the network as a whole rather than in a piecemeal fashion. A systematic approach minimizes confusion and cuts down on time that would be wasted with trial and error.

T

TACACS/TACACS+ An authentication protocol, developed by the Defense Data Network (DDN) community, that provides remote-access authentication and related services, such as event logging. User passwords are administered in a central database rather than in individual routers, providing an easily scalable network security solution.

teleworking Working from a nontraditional workplace such as at home, offers many benefits to the worker and to the business.

three-tier hierarchical design A hierarchical design that maximizes performance, network availability, and the ability to scale the network design. Consists of core, distribution, and access layers.

time-division multiplexing (TDM) A technique in which information from multiple channels can be allocated bandwidth on a single wire based on preassigned time slots. Bandwidth is allocated to each channel regardless of whether the station has data to transmit.

time-division multiple access (TDMA) This is a channel access method that allows several users to share the same frequency channel by dividing the signal into different time slots. The users' station quickly transmits packets in rapid succession using its own time slot that allows multiple stations to share the same transmission medium while using only a part of its channel capacity.

toll network Consists of the long-haul, all-digital, fiber-optic communications lines, switches, routers, and other equipment inside the WAN provider network.

top-down troubleshooting You start with the end-user applications and move down through the layers of the OSI model until you find the cause of the problem. You test end-user applications of an end system before tackling the more specific networking pieces. Use this approach for simpler problems or when you think the problem is with a piece of software.

transmission link A network communications channel consisting of a circuit or transmission path and all related equipment between a sender and a receiver. Most often used to refer to a WAN connection.

Triple Data Encryption Standard (3DES) Popular encryption standard used for IPsec VPNs. It is considered stronger than DES but weaker than AES. Contrast with DES and AES.

trunk lines   A telephone line that is switched over a telephone carrier network and provides voice and data transfer between two customers.

Two-tier hierarchical design   A two-tier hierarchical design where the core and distribution layers are collapsed into one layer.

U–V

unique local addresses   IPv6 unique local addresses (ULA) are similar to RFC 1918 private addresses in IPv4, but there are significant differences as well. The intent of ULA is to provide IPv6 address space for communications within a local site; it is not meant to provide additional IPv6 address space, nor is it meant to provide a level of security.

very small aperture terminal (VSAT)   Very small aperture terminal (VSAT) is a solution that creates a private WAN using satellite communications. A VSAT is a small satellite dish similar to those used for home Internet and TV. VSATs create a private WAN while providing connectivity to remote locations.

virtual circuit (VC)   A logical circuit created to ensure reliable communication between two network devices. A virtual circuit is defined by a VPI/VCI pair, and it can be either permanent (PVC) or switched (SVC). Virtual circuits are used in Frame Relay. In ATM, a virtual circuit is called a virtual channel.

virtual private networks (VPNs)   A VPN extends a private network across a public network, such as the Internet. It enables a computer to send and receive data across shared or public networks as if it were directly connected to the private network, while benefiting from the functionality, security, and management policies of the private network. This is done by establishing a virtual point-to-point connection through the use of dedicated connections, encryption, or a combination of the two.

Virtual Private LAN Service (VPLS)   Virtual Private LAN Service (VPLS) is a class of VPN that supports the connection of multiple sites in a single bridged domain over a managed IP/MPLS network. VPLS presents an Ethernet interface to customers, simplifying the LAN/WAN boundary for Service Providers and customers, and enabling rapid and flexible service provisioning, because the service bandwidth is not tied to the physical interface. All services in a VPLS appear to be on the same LAN, regardless of location.

W–Z

WiMAX (Worldwide Interoperability for Microwave Access)   Described in the IEEE standard 802.16. WiMAX offers high-speed broadband service with wireless access. It provides broad coverage like a cell phone network rather than using small Wi-Fi hotspots.

W

X-Y-Z

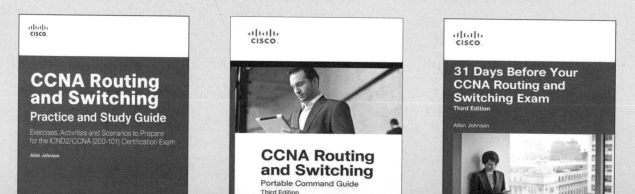